THE ENCYCLOPEDIA OF

ANTIQUES

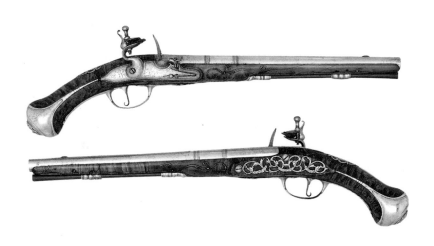

THE ENCYCLOPEDIA OF
ANTIQUES

INTRODUCTION BY DAVID BATTIE

ACROPOLIS BOOKS

THE ENCYCLOPEDIA OF ANTIQUES

This edition first published by
Acropolis Books
© 1991 Bookmart Ltd
Desford Road, Enderby,
Leicestershire LE9 5AD
United Kingdom

ISBN: 1 873762 01 1

A CIP catalogue record for this book is available from the
British Library

Edited, designed, and produced by
Anness Publishing Limited, London

Editorial Director: *J o a n n a   L o r e n z*
Project Editor: *N i c k y   A d a m s o n*
Art Director: *P e t e r   B r i d g e w a t e r*
Designer: *J a m e s   L a w r e n c e*
Typesetter: *C e n t r a l   S o u t h e r n   T y p e s e t t e r s ,*
E a s t b o u r n e
Printed and Bound in Hong Kong

**FLINTLOCK HOLSTER
PISTOLS**
FRENCH c.1680
*A pair of fine quality
pistols made in Paris for
the Danish Statholder of
Holstein. Like many
pistols of this period the
barrels are fairly long.*

KOGO AND KOBAKO
*JAPANESE 18th and 19th c.
These small lacquer boxes
(the largest is 12.6cm −
5in wide) were made to
hold incense.*

CONTENTS

INTRODUCTION

BY DAVID BATTIE

Collecting has a long history. It seems that man has inherited an inbuilt aesthetic sense and while still living in caves he was producing flints polished to a degree higher than was necessary for strictly functional purposes.

These flints became items of barter all over the continent of Europe, and it is not beyond the bounds of possiblility that there was a Neanderthal J. Paul Getty lining up a collection in his cave. Certainly, by the time of recorded history the wealthy were accumulating hordes of objects both for temporal appreciation and for their well-being in the afterlife. By Roman times they were complaining about the high price of antiques at auction.

There are fashions in antiques as there are in any other aspect of life. For example, in the mid 18th century excavations of Roman objects changed taste from the wild extravagance of the rococo to restrained Neoclassicism. Disinterred vases, bronzes and sculpture changed hands for considerable sums. Changes of style meant that those members of the aristocracy who wanted to remain in fashion had to remodel their houses, inside and out. Then, as now, second-hand furniture and works of art were unsalable, and many of the objects in the previous fashion were stored away in the attics and outhouses or relegated to servants' quarters. These rejects are today's masterpieces.

The idea of collecting yesterday's castoffs simply because they are old is, in fact, of recent origin. It was not until the middle of the 19th century that a gentleman would consider collecting much but books and manuscripts. Admittedly antiquities were acceptable, as were prints and maps and coins, but even paintings attracted very few dedicated collectors. There were almost no books on antiques (as opposed to antiquities) until the second half of the 19th century when research began to be conducted into objects made in previous centuries. Then the Victorians,

enthusiastic recyclers of early styles as they were, set in motion the modern drive to know the last tiny fact about one's prized antique.

There is, in fact, nothing wrong with wanting to know everything about the history of a piece, unless – and it happens all too frequently – the collector becomes blinded by background and stops looking with an unbiased eye at what it is he is collecting. This failure to look afresh at every piece, often the product of a slavish following of fashion, can upset the market. Once a group of objects suddenly comes into vogue – the crazes for Clarice Cliff in 1988 and minor Impressionist paintings in 1989/90 are two recent examples – too many unknowledgeable collectors and investors jump on the bandwagon, which rolls for a year or two and then grinds to a halt. The market collapses and for a matter of months, or occasionally years, the outlook seems bleak. But the market always recovers, as collecting works of art will never go out of fashion for long. The intelligent collector follows his own instincts and buys what he believes in, even if the market presently scorns it. Fashion will eventually catch up with him. From this follows the first and only real rule of collecting: buy what you like. No matter what the fluctuations in the market, you will own something that you love.

The hobby of collecting has spread from a very few dedicated amateurs at the beginning of this century to millions today. As every year passes, it seems, a new area is discovered, usually one previously despised and ever closer to the present day. The British government defines an 'antique' as an object over one hundred years old which then escapes import duty. Now the term has come to mean almost anything second-hand and collectable. While this may exclude the kitchen sink it certainly does include refrigerators, typewriters and old Coca Cola bottles.

Even jumble sales can turn up the most extraordinary finds. In 1977 a lady came into Sotheby's with a box full of bits and pieces for them to look at. Nothing proved of any value. Sadly she packed away what were no longer her treasures and turned to go. Shen then remembered a small plaque, only a few inches high, that her daughter had asked her to take along. It was black and almost unrecognizable, but it looked promising. Proper cleaning revealed a Carolingian ivory plaque from a 9th century bible. It sold for £280,000 ($518,000). Her daughter had bought it at a jumble sale for 25p (45¢).

Antiques programmes on television have had two important effects on the market. One, they have stopped families, when Aunt Matilda dies, throwing out everything onto the local tip, and, two, they have made the chance of finding a bargain in a shop that bit more unlikely. However, the drive to strike it rich should not be the overriding drive for anyone interested in works of art. Certainly the possibility is there, but it is a very small possibility. Many antique dealers spend their lives, all day every day, buying and selling, and never finding the one-off bargain on which to retire. It has to be faced, however, that one way for a collector to support buying for his collection is to undertake a little trading on his own behalf. Certainly, the true collector is forced into selling if he is to weed out poor or damaged examples and replace them with other, better pieces. This constant upgrading of a collection should always be undertaken if one wants the greatest satisfaction from ownership.

☞ *right*
MAHOGANY LONGCASE CLOCK
ENGLISH c.1780
In the mid-18th century mahogany replaced walnut as the most popular material for clock cases. This example has an arched dial and a trunk door.

Works of art can give hours of pleasure in the search, buying, research and ownership. Against this they do cost money to own – one has to pay insurance on them and, if one is at all serious, probably have the house burglar-alarmed – and there is, in many cases, the risk of breakage. But they do, it must be admitted, have the marvellous advantage of increasing in price year by year (well, most years).

There is little doubt that there is such a thing as an 'eye'. This is the term used by those in the antiques profession to describe the natural ability that some people have of recognizing the only promising piece from a sea of junk. Undoubtedly, that 'eye' can be improved by looking long, hard and frequently at objects in one's chosen field. Museums have their place, but touching is forbidden in them. Flogging round car boot sales, yard sales, junk shops, flea markets, fairs, antiques shops and auctions is the only real way to learn. Much is absorbed through the eyes and the finger tips, and nothing can replace this continual contact with objects. The ear is the other receptor well worth cultivating, for a willing teacher is a most valuable asset. The smallest scrap of information from a friendly dealer, auctioneer or fellow collector can make a whole set of previously confusing facts suddenly fall into place. Nevertheless, however much time one dedicates something will be lacking from one's knowledge – background. To be able to sit in a comfortable chair and browse through a book at one's leisure will be time well repaid.

Antique dealers should be looked on as valuable allies. A good dealer can guide the collector as he slowly gains confidence in his collecting area. He will advise on pieces that he has in stock, and buy at auction for you if attending yourself is impossible or unnerving. He will take back into stock as you upgrade. All these services will cost money, but it is money well spent, and you have the security of knowing that he will not risk offending a valued customer. Once you have enough confidence and knowledge in your own expertise, then you can set off on your own and buy at auction. This pits the knowledge of the auction house against the knowledge of the dealers and collectors and, certainly in small country auctions, there are wrongly or under-catalogued bargains awaiting those lucky enough to spot them. On the other hand, country auctions abound with modern reproductions or blatant forgeries over which the unwary can easily trip. And there will be no comeback: let the buyer beware. If you buy from a dealer, get a receipt on which all the details of the piece are written, including its condition. If there turns out to be a problem in the future you can get your money back – but no receipt, no money back.

The tyro collector will need a general book which will guide him through the thousands of terms, definitions, periods, techniques and so on, which seem to bedevil the antiques business. At some later date, once settled on a particular group of objects on which to lavish his love, time and money he will need a book, or books, with more detail and depth. Even so, few collectors are completely single-minded, and the eye to the bargain in a different field will always be there. For that reason no collector's library should be without its general encyclopedia.

In fact, thumbing through an encyclopedia can have hidden benefits. By constantly coming across objects which the reader had never previously considered, a change of direction may take place. The collector who only has eyes for, say, first-period Worcester porcelain, is going to have his understanding of that factory widened by looking at porcelain from contemporary English factories. Still more will he benefit from looking at Chinese and Continental porcelain, from which Worcester drew much of its inspiration. Ceramic shapes usually imitate those of silver, and the silver follows in its turn the decoration of the furniture-makers and architects. All these interwoven themes and movements will only be appreciated in a comprehensive volume such as this.

FURNITURE

☞ *above*

COMMODE

FRENCH c.1860

This particularly fine copy of a Louis XIV original is
typical of the 19th century fascination with the past.

ENGLISH FURNITURE

JOHN TAYLOR

From the Tudors to the Commonwealth

LITTLE FURNITURE from before about 1500 can be seen outside museums or medieval buildings preserved as historic monuments. Most antiques that might come on the market probably date from the Tudor period and later.

From 1500 to about 1650 oak was the timber most commonly used for furniture as a whole. Although often painted, few pieces bear traces of original decoration. Grander pieces of furniture were inlaid with arabesque patterns, occasionally in bone or mother-of-pearl. However carving is the most common form of decoration during this period and is usually a corruption of continental renaissance or mannerist motifs, such as grotesque figures or architectural details. The techniques of construction were comparatively simple. Furniture was usually panelled and joints were secured by pegs.

The most commonly found pieces dating from this period are the simple oak chests used to contain linen. These have a hinged lid, a panelled front and sides within a simple pegged frame-work. Sometimes the panels were carved with patterns although often a mechanical feel to the carving betrays the 19th or 20th century improver's hand.

The court cupboard is another typical piece dating from this period. Literally a cup-board, it would have been used for the display of plate. Typically it consists of a series of open shelves supported on heavy turned baluster supports, usually carved. Hall or livery cupboards were constructed in the same way but either the upper or lower section, and often both, were partially enclosed by panelled doors.

As the 17th century wore on case furniture increasingly began to include drawers and gradually the modern chest-of-drawers evolved. Drawer fronts were usually heavily panelled often with geometric designs. Often chests were carried on stands incorporating further drawers or supported on turned legs.

The simple turned forms of seat furniture used in the earlier 17th century began to be superseded in fashionable circles towards 1670, and gradually arms and backs, together with legs and stretchers became the subject of the carver's lavish attention. On the grandest examples the frames resembled a continuous deeply-carved pattern of scroll-work. Panels of cane were introduced to fill seats and backs at about this time, although the upholstery of the grandest chairs became ever more extravagant. In general backs became higher towards the end of the century while seats were a little lower.

By this period the practice of veneering case furniture was beginning to become increasingly prevalent. This technique consisted of glueing thin layers of a decoratively figured or unusually coloured wood to the solid structural members or carcase of a piece. Initially small areas were treated in this way but gradually the whole piece was covered in veneer. Borders of contrasting veneers were laid with the grain running at right angles to the main veneer, a practice known as cross-banding. Patterns could also be in chevrons or feather banding. The change to veneered case furniture was gradual and outside London and main provincial centres relatively simple oak pieces remained the staple of the furniture industry.

Hand in hand with the fashion for veneering went the introduction of marquetry and parquetry, processes whereby elaborately cut, contrasting veneers were applied to the carcase to create a striking decorative effect. Parquetry decoration is the arrangement of veneers in abstract geometric patterns: the most common type of parquetry found in Britain during the late 17th and early 18th century is oyster-veneering, whereby cross-cut veneers were laid to give the effect of opened oysters. Marquetry inlay is figurative and during this period consisted usually either of panels of flowers or of the tightly scrolled arabesques known as 'sea-weed' marquetry.

☞ *below*
WALNUT SIDE TABLE
ENGLISH *c.1690*
This simple side table is flanked by two contemporary torcheres. *The late 17th century saw*

a revolution in furniture design with the influx of Continental craftsmen following the accession of William of Orange to the English throne.

The expansion in trade with the East during this period was paralleled by a fashion for all things Oriental. Lacquer cabinets, usually with two doors enclosing an arrangement of small drawers, were imported from China and Japan and mounted on domestically produced stands. English cabinet-makers took advantage of this trend by mimicking eastern lacquer cabinets 'japanning' and mounting them on elaborate gilded stands.

The golden age

THE LATER part of the 17th century saw a revolution in the construction and types of furniture produced in England. This revolution was largely instigated by the influx of foreign craftsmen following the expulsion of Huguenots from France in 1685 and the arrival of the Dutch Prince of Orange, William, on the English throne in 1688. These changes were to see the establishment of basic types of furniture which were to remain in favour through the 18th century and beyond.

Among the new types to evolve were the bureau, a writing table with a hinged

☞ *left*
WALNUT BUREAU-BOOKCASE
ENGLISH c.1720
The bureau-bookcase was an innovation of the early 18th century. A good example such as this could
fetch well over £20,000 ($37,000) at auction.

flap enclosing an arrangement of drawers and folding out to form a horizontal writing surface. Initially these were supported on turned legs but gradually were supported on a solid carcase with an arrangement of long and short drawers. By the early 1700s bureaux of this type were often to be seen with a cabinet with one or two doors above the writing flap. Doors were often mirrored to reflect light onto the writing surface and took on a quasi-architectural form, often pedimented, domed or double-domed. Another common piece of writing furniture was the escritoire, a cabinet with a vertical hinged flap which opened to form a writing surface. Again these could be supported on chests containing drawers or on legs.

It was towards the end of the first decade of the 18th century that a new type of chair began to evolve. The back had a gently moulded frame which contained a single shaped splat. The seat was upholstered, contained within a frame and supported on gently curved or cabriole legs. The grandest chairs had splats veneered with burr walnut and the knees of the legs were carved, perhaps with shells, while the feet were carved with claw-and-ball motifs.

In about 1730 walnut began to be superseded as the most fashionable timber by mahogany imported from the Spanish colony of San Domingo. This particular wood was darker than walnut and with a much less pronounced figuring, but considerably tougher.

The middle of the century saw the influence of the French rococo style on English decorative arts and the furniture produced in this style introduced a golden age of furniture making. The more ponderous forms of the early part of the century were

abandoned as English furniture makers responded to the lightness of the new trend. The style drew its inspiration from the organic forms of nature: flowers, foliage, rocks and shells, even waterfalls, freeing them from the rigidly architectural forms of early styles. The most common decorative motif was the scroll, often in the form of a 'c'.

At the same time other influences were at work on furniture designers. A resurgence of interest in the arts of the East produced a range of decorative motifs culled from Chinese ceramics and wallpaper. These included geometric fretwork patterns, pagoda-like canopies, and ho-ho birds. Other designers turned for their inspiration to the gothic forms of the medieval period. Ogival arches, lancet panels, finials and clustered columns began to find their way into fashionable pattern books such as Thomas Chippendale's 'Gentleman and Cabinet-Maker's Director' of 1755. However most designers drew on these forms to create an eclectic whimsical style. Often elements from rococo, gothic and *chinoiserie* styles can be found side-by-side in the same piece.

Among the most interesting pieces dating from this period are the elaborately carved pier-glasses and console tables. More expensive chests were given serpentine fronts and occasionally the *bombe* forms of French commodes were imitated by the most expensive firms, such as Mayhew and Ince, John Cobb, and emigré Frenchman Pierre Langlois.

One of the most innovative furniture types to appear at this time was the tripod table. Originally designed for the taking of tea, these have circular tops carried on a pillar and supported on three cabriole legs. The tops normally fold down when not in use, and some tops revolve, as well. On this essentially simple form designers were able to make the most elaborate decorative pieces of furniture using rococo, gothic and *chinoiserie* motifs. Tops were often shaped and dished, carved with elaborate borders or given fretted or spindle galleries.

☞ *above*

**ROSEWOOD CYLINDER
BUREAU**
ENGLISH c.1780
*This delicate and
uncluttered bureau shows
the influence of
Neo-Classicism on
furniture design.
An example such as this
would command five
figure prices at auction.*

Neo-classical forms

~

THE FLOWERING of the rococo style
in England was comparatively brief and
by 1770 the neo-classical style championed
by Robert Adam (1728–92), William
Chambers and James Stewart, had established itself, although residual rococo
forms continued to linger until about
1780. Drawing on classical antiquity, the
new style saw a return to simpler architectural forms. The cabriole leg gradually
disappeared to be replaced by square
tapering legs or tapering, fluted legs.

Carved decoration ceased to be as
important as it had been during the height
of the rococo fashion, but attention was
lavished on the surface of furniture.
Mahogany continued to be the favoured
timber but more richly figured veneers
had begun to be imported from Cuba and
great pains were taken to match grains to
create a decorative effect. At the same
time there was a revival of interest in
marquetry decoration. Neo-classical
motifs such as urns, swags and fans
derived from the wall-paintings of the
newly unearthed Pompeii and Hercu-

laneum were inlaid into case furniture and
the cabinet-maker seems to have employed a wider than ever range of veneers
to create his effects.

Among new forms to appear during
this period were the sideboard and the
dining table. Typically the sideboard had
a long top often of serpentine or bowed
outline, and a single long drawer flanked
by a pair of short deep drawers. Dining
tables were made of various sections
which could be placed together in different combinations. There were two
main types. The pedestal table was the
more prized; the top of each section was
carried on a pillar and supported on
splayed legs. The tops of the end sections
had rounded corners on one side, and
could be placed against the wall when not
in use. The table could be extended by the
use of separate leaves.

Chairs during this period retained the
proportions of rococo chairs but were
normally carried on tapering legs. Backs
were rectangular, oval or shield-shaped
and the splats were carved with classical
motifs. Drawing room chairs were of a
similar form but the backs were upholstered. While dining room chairs
tended to be made almost exclusively in

☞ *left*

MAHOGANY WINE TABLE
ENGLISH c.1750
*Mahogany took over from
walnut as the most
fashionable timber for
furniture making.
Imported from San
Domingo, it was darker
and tougher than walnut.*

☞ *left*
MAHOGANY DINING TABLE
ENGLISH c. 1790
This three pedestal dining table is a particularly fine example of a form that was developed during the late 18th century. A good quality example with its original leaves could fetch as much as £30,000 ($55,000) but smaller tables and those with alterations may be obtained for less.

mahogany, drawing room chairs were often of beech, gilded or painted.

The growing pace of change in fashion is testified to by the pattern books of the late 18th century. Hepplewhite's 'Cabinet-maker's and Upholsterer's Guide of 1788' was quickly supplanted at the forefront of fashion by the French-influenced designs that appeared in Thomas Sheraton's 'The Cabinet-Maker's and Upholsterer's Drawing Book' of the early 1790s. Satinwood was the most highly prized timber during this period and was frequently embellished with painted decoration.

The 19th century

THE TURN of the century saw a change in direction in the design of furniture. Designers such as the wealthy amateur Thomas Hope and the cabinet-maker George Smith were influenced by the designs of the French decorators Percier and Fontaine and produced designs for furniture that were archaeological in character. Chairs were modelled on the Klismos chair of ancient Greece, while tables were supported on lion monopodia. Many of these designs were much heavier than the light elegant designs of the Sheraton period. Rosewood began to replace satinwood as the most fashionable timber

although mahogany continued to be generally used. Cut-brass inlay inspired by the work of the 17th century cabinet-maker André-Charles Boulle (1642–1732) was a favourite form of decoration.

Heavy neo-classical forms were used throughout the first quarter of the 19th century but increasingly the style was rivalled by historicist styles. Jacobean and Gothic revival furniture became increasingly popular in the 1820s. The so-called 'Louis Quatorze' style adapted various French 18th century styles to create a hybrid. Thus, by the beginning of Queen Victoria's reign seat furniture had acquired the sinuous contours and naturalistic carving of the rococo style but they were grafted to much heavier forms. Among the more popular pieces was the credenza, a side cabinet, often of serpentine outline and frequently set with mirrored or glass panels. These could be in walnut, sometimes with inlaid decoration, although boulle-work was also popular.

Certain designers reacted against these eclectic styles. Among the first was A. W. Pugin (1812–1852), who was responsible for much of the decoration of the new Houses of Parliament and who wanted a return to authentic Gothic forms. Later in the century the designer William Morris produced simply constructed furniture which broke away from the mechanized

techniques which had taken over so much of the furniture industry.

The end of the century saw a revival of interest in English 18th century furniture, and in particular that of the Sheraton period. Once again satinwood enjoyed a spell of popularity, while firms such as Maples produced dining room suites inspired by Chippendale's designs.

CONTINENTAL FURNITURE
J O H N   T A Y L O R

The Italian Renaissance and its influence

DURING THE 14th and 15th centuries the innovations of its painters, sculptors and architects gave Italy a pre-eminent position in the development of the decorative arts. Looking back to the past splendours of the classical world and guided by theorists such as the humanist scholar, Leon Battista Alberti, designers were able to forge a new decorative vocabulary based around the five orders of architecture.

The furniture type most suited to this new style was the *cassoni* or marriage chest. Craftsmen took as their inspiration the forms of antique sarcophagi and embellished the chests with carved putti, swags, and volutes, and supported them on feet carved as lion's paws. Usually in polished walnut, they were also gilded and set with elaborate painted panels.

The influence of the Italian Renaissance was felt in France in the early part of the 16th century. Designers such as Jacques Androuet DuCerceau, who published a series of influential designs for furniture in 1550, applied Italian mannerist ornaments, such as swags and caryatids, to a whole variety of beds, tables and wardrobes or *armoires*.

The most important piece of furniture during this period was the dresser with an upper stage, usually of architectural form, enclosed by cupboard doors, and supported on columnar supports. Gradually a new form of cabinet appeared with upper and lower sections each with two doors and often with a pediment cresting.

In Germany too, Italian influence was of paramount importance during the 16th century. Hans Holbein the younger and Albrecht Dürer had both visited Italy in the first decade of the century and Italian applied arts had clearly made a deep impression on them. However it was not until the middle of the century that de-

signers such as Peter Flottner of Nuremburg began to evolve a mature approach to the new decorative trends from the south. Decoration culled from Italian souces and grafted on to simple German forms was typified by dense floral arabesque carving in low relief, often centred by classical portrait medallions. Carving of this type was incorporated into low chests and large cupboards. Different regions interpreted the new style in varying ways. In the south soft woods were favoured and these were usually applied with painted decoration or inlaid with classical-type motifs. The city of Augsburg produced high quality panels of pictorial marquetry, which were then set

☞ *left*

DISPLAY CABINET

ENGLISH *c.1840*
Showing Gothic forms, this early Victorian parquetry display cabinet has porcelain plaques.

☞ *below*

CARVED WALNUT CABINET

FRENCH *c.1580*
16th century French cabinet-makers, influenced by the Italian Renaissance, applied Italian mannerist ornament to a variety of pieces. This cabinet is valued in the region of £12,000 ($22,000).

☞ *right*

WALNUT ARMOIRE

GERMAN c.1750
A walnut armoire from
the south of Germany
with marquetry
decoration, a particular
speciality of the area
around Augsburg.

☞ *opposite above*

CARVED WALNUT
ARMCHAIR

FRENCH c.1730
The simple contours of
Louis XIV chairs became
more undulating during
the Régence under the
influence of the French
version of rococo.

☞ *below*

EBONY TABLE CABINET

FLEMISH c.1650
The cabinet-on-stand was
introduced throughout
Europe in the mid-17th
century, though there
were distinct regional
differences. This example
has painted panels, while
others in the Low
Countries featured red
tortoiseshell.

into cabinets. In the north of Germany oak was the favoured timber and although cabinets and chests were carved with decoration in the new style they retained a sober outline.

Many of these furniture types remained the same throughout the first half of the 17th century as cabinet-makers and designers refined their interpretations of the mannerist style and as Germany found itself engulfed in the tragedy of the Thirty Years War.

From 1650 to 1720

THE MIDDLE of the 17th century saw the introduction of the cabinet-on-stand throughout Europe. Although of much the same form, they were developed in different ways. In Italy they were frequently set with *pietra dura* panels, a form of marquetry executed in marble and semi-precious stones. In the Low Countries they were embellished with panels of red tortoiseshell. The unrivalled splendour of Louis XIV's court demanded furniture of the utmost luxury. Highly sophisticated floral marquetry in wood was developed by Pierre Gole and later by André-Charles Boulle. Boulle also developed a type of marquetry which juxtaposed veneers of

ebony, cut-brass and tortoiseshell, a technique to which he gave his name. Boulle seems to have been responsible for the development of the commode – a chest with drawers and usually with a marble top. It was to be among the most important of 18th century furniture types. German cabinet-makers, notably those of Augsburg, continued to show an interest in using new materials.

The mid-18th century

TOWARDS THE the end of Louis XIV's reign a new informality was discernible in French decorative arts. Ornamentalists such as Berain, Audran and Gillot re-worked the grotesque work of the Renais-

sance into a new, much lighter style based around sinuous curved lines. The first fruition of this style was fostered under the patronage of the Regent, the Duc d'Orléans, the young Louis XV's guardian. He employed the architect and decorator Oppenord and the cabinet-maker Cressent on the interiors of the Palais Royal, his Paris residence, and there they created the style which has become known as *Régence*.

Commodes gradually became more sophisticated in shape. They were normally serpentine in plan and bombé in profile. Early *Régence* commodes are quite bulky but they became increasingly graceful; the initial three drawers were reduced to two drawers and were raised on slender cabriole legs. The design of mounts evolved so that instead of defining the form and structure of a piece, they appeared to float on the surface of the veneers. The simple scrolls and grotesque masks favoured by Berain and Boulle were gradually replaced by abstract *rocaille* decoration based on organic forms. Commodes were veneered *sans traverse* so that the two drawer-fronts were treated as a single uninterrupted decorative surface rather than as two surfaces, and the division between them was ignored or obscured. The arrangement of mounts reinforced the illusion. Case furniture was

usually veneered in kingwood or tulipwood and arranged in quartered panels whereby the veneers of any section were cut into quarters and positioned with the grain converging on the central join. Often floral marquetry was inlaid into quartered panels. However, the increasing taste for luxury stimulated the search for new decorative finishes. The most luxurious models were japanned, or incorporated panels of Japanese or Chinese lacquer, while others were mounted with decorative panels provided by the royal porcelain factory at Sèvres.

An increasing informality in domestic life necessitated the creation of new forms such as ladies' writing desks (*bureaux-en-pente*), usually with a hinged sloping flap. Small, easily portable tables (*tables-à-milieu*) were another innovation of this period.

The same influences affected the design of seat furniture. The simple contours of Louis XIV chairs were replaced by undulating lines. The wooden frame of the chair was exposed and contained the upholstery within a border of moulded curves. The arms of chairs were brought back from the front of the seat-rail to accommodate new dress fashions. In some cases (known as a *fauteuil-en-cabriolet*) the back itself was curved while the seat was usually bowed at the front. Chairs were still made largely from beech or walnut and frequently painted or gilded. Carved decoration took the form of scrolls, cartouches and small sprays of flowers.

The early part of the 18th century found German cabinet-makers producing bureau cabinets of complex serpentine and canted form. Usually veneered with walnut, they were decorated with inlaid strapwork borders and much play was made of contrasting figured veneers. The upper sections were often domed and could be carved with elaborate mouldings. Among the most exuberant in profile were those made by the cabinet-makers of Mainz, notably J. F. Raab. The armoire continued to develop in various centres. Those made in Frankfurt had doors carved as a series of concentric rectangular concave mouldings. Others had doors divided by Corinthian pilasters.

The influence of the French *Régence* and Louis XV styles was soon felt in Germany through designers who had trained and worked in Paris. However, the forms of

☞ *left*
VENEERED COMMODE
FRENCH *c*.1750
A relatively plain, kingwood-veneer commode from the Louis XV period. An example

such as this might fetch between £5–7,000 ($9–13,000) at auction.

☞ *left*

MARQUETRY COMMODE
FRENCH *c.1760*
The use of rectangular forms with cabriole legs reflects the transition between the Louis XV and Louis XVI styles.

the German rococo style tended to be more robust and vigorous than their French counterparts. The asymmetry which was a natural part of the style was exaggerated to extraordinary lengths.

Italian designers began to be influenced by the new French styles during the 1730s and it was in Italy that the style was to find its most vigorous expression. In the North, Venetian craftsmen in particular used exaggeratedly bombe forms. Walnut veneers were wisely used although furniture was also frequently painted. In Venice craftsmen developed a form of Japanning known as *arte povera,* whereby cut-out pieces from engravings were stuck to furniture and then varnished over. In Piedmont the royal cabinet-maker, Pietro Piffetti, developed a highly idiosyncratic style of marquetry using a wide range of unusual veneers including mother-of-pearl.

The revolutionary period

A REACTION TO the curved lines of the Louis XV style began to set in after about 1750. Designers looked back to the more architectural furniture of the Louis XIV period and searched for a more authentically classical style. At the same time they were influenced by a new interest in antiquity which swept Europe, fuelled by discoveries at Herculaneum and Pompeii.

At first the new fashion was confined to a few wealthy patrons such as Madame de Pompadour and the Prince de Condé, but towards the middle of the 1760s there was a noticeable change in the form and decoration of furniture. The relaxed curves of the Louis XV style began to stiffen. Commodes retained their cabriole legs but lost their bombe profiles and serpentine outlines. Mounts ceased to be moulded as abstract *rocaille* and took the form of classical architectural features.

New forms of writing furniture appeared during this period. The *secretaire-à-abattant,* a fall-front secretaire, had existed in a rococo form but its rectangular shape came into its own against the background of neo-classicism. The *bureau-à-cylindre* had a writing surface covered by a cylinder formed from slats.

By 1770 the new style was beginning to influence the design of seat furniture. Gradually chair backs lost their sinuous curves and became rectangular or oval, and cabriole legs were replaced by turned, fluted legs. The elaborate scroll work and naturalistically carved flowers disappeared to be replaced by formal architecturally derived motifs such as *guilloche* and wreaths.

Commodes gradually lost their cabriole legs and were supported on short fluted legs or feet, while their proportions became more bulky. Commodes with three drawers returned to fashion. Once again furniture mounts were used to define the

form of furniture. While lacking the relaxed swagger of rococo mounts, they were increasingly finely chased and the mounts on the furniture of Riesener, Marie-Antoinette's favourite cabinet-maker, have an almost lapidary crispness. Although marquetry continued to be popular, advanced taste increasingly favoured simple, unadorned mahogany veneers after the English fashion. This enthusiasm for furniture *à l'anglais* even led to a fashion for mahogany chairs with pierced splats rather than upholstered backs.

The period immediately after the French Revolution, known as the Directoire, saw a continuation of many of the themes of this simpler late Louis XVI furniture. The privations of war necessarily led to a fall-off in the quality of much furniture and brass was often used for mounts instead of gilt-bronze. Among the most popular forms during this period were the so-called Etruscan chairs which had been pioneered in the late 1780s by the *menuisier* George Jacob (1739–1814). They took their sabre legs and over-scrolled backs directly from antique forms such as the Klismos chair.

In the late 1790s the architects Percier and Fontaine produced a series of lavish interiors for an exclusive clientele which

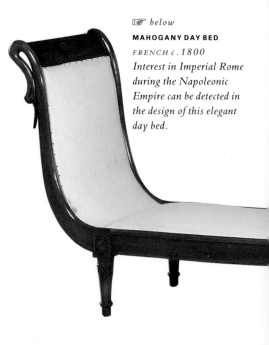

☞ *below*

MAHOGANY DAY BED
FRENCH *c.1800*
Interest in Imperial Rome during the Napoleonic Empire can be detected in the design of this elegant day bed.

culminated in the refurbishment of the Château de Malmaison for the wife of the First Consul, Napoleon Bonaparte. The style derived directly from late Louis XVI and Directoire taste, but the architects' interest in archaeology and in particular the splendour of Imperial Rome led them to develop a new style, which reached fruition with Napoleon's coronation as Emperor in 1805.

Typically, Empire Furniture is sombre and architectural in character. Often case furniture has a projecting frieze drawer directly below the marble top which is supported by colonettes with engine-turned capitals. Although initially executed in mahogany, the naval blockade imposed by the Allies in the Napoleonic Wars led to the adoption of native timbers such as maple. Decoration was usually confined to a few mounts in shallow relief. Seat furniture became stiffer even than Directoire forms. Chair backs were rectangular and front legs were either turned as balusters or of square section. Often armrests were carried on small caryatid supports. Towards the end of the Empire, armchairs acquired scrolled arms and simple scrolled front legs. Pier tables and circular centre tables, or *gueridons,* were often carried on monopodiae, or simple columns.

The massive forms of Empire furniture continued to find favour under the restored Bourbon monarchy. However, gilt-bronze mounts were used less frequently and furniture was decorated with abstract patterns of inlaid lines derived from Greek motifs. Light-coloured woods

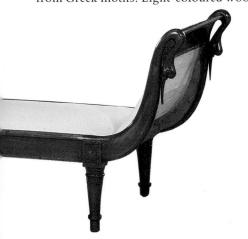

☞ *above*
SIDE TABLE
FRENCH c. 1805
This mahogany and bronze side table is typical of the heavy, architectural character of Empire furniture.

☞ *below*
DEMAY MAHOGANY CHAIR
FRENCH c. 1785
One of a set of six designed by Jean-Baptiste Bernard Demay, this chair reflects the pre-revolutionary taste for simple unadorned furniture a l'anglais.

(*bois clair*) such as maple were often used in preference to mahogany. The harsh contours of Empire furniture became softer.

In Germany the Louis XVI style was quickly adopted. Typically, northern German furniture of this period is of simple geometric form, executed in mahogany and applied sparingly with gilt-metal or brass mounts. This type of furniture was taken to its pinnacle by the Neuwied cabinet-maker David Roentgen (1743–1807). Roentgen furniture of this period is distinguished by the quality of its construction and by unusual mechanical devices such as complex locking systems and spring-operated drawers and compartments. Roentgen's visit to Catherine the Great and the presence of German craftsmen in St. Petersburg such as Heinrich Gambs led to the adoption of this style in Russia during the 1790s.

Although it owed much to French fashions, neo-classicism in Italy acquired its own distinctive flavour. In Milan cabinet-makers, of whom the most famous was Giuseppe Maggiolini (1738–1814), produced commodes of simple rectangular form raised on tapering legs lavishly inlaid with marquetry based on neo-classical motifs. In Turin the virtuoso wood carver Giuseppe Maria Bonzanigo produced elaborate neo-classical cabinets, commodes and a whole range of other pieces, profusely carved with swags and foliage.

Napoleon's conquests meant the diffusion of the Empire style throughout Europe. In Italy indigenous cabinet-

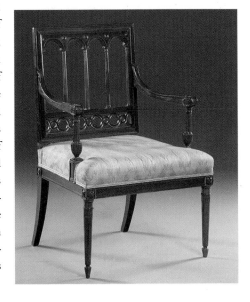

makers such as Giovanni Socchi of Florence produced sophisticated interpretations of French styles. The designer Agostino Fantastici created furniture in the Egyptian style with an exuberance lacking in French design. After Napoleon's demise neo-classicism continued to be favoured by the aristocracy throughout Italy. The highly sculptural gilded furniture designed by Pelagio Pelagi for the Palazzo Reale in Turin typifies this heavy style.

Empire influences were also strong in Germany and Austria in the early part of the century. Court furniture was often based on the latest Paris models. At the same time a distinctive style of furniture, known as *Biedermeier*, began to appear in the homes of the middle classes. Using the same austere architectural forms as the Empire style, *Biedermeier* furniture was shorn of ornament and executed in local timbers such as yew and maple.

The 19th century

AT A time when cabinet-makers were able to exploit new industrialized techniques, the character of French 19th century furniture was determined, ironically, more and more by a fascination with the past. A renewed interest in the Middle Ages led to the increasing appearance of gothic decorative details on furniture. Occasionally chairs were of completely gothic form with lancet backs carved to resemble tracery. The forms of the Renaissance were also admired and cabinet-makers began to produce enormous walnut buffets.

However, designers did not have to look so far back to find models. Throughout the 1830s cabinet-makers were taking as their inspiration the decorative arts of the 18th century. Initially this revived style was an eclectic mélange of 18th century styles. Thus Boulle marquetry was often applied to Louis XV forms. However, by the middle of the century, cabinet-makers such as Henri Dasson were producing accurate copies of royal 18th

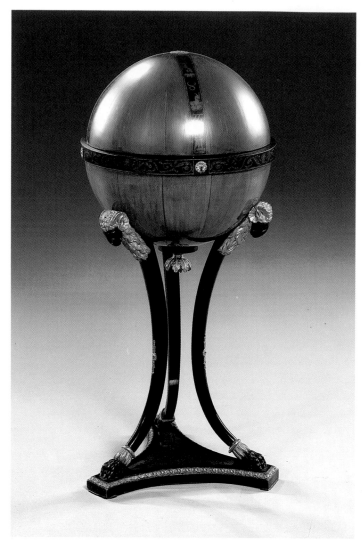

century furniture. At the same time designers continued to innovate. Towards the end of the century the cabinet-maker Francois Linke produced high quality furniture which, although clearly Louis XV in inspiration, betrayed the influence of Art Nouveau in its sinuous contours.

Late Biedermeier furniture had often incorporated gothic motifs but during the 1830s the wave of historicism which had swept European decorative arts produced a new, more serious gothic style. Other periods also found favour with German furniture makers. The rococo style was a particular favourite, while from around 1860 onwards Renaissance forms were increasingly popular.

Italian furniture was subject to the same influences as the rest of Europe but inevitably it was to the Renaissance that most

designers turned for inspiration. Cabinet-makers such as Pogliani of Milan specialized in the production of enormous architectural cabinets of ebony inlaid with ivory. The highly sculptural blackamoor figures produced in the 17th century by the virtuoso wood-carver Andrea Brustalon were now imitated on a wide scale.

From the early 19th century the use of mechanical tools inevitably affected the quality and individuality of pieces, wherever they were being produced. However, well-proportioned suites of early 20th century Chippendale-style furniture have recently come into demand and now fetch fairly high prices. It seems that, whatever the method of production, good quality furniture in popular styles will eventually acquire value.

AMERICAN CHIPPENDALE FURNITURE

LEIGH KENO

Among the most popular items of antique furniture in the United States are those made in Colonial America in the Chippendale style. American Chippendale pieces date from a time, after 1750, of unprecedented peace and prosperity. A growing merchant class exported raw materials to Africa and the West Indies, and purchased English goods with the money in what was known as the Triangle Trade. Although thousands of pieces of furniture were imported from England throughout the 18th century, a vital domestic cabinet-making industry developed. Cabinet-makers could choose from an abundance of native woods, such as cherry, walnut, white pine, poplar and chestnut, as well as West Indian or Honduran mahogany. They found that native woods were not subject to worm infestation or damage from a dry climate, as were those imported from England at considerable expense.

☞ *below*

PAIR OF WALNUT SIDE CHAIRS

*RHODE ISLAND c. 1760
In the Queen Anne style, these balloon seat side chairs have carved and water gilt decoration. They are probably from Newport.*

The 'Queen Anne style' (which came into fashion in America some ten years after her death in 1714), was characterized by a use of the S-shaped line and a consideration of the scale of the human body. Form, order, and comfort became integrated in the furniture of the Queen Anne period. In America this style has come to mean graceful walnut pieces with cabriole legs ending in pad, trifid, or in some cases, claw-and-ball feet.

The Chippendale style, which would integrate these Queen Anne design elements with a new decorative repertoire, takes its name from Thomas Chippendale whose pattern book called *The Gentleman and Cabinetmaker's Director* discussed three basic styles: Gothick, Chinese and French, stressing imaginative and fanciful variations of each one. What Chippendale called 'modern taste' is actually what we know today as rococo, characterized by the interplay of decorative asymmetrical forms.

American furniture made in the Chippendale style did not differ drastically at first from Queen Anne furniture. For example, in some cases the only difference lies in ornamentation. The hybrid forms that resulted from this meshing of styles are often known as 'transitional'. They are reminders that it is not always easy to assign a stylistic label to a piece of American furniture. Noticeable decorative changes in the Chippendale period include flared ears on chairs and balloon seats giving way to more a right-angled format. In contrast to the subdued walnut prominent in the Queen Anne period, richly figured imported mahogany was the wood of choice, selected to showcase both the movement of swirled patterns in its grain and superb reflection of light.

Regional variations in style

COLONIAL CENTRES of cabinet-making were separate entities. While substantial interaction existed, each region answered to England in its own way. While the primary wood used in urban areas was mahogany, each region relied on available native woods for secondary structuring. Collectors today can use wood identification to help pinpoint the origin of a particular piece.

Each area interpreted the Chippendale style in its own way. Boston, the first great American cabinet-making centre, was not directly affected by Chippendale's design book. Instead, imported pieces in the Chippendale style seemed to be the primary inspiration for local artisans. A patron might bring in a London-made side chair, and ask a local craftsman for ten copies. In case-pieces, the bombe and blockfront forms reached their zenith in

this city. Claw-and-ball feet with raked-back talons and cabriole legs with flat, stylized leaf-carving characterized the best work of this city.

From 1750–76, Newport, Rhode Island, had a large number of craftsmen making simple furniture for export to New York and the West Indies. Yet this area has become famous for the monumental and work-intensive block-and-shell case pieces of Honduran mahogany made by the Townsend and Goddard families. The originality, design and quality of materials and workmanship found in furniture produced by these two clans is unmatched in other Colonial urban areas

☞ *left*

MAHOGANY, CHEST OF DRAWERS

BOSTON, MASS. c.1770
Boston was the first great American cabinet-making centre, and this blockfront chest is typical of the work done by local craftsmen inspired by genuine Chippendale pieces imported from England.

☞ *left*

**CARVED MAHOGANY CARD
TABLE**

*NEWPORT, RHODE
ISLAND c. 1770*
*Made from Honduran
mahogany, this table is
authenticated to the
workshop of John
Goddard. The Goddard
and Townsend workshops
are famous for producing
some of the most original
pieces of Chippendale
style furniture in colonial
America.*

native cherrywood, the often whimsical
and charming pieces made there seem to
have been influenced more by neighbouring colonies than England. For collectors,
a fascinating aspect of Connecticut furniture production is the distinctive stylistic
and structural characteristics found in
each of the State's many counties.

New York produced pieces which
closely followed English practices. And,
with the exception of the famous ser-
pentine-side card table, its craftsmen did
not create any uniquely American forms.

Philadelphia would become the centre
of American cabinet-making by the 1770s,
at a time when the rococo style reached its
zenith in the colonies. The furniture from
this period comprises some of the most
elegant and elaborate interpretations of

and was not greatly influenced by English taste. Cabriole leg furniture from
these shops – including highboys, low-
boys, card tables, chairs and tea tables –
is greatly cherished by collectors today.
The knees, embellished with graceful stylized scrolls, lobes and leafage, have no
precedent: they are uniquely American
designs.

Furniture from Connecticut does not
have a single style. Fashioned primarily of

Chippendale design found on this side of the Atlantic. Typical motifs used on mahogany pieces produced in that city from 1750 until 1785 included claw-and-ball feet, acanthus carved knees, pierced and carved splats, and shell- and acanthus-leaf drawers.

Upper-class Philadelphians looked to England as a barometer of taste, and many citizens ordered furniture from London shops. General John Cadwalader, a widely travelled merchant, furnished his home in the grand manner. In 1771, he commissioned Thomas Affleck (1740–1795), an immigrant cabinet-maker, strongly influenced by Chippendale's *Director,* to make one of the most ambitious suites of 18th century American furniture on record. Decorative details included elaborately carved C-scrolls, cabochons, acanthus leaves and hairy paw feet.

Williamsburg and Charleston were, in contrast, relatively minor centres of cabinet-making. Each had its own styles, but basically adhered to English designs.

Value and authenticity

CHIPPENDALE FURNITURE from Newport and Philadelphia brought record prices in pre-Depression days. The same

☞ *right*

MAHOGANY SIDE CHAIR

PHILADELPHIA, PA

c.1765

This scroll-foot chair features carving attributed to the shop of Nicholas Bernard and Martin Jugiez, in partnership between 1762 and 1783. Inset (far right) is a detail from the knee carving.

is true now. For example, in 1930, when the collection of Philip Flayderman was sold, at a time when prices for the very best American pieces rarely surpassed $4,000, a mahogany Chippendale tea table made for Jabez Bowen by John Goddard of Newport brought the record-breaking sum of $29,000. In a subsequent sale, this figure was surpassed when a Philadelphia Chippendale highboy sold for $33,000. In 1986, an easy chair from the famous Cadwalader suite broke all records for furniture, fetching $2,750,000. This high-water mark held until 1989, when a mahogany six-shell Newport secretary-desk brought $12,100,000.

The condition of a piece of American furniture affects its value more than any other factor. Collectors who are interested in purchasing an American Chippendale piece should consult an expert whom they can trust. Many fakes abound in the current market, and examples that are seemingly intact may have parts replaced or recarved within the last hundred years. If found to have a new leg, a highboy valued at $150,000 is worth perhaps $20,000. To avoid such a pitfall, you should ask your dealer to guarantee the piece being purchased, and to provide a detailed description and condition report with the bill of sale.

Knowledgeable buyers use four criteria for authenticity: quality, rarity, condition and provenance. In terms of quality, you

☞ *right*

MAHOGANY TILT-TOP TABLE

BOSTON, MASS. c.1765
A fine Chippendale tilt-top tea table from Newport, Rhode Island sold as long ago as 1929 for $29,000!

history of ownership can often give a clue as to the specific region of its manufacture.

Remember that while a beautiful, authentic object of high quality can stand alone, without provenance, a poorly made artifact with an impeccable history of descent is of little value to the collector. The object must always stand on its own. In judging a piece of Chippendale furniture, the best overall advice is to consider it guilty until proved innocent!

need to be sure if the piece is well constructed. Is the wood richly figured or of dull grain? Are the decorative elements well done, and do they relate to other known pieces? In terms of rarity, find out if the form is unique. Does it have a precedent? Too rare a form suggests that the piece is possibly a fake, made up from old parts or altered from a genuine item.

To judge condition, look for an old surface. Has it been completely stripped and refinished? Fakers today can simulate antique finishes with uncanny accuracy. A Chippendale lowboy with a replaced top, even one that might have been coloured and falsely aged, is worth about one-tenth the value of an intact piece.

Finally, in terms of provenance, where has an alleged antique been from the time it was made until the present day? The

☞ *right*

MAHOGANY EASY CHAIR

PHILADELPHIA, PA.
1770
This hairy paw foot Chippendale chair from the home of General John Cadwalader is attributed to the workshop of Thomas Affleck, and features Bernard and Jugiez carving.

SHAKER FURNITURE

American Shaker furniture

IN ORDER TO fully understand and appreciate Shaker furniture and objects, it is necessary to know a little about the spiritual and philosophical background against which the work was created.

The Shakers were a group formed in England in the 1760s and 1770s by a splinter faction of the Quaker movement, led by the visionary Mother Ann Lee.

☞ *right*

SHAKER TILTER SIDE CHAIR

AMERICAN c.1830
A red-stained cherrywood tilter side chair from Harvard, Massachusetts.

Naming themselves 'The Society of Believers', they left England for America in 1774 to avoid persecution, and founded a settlement at Watervliet, New York. There, deserted by a husband with whom she had borne four children, Mother Ann declared that the Shakers were to be henceforth a celibate community which would grow by converting others to their beliefs rather than by reproducing among themselves. Less than one hundred years later there were eighteen Shaker communities spread as widely as New York, Ohio, Kentucky, and New England, consisting of nearly 6,000 members in total. Since this heyday, the sect has dwindled until there are only a handful of true Shakers alive. Mother Ann had foreseen this, predicting two hundred years ago that when fewer than seven Shakers remained, there would be a resurgence. This has yet to happen in the community itself, but the fantastic reawakening of current interest in the Shakers and the work they produced cannot be denied.

The craft ethic of the Shakers was shaped by their beliefs : everything fashioned was made for God, and therefore had to be as perfect as possible. All Shaker objects and pieces are as finely finished underneath, behind and inside as they are on the obviously visible surfaces – this philosophy extended through everything they made, from apple pies to rocking chairs. In addi-

☞ *right*

SHAKER MAPLE TILTER SIDE CHAIR

AMERICAN c.1840
Shaker craftsmen used available timber as with this curly maple tilter side chair from New Lebanon, New York.

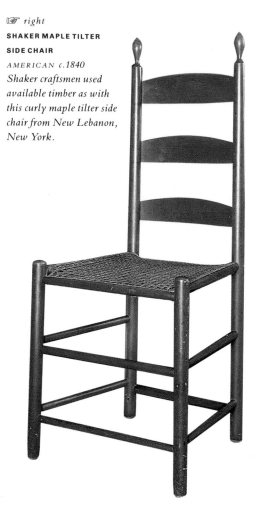

☞ *left*

SHAKER MINISTRY TABLE

AMERICAN c.1830
A Shaker drop-leaf ministry table made of cherry and birch at Hancock, Massachusetts.

tion their work rate was phenomenal: in effect, outside of their worship, their craft was their lives, and they devoted themselves to it with incredible energy.

In terms of design, the Shakers were extraordinarily inventive. Their inspiration mainly came from the English country styles in which they had been raised, but was further driven by their immediate responses to the difficult lifestyle that they had determined for themselves. The list of creative solutions they developed is as wide-ranging as it is eccentric: the Shakers can lay claim to having invented the modern square-headed broom, forms of threshing machinery, a washing machine, the circular saw, and the clothes peg, as well as innumerable domestic labour-saving and storage devices.

The principal stylistic concern was simplicity: frippery and embellishment was scorned, as was the making of anything that did not have a specific and valuable function within the community. This attitude was summed up in one of Mother Ann's most famous aphorisms: 'Whatever is fashioned, [let] it be plain and simple, unembellished by any super-fluities which add nothing to its goodness or durability.' The result was a range of

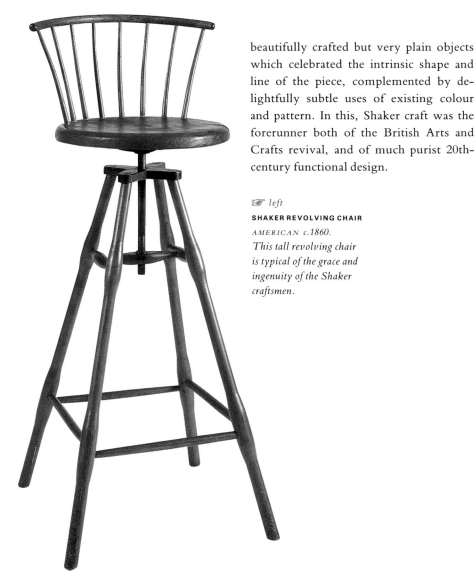

beautifully crafted but very plain objects which celebrated the intrinsic shape and line of the piece, complemented by delightfully subtle uses of existing colour and pattern. In this, Shaker craft was the forerunner both of the British Arts and Crafts revival, and of much purist 20th-century functional design.

☞ *left*
SHAKER REVOLVING CHAIR
AMERICAN c.1860.
This tall revolving chair is typical of the grace and ingenuity of the Shaker craftsmen.

☞ *left*
SHAKER CHEST
AMERICAN 1837
Made by Brother Gilbert Avery of Canaan, New York, this red-painted blanket chest is made of pine.

CHINA AND CERAMICS

JOHN CUSHION

☞ *above*

DERBY PORCELAIN LEOPARDS

ENGLISH *c.1765–70*

A pair of soft-paste porcelain leopards, painted with enamel
colours, from the Derby factory of William Duesbury.
Length: About 14cm (5½in).

The wares of China's Han-Song dynasties

FOR MANY centuries potters throughout the world have been indebted to the Far Eastern ceramic craftsmen and artists for their inspiration which is still evident today when one studies the techniques and designs of many studio-potters. From as early as 4000–3000 BC the Chinese potter was making useful wares of great beauty. Before the introduction of the potters' wheel, these were produced by hand-forming or coiling and were sometimes painted with exciting and vigorous patterns using coloured earth pigments.

It is due to the Chinese practice of tomb burials, including the interment of

'wares for the usage of the dead', that we have so many fine examples of ceramics available for study today. The excavations of these tombs, usually dating from the 1st century AD, have over recent years provided a wealth of information concerning the people and their way of life. The wares included figures in costume, sometimes from other countries, houses, animals and even entertainers, such as acrobats, dancers and musicians.

During the Tang dynasty (618–906 AD) many tomb figures of this kind were still produced, but decorated from about the 8th century with lead-glazes stained with high temperature oxides to produce greens, blues, yellows and rich browns. It was at this time also, that many important discoveries or inventions occurred, enabl-

ing refined stonewares to replace the coarser earthenwares. This led to the production of a white-bodied porcellaneous ware, referred to as 'Samarra' (a reference to the name of the site on the Euphrates where the shards of this type were first discovered in the 9th century), and it was this type of ware which seems to have evolved into the white porcelain that we know today.

Despite a barbarian invasion from the north in 1127 which virtually divided the country, making it necessary to establish a new capital in the south at Hangchow, the Chinese potter enjoyed the patronage of the Court during the Song dynasty (960–1279 AD). A new scholarly class had also arisen who appreciated the fine wares which were produced.

New kiln firing techniques resulted in many new and beautiful monochrome glazes, individual kilns producing their own particular type in different areas. It was nevertheless in the northern area in the province of Hebei that the first Ding porcelains were produced, a ware much admired by the Court.

Equally beautiful are the late Southern Song porcelains named Qingbai (bluish-white), which often have delicately incised or moulded decoration. During this period also, a form of ware was produced known to us as 'Celadon'. This term refers to the grey-green glaze applied to a stoneware, the colour resembling jade, the mineral so highly regarded by the Chinese.

It was during the short-lived Yuan dynasty (1279–1368 AD) of Khubilai Khan, that the use of the metallic oxide of cobalt (underglaze-blue) and the rarer copper (underglaze-red) was first used as a means

of decoration. A pair of vases decorated with underglaze-blue which are on exhibition at the Percival David Foundation in London are dated 1351 and are the earliest documentary pieces from this period.

The Ming dynasty

DURING THE Ming dynasty (1368–1644 AD) the kilns at Jingdezhen in Jiangxi Province were further developed and became the centre of production. The tradition of underglaze-blue decoration was continued and improved. Under the Emperor Chenghua (1465–87) a particularly fine

☞ *above left*
EARTHENWARE
WATCH-DOG
CHINESE HAN DYNASTY
(206 BC–220 AD)
An earthenware figure,
37cm (14½in) long, of a
watch-dog with green
lead-glaze, made for
burial in a tomb. Note the
ring for a leash.

☞ *right*
EARTHENWARE FIGURE
CHINESE TANG DYNASTY
(618–906 AD)
The figure of a western
Asian groom, 37.5cm
(15in) high, in
earthenware decorated
with high-temperature
glazes.

and delicate porcelain was made. It was decorated with an underglaze-blue outline with a fired glaze to which colourful enamel colours were added and then re-fired at a lower temperature. It is said that these beautiful wares were made especially to satisfy the wishes of the Emperor's extravagant mistress, Wan Kuei-fei.

Another fine white porcelain was pro-duced at this time, known as *blanc de chine*. It was made at the kilns of Dehua in the Fujian Province. These wares are mainly in the form of sculptural figures of deities, libation cups and items for the scholar's table.

During this period also, a reddish brown stoneware was made at Lake Tai in the Jiangsu Province at potteries in Yixing Xian. Many teapots of this material were later exported to Europe. It was during the later reigns of the Ming dynasty that direct foreign trading began, and by 1557 the Portuguese had been granted con-cessions to trade from off-shore Macao.

The years following the death of the Emperor Wanli in 1620 until about 1683, cover the so-called 'Transitional Period' (from the Ming to the Qing dynasties) after which time a new director was appointed at the Imperial kilns of Jingdezhen.

It was from the commencement of the Ming dynasty that the Chinese potter began to mark his wares in underglaze blue with the reign-name of the incum-bent Emperor. However these marks are sometimes an unreliable guide, for they were at times back-dated as a form of reverence to outstanding periods of production.

The Qing dynasty

ALTHOUGH THE Qing dynasty (1644–1912) started in 1644 it is the Emperor Kangxi to whom we most frequently refer. He reigned from 1662–1722, during which time many excellent porcelains were made. The blue and white of this period show a rich royal blue on a pure white ground, often favouring wrap-around landscapes, the quality sometimes varying depending upon whether they were intended for Court use or for export. During the reign of Kangxi the use of underglaze-red, which had virtually ceased by about 1425, was re-introduced, sometimes together with underglaze-blue, a difficult combination to fire successfully.

A new range of enamel colours was introduced at this time, taking their name from the predominant colour used. They are referred to in French terms, such as *famille noire,* when black dominated, *famille verte* or *famille jaune* where greens or yellow were the main colours. The ex-planation for the use of French terms for Chinese porcelain is that the best books written on the subject appeared in France during the 19th century.

Other wares were introduced during this reign such as 'enamel on the biscuit', which is simply enamels painted onto a ware fired without a glaze. Many fine monochromes were also made, from the pale blue *Clair de Lune* to the 'mirror-blacks' which were often further decor-ated with gilt.

The porcelains produced during the short reign of the succeeding Emperor Yongzheng (1723–35) were usually more delicate, and the fashion for blue and white was giving way to colourful copies of Ming times. At the same time a new enamel was introduced, the *famille rose,* composed of varying shades of pinks to a deep ruby.

During the long reign of the Emperor Qianlong (1736–95) the early wares con-tinued under the influence of the previous reign, but by the middle of the century, heavy bronze forms, and a tendency to overdecorate, heralded a decline in the manufacture of Chinese porcelain.

Chinese export porcelain

AS EARLY as the Tang dynasty wares were being exported to the Near East, but today we are familiar with those made for Europe and dating from the 17th century. The first English East India Company was formed in 1600, soon followed by the Dutch *Vereenigde Oestindische Compagnie* (V.O.C.) in 1602, who were to monopo-lize the China trade during the 17th cen-tury, when the English were more involved with India. It was from 1699, when Canton was opened to foreign traders, that the English Company began to dominate the trade, despite newly established competition from the French, Danes and Swedes. One must remember, however, that the major trade was in tea, silks and spices. Trading with the Chinese was not easy, and from 1757 merchants were confined to a small area in Canton where European 'Hongs' or warehouses were built outside the walls. It was in 1784 that the first American ship, *The Empress of China,* sailed from New York, and although no American East India Com-pany was formed, the 'New People' as they were called had sent 28 trading ships to Canton by 1790.

During recent years there has been con-siderable publicity given to the recovery of shipwrecks that had been engaged in the China Trade, and these have provided much useful information regarding the many wares involved. Most of the wares recovered are of the blue and white type, but some interesting enamel wares are also found of the type allowed as 'private trade' for crew members and company officials. Some of these became very wealthy and had services made bearing the coat-of-arms or crests of their families, or at times of their own invention. These so-called 'Armorial' wares are of great interest today.

Japan

DURING THE the middle decades of the 17th century, China was engaged in political strife, the kilns at Jingdezhen had practically been destroyed, trading in porcelain virtually came to a standstill, and the industry was not revived until about 1682. The East India Companies sought an alternative source of supply, and trading with Japan began.

☞ *above*

KAKIEMON GOURD-SHAPED VASE

JAPANESE 1660s or 1670s
43cm (17in) high, 20cm
(7¾in) max. diameter
This type of high-waisted
gourd vase, often known
as 'double' gourd-shaped,
derives its form from
Chinese types, especially
from the Transitional
period of around 1640.

early 17th century, when Korean potters are credited with locating the source of the necessary clays at Arita. Their early production of blue and white wares was much in demand by the Dutch, who established a trading post on the island of Deshima in Nagasaki harbour. Many of these wares were of European form, but decorated in Oriental styles.

Much appreciated and much copied polychrome-decorated porcelains were produced from the later decades of the 17th century, known as Kakiemon, the name of the family attributed with the introduction of these colourful wares which were to prove so popular in Europe. They are to be seen among the Far Eastern wares purchased by Augustus II of Saxony, and which were later copied at Meissen, Chantilly, Bow, Chelsea and other English factories.

The wares made during the 17th century at Kutani in central Honshū are in complete contrast to those at Kakiemon and are decorated with thickly applied strong greens, yellows, purple and blue, usually with foliage and flowers. Other Japanese regions are known for their exclusive styles of decoration, such as Nabeshima wares, which were reserved for the Lords of that area, often decorated in rather formal patterns, as if drawn by architects. The wares of Hirado are distinctive with their sparse decorative scenes painted in a bright blue.

Although much of the highly decorated cream-coloured earthenware known as Satsuma is enjoying a period of popularity today, many of these wares are of a very poor quality, as are some of the so-called Imari wares. Most of these pieces were produced in Japan after it was forced to open to European trade by the American Commodore Perry in 1854. There are few pieces of Satsuma wares which can be dated to the Edo period, which came to an end in 1868, and regrettably there is very little reliable material written on the wares produced during the succeeding Meiji period, when the popularity of Satsuma encouraged similar productions at many other Japanese pottery centres.

It is known that various areas of Japan had been producing earthenware for over three thousand years. The earliest wares were shaped by hand, resulting in a ruggedness which is still much admired and emulated today especially for the various vessels used in the cult of the 'Tea Ceremony', which came to Japan from China during the Song period (960–1279) and was associated with Zen Buddhism.

The production of porcelain does not appear to have started in Japan until the

Islamic pottery

THERE SEEMS little doubt that it was the awareness of the pottery made in China during the Tang dynasty (618–906 AD) that provided the Islamic potter with the initial impetus to produce similarly decorated wares with green, yellow and purple glazes, as seen for example on Tang pottery horses and camels. Very few of these wares, dating from about 800 AD, have survived intact, the majority having been restored from fragments found on rubbish tips.

It was during the 9th–10th century that the influence of Tang wares was most obvious, and the Islamic potter began to produce pieces which not only served a useful purpose, but also were pleasing to the eye. At Samarra and Nishapur (in present-day Iraq and Iran) excavations unearthed important evidence of the early Chinese porcellaneous white wares being imported during the 9th century.

It was probably due to the fact that Islamic potters were unable to locate the necessary ingredients to make a Chinese type of porcelain that led them to apply a white, opaque tin-glaze to their earthenware. This was often decorated prior to firing with simple floral designs of Kufic

inscriptions in cobalt-blue, copper-green and antimony-yellow.

A further important decorating technique was that of lustre decoration, probably first discovered by the early Egyptians when decorating glass. These metallic lustres vary from a deep red, or copper-tone, to a pale yellow, and were applied on to a previously fired glaze, and then subjected to a further firing in a reduction kiln, where the intake of air was restricted in order to create the necessary atmosphere. This technique became very popular on decorative tiles, but declined in Mesopotamia from about 950 AD.

The main pottery centres producing these wares during the 9th and 10th centuries, were Baghdad and Basra in Iraq. During the 9th to the 11th centuries, Iran and Afghanistan also became important centres of pottery production, and excavations during this century have revealed a wide variety of slip-decorated bowls and dishes in the regions of Samarqand and Nishapur.

During the reign of the Fatamid dynasty in Egypt (969–1171 AD), lustre continued to be a favourite method of decoration for their buff or reddish clays. These were often signed by the potter, who painted subjects as diverse as the figure of Christ,

or a cock-fight.

From the beginning of the 11th century new pottery centres developed in North and North-West Iran, making a type of ware not previously encountered in Islam. This involved a technique known as *sgraffiato*, which is a method of scratching into the clay body through a thin layer of applied clay to reveal the underlying contrasting coloured body. The designs on the early wares were usually influenced by the metalwork of the period. Later, during the 12th and 13th centuries, the incised lines were coloured in green or brown. When larger areas of the thinly-applied slip were removed to produce designs in the contrasting coloured clay body, the technqiue is referred to as *champlevé*, and was a form usually associated with Western Iran.

During the mid-11th century, Iran, Iraq, Syria and Asia Minor were conquered by the Seljuq Turks, and a period of fine architecture and arts followed into the 13th century. During this time a white-bodied ware was introduced which was then painted under a stained glaze, or painted in a wide range of polychrome enamels. These white wares were influenced by the Chinese Ding wares of the Song period, and although we know that the Persian potter was unable to produce porcelain, the penetrating glaze, combined with the soft porous clay, produced a near-transluscent body, much akin to a soft-paste porcelain. This same ware was equally attractive when covered with a monochrome glaze, especially the popular turquoise-blue. A common shape was the double-walled ewer, which was pierced with designs in the outer-wall (reticulated).

An early form of drug-pot or *albarello* was also a favourite vessel, which the Persian potter decorated by carving and then sparsely decorating with polychrome glazes. These were made at both Rayy and Kashan. The best known wares of this period, associated with the same centres, are decorated with black or other dark colours applied to the white body and then covered with a colourless or trans-

☞ *left*
EARTHENWARE BOWL
EGYPTIAN Early 12th c.
From the Fatamid period, this bowl painted with a Coptic priest in brownish-gold lustre is signed on the base by the painter Sa'ad. Diameter: 22.5cm (8¾in)

☞ right
EARTHENWARE DISH
TURKISH 1550–1600
An Isnik dish painted in
high-temperature colours,
on a white ground under a
clear glaze.
Diameter: About 25cm
(9¾in)

parent blue glaze.

By the 12th century migrating Egyptian potters had brought the technique of lustre decoration to many Mesopotamian and Iranian centres, including Rayy, Hashan, Sava, Gurgan and Sultanabad. The Victoria and Albert Museum in London, and the Fitzwilliam Museum in Cambridge, exhibit some amazing pieces of this period, which were buried in sand in large jars during the 13th century, where they remained until discovered in the 1940s, appearing as if recently made!

The study of Islamic wares covers a long period, and the same techniques were to continue for many years. They were increasingly concerned with architectural decoration, which almost dominated their production. By the 15th century many Persian wares were decorated in blue and white, in styles similar to that of contemporary Chinese porcelain, which continued into the 19th century.

The known Turkish wares are those which were for many years wrongly termed 'Rhodian', but are now recognized as having been made in Isnik, in Western Anatolia, dating from between 1555 and 1700. These wares are remarkable for their use of rich 'sealing-wax' red, together with greens and blues painted onto

a white slip under a clear glaze.

Some interesting pottery was also made during the 18th and 19th century at Kütahya, which had become the centre of, the Turkish pottery industry by this time. The decoration on these wares reminds us that the kilns were in the midst of the Armenian and Christian communities of the Ottoman Empire of that day.

The interest of most scholars in this field is concerned primarily with the early wares and very little research has been carried out into the production of Iranian wares made from the 16th century. At times these appear to be very sophisticated, although many of their lustres, which often appear to be of the 19th century, were in fact made much earlier.

Spanish pottery and porcelain

TWELFTH CENTURY Spain may well be considered the converging point of Eastern and Western pottery styles. The Arabs had invaded the Iberian Peninsular in 711 AD and by the mid-13th century Moorish potters were at work in Malaga producing tin-glazed earthenware with blue and lustre decoration, which we today term Hispano-Moresque ware. This pro-

duction continued in the following century in Granada, Manises, and Valencia.

The most common shapes produced in these centres were dishes and tall, waisted jars, called *albarellos*. Made for the apothecary, they were often decorated with mock-Arabic script, together with the arms of the owner. The high quality of these early pieces continued well into the 16th century, from which time the fine pale greenish-tinged, much admired 'golden pottery' began giving way to wares decorated with a deep metallic copper-lustre of a reddish hue. The manufacture of lustre wares has continued until today at Manises, near the city of Valencia, where they cater primarily for the tourist requiring pottery at least similar to the traditional wares.

It was the influence of the Arabic potter which was doubtless responsible for the large production of Spanish tiles (*azulejos*) starting during the second half of the 15th century, with a form of decoration called *cuerda seca* (dry-cord). The lines incised into the unfired clay to form the required pattern were filled with a greasy substance, which acted as a barrier to prevent the merging of the various coloured glazes used in the decoration. The later alternative method, used at Toledo and Seville, served the same purpose, but here moulds into which the design has been incised were pressed on to the unfired clay, resulting in raised ridges, so forming compartments into which the liquid glaze was applied, perhaps suggested by early Chinese *cloisonné* enamels. This technique was called *cuenca*.

By the 16th century new and original styles of decorating tin-glazed earthenware were introduced in Toledo and Talavera, together with new shapes, which became popular throughout Spain. It is recorded that in 1575 King Philip II gave 359 pieces of pottery to the Escorial Monastery, many of which were for the use of the apothecary.

It was during the mid-18th century that the Talavera potters began to make more fashionable forms as introduced at Alcora in the Province of Valencia. This factory

was established in 1726 by Count Aranda and owed its success to a French potter, Joseph Olery. The finest of the Alcora wares rivalled the quality of some of the earlier Italian *maiolica,* when painted with biblical or mythological subjects in powerful high-temperature colours. During the second-half of the 18th century, Alcora was one of the many European factories where the potters were forced to produce a form of cream-coloured earthenware in an attempt to survive against the extensive importation of Josiah Wedgwood's Queen's Ware.

When the production of Capodimonte porcelain was transferred to the grounds of the Buen Retiro Palace, near Madrid, in 1759, a certain amount of the clays such as had been used in Italy were transported together with a mass of equipment to the new premises. In consequence, the earliest wares produced at Buen Retiro were better than those which followed. These were made from Spanish clays and often have the appearance of a cream-coloured earthenware.

Buen Retiro porcelain is seen at its best in the porcelain room, completed in 1765, at the Aranjuez Palace, which lies about 30 miles south of Madrid. The large rococo mirrors are surrounded with porcelain panels modelled in high relief with chinoiserie figures by Giuseppe Gricc. Although frequently modelled by Gricc, compared with those produced at Capodimonte, the figures are large to a point of clumsiness, and the colours used are garish.

Portuguese earthenware

~

DUE TO their early association with China during the 16th century, Portuguese potters were familiar with the blue and white porcelain of the Ming dynasty. In consequence much of the high quality tin-glazed earthenwares made in Lisbon were decorated to resemble the Oriental wares made for export to Europe. Portugal was one of the many European countries which produced tile-pictures during the

☞ *left*
ALBARELLO (DRUG JAR)
SPANISH c.1435
A typical tin-glazed earthenware albarello or drug jar, decorated with high-temperature blue and copper lustre, with illiterate Kufic script, from Manises in Valencia.
Height: About 30cm (11¾in)

16th century. These were made from painting continuously over a number of square tin-glazed tiles, which was also a favourite art form in Spain.

The average collector is more likely to be familiar with the lead-glazed wares made by Mafra & Son at Caldas da Rainha from 1853, at a time when there was great interest in Bernard Palissy pottery made at Saintes in France in the 16th century. These imitations favour the more grotesque of Palissy's creations and are very poor quality and should not be mistaken for the original light, brightly glazed pieces.

Italian earthenware

THE ITALIAN term for tin-glazed earthenware is *maiolica*. It is thought that the name derives from the fact that Hispano-Moresque wares from Spain were imported to Italy via the trading-ships from the Balearic island of Majorca. The earliest Italian productions appear to date around 1400, and were made at the small town of Orvieto in Umbria. Because most examples of these wares have been excavated, they are usually discoloured and not seen at their best.

It is to Florence that we look for finer mid-15th century pieces, such as the so-called 'oak-leaf' jars. These were large drug-pots, often necessitating robust handles, which were painted in a blackish-blue often with heraldic beasts set against a background of stylized oak-leaves. Another popular Florentine type of ware was the large pan-shaped dishes, painted in purple, green and yellow high temperature colours with human heads or animals.

Fine Italian maiolica is not seen at its best until the first half of the 16th century. Due to the roving habits of so many of the finer painters it is sometimes difficult to relate certain styles of painting to a particular centre of distribution. The colours available to the early maiolica painter were confined to those derived from metallic oxides which could be painted on the raw tin-glaze and fired at the same temperature. Colours included blue from cobalt, yellow from antimony, orange and shades of violet and purple from manganese, with a very occasional use of red derived from an earth known as Armenian bole, which was a very difficult colour to fire successfully. Today maiolica commands very high prices – an Urbino dish sold at auction in 1987 fetched £6,000 ($11,000), while a Denita piece fetched £3,800 ($7,000).

From the very beginning the city of Faenza became the centre of influence for these wares, and it has remained an important area to this day. There are very few collectors of this colourful pottery, the finest having been acquired by the

☞ *above*
MAIOLICA PLATE
ITALIAN c.1510
An example of the Italian tin-glazed earthenware known as maiolica *from Cafaggiolo, near Florence. Attributed to the painter Jacopo, it depicts an artist watched by his patrons, painted in high-temperature colours. Diameter: About 23.5cm (9¼in)*

major museums throughout Europe during the second half of the 19th century, when they were much in demand. They were frequently referred to as 'Raphael Fayence', a term almost certainly due to the similarity of the painting to the style of Raphael's painting in the *loggie* of the Vatican. This style of painting particularly appealed to 19th century potters engaged in reproducing wares of this type, such as Ulysse Cantagalli, whose work can often be identified by a broadly painted cockerel in blue on the reverse. Cantagalli worked in Florence from 1878 until his death in 1901.

Italian porcelain

THE FIRST attempt to produce porcelain in Europe which in any way resembled that made in the Far East was made in Florence, between 1575 and 1587, when an early soft-paste, or artificial porcelain, was made from white-firing clays, with about 20% of frit (glass). This production, of which only about sixty examples are known to have survived, appears to have been made for the personal needs of the family of the Grand Duke Francesco I de'Medici. Being a soft-paste porcelain, the body was first fired to a biscuit, then painted with cobalt-blue and occasionally with manganese-purple, after which it was covered with a transparent lead-glaze and again fired.

This material was inclined to slump in the kiln if overfired, and the wares consisting of plates, small jugs and bottles for table-use are often distorted. All but a few of these pieces are marked in underglaze-blue with a drawing of the dome of the Cathedral of Florence.

The first hard-paste porcelain to be made in Italy was produced between 1720 and 1727 by Francesco Vezzi, aided by C. H. Hunger, the arcanist previously employed at Meissen. He is considered responsible for the closure of the factory, when in 1727 he returned to Saxony and stopped the export of the necessary clays to Vezzi. During this seven year period some very good table-wares were made in silver baroque forms, decorated in enamel colours, which favoured a very distinctive iron-red.

There were few serious attempts to produce porcelain again in Italy until 1764, when Geminiano Cozzi founded a production of hard-paste porcelain, which survived until 1812. In consequence it is one of the few Italian porcelains frequently seen outside of museums. Cozzi's porcelain was not of a high quality; it had a rather thickly potted grey body, with an ill-fitting glaze, but was often decorated with fine gilding.

From about 1780, the influence of Sèvres on Cozzi shapes and decoration

☞ *above*

HYBRID-PORCELAIN FIGURE

ITALIAN c. 1770
The figure of a peasant from Deccia, near Florence, painted in strong enamel colours with stippled flesh-tints.
Height: About 11cm (4¹/₃in)

☞ *right*

SALT-GLAZED STONEWARE JUG

GERMAN 1691
This jug from Grenzhausen with a pewter lid is decorated with cobalt-blue and manganese-purple, and features an applied relief of William and Mary of England.
Height: About 30cm (11³/₄in)

becomes very apparent, but their output included a range of interesting figures, enamelled with a typical Italian palette, including iron-reds, blues, purple and a yellowish-green, but unlike the useful wares these figures were rarely marked with the red-anchor mark adopted by the factory, making certain attribution difficult.

The important factory at Doccia, near Florence, was founded by the Marchese Carlo Ginori, who started marketing a coarse, greyish, hard-paste porcelain in 1746, which between 1770 and 1790 was made to look more attractive by the addition of a white, opaque tin-glaze, which

was sometimes painted with enamel colours in a Japanese porcelain manner.

From 1745 to 1755, large vases, plaques and table-wares were frequently moulded with high relief mythological subjects, painted in colours. A class of ware sometimes wrongly attributed to the factory of Capodimonte, these wares are not in fact tin-glazed. The figures produced at Doccia are lively and pleasing in typically exaggerated theatrical poses, usually on simple square bases, painted to resemble marble.

The really beautiful soft-paste Italian porcelain was made between 1743–59 in the factory of Charles of Bourbon, at Capodimonte. These wares are extremely rare and are very expensive, especially the figures, all of which are invariably marked with the *fleur-de-lis,* impressed or in blue. This same mark continued to be used when the entire production was moved to Buen Retiro in Spain, when Charles succeeded to the throne of that country in 1759.

Their table wares, which were mostly in the baroque style, were very much under the influence of the Meissen factory in Saxony. At this same time they produced some beautifully designed and painted snuff-boxes, cane-handles and other small pieces. Their fine figures, often based on characters from the Italian Comedy *(Commedia dell'Arte),* were frequently modelled by Guiseppe Gricc, whose work can easily be identified by the diminutive heads of the characters.

It was at the Royal Factory of Naples, established by Ferdinand IV in 1771, that we first find wares marked with a 'N' under a crown in blue. This mark was never used at Capodimonte, to which it is often attributed, but was frequently copied on later Doccia wares and the porcelains of Ernst Bohne, who operated at Rudolstadt in Germany from 1854.

The majority of porcelain made at Naples came under the influence of the early finds that had been made during the excavations on the sites of Herculaneum and Pompeii, which were to bring about the fashion for neo-classical art in all forms. Many of these pieces which are of a soft-paste are well painted with views of the excavations, whilst the border decorations resemble those used by Josiah Wedgwood on his creamwares.

German, Austrian and Central European earthenware

THE POTTERS of Germany, Austria and other Central European countries, did produce tin-glazed earthenware, but not on the scale of the Italians. Probably the most important contribution of German potters to the history of ceramics was salt-glaze stoneware. In this a clay body was fired to a temperature ranging between 1200 and 1400°C, with salt (sodium chloride) being shovelled into the kiln at the peak temperature. The sodium combined with the clay silicates to form a thin, hard glaze, with a texture often likened to orange-peel. In order to produce a rich brown or blue decoration, the body was brushed with a slip containing iron-oxide or cobalt.

The manufacture of salt-glazed stoneware began in the Rhineland in the 14th century with Siegburg remaining as the centre of the industry until devastated by the Swedes in 1632. The majority of these stonewares were jugs or drinking vessels, in a wide variety of shapes. Some large jugs were fitted with candle-sockets,

flasks were made in the form of hollow rings and small jugs, in the form of owls, had detachable heads, which formed the lid.

The further important centre was Cologne, until production was halted in about 1600 and moved to Frechen. It was in these two major centres that the majority of the bearded bottles, or Bellarmines, were produced. Drinking vessels in grey salt-glaze with blue decoration have remained a popular form of tourist souvenirs which are sold in that region to this day.

From the 17th century Hamburg, Hanau, Nuremberg and Frankfurt-am-Main were among the major cities where tin-glazed earthenwares were made, often decorated in imitation of Chinese styles of the late Ming dynasty, or in some of the popular styles being applied at the same period to Delftware. It is sometimes difficult to separate these German wares from the Dutch, but nothing was ever achieved to match the painting of 16th century Italian maiolica.

Prior to making porcelain several other German factories, including Höchst, Ansbach and Fulda, also produced some colourful, well painted tin-glaze wares. During the second half of the 18th century tin-glaze earthenware was also made at Proskau in Silesia and Holitsch in Hungary, both productions lasting well into the 19th century.

Meissen porcelain

THE PRODUCTION of a Chinese type of hard-paste porcelain was eventually started in Europe with the establishment in Saxony of the Meissen factory, situated 25 kilometres from Dresden and the Court of its patron, Augustus the Strong, in 1710.

Experiments had been taking place since about 1701 under the direction of Johann Friedrich Boettger, a young alchemist, whose experiments first resulted in the production of a hard, red stoneware, which was of such a fine grain that it could be engraved and polished in the

manner of a semi-precious stone. The production of this material continued until about 1730 and the later pieces are frequently marked with the incised crossed swords, the mark adopted by the factory from about 1723, taken from the arms of Saxony.

The first Meissen porcelain was not a good colour. At the time they were using alabaster as an alternative to china stone, which they did not discover until about 1718. Their earliest wares were mostly tea or coffee-services, tankards or vases, most of which were moulded or decorated with applied reliefs, whilst their earliest figures were left in the white or with touches of gilding.

Following the arrival from Vienna in 1720 of J. G. Höroldt, a skilled painter and designer, Meissen wares were decorated with stylized flowers, *chinoiserie* and harbour-scenes, all in bright enamel colours. Some of the larger pieces of this early period were marked with an underglaze-blue monogram of 'A. R.' (Augustus Rex). This indicated that they were made for the Elector to help decorate the *Japanisches Palais* he had purchased in 1717 to house his collection of porcelain, which included large quantities of Japanese and Chinese wares.

In 1727 the sculptor, J. G. Kirchner, was appointed to produce the original models from which moulds were made to make the porcelain figures, including large fantastic models of animals and birds. Kirchner was soon to be replaced by a more skilful modeller, J. J. Kaendler, who, with his assistants, produced a wide range of figures which were at times also used to decorate useful wares. Kaendler's best figures must be those of Harlequin, Columbine and other characters from the *Commedia dell'Arte,* which were modelled from about 1738.

Following the death of Augustus II in 1733, the factory was under the direction of Count Brühl, for whom the famous Swan Service of over 2,000 pieces was produced, including figures of swans, which 'swam' around the table on lakes of mirror.

building, erected by the State at Trie-
bischtal, in the suburbs of Meissen. A
limited range of wares are still made there
today, often from some of the old moulds,
but decorated to appeal to 20th century
taste.

Other porcelain factories

BY THE middle years of the 18th century, many workmen who had acquired
their knowledge of porcelain manufacture
at Meissen, were prepared to sell their
skills to Electors, Kings and Princes of
other German States. Within a short
period porcelain factories, some of which
had previously only made tin-glazed
earthenwares (faience), were in production at Höchst, Fürstenberg, Berlin,
Nymphenburg, Frankenthal, Ludwigs-
burg and about sixteen other minor factories, all making porcelain from the original Meissen formula. Some were short-
lived but others extended well into the
19th century.

Although established in 1717, Du
Paquier's Vienna factory had little success
until aided by S. Stölzel and C. H. Hunger,
whom he had lured away from Meissen
with a promise of rich living (which did
not materialize). After their departure the
factory was continued until 1744, when
for financial reasons Du Paquier was
forced to sell to the Austrian Empress
Maria Theresa, under whose patronage

☞ *above*

**MEISSEN PORCELAIN
HARLEQUIN**

GERMAN c.1750
*A figure of the Greeting
Harlequin in hard-paste
porcelain decorated with
enamel colours. The
original design was
modelled by J. J.
Kaendler in about
1739–40.
Height: About 14cm
(5½in)*

During the Seven Years War the Meissen
factory was occupied by the troops of
Frederick the Great of Prussia and by the
end of the war in 1763, the age of the
baroque, during which Meissen had
excelled, had given way to the new
fashionable rococo, in which the new
French factory at Sèvres was to become
the trend setter. Meissen were never again
to regain its lead, and could only endeavour to reproduce, in hard-paste, the
beautiful soft-paste wares of the French
factory.

In 1864 the Meissen factory was moved
from the Albrechsburg Castle to a new

☞ *right*

**NYMPHENBURG
PORCELAIN FIGURES**

GERMAN c.1760
*Modelled by Franz
Anton Bustelli, this hard-
paste porcelain piece
features Octavio and a
mushroom seller, painted
in enamel colours.
Height: About 18cm
(7in)*

the factory ran until 1784. It was from the start of this State Period that the much-copied two-bar shield of Austria was adopted as a factory mark. From 1784 until its final closure in 1866, during part of which time the production was under the management of a wool-merchant, Konrad von Sergenthal, some highly decorated wares were produced.

The unmarked wares of the Du Paquier period were usually decorated in enamel colours and gilding with extreme baroque ornament, scrollwork, shell-like palmettes, lattice-like gilding, *chinoiserie,* or Meissen-type flower painting; only very few figures were made. The wares and figures made during the State Period (1744–84) continued to owe a great deal to Meissen and produced few original wares, until coming under the influence of the neo-classical styles.

The wares made under Sorgenthal in the early years of the 19th century attracted many other later European porcelain makers. They produced copied wares often termed 'old Vienna', often complete with bogus marks, usually applied in enamel rather than the correct under-glaze-blue. The very fine gilding on the original wares can often be clearly seen to have been reproduced by means of a rubber-stamp.

French earthenware

THE MAIN production of French potters was of tin-glazed earthenware, known in France from the early 17th century as *faience* after Faenza, the large distribution centre of Italian *maiolica.* Before considering these wares it is worth noting that two outstanding and rare types of lead-glazed earthenwares were also produced, important in that they have both been reproduced in large quantities during the 19th century.

The name of the potter who made the particularly fine ivory-coloured pottery sometimes known as Henri II ware, is not known, but 16th century references leave little doubt that it was made in St Por-

☞ *left*

FAIENCE POT-POURRI AND DISH

FRENCH *c.1755*
A tin-glazed earthenware (faience) pot pourri and dish, painted in enamel colours, from Paul Hannong's Strasbourg factory.
Height: About 20cm (7¾in)

chaire, in the department of Deux-Sèvres. It was at one time thought that the very precise decoration in contrasting coloured clays was inlaid, but this is not now accepted, and French ceramic specialists are of the opinion that the underglaze coloured clays were applied to the surface of the ivory tinted body, with the 'possible collaboration of a printer'. There are only about 64 genuine examples of this work recorded. During the 1860s some very good reproductions of these wares were made by the Staffordshire firm of Minton and that of Charles Avisseau at Tours, in France.

The other much reproduced earthenware was of the type attributed to Bernard Palissy, who was potting at Saintes from about 1542. Palissy's best known wares are decorated with snakes, lobsters, lizards, fish and shells etc. His naturalistic modelling is said to have been achieved by taking moulds of the actual creatures or objects and using the casts to create these rather macabre wares. Likewise, many of the 19th century reproductions were made from casts of moulds taken from original and genuine pieces. These can often be detected, due to the fact that they are always smaller than the originals, remembering that all clays shrink approximately ⅙th–⅐th during the initial firing, and so only by modelling an oversize copy could one arrive at the correct size.

There is little doubt that the production of French tin-glazed earthenwares was

started in the early decades of the 16th century by immigrant potters from Spain and Italy, which at times make it difficult to be certain of the country of origin. This is the case with those of Lyons, Nîmes and Rouen. From the early 17th century, Nevers was to become the fashionable centre for this industry, producing pieces made in imitation of Chinese blue and white, and wrongly termed '*blue-persan*', in which tin-glaze was stained to a dark royal blue and then decorated in white and sometimes yellow, with flowers or a Chinese landscape. From the late years of the 17th century Rouen potters produced a wide range of wares, painted in dark blue on a white ground, with so-called *lambrequin* designs; introduced by Jean Berain, *style rayonnant* and *ferronerie* (ironwork) was technically very skilful painting, but a fashion that soon became too tedious and monotonous.

At Strasbourg and Marseilles we find the well-painted and original styles of decoration where the tin-glaze was first fired and then the decoration applied in a wide palette of enamel colours. Due to the close proximity of the German border, the wares of Strasbourg catered primarily for German taste. First established in 1721 by Charles-François Hannong, their earlier wares were decorated with the limited range of high temperature oxides, as used on Italian maiolica, but by the middle of the century they were using enamels to paint some very beautiful flower groups in the manner of Meissen porcelain.

Marseilles, in the south, had several factories during this period, but the best known is certainly that of *Veuve Perrin* (Widow Perrin) who continued to run the pottery after the death of her husband in 1748, until she died in 1793. Here the painting was characteristic of the area in which the pottery was situated, and depicted fish, vegetables and insects etc, although some chinoiserie also appears, but all painted in a delightful free manner.

Among the other French faience factories worthy of note are those of Niderviller, Lunéville, Saint-Clement, Les Islettes, Pont-aux-Choux, Creil and Montereau. Several of these factories also produced forms of cream-coloured earthenware in an endeavour to survive against the large importation of this form of earthenware from England.

French porcelain

PRIOR TO the establishment of the Vincennes factory in 1738, there were only a few concerns making porcelain in France worthy of mention, Rouen being the first. The limited wares that are attributed to Louis Poterat, who was working at Rouen from 1673, are difficult to attribute with any degree of certainty, but the few pieces that are, were made from a very glassy soft-paste body, decorated with dark inky-blue in the styles of the contemporary faience, marked with an inexplicable 'A. P.'

From about 1690, a porcelain production of soft-paste was probably started at St-Cloud, near Paris, by the family of a maker of faience, Pierre Chicaneau. Chicaneau had passed the secret to his widow, who later married Henry Trou, under whose name the factory continued until 1766. They obviously experienced firing problems and their wares are very thickly potted and confined mostly to smaller useful wares and figures, which at times closely resembled Chinese *blanc de chine*. Whilst underglaze-blue, similar to

☞ *left*

PORCELAIN TEAPOT

FRENCH *c.1730–40*

A soft-paste porcelain teapot made in Chantilly, with an opaque tin-glaze and decorated in enamel colours in the Kakiemon style.

Height: About 9cm (3½in)

that thought to have been applied at Rouen, remained the favourite form of decoration, many of their small wares were painted in Japanese Kakiemon styles with bright enamel colours.

From 1725 the factory of Chantilly, under the patronage of the Prince de Condé, produced a range of wares confined almost solely during its first 20 or so years to pieces fashioned after the large collection of Japanese porcelain already in the Prince's possession. To provide a suitable ground for the Kakiemon styles, the soft-paste creamy-toned Chantilly porcelain was covered with a white tin-glaze, as used on faience, marked with a red enamel French hunting-horn.

Towards the middle of the century, the tin-glaze was replaced with a normal colourless glaze and the decoration consisted mostly of well-painted flowers, often in the Meissen style. From about 1770 until the closure of the factory in

1800 the majority of their wares were decorated in either blue enamel or underglaze-blue, often with the popular 'Chantilly sprig' pattern, later copied at Caughley in England at Thomas Turner's factory.

The other important French factory to be established prior to that of Vincennes, was at Mennecy, under the protection of the Duc de Villeroy. Established in 1734 in the rue de Charonne by François Barbin, the factory was moved to Mennecy in 1748, where it continued until 1773, when it was again transferred to Bourg-la-Reine until eventually closing in 1806.

The body of early Mennecy porcelain soft-paste is a milky-white, the glaze 'wet' and brilliant, absorbing the well-known Mennecy rose-pink enamel until it almost appears to run. Due to the harsh monopolies granted to the Vincennes and Sèvres factories, Mennecy were prohi-

☞ *left*

MENNECY PORCELAIN SAUCE TUREEN

FRENCH *c.1750–60*

A soft-paste porcelain sauce tureen with cover and stand, painted in enamel colours with flowers in the Meissen style.

Length: About 16cm (6⅛in)

bited from applying gilding to their wares.

Their shapes were few and simple, providing ample space for their versions of the *Deutsche Blumen* of Meissen. In common with the contemporary French factories they produced many small ware, including snuff-boxes, scent-bottles, knife-handles and some charming covered so-called 'custard-cups' with close spiral reeding. The most common mark used at Mennecy is an incised 'D.V' for 'de Villeroy', occasionally in red or blue enamel.

☞ *left*

SÈVRE PORCELAIN BASIN AND EWER

FRENCH 1761

A soft-paste porcelain basin and ewer from the Sèvre factory, painted by Nicholas Catrice in enamel colours on a jaune jonquille *ground. Height: About 20cm (7³⁄₄in)*

Vincennes and Sèvres

THE IMPORTANT French production centre at Vincennes was established in about 1738, but very little porcelain was produced, with the exception of flowers, until after 1745, when a new company under the name of Charles Adam was formed. In 1756 a new building, close to Versailles and near Madame de Pompadour's château at Bellevue, was occupied, surviving as a museum to this day. Few profits were being made and to avoid closure, Madame de Pompadour, who had shown great interest in the factory, persuaded King Louis XV to become the sole owner, which he did, making Sèvres a Royal Factory. This royal interest was continued by Louis XVI and Marie Antoinette from 1774. In 1793, the factory was taken over by the Republic, since when the production has continued to this day.

The most admired of the Vincennes and Sèvres wares are those produced in the beautiful, early, soft-paste. Although after 1768 the necessary clays for the production of a hard-paste were discovered near Limoges, both materials were produced over many years, and it was 1804 before the use of the soft-paste finally came to a halt.

It was probably due to the interest of the King and Madame de Pompadour that so many talented designers, sculptors and painters were called upon to apply their skills to production resulting in the graceful shapes of the period. These included ice-pails, jugs with long cylindrical necks and slender vases, sometimes decorated only with outstanding quality gilding or coupled with the first of their fine ground colours, *blue lapis,* the underglaze-blue introduced in 1749.

Other popular colours were added in quick succession, *bleu céleste* or turquoise in 1752, *jaune jonquille,* yellow, 1753, green in 1756 and *rose,* not Rose Pompadour, 1757. It was not until 1763 that use was made of a dark-blue enamel, *blue de roi,* a colour much copied by such English factories as Minton and Coalport.

The very informative marks used at the factory are a great aid to the collector. The interlaced 'L's of the French crown were used as a mark from about 1750, into which from 1753 a series of date-letters were introduced: A–Z means 1753–77, AA–PP 1778–93. In addition many of the 385 painters and gilders applied their initials or a distinctive symbol, to help identify their work. These date letters are a good guide in helping to decide whether the piece in question is genuine; for example any piece with *rose* as a ground colour, should not bear a date-letter prior to 'E', 1757, when the colour was first used. Similarly any piece of hard-paste porcelain is unlikely to be dated prior to 'R' or 'S', 1770 or 1771.

From 1793 into the early 19th century many pieces of soft-paste Sèvres, which had been sold by the factory after 1793 either blank or slightly faulty, were frequently re-decorated in a popular style, sometimes by painters who had previously been employed at the factory. Production has continued to the present day, but the quality of their early wares has never been equalled. There were many bogus pieces of Sèvres made in and around Paris in the late 19th century, usually wrongly marked.

Scandinavian earthenware

THE COUNTRIES of Scandinavia produced very few original wares, and apart from those on show in museum collections, they are rarely seen. The major styles followed those of Holland and Germany.

One of the most interesting potteries was founded by a German potter, Johann Christoph Ludwig von Lücke, at Schleswig in 1755. The wares produced were different from the majority of their contemporaries, being mostly painted in a manganese-purple. The most interesting forms produced were those in the shape of a Bishop's mitre, which were intended to hold a local punch known as 'Mitre'. They also produced some very large wares including table-tops.

The Rörstrand factory in Sweden has a very long history, and celebrated its 233rd anniversary with a fine exhibition at the

☞ *left*
FAIENCE PLATE
SWEDISH 1768
A tin-glazed earthenware
(faience) plate from
Marieberg, decorated
with a transfer-print.
Diameter: About 20cm
(7¾in)

An early attempt to produce a true porcelain on the estate of Marieberg, Stockholm, ended in 1759 in a disastrous fire, no further porcelain was produced in Sweden until 1766. Then, the Frenchman Pierre Berthevin, who had formerly been a modeller at Mennecy, made a very similar soft-paste porcelain, decorated in much the same manner with flower painting in pastel shades, favouring the so-called covered custard-cup.

True hard-paste porcelain was eventually made by Jacob Dortu, who had gained his knowledge from Berlin, but the production only continued until 1782, when the factory was closed.

Dutch Delftware

TIN-GLAZED wares were being made in the Low Countries at Antwerp, Haarlem, Rotterdam, Amsterdam and Middelburg for many years before 1609, when Holland together with six other Provinces in Northern Netherlands became independent of the County of Flanders and duchy of Burgundy. These 16th century wares were often the work of Italian migrant potters and are difficult to attribute, but it is the later Dutch wares which are most frequently seen, made from the middle of the 17th century in the town of Delft. Many potters had moved there, occupying buildings previously housing breweries whose trade had declined, hence the adopted names of many of the potteries, such as 'The Hatchet', 'The Golden Flowerpot' and 'The Two Little Ships'.

Victoria & Albert Museum in London. The factory was founded in about 1726, but it was nearer the middle of the 18th century before they began to produce fine tin-glazed wares, which were often decorated with so-called *bianco-sopra-bianco*, which involved decorating a tinted glaze with white enamel. From 1767 some tin-glazed wares were decorated with English-style transfer-printing, but these pieces are very rare.

Scandinavian porcelain

THERE WAS a short-lived porcelain production at Copenhagen under the direction of the Frenchman, Louis Fournier, between 1759 and 1765, when it came to a halt due to high costs. It was in 1775 that the present-day production of fine hard-paste porcelain was first established in Copenhagen under F. H. Müller; in 1779 this concern was taken over by the King and became The Royal Danish Porcelain Factory. Their early wares were of a poor quality and greyish in colour, their styles following those of Meissen, often decorated in underglaze-blue in similar patterns. By 1789 however their material

and enamel decoration had been sufficiently improved to enable them to produce the famous 2,000 piece *Flora Danica* service, intended for Catherine II of Russia, but taken over by the Danish King. The service was painted in enamel colours by Johann Christoph Bayer, a task lasting thirteen years, and it can be seen today in the Rosenborg Castle, Copenhagen.

From about 1780 the factory produced a wide range of figures, many left in white biscuit porcelain and modelled under the direction of Anton Carl Luplau, who had previously been a modeller at the Fürstenberg factory. After 1835 many new models were introduced after the many statues by the Danish sculptor Thorwaldsen.

☞ *left*
ROYAL DANISH PORCELAIN
BOWL
DANISH Late 18th c.
A hard-paste porcelain
bowl painted in enamel
colours and gilt from the
Royal Danish Porcelain
Factory in Copenhagen.
Diameter: About 20cm
(7¾in)

Some of the best Delftware, made between 1650 and 1710, was decorated in the fashion of the Chinese blue-and-white porcelain of late Ming times, which at the time The Dutch East India Company was importing in large quantities. Their reproductions in tin-glazed earthenware are at times so good that they are difficult to separate from the Chinese porcelain, without the opportunity of handling. This was partly due to the fact that they generally applied a second transparent glaze upon the opaque tin-glaze, in order to acquire a porcelain-like brilliance.

Some of the finest examples of Dutch Delft, made by such potters as Adrianus Kocks, to the designs of Daniel Marot, were made for the English nobility at the time of the reign of William and Mary (1689–1702).

At the beginning of the 18th century, Delft potters extended their high-temperature palette to include green, iron-red and yellow, which enabled them to copy the Oriental *famille-verte* colours of the Kangxi period and the Japanese porcelains of Arita.

English pottery

PRIOR TO the 17th century there were very few pieces of pottery made in Britain which can be considered popular collectors' items, although justifiably exhibited in many museums. The majority of these early wares were unglazed and it was not until the 12th century that a raw lead-glaze was 'pounced' on to the surface of the clay before firing.

The area of Stoke-on-Trent in North Staffordshire has remained the centre of the English ceramic industry since the early 17th century, when the early form of bottle-kilns were being fired with local coal and all the necessary clays were available nearby. The majority of the decorative wares made there are 'slipwares', usually thrown or moulded from a warm-red clay, often with a surface dressing of a filtered slip of a buff-tone, decorated with trailed or dotted slip of a contrasting

☞ *right*

DELFT EARTHENWARE DISH

DUTCH c.1650
A tin-glazed earthenware dish painted in high-temperature blue in the style of Chinese export wares of the late Ming period.
Diameter: About 36cm (14in)

colour, after which the surface was covered with a thick treacle-like lead-glaze. The best of these slipwares were produced to order, to commemorate a coronation, birth, marriage or some special event. Wares signed 'Thomas Toft' as part of the decoration date from the reign of Charles II.

At this same time an important English potter was at work in Fulham, London. John Dwight took out a patent in 1672 to make salt-glazed stoneware, or 'Cologne Ware', but despite the patent, by the end of the century other potters were making similar wares in Nottingham, Derbyshire and Staffordshire. Among the potters John Dwight accused of infringing his patent were John and David Elers, who worked with Dwight for three years before moving to Bradwell Wood, Staffordshire. Here during the last years of the 17th century they made some fine red-stoneware mugs and tea-wares, all unglazed and often decorated with moulded sprigs of flowers and leaves, a type of ware which was continued well into the 18th century by other Staffordshire potters.

From the beginning of the 18th century we follow the development of two types of ware, salt-glazed stoneware and lead-

glazed earthenware. The former was soon improved upon to become a fine white body, with a glaze often likened to orange-peel, and used to produce a wide range of table-wares and simple but pleasing figures, such as 'pew groups'. By the middle of the century some salt-glaze was decorated with enamel colours, which at times can be likened to that applied to Longton Hall porcelain. When fired to a lower temperature, this material remained earthenware, upon which a lead-glaze was applied at a second firing. This resulted in the first English cream-coloured earthenwares, a type which was to be perfected by Josiah Wedgwood and used for the production of wares in Neo-Classical style.

From about 1740 Staffordshire potteries began to produce many delightful human and animal forms, using the natural colour clays under a rich-lead-glaze. This is known as Astburyware, or, when further decorated with metallic oxides, Astbury-Whieldon, although other potters made similar wares. The most famous English potter was Josiah Wedgwood (1730–1795), who after serving his apprenticeship with his elder brother was in partnership with Thomas Whieldon from 1754–59, when

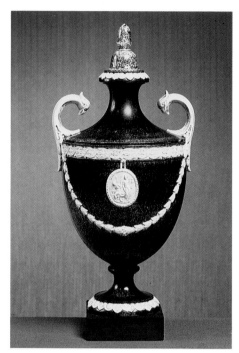

look like Chinese porcelain, they have become much sought after collectors' items, especially if dated, and have a unique naive charm.

Returning to Staffordshire, it was from about 1770 that the Wood family of Burslem produced a wide variety of well-modelled figures, decorated with glazes which had previously been coloured green, yellow, blue or purple. This gave them the advantage of applying the colours where required, rather than the earlier Whieldon method. It is at this time that so many Toby Jugs are credited to John Wood.

Similar figures were produced during the 1790s, but now coloured with enamel colours on a clear glaze in the porcelain manner, soon to be followed in the early decades of the 19th century by earthenware

figures, also decorated with enamels, often with a *bocage,* composed of a tree or foliage sprinkled with flowers, which formed a background to the figure or group. Walton and Salt are two Staffordshire potters known to have specialized in this type of figure. Many similar interesting groups with table-like bases are attributed, without any good grounds, to a potter named Obadiah Sherratt.

The mass production of the simple flat-backed earthenware Staffordshire figures began at the start of Queen Victoria's reign in 1837, often made by young children, working very long hours for very poor pay. These models which portrayed figures from all walks of life, from royalty

he became an independent master-potter in Burslem, Staffordshire. Among his first productions were useful wares covered with a fine green glaze, soon to be followed by a refined creamware, which he was permitted to name 'Queen's Ware'. In 1767 he produced black basalt stoneware, from which the famous vases were made to commemorate the start of his partnership in 1769 with Thomas Bentley, who died in 1780. It was during this period that the now famous blue-jasperware was first introduced, decorated with white moulded reliefs. One of Wedgwood's outstanding achievements was his 1790 copy in black jasper ware of the early Roman glass vase, the Portland Vase.

During these years the British potter had also been producing English delftware, (small 'd'). Starting in Aldgate, London, in about 1575, it was soon being made in Southwark, Lambeth and Vauxhall, before spreading to Bristol, Liverpool, Glasgow and Dublin. Unlike later European potters engaged in this manufacture, the British potters only rarely used enamel colours, an exception being the delftware tiles made at Liverpool and decorated by the firm of Sadler and Green. Because British potters did not try to make wares

☞ *above left*
WEDGWOOD
EARTHENWARE VASE
ENGLISH c.1775
A cream-coloured
earthenware vase, marked
'Wedgwood & Bentley',
on a black basalt base. It
is decorated with high-
temperature colours to
resemble stoneware.
Height: 31cm (12¹⁄₈in)

☞ *right*
WOOD OF BURSLEM
EARTHENWARE GROUP
ENGLISH c.1775
An earthenware group of
figures entitled 'The
Vicar and Moses',
decorated in high-
temperature colours.
Made by John or Ralph
Wood at Burslem in
Staffordshire, it bears the
impressed mark, 'Ra
Wood/BURSLEM'.
Height: 22cm (8¹⁄₂in)

to criminals, are eagerly sought by today's collectors, especially if the characters are named.

Among the many earthenwares made during the last century, there is little doubt that those decorated with underglaze-blue prints, taken from an engraved copper-plate, formed the bulk of the output of Staffordshire until well into the 19th century. The most common design used was one of the various versions of the popular Willow pattern. In addition to the numerous *chinoiserie* designs, plates and other table-wares show typical British scenes, stately homes, views of Italy and India, and views of excavations taking place in Asia Minor, many of the latter taken from contemporary topographical prints. The American market was also well catered for, with views of American scenes and buildings. These wares are particularly interesting when marked with the maker's name, and sometimes with the name of the pattern or place depicted.

Among the many highly collectable Victorian wares are the so-called 'majolicas', which include a wide range of useful and decorative forms, painted with highly coloured lead-glazes. Wares of this type were first exhibited by the Staffordshire firm of Minton, at the Great Exhibition held in Hyde Park in 1851. Other neighbouring firms, such as George Jones and

☞ *above*

SPODE EARTHENWARE COMPORT
ENGLISH c. 1815
An earthenware comport from the Spode factory at Stoke in Staffordshire, decorated with an underglaze blue print of a 'Citadel near Corinth'. Length: 27cm (10½in)

☞ *below*

STONEWARE BIRD
ENGLISH c. 1815
This salt-glazed stoneware bird, with detachable head, was made by the Martin brothers in their London & Southall studios. Height: About 20cm (7¾in)

Adams & Co. soon produced similar wares.

During the second half of the 19th century the Lambeth firm of Doulton produced some interesting art-pottery, which was decorated from 1871 by artists who had been trained at the Lambeth School of Art. Each piece was signed and dated, often by Hannah, Florence or Arthur Barlow, George Tinworth or Frank Butler, whose names, among others, are known for their excellent work.

A further range of late salt-glazed stonewares which attract today's collectors are those made by the three Martin brothers, the fourth taking charge of the business. Their decoration was confined to the colours of the natural clays, with an occasional use of a high temperature colour, and usualy took on a distinctive Japanese style. They also produced some rather grotesque drinking vessels in the form of human faces or birds, which are highly regarded today. They established their pottery in Fulham, London, in 1873, moving to Southall in 1877, but by 1915 three of the brothers had died, and the firm had virtually ceased trading, although Robert Wallace Martin endeavoured to continue alone into the early 1920s. These brothers might well be considered to be the first English studio-potters.

Another interesting figure in the pottery world at this time was William De Morgan (1839–1917), who was more concerned with design and decoration than the production of pottery forms, and he is known to have purchased undecorated 'blanks' on which to apply many of his Persian and Near-Eastern lustre decorations. De Morgan was very much under the influence of the William Morris School, as can be seen on some of his beautifully decorated tiles. Following his training at the Royal Academy School, he commenced working at Chelsea in 1872, where he mainly produced large dishes and tiles. In 1882 he moved to Wimbledon, where he stayed for six years, before returning to Fulham, where he went into partnership with Halsey Ricardo. De Morgan retired from business in 1905, due to ill health, but other partners and decorators continued to run his establishment for several more years.

English & Welsh porcelain

ALTHOUGH SINCE about 1745 British porcelain manufacturers have produced an enormous number of wares, unlike the earthenware potters they only rarely showed any great originality in shapes or forms of decoration. They looked first to the Meissen factory, then to Sèvres and during the 19th century revived many of the earlier fashions.

The Chelsea factory was started in 1745 by a Huguenot silversmith, Nicholas Sprimont, who produced a wide range of useful, ornamental wares and figures until 1769, when just prior to his death in 1771 the Chelsea concern was purchased by William Duesbury, the proprietor of the Derby factory, who ran both productions until 1784, in the so-called Chelsea/Derby period.

Over recent years information has come to light concerning a second Chelsea concern, which seemingly only ran from about 1749 to 1754, producing a few useful wares and figures, making them very expensive collectors' items. It appeared to specialize in small scent-bottles, mostly of human form. This factory, of which

☞ *right*
CHELSEA PORCELAIN
ASPARAGUS DISH
ENGLISH *c.1755*
A soft-paste porcelain asparagus dish and cover, made at the Chelsea pottery during the 'red-anchor' period.
Length: About 18cm (7in)

☞ *below left*
CHELSEA PORCELAIN JAR
ENGLISH *c.1750–54*
From the Chelsea 'Girl-on-a-swing' factory, a soft-paste porcelain jar.
Height: 13.4cm (5¼in)

we still have much to learn, is called 'The Girl-in-a-Swing' group on account of one rare model. No factory-marks are recorded.

Chelsea frequently used factory-marks, first an incised triangle, c.1745–49, then a raised-anchor on an applied oval medallion, c.1747–52, followed by a small red-painted anchor, c.1752–c.58, and finally the much copied gold anchor. This was used until the takeover, after which the anchor was often used together with a 'D' for Derby until nearer 1784, usually in monogram form.

Few of the actual workers involved at the Chelsea factory have been identified,

but the best of their models are considered to be work of Joseph Willems. Some of the most pleasing painting, in colour, of Aesop's Fables is attributed to Jefferyes Hamett O'Neale, who from about 1768 was engaged at the Worcester factory or decorating their wares independently.

The Bow factory, just in Essex, east of London, was also producing a soft-paste porcelain which contained calcined animal-bone from about 1747, continuing until 1776. They produced a large quantity of table-wares and figures and at the peak of their prosperity were employing three hundred hands in their 'New Canton' factory. Unlike Chelsea, their main produc-

tion was of useful wares decorated in a Chinese manner with underglaze-blue, although they did in addition produce a great variety of poorly modelled figures, some of which were sold 'in the white' and decorated by such independent painters as William Duesbury, who was working in London prior to becoming involved with Derby.

Recent excavations carried out in London on the mid-18th century factory sites of Limehouse and Vauxhall have enabled us to learn more of two groups of porcelains which have previously been thought to have been made in Liverpool.

The Derby factory continued with an unbroken history until 1848, and then there was a period during which production was continued to a lesser degree, by previous employees, until 1876, when the present-day Royal Crown Derby was established. The best wares made at Derby are those in neo-classical style, which were produced during the partnership of the two factories between 1770 and 1784.

The only English factory that has survived until today with an unbroken history is that established by Dr Wall and his partners in 1751 at Worcester. To obtain the necessary licence to quarry one of their essential ingredients, soaprock or steatite to make a soapstone porcelain, it was decided to take over an existing Bristol factory, which had been producing this new-type body from about 1748.

There are some early wares which we have to term Bristol/Worcester as it is difficult to decide at which factory they were made, as only very few of the Bristol pieces are marked. Until about 1755, the majority of the Worcester wares were decorated in underglaze-blue painting, but from about that time they also produced many very attractive pieces painted in enamel colours in a variety of styles with gilding, concentrating on fine tablewares and only making a few poor quality figures. Some very high quality decoration was added to Worcester 'blanks' or those only decorated with underglaze-blue grounds, by James Giles, an independent decorator working in London

☞ opposite below
CHELSEA PORCELAIN BASKET-FIGURES
ENGLISH *c. 1760–65*
A pair of soft-paste porcelain basket figures painted with enamel colours and gilt. They are marked with an anchor in gold.
Height: About 17cm (6½in)

from about 1765 into the early 1770s.

The potters of Staffordshire produced a very glassy type of soft-paste porcelain at Longton Hall from c. 1749 to 1760, but the undertaking was far from a success, although these sometimes very poorly produced wares are much sought by today's collectors, as also are those of the manager, William Littler, who continued a production of similar quality at West Pans in Scotland from about 1764 into the mid-1770s.

Some small, pleasing, useful wares were made from bone-porcelain at a Lowestoft factory on the east coast of Suffolk, where they operated from 1757 until c.1799. Prior to 1768 all their porcelains were decorated in only underglaze-blue and have a lot in common with those made at Bow, but from that time they also decorated a wide range of wares in Chinese styles. The most interesting pieces made at Lowestoft are those named and dated for the recipients and those which are painted with 'A Trifle from Lowestoft', an early form of a 'Present from the Seaside'.

Thomas Turner ran a successful factory

☞ above
LONGTON HALL PORCELAIN FIGURE
ENGLISH *c. 1756–7*
A soft-paste porcelain figure of Cupid on a galloping horse, painted in enamel colours, and modelled on an original bronze by Francesco Fanelli.
Height: 15cm (5⅞in)

at Caughley, in Shropshire, from about 1772 until 1799, when it was taken over by John Rose, the owner of the Coalport factory. Many Caughley wares decorated with underglaze-blue prints have a lot in common with the contemporary wares of Worcester, but over recent years excavations on both factory sites have proved that around 1785 the Caughley wares are superior to their rival. Some of the finest Caughley jugs, decorated with enamel colours and gilt are now recognized as

☞ *above*

**ROCKINGHAM BONE-
CHINA VASE**

ENGLISH c.1830
*A bone-china vase
painted in enamel colours
and gilt by Edwin Steel,
and manufactured at the
Rockingham factory at
Swinton, Yorkshire.
Height: About 30cm
(11¾in)*

☞ *right*

PORCELAIN HARE

ENGLISH 1768–70
*A hard-paste porcelain
hare from Plymouth in
Devon, painted in enamel
colours.
Height: 16cm (6¼in)*

being the work of Chamberlain, who had broken away from the Worcester factory.

It was 1768 before William Cookworthy put to use the materials he had discovered in Cornwall for the production of a hard-paste porcelain. His first factory at Plymouth was moved to Bristol in 1770, where it continued under the charge of Richard Champion until 1781. During this period many well-decorated table-wares were made, together with some rather large figures of the Seasons and the Continents, but their hard-paste useful wares were inferior and more expensive than those which were being imported from the Far East in great quantities at the time.

In 1781, a group of Staffordshire potters purchased the unexpired years of Champion's patent for the production of hard-paste porcelain and established the New Hall factory, where they continued to make hard-paste teawares and other small table-wares until about 1812, when in common with many other English factories, they made bone-china, until closing in 1835.

There are numerous other British factories which produced hybrid porcelains and bone-china from the early 19th cen-

tury, including, Coalport, Spode (later Copeland), Minton, Davenport, Rockingham and Daniel, to name but a few.

Among the many porcelains sought by today's collectors are those made in South Wales at Nantgarw and Swansea, where the previously mentioned William Billingsley was involved with both concerns from 1813–20, but his fine soft-paste porcelain proved very difficult to fire and there were many kiln losses. However 'blanks' of these wares were much in demand by independent decorators in London and elsewhere, working mostly for retailers.

American pottery & porcelain

MOST OF of our knowledge concerning the manufacture of earthenware and stoneware among the early American colonies centres around New England, where prior to the early 17th century all their needs were imported from Europe. From the mid-17th century and well into the 1800s the settlers were producing their own basic ceramic requirements from a red earthenware, covered with a honey-coloured lead-glaze. It was sometimes decorated in a simple fashion with manganese, which fired to a dark-brown or black.

Although salt-glazed stonewares were imported from both Germany and England prior to the Revolution at a low rate of tax, the higher duties later imposed saw a growing production of stoneware in New York, New Jersey and New England, which in turn gradually replaced the softer and more vulnerable earthenwares. One of the major suppliers was Edmands Pottery, in Charlestown, Massachusetts. Local productions were still not in sufficient quantity to cater for demand by the increasing population and Britain continued to be the main supplier of salt-glaze, creamware and pearlware, much of which catered for American taste. From 1784 there was also a large amount of Chinese porcelain being made for the

☞ left
PORCELAIN BASKET
AMERICAN c.1770
*A soft-paste porcelain
basket painted in
underglaze-blue, and
made at the Philadelphia
factory of Bonnin and
Morris.
Diameter: About 18cm
(7in)*

American market and imported direct by
their own trading vessels.

A wide variety of red earthenware and
salt-glaze continued to be produced in
New York and Bennington, Vermont, to
serve the local communities well into the
mid-19th century, including jugs, pans,
porringers and storage jars, often decorated with cream-coloured slip and so
similar to the 17th and 18th century English wares that sure attribution is often
difficult. One major pottery was that of
Hervey Brooks, a farmer-potter of
Connecticut, who was potting from 1802
until firing his last kiln in 1864 at the age
of 84.

Our knowledge of a soft-paste porcelain thought at one time to have been
produced by Andrew Duché, in Savannah,
Georgia, in about 1740, is too vague to
record, but we do have knowledge of
Gousse Bonnin and George Morris, who
in the early 1770s established a short-lived
factory in Philadelphia, where they made
soft-paste porcelain tablewares, decorated
in underglaze-blue, sometimes resembling
those made at Bow and Derby in England,
although usually more heavily potted.

Another American porcelain factory of
note was that of William Ellis Tucker,
who produced a hard-paste porcelain in
Philadelphia from 1826, after which
various partners were involved. In 1831
Alexander Hemphill became a partner and
the concern continued to produce porce-

lain under members of the two families
until 1838. During these twelve years it is
difficult to identify their productions
from those of the Empire styles being
made in Paris, if unmarked. Fortunately
the original pattern books are preserved in
the Philadelphia Museum.

Many other later 19th century potteries,
including the United States Pottery
Company at Bennington, Vermont and
Christopher W. Fenton, also from Bennington, and the Trenton Pottery Company, New Jersey, all made large quantities of Parian ware figures and decorative
tablewares. The best known of these
Parian figures must be that of 'The Greek
Slave' of which the full-size marble statue
was shown at the Great Exhibition of 1851,
under a specially erected canopy in the
American Section.

Production of art pottery did not become popular in the U.S.A. until the
1870s, at the time of the Centennial Celebrations, when at least six major concerns
started up in Cincinnati alone, but by 1890
only that of Rookwood was still active.
Rookwood was started by Mrs Maria
Longworth Nichols, daughter of a
wealthy local family, in 1880 and survived
until 1941. The early years were financially
supported by the founder's wealthy father,
but from 1883, after the appointment of a
manager, the pottery began to flourish,
aided by the production of commercial
and utility wares. Some of the finest of the

art pottery wares are those decorated with
skilfully applied slip decoration under a
wide range of translucent coloured glazes.
Other forms of decoration consisted of
carved, incised, or impressed designs,
under similar fine glazes, all of which are
widely sought today.

In 1889 the Rookwood factory was
transferred to the ownership of the
manager, William Watts Taylor, who
from that time concentrated on decorative
wares, rather than functional, and moved
to a larger building, where by 1899 he was
employing thirty-six artists in the art
department alone, one being Artus van
Briggle, who later founded his own pottery at Colorado Springs. Up until about
1910, nearly all the Rookwood artists
signed their own work.

Collecting ceramics

BECAUSE OF their beauty and historical
interest, and also because they are easy to
transport and display, ceramics are highly
sought after by collectors. Prices can be
very high – for instance an 11th century
Chinese celadon dish was sold at auction
for £7,500 ($13,500) in 1987, an Isnik
piece of 1580 reached £10,500 ($19,500)
a 19th century fake even achieved
£2,200 ($4,000), and a pair of Meissen
Commedia dell'arte figures went for £4,800
($8,800). Fashions do change however; in
1990 some of the highest prices were paid
for English wares: a Minton maiolica
fountain went for £6,100 ($11,200), a
Wedgwood fairyland lustre vase went for
£8,500 ($15,700), while a pair of Whieldon
figures reached £32,000 ($59,000).

Although it could be said that there are
no 'cheap' antique ceramics, there is scope
for the more modest collector to buy
good pieces for between £300 and £500
($500–$900) or less. Excellent pieces of
New Hall porcelain, made in Staffordshire
between 1781–1835, can be obtained for
quite modest prices. It is also a good idea
to look at the work of modern studio
potters, for their work will be the antiques
of the future.

GLASS

SIMON COTTLE

☞ *above*

RUBINGLAS

GERMAN Late 17th c.

*Early rubinglas with silver-gilt mounts, amongst the first
pieces to be made in Germany, in the late 17th century. The
ruby colour was achieved by adding gold to the molten glass.*

Glass is one of the most undervalued of collectable antiques. From stained glass windows to paperweights and from decanters to scent flasks, glass has been used throughout history in many different ways, sometimes as a substitute for ceramics, wood or metalwork, but often as a wonderfully adaptable material in its own right. The development of the wine glass and goblet especially in the last 300 years now provides much interest for collectors and historians alike, not to mention the social historians for whom the traditions and rituals associated with wine drinking can be so fascinating. This crystal clear product, so often overlooked in its colourless state, may embody skills which in the present machine age can hardly be rivalled.

Glass is essentially made from mixing silica (usually sand) with an alkali (potash or soda) and sometimes another base (lead or lime) and melting at high temperature. The manufacture of glass has its origins in the Eastern Mediterranean where it was developed by the Egyptians in the 3rd century BC. Most glass at this date was made by casting methods. Molten rods of variously coloured canes of glass were wound round a core of sand or clay and then combed into feathered patterns often resembling the markings on semi-precious hard stones. At this date glass was considered as a substitute for precious and semi-precious gemstones and was made into beads for bracelets and necklaces and as insets in furniture.

Early glass
~

THE EARLIEST type of glass known, soda glass, was used by the Egyptians, Romans and, from the 15th century AD, by the Venetians who called it 'cristallo'. From the 1st century BC entire glass vessels were produced by a simple yet revolutionary new method which involved the aid of a long pipe. The technique of free-blowing glass is still today the chief method used for producing high quality tablewares and studio glass.

Much early glass is incomplete and bears an iridescence which is largely due to a degrading ageing process or from burial in the ground. This unintentional decoration has inspired artists, such as Emile Gallé and L. C. Tiffany at the turn of the 20th century and recent contemporary studio artists, to reproduce this attractive effect by chemical methods. Together with bowls and drinking vessels, large numbers of mould-blown flasks for holding ointments and oils were made, most in imitation of common pottery and metal shapes. The rarer and more intricate examples command high prices and faithful 20th century reproductions of genuine glass antiquities, particularly from Damascus, can fool the unwitting collector.

Cameo glass was known to the ancient Egyptians but was perfected by the Romans in the 1st century BC and the 1st

☞ *below*

CLASSICAL GLASS

ROMAN 2nd c. BC – 2nd c. AD
Various pieces from Ancient Rome and the Mediterranean. The Romans perfected cameo glass, and also used the oldest known form of glass, soda glass.

century AD. The Portland Vase at the British Museum is one of the best known examples of an art form which required the casing of a glass vessel within a second or even third layer which was then carved to expose the different layers. The technique was revived by the Chinese in the 18th century on Peking Glass, especially for snuff bottles, and used highly creatively at the end of the 19th century by artist-glassmakers in the West Midlands – notably John Northwood and George Woodall. It was popular during the Art Nouveau period in France and in the United States where Gallé and Tiffany were the leading exponents.

Glass-making in Venice

By 1292, when glass was in production on the island of Murano, Venice was a well-established and influential glass-making centre. Its early glassware consisted of beads, jewellery, mirrors and window glass. Enamelled ceremonial cups and winged goblets were popular in the 15th century and by the 16th and 17th centuries glassmaking in Venice had reached its height of popularity and its products were copied throughout Europe – especially in Spain and the Low Countries (known as *façon de Venise*), where immigrant Italian glassmakers practised their skills.

Besides *façon de Venise* bottles, flasks, wine cups and goblets, a more compli-cated and ambitious range of products was manufactured. This glass was made from soda which is very light in weight and consequently extremely brittle. It is a wonder that so much has survived. Ele-gant bowls and goblets with white enamelled threads forming gauzes and intricate lace-like networks, pincered decoration and trailed coloured rims (especially deep marine-blue) are typical. Efforts to reproduce this glass in the 19th century in Venice and elsewhere were only partially successful, but collectors should be aware of the high quality reproductions made by the Anglo-Murano Glass Co. in

Venice under the direction of Antonio Salviati. Salviati's glass is generally heav-ier both in weight and style than the ori-ginal on which it is loosely based and is too perfect to be considered as deliberate forgery.

Early Northern European glass

A SEPARATE PROVINCIAL tradition of glassmaking occurred in Northern medieval Europe, especially in the areas that we now know as Germany, and in the South of England. *Waldglas* or forest glass was made in the woodland regions of central Europe, and generally stained green in colour by the wood ash from the timber furnaces. Some of the best-known vessels are *roemers* with spiral trailed feet and applied prunted decoration. These have been widely reproduced in the 19th and present centuries and the roemer form is still popular today.

Later, in the 16th and 17th century,

German glassmakers based in towns and small settlements rather than in forests or woodland, produced some of the finest communal drinking vessels – *humpen* – of a straw-tinted glass decorated with brightly enamelled coats of arms, many of which were dated. These large and impressive drinking vessels, perhaps inspired by contemporary silver tankards and flagons, were reproduced in the 1870s and 1880s even to the extent of adding appropriate 16th and 17th century dates. The decoration on these later productions is, however, usually rather too stiff and formal for most tastes.

The decline of glassmaking in Venice at the end of the 17th century is traditionally considered to have resulted from the development in the 1680s of the superior lead crystal glass in England by George Ravenscroft. However, whilst this may have seen the emergence of a stronger English glassmaking tradition, the intro-duction of lime to Continental soda glass at the beginning of the 18th century and

☞ *right*
HUMPEN
GERMAN 1652
Humpen *were communal drinking vessels, bearing enamelled coats of arms. This one has the arms of Brandenberg, and is clearly dated 1652.*

☞ *right*
WINE GLASSES
ENGLISH *Early 18th c.*
*A group of early 18th
century English lead
crystal wine glasses,
including several heavy
balusters.*

the recently acknowledged development
of lead crystal in the Low Countries in the
1730s and in Scandinavia in the 1760s,
highlights the 18th century as a distinct
period of change and excitement for glass
collectors.

The emergence
of the English style

THE DEVELOPMENT of lead crystal
meant that not only was the glass a great
deal more robust and less liable to the
'crizzling' which affects much soda glass
causing it to disintegrate internally, but it
was also more brilliant in colour and
softer so that it could be deeply engraved.
English glassmakers at first continued to
produce glass in the style that they were
used to – namely Venetian. However, a
more idiosyncratic approach was adopted,
influenced in particular by architectural
forms, and a definite English style began
to emerge.

Trailed decoration, whereby threads of
glass were laid onto the surface of the
vessel, is perhaps a continuation of the
earlier Venetian tradition, whilst the
moulded 'gadroons' found on posset pots
and sweetmeat glasses closely resemble
silverware at this date. For collectors,
however, it is drinking glasses which are
amongst the most collectable items of the

18th century. Traditionally made in either
two or three sections – the bowl, stem
and foot – the variety of bowl shapes,
stem forms and foot types provides a rich
range of wares from which one may form
a collection. Although the rarer items can
fetch several thousand pounds it is still
possible for collectors to purchase early
18th century glasses for under £200
($350).

With changing fashions, each section of
a wine glass was adapted, too. Economic
influences have also had an important
part to play in these developments. The
changing shapes provide a guide for
collectors to date their glasses more
accurately, though it is apparent that
some forms remained popular for very
long periods. From the heavy balusters of
the first quarter of the 18th century, their
stems based on the architectural baluster,
such as one finds on a staircase, and combining a variety of 'knops' such as mushroom, acorn or simple ball shapes, to the
light balusters of the mid-18th century
with their slender multi-knopped stems,
one can see the evolution of what is now
accepted as the characteristic English
wine glass.

The shape of the bowl has evolved
generally from the Anglo-Venetian styles
of the 17th century, but by the mid-18th
century there are recognizable types
appearing which are peculiar to England

alone. The capacity of bowls continued
to decrease throughout the century and
with the introduction of the glass excise
tax in 1745 with its emphasis on the weight
of the glass, the style of drinking glasses
generally became much lighter. The size
of the bowl in proportion to the stem
may also be an indication of its intended
use. Deep and rounded funnel bowls, for
example, often engraved with barley and
hops motifs and with short stems, were
most probably designed for drinking
short ale, much stronger than the ale we
drink today. Smaller capacity bowls on
tall stems may have been intended for
cordial, whilst the average-sized bowl
engraved with fruiting vine decoration
obviously relates to drinking the grape
and can correctly be referred to as a wine
glass.

Single bubbles, or tears, of air found in
the stems and knops of the earlier heavy
balusters were incorporated as concentric
beading in ball knops on light balusters
and used more elaborately from the 1740s
to produce airtwist-stemmed wine glasses
and goblets. In this instance, tears of air,
trapped in a gather of glass, are drawn
out into short slender stem lengths, twist-
ing all the while to produce either close
knit spirals, gauze or sharper and more
brilliant corktwists – in some cases resembling mercury. The domed and folded
foot, a typical feature of pre-1745 glass, is

generally abolished (though in some provincial areas it continued in fashion until the end of the century) and a plain conical foot – which uses less glass – takes its place.

A further development from about the 1760s is the introduction of opaque-white enamel canes into the stems to form intricate spirals and gauzes of a similar nature to the earlier airtwist variety. Closely resembling Venetian glass *latticinio* and *lattimo* techniques of the 15th and 16th centuries, these were made by initially juxtapositioning the required number of short thick canes of enamel and encasing them in a gather of clear glass. The glass was then drawn out, sometimes to a length of thirty feet – the canes being twisted at the same time. On completion the rod of twisted glass was cut into three-inch lengths, each length applied to a previously-blown wine-glass bowl. A disc foot, shaped from a gather of glass held by the glassmaker's assistant on the tip of a pontil rod, is added to the other end to produce a three-piece wine glass. Coloured canes of various shades of red, blue, yellow and green were popular in the 1770s but this fashion was short-lived. This makes colour-twists, as they are generally known, quite rare and consequently highly desirable and over-expensive for the average collector.

The advent of glass-cutting in the mid-century saw by the 1770s the introduction of facet-cut stems. Bowls and feet were usually left plain, though the pontil – the rough mark often found on the underside of the foot where it was originally broken away from the pontil rod – was often ground away. The existence of a pontil mark is not a guarantee of age as this method of attaching feet to stems is still used by glassmakers today.

Glass decoration and engraving

~

THE WORK of glass decorators – engravers, enamellers, gilders and cutters – adds greater value to the product. En-

graving techniques were perfected in the 18th century both in England and on the Continent. The use of a diamond-point on Venetian and Dutch glass either to incise or stipple-engrave – i.e. building up feint pictures from a series of dots leaving one with the impression that the image has been breathed on to the glass surface – was popular in the 17th and 18th centuries. By 1720, wheel-engraving, using a spinning copper wheel, had been developed which allowed the engraver literally to slice away at the surface of the glass. Some of the leading exponents of this technique were Dutch, Jacob Sang (1725–69) being one of the best known. Sang decorated light baluster wine glasses with ship portraits in particular. This type of glass has until recently been called a 'Newcastle light baluster' since it was thought for almost a century that the Dutch engravers imported their wine glass blanks from the long-established glass-making centre at Newcastle-upon-Tyne. We now know, however, that lead crystal was also manufactured in the Low Countries in styles similar to those which have long been considered to be typically

English, so much of this Dutch engraved glass is probably of local origin. It is now known, too, that the Dutch also made opaque-twist and colour-twist glasses, and experts are still endeavouring to differentiate between English and Continental lead crystal examples.

English 18th century glass engravers were also responsible for some fine work. Engraved decoration can add a substantial amount to the value of a glass, especially if the engraving commemorates a significant datable event. Toasting or commemorative glass associated with the Protestant William III, bearing equestrian portraits of the king as a celebration of the Battle of the Boyne of 1690, and Jacobite glass in support of the Old and Young Pretenders, James Edward Stuart and his son Charles, fetch very high prices at auction. As a result this type of glass has been forged – especially in the 1920s and '30s following the publication of extensive research on English glass, drawing attention to the special clandestine nature of such glasses. As much 18th century engraving was of poor quality it is not difficult for a 20th century engraver to acquire a plain 18th

☞ *left*

WINE GLASSES

ENGLISH *c.1750–70*
A group of lead crystal glasses. The wine glasses include fine examples of airtwist, opaque-twist and colour-twist stems.

under the direction of William Beilby. Beilby trained initially as an enameller of metal boxes at Bilston. With his brothers and sister he decorated wine glasses purchased from the local glasshouses with exquisite opaque-white painted images of architectural ruins, sporting pastimes and rural themes. However, it is their goblets and decanters painted with highly elaborate armorials, a few of which are signed, which fetch the highest prices. Traditionally a Continental art form, Beilby enamelled glass, of which some 400–500 examples exist, is amongst the most desirable and the most expensive of 18th century English glass.

The gilding of glass was perfected by decorators around the country in the 1770s, the most notable of whom was James Giles, who also decorated Chelsea porcelain. Gilding of coloured glass towards the end of the 18th century was a speciality of Bristol glasshouses. Coloured glass – especially blue, green and amethyst – produced in Bristol and in other parts of the country, often bears gilt decoration. Decanters, cruets, wine glasses and other table wares of coloured glass were generally made between 1790 and 1820. The rarest and most collectable of coloured glasses are generally earlier in date, circa 1750–60, and possess composite stems – such as a green-tinted ribbed mead or champagne glass with an opaque-twist stem encased in colourless glass and a green-tinted foot – or have unusual bowl

century glass and copy the engraved subject of an original example from either a photograph, book illustration or a drawing. Collectors beware!

In the 1930s several Midlands glassmakers produced airtwist glass, Jacobite glass and other popular 18th century styles which were widely advertised as legitimate reproductions. Today, some unscrupulous antique dealers have taken these later examples and aged them by adding wear to the feet – old wear normally takes the form of a dull roughened network of scratches whereby new wear, produced by means of emery paper, is often too deeply scratched. Reproduction Jacobite glasses generally combine too many if not all of the known disguised motifs on Jacobite glass – from the rose and bud (representing the Old and Young Pretenders) with an oak leaf (the badge of the Jacobite Oak Leaf Society, a loyal drinking club) to the title 'Fiat' ('so be it') and a starburst.

Enamelling of English glass is generally quite rare, with the exception of that produced in Newcastle-upon-Tyne between 1760 and 1775 by the Beilby workshop

☞ *below*

TWO FINGER BOWLS

ENGLISH *c.1810*
The Bristol glasshouses, where these finger bowls were made under the direction of Isaac Jacobs, specialized in very fine, blue gilded glassware.

☞ *left*

GLASS VASE

ENGLISH *c.1760*

A small English opaque white glass vase enamelled in the Chinese manner. This piece probably originates from South Staffordshire, where enamelling on white glass was particularly prevalent in the 1760s.

on the weight of glass. This style reached the peak of its perfection in the period 1800 to 1820. There were several factories operating in Ireland, established after 1780 when the ban on exporting glass from Ireland was removed and several Irish financiers and English glassmakers saw the opportunity to avoid English taxes.

A distinct Irish style emerged, especially for mould-blown decanters and stoppers. However, unless clearly marked with the name of an Irish glasshouse – applied to the bottom of the mould and thus reproduced on the decanter's base – this glass is not as popular with collectors as the earlier plainer English forms. Surprisingly, it is still possible to buy intricately and heavily diamond cut and faceted Irish jugs, boat-shaped bowls and covered jars for half the price of a plain English 18th century decanter. A marked Irish decanter, on the other hand, usually exceeds all expectation at auction. A duty on Irish

☞ *below*

CUT GLASS

ENGLISH AND IRISH

Early 19th c.

A selection of cut glass pieces from England and Ireland. Cut glass emerged in part to avoid the tax on glass, which was levied by weight. Several English glassmakers moved to Ireland in the late 18th century to avoid English taxes altogether.

and stem forms – honeycomb-moulded bowls, for example, and incised or air-twist stems.

Bowls, vases, candlesticks and tea cannisters in opaque white glass, enamelled in the manner of porcelain, or gilded, was a speciality of the South Staffordshire area in the 1760s, and although often highly attractive, disappointingly their value is considerably less than their porcelain counterparts. Perhaps it is because the glassmaker was trying to imitate the more popular porcelain that opaque white glass has been unfairly ignored by the serious collector. Some coloured glass in the style of the 1770s and 1780s continued to be produced throughout the 19th and early 20th centuries. Reproductions are often too brilliant and the gilding is much brighter than one finds on the earlier examples.

Cut glass

CUT GLASS was also produced in Ireland and in England in response to the penalties imposed by the glass excise tax

glass was imposed in 1825, largely bringing to an end a productive period in the history of cut glass.

European glass

From the late 17th century separate traditions evolved from the various glassmaking areas based especially in Central Europe. Elaborate covered goblets engraved with baroque *laub-und-bandelwerk* (literally leaf and strapwork ornament), coats of arms, mythological scenes and military battles – derived from printed sources – were ever popular, together with themes associated with drinking. The engravers of the Low Countries – especially the Dutch – were responsible for some of the finest copper-wheel engraved wine glasses, many of which portray elaborate ships or bacchanalian scenes and are inscribed with sentiments of goodwill and friendship. The names of some of these engravers have survived, of whom the best known is Jacob Sang (already mentioned).

Stipple engraving – the effect of creating an image by striking a diamond or hardened steel point against the glass, so that the image desired is produced by many tiny shallow dots indented in the surface – is amongst the finest of the work of Dutch engravers such as Frans Greenwood and, later, David Wolff. They employed images which include attractive coats of arms – particularly those of the House of Orange, also reproduced by

☞ *below*

HUNTING BEAKERS

BOHEMIAN c.1730
Two Bohemian beakers made of 'Zwischen-goldglas' – engraved pieces decorated with gold and with a further layer of glass on the outside. The technique is Roman in origin, but was revived in Germany and Bohemia in the 18th century.

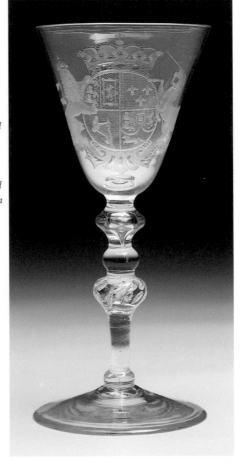

☞ *above*

GOBLETS

ENGLISH AND GERMAN c.1750
Royal motifs were frequent subjects for English glass-engravers. This Lauenstein goblet has the monogram of Frederick, Prince of Wales. It is accompanied by two engraved goblets from Saxony.

☞ *left*

WINE GLASS

DUTCH c.1750
An engraved lead crystal light baluster wine glass, bearing the arms of Anne, daughter of the British king, George II. Dutch engravers of this time were expert at producing fine work by cutting the glass with copper wheels.

wheel engravers and enamellers – and portraits.

Engravers in Germany from the late 17th century onwards decorated characteristically tall goblets and covers using *hochschnitt* (relief cutting) and *tiefschnitt* (intaglio cutting) methods. From 1700, *blankschnitt* (polished highlights) enhanced the engraving's sculptural effects. The heavier soda-lime glass, developed from the Venetian 'cristallo', is almost as soft for an engraver to use as is the finer English lead crystal. Engravers of German glass were often itinerant, peddling their wares around the Continent and undertaking commissions when called upon to do so.

The products of Saxony, Silesia and Thuringia can often be distinguished by their characteristic bowl shapes, stem forms and foot types. The many glassmakers of Bohemia, however, copied some of these forms but in a less elaborate manner. Deeply engraved sweetmeat or ambrosia glasses, wine goblets and flasks are most typical. Coloured glass, especially ruby which was to become so popular during the 19th century, emerged in the last quarter of the 17th century when Joseph Kunckel developed *rubinglas* by adding gold to the clear molten glass. Such items often have silver or silver-gilt mounted feet and covers. This glass is highly prized and, like the precious metal mounts adorning it, an example can be quite costly. The silversmiths of Augsburg and Nuremburg were closely associated with the glassmakers and supplied much of the metal mountings.

Scandinavia was much less influenced by Venice than other countries, producing by around c.1780 German-style cut and engraved glass and chandeliers and wine glasses which closely resemble typical English products. One suspects this may have something to do with a small number of immigrant English craftsmen from Newcastle-upon-Tyne. Some Norwegian glass bears engraved decoration which is highlighted with gilding, the glass being of a slightly cloudy nature. Although closely resembling English and Dutch glass, 18th century Scandinavian glass is inexpensive and not highly regarded by collectors.

Some of the coarsest glass was produced for the Russian market by Saxon and Bohemian glasshouses. Whilst a limited number of glasshouses operated in St Petersburg and elsewhere in Russia, they were unable to satisfy the local demand for glass and cheaper imports sufficed. Such imported glass often bears Russian crests and sentiments in cyrillic characters or is decorated with the imperial arms of the Czars and Czarinas.

American glass

AMERICAN 18TH century glass, like that of Scandinavia, was largely based on English imports or on small pockets of immigrant German makers working in Pennsylvania in the glasshouses of the Cologne-born Henry William Stiegel (1729–85). It was in the 19th century with the development of press-moulded glass,

☞ *right*
GROUP OF GLASSES
FRENCH mid-19th c.
A group of French glasses with coloured enamel threads. The development of skills during the 19th century led to greater novelty and innovation as the century progressed.

in the 1820s, that American glassware developed an independent style which was later to be partly copied by the Europeans.

The 19th century

DURING THE first half of the 19th century cut glass was the dominant style in Europe, affecting most of the popular glass shapes. By 1850 elaborate cut glass centrepieces, especially from Bohemia and France, highlighted the innovation and skills which characterized the century. Later in the period novelty was all important and a variety of naturalistic designs were applied to glass, including acanthus leaves, fish, reptiles, flowers and fruit.

Developments in design in the decorative arts throughout the 18th and 19th centuries were mirrored in glass products. This is especially true of the period after 1800 when Continental glass was greatly affected by the strong design elements embodied in the Empire and Biedermeier styles, which engendered a close harmony between glass, porcelain and furniture. This encouraged a revival of glass-making and engraving in Bohemia. Spa beakers – drinking vessels produced by glasshouses in spa towns in Germany – were popular at this time. Their waisted cylindrical bodies were often partly stained and attractively decorated in translucent enamels, with diamond and hobnail cutting, or were gilded, the bases being star-cut. New-style opaque glass called lithyalin was made in imitation of minerals, or in imitation of Oriental black and red lacquer, called hyalith. These bodies were occasionally decorated with gilding.

Clear cut glass was superseded by vividly coloured glass made by flashing or staining the glass. The new forms became massive, were intricately cut, and generally quite coarse in appearance. New techniques of glass staining were developed, the most popular colours adopted being ruby and amber. The surfaces were cut through or engraved to reveal the

☞ *above*

GOBLETS AND COVERS

BOHEMIAN c.1850–60
A group of tall Bohemian flashed and engraved goblets and covers. Flashed pieces of this period were intricately cut, but still often appeared quite coarse.

colourless glass below. This style was particularly popular between 1815 and 1848 where new shades of yellow were developed from uranium. Engraved decoration often features scenes of deer – especially stags – in continuous woodland landscapes wrapped around the bowls of covered goblets, vases and jars.

Towards the end of the 19th century cranberry glass, pinkish ruby in colour, was fashionable, some of which was turned into unusual decorative items for Indian palaces. Popular Bohemian products were overlaid decanters and vases made by coating transparent coloured or colourless glass with a layer of opaque coloured glass, particularly white. They were often picked out with gilding and enamelled flowers, occasionally depicting chocolate-box portraits of young girls or embellished with paste gemstones. There

Press-mounted glass
—

THE TECHNIQUE of making press-moulded glass was initially patented in the United States in the 1820s and introduced to Europe at some point in the 1830s. It was made in the English Midlands and in France and Belgium, particularly, and was to revolutionize the glass industry. The intention behind its production was to provide cheap mass-produced copies of luxury glasswares – especially cut-glass – for a growing, wealthy middle-class market. In this it succeeded. Today, pressed glass is widely collected because unlike so much antique glass it can be identified either from the manufacturer's trademark or on the basis of designs published in trade catalogues. The attaching of a label to a product is always significant for the collector which

☞ *below*
EWER
VENETIAN c.1870
A façon de Venise opalescent glass ewer, made by Salviati & Co. Salviati's reproduction pieces are sometimes taken for 16th or 17th century Venetian work, though they are generally heavier in character.

☞ *above*
OVERLAY LUSTRES
BOHEMIAN Late 19th c. A pair of green glass overlay lustres with gilt and enamelled decoration.

were many glasshouses in North and South Bohemia (part of modern Czechoslovakia and southern Germany). Some years ago their products were considered tasteless – kitsch, even – and were dismissed by serious collectors of glass. Today they are amongst the most sought after of glass types.

After about 1860, historical revival glass – or 'historismus' as it has become known – was a speciality of Bohemian, Venetian and Austrian glasshouses. Direct reproductions were made in these countries as well as inspired copies of earlier glass examples. The fine quality glass of Salviati & Co. which is often mistaken for 16th or 17th century Venetian or *façon de Venise* glass, is generally heavier and characteristically 19th century in feel. It was not produced with the intention of deceiving and is today greatly undervalued and sadly ignored by collectors. On the other hand, the similar *façon de Venise* revival wares of some English manufacturers, such as James Powell and Sons' Whitefriars Glass at the turn of the 20th century, is highly desirable because it is considered to have artistic merit, complementing a wider interest today in the British Arts and Crafts movement.

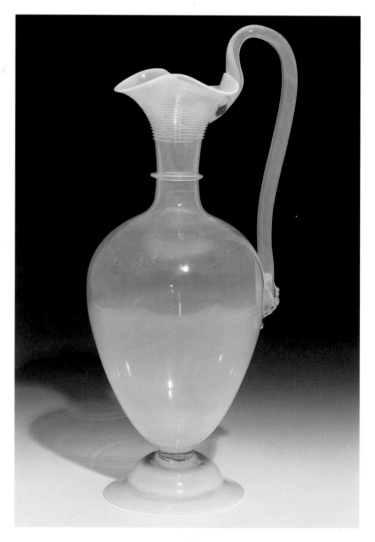

☞ *left*
GROUP OF GLASS PIECES
ENGLISH *Late 19th c.*
*This group of late
Victorian English pieces
includes North-eastern
and Midlands press-
moulded glass,
Stourbridge flower-
encrusted glass and
Webb's 'Burmese' glass.*

is why this market has grown so convincingly within the last the ten years.

The fancier ornamental wares of Midlands and Northern glassmakers are highly
sought after, with collectors eager to find
unusually coloured or limited production
examples. The manufacture of pressed
glass has continued into this century and
is perhaps now the standard method by
which most cheap glass is made. Collectors should be aware, therefore, of the
problems associated with the possible
continuance in use of an earlier mould.
Whilst the design of a glass may be known
to have been introduced in a certain year,
it is not always the case that the product

was produced at that time and in fact it
might have been made a great deal later.

19th century
engraved and cameo glass

COLOURLESS ENGRAVED glass continued to be produced in most glassmaking countries during the 19th century,
often accompanied by cut decoration such
as strawberry diamond or hobnail cutting
and facets. Subjects found engraved on
English glass include commemorative
themes, masonic devices, racehorses,
inscriptions representing marriages or

☞ *right*

**COIN GOBLETS AND
RUMMER**

*ENGLISH Early and
mid-19th c.*
*The goblet in the centre
bears a view of the High
Leel railway bridge over
the River Tyne, which
was opened in 1849.
Rummers are large
drinking glasses with
short stems, common in
the late 18th and early
19th centuries.*

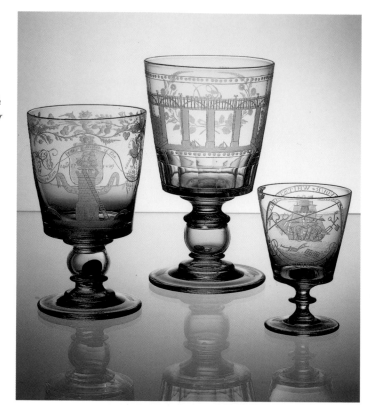

christenings, views of buildings and popular sentiments amongst many others. By the 1860s tableglass was manufactured in large quantities in the Stourbridge area, much of it decorated by acid-etching, a technique which was less costly than wheel or diamond engraving methods but which produced often stylish and complicated images in series. As acid-etching was developed during the revival of neo-classical decoration, the emblems on the earlier examples are often Graeco-Roman in character.

The revival of cameo techniques in Stourbridge in the 1870s saw the production of some of the finest examples of 19th century English glass by artist-designers such as John Northwood and George Woodall, many of which went on display at the Paris International Exhibition in 1878. Their classically-inspired hand-carved vases created a great deal of interest and inspired their employers to develop production lines of their popular cameo glass, using industrial rather than hand techniques. By 1900 the Stourbridge firm of Thomas Webb led the field in this production whereby robust designs of overlapping flowers, delicately drawn marine life or intricate interwoven scrollwork,

☞ *left*

CAMEO GLASS VASES

ENGLISH c.1880–90
*Thomas Webb's firm in
the West Midlands town of
Stourbridge was a leading
maker of cameo glass.
The decoration was
carved by hand out of
semi-translucent white
glass laid over a coloured
glass ground.*

amongst a variety of decorative motifs, were carved out of semi-translucent white glass which had been laid over a coloured glass ground. The most popular ground colour is blue with yellow being the least fashionable. Vases and scent bottles were the most popular carriers of this art form.

Encased glass

ENCASED GLASS such as paperweights and *crystallo ceramie* (or sulphides) was popular from the early 19th century. The technique of encasing white porcellaneous cameos and medallions of prominent people in colourless glass was first developed in Bohemia and then patented in France by Barthelemy Desprez (*fl.* 1773–1819) in 1818 and by Apsley Pellatt in England in 1819. Paperweights were manufactured in large quantities in France, Germany and in Bohemia from the 1830s. The finest were made in France – at Baccarat, Clichy and St Louis – from 1843 onwards, the classic period being 1845–55.

Paperweights were the cornerstone of the glass industry for which France is remembered now. These paperweights came in three different sizes: miniature (under 5cm), average (between 5 and 10cm) and the magnum weights, which were over 10cm in diameter. Baccarat dated several of their weights from 1846 to 1849 and sometimes put a small 'b' beside the date. They are the easiest of the French paperweights to identify, having many small distinguishing 'trade marks'. Typical of these were the silhouettes set into canes, broad arrows and whorls, as well as stardust clusters and honeycomb moulding; but in addition Baccarat produced mushrooms, snakes, butterflies and flower weights in profuse variety.

The St Louis weights are also quite distinctive. Their colours are far softer than those of Clichy or Baccarat and for some years they were also dated, sometimes with the initials 'S.L.' preceding the date. St Louis was also famous for its flowers, mushrooms, salamanders and snakes, but it is the fruit weights set on latticinio

☞ *above*

PAPERWEIGHT

FRENCH c.1850

The invention of the technique of encasing glass in the early 19th century made the production of paperweights possible, and they soon became popular. This pansy paperweight is from Baccarat, one of the sources of the finest examples.

baskets and the hollow-blown crown weights for which it is most famous.

The Clichy weights were very different. Their colours were bright and attractive, although it is rare to find Clichy flowers. Probably the most distinctive features of Clichy weights were their swirls and colour grounds. Only occasionally did Clichy mark their weights with an initial C. The most famous of their 'trade marks' was a very small stylized rose, which came in several colours and varieties, the most common being a distinctive pink.

Paperweights were also made in Italy at Murano by Pietro Bigaglia and by English firms such as Whitefriars and George Bacchus and Co. In the United States the most notable were made in the 19th century by the New England Glass Co. and the firms of Sandwich, Gillender and Mount Washington. Their weights are similar to many of the more superior French examples, the result of using immigrant French paperweight makers. Charles Kaziun and Paul J. Stankard produced some outstanding weights in this century. The French weights are the most collectable with some examples attracting many thousands of pounds. Imperfections in the glass and the general condition of a weight can affect its value. The few weights made by the French firm of

Pantin which incorporate snakes and lizards are highly sought after, one example with silkworms reaching $143,000 at auction in 1983 at Sotheby's in New York.

Apart from paperweights, a great variety of coloured glass was manufactured at the various factories all over France during the 19th century. This included some wonderful coloured chandeliers and very fine opaline with richly tinted colours, some plain, others gilt, silvered and enamelled and mounted in ormolu.

The use of the artist designer

TOWARDS THE end of the century the role of the artist designer was developed and glass vessels and ornaments incorporated the designs and styles of leading craftsmen of the period. During the 1890s the Art Nouveau style was adapted to glassware – especially vases – using *pâte de verre* (literally glass paste made from ground glass, fused together in a mould) and cameo techniques. At the Paris Exhibition of 1878, for example, revolutionary new styles of French glass were shown by artists like Émile Gallé, Antoine Daum, Legras and Le Verre Français. It marked a turning point in the history of modern glass-making. Gallé's oriental-inspired carved cameo glass and pâte de verre, with its fluidity, subtle colour tones and its emphasis on natural forms, has in recent years become amongst the most sought after glass. His enamelled work, which like his cameo, was generally signed, was also inspired by oriental forms. It reveals, too, his interest in nature, an idea central to the Art Nouveau movement of which he is one of the leading lights.

In the United States the style was promoted by Louis Comfort Tiffany, who has produced some of the most glorious coloured glass of the 20th century. From iridescent stained glass windows to vases and tablelamp shades, Tiffany's products now attract high sums at auction. His

ideas were copied especially in the United States by many other factories, who snapped up some of Tiffany's well-trained apprentices and designers. In some instances the copies can be very close indeed.

Contemporary European glass firms such as that of Loetz in Austria were influenced by the iridescent favrile glass of Tiffany and they even exported their Tiffany-like products to the United States. Today, as this glass increases steadily in value, the similar but poorer quality unmarked wares of rival Bohemian firms are frequently passed off as Loetz.

By the early 20th century glassmaking had reached a significant point in the development of style. Despite the conservatism of much industrially-produced glass of this time, experimentation in the 1920s and 1930s led to a broadening of the distinction between glass as a luxury ornament and the work of art in glass. In France, especially, art glass had become more sculptural. However, in Scandinavia, functionalist, Modernist theories were being applied to glass manufacture. New mass-produced ranges from European and American glassmakers included a limitless variety of vases, tableware, dressing-table items, jewellery, car mascots, clock-cases, sculptures, lamps and even decorative glass furniture and architectural fittings.

It is through the artist-designer René Lalique, who was both versatile in glassmaking and jewellery manufacture, that the gap between Art Nouveau and the later Art Deco style is bridged. Initially manufacturing perfume bottles for Coty, he established a glass factory near Paris around 1908 making large quantities of moulded, pressed and engraved glass. He was interested in surface treatment by acid or sand-blasting, resulting in a frosty opalescence. As a follower of Emile Gallé, Lalique made pieces in Art Nouveau fashion until he developed his own original style. His best-known glass was produced after 1925 which, although colourless, has a pale blue opalescent matt

surface and uses motifs based on plants, animals and often the female body.

After 1900 many artist designers became involved in the mass-production of glass. In England, the United States and in Continental Europe ranges of glassware produced by cheap factory methods such as press-moulding were created by some of the leading designers of the day. Important Austrian and German architects designed glass tablewares, as well as other domestic items in wood, ceramics and metal. This is particularly true of the Vienna Secession movement prior to the First World War, where Josef Hoffman and Kolo Moser were chief among those involved in a unique design production. This helped to produce a comprehensive personal style into which all the decorative arts could fit.

Whilst individual pieces by leading designers command high prices today and may be in many cases outside the pocket of the average collector, it is glass of a more popular mass-produced nature which is attracting the attention of many glass devotees. In Europe the press-moulded wares made for table and sideboard are actively pursued. Prices can be quite low for the more common productions. In America the most popular type of glass is known as 'Depression' glass, a term applied to a wide range of cheap ornamental and useful wares. Often coloured pink, green and yellow and generally but not always translucent, this group of wares was made in the 1920s and 30s by numerous American glass manufacturers. Depression glass is often confused with 'Carnival' glass, a similar cheap massproduced ware which was given away as prizes at fairgrounds and bought as trinkets at inexpensive stores. Such wares – plates, jugs, bowls, etc. – are iridized in either rich peacock-feather hues or an orange marigold colour and were made both in Europe and in the United States generally around the time of and just after the First World War.

Apart from Lalique, high quality glass of the 1920s and 30s in the Art Deco style is still comparatively inexpensive. Individual French and Swedish designer wares are naturally keenly sought after and their productions in part heralded what is now termed 'studio' glass – a movement which emerged more strongly in the early 1960s. However, the wares of British manufacturers of the 1930s, like Thomas Webb & Sons, Stuart and Sons and others working in the Stourbridge region of the West Midlands, are by comparison relatively undervalued. Some of these firms employed leading designers of ceramics –

such as Keith Murray – to design wares and engraved decoration which was intended to stimulate interest at that time in their high quality free-blown glass production. In this they succeeded and collectors may be richly rewarded if they find examples today, as such glasses – together with those products of the current studio glass movement – are likely to be amongst the leading glass antiques of the future.

☞ *below*

SELECTION OF GLASS VASES

ENGLISH *1930s*
A selection of glass vases made by leading designers for Midlands' glass-houses, including pieces by Clyne Farquharson for John Walsh of Birmingham.

SILVER

CHARLES TRUMAN

☞ *above*

EWER

ENGLISH 1705

Ewer from the reign of Queen Anne by David Willaume,
engraved with the royal arms.

Because of its comparative scarcity, its weight, solidity and immediate appeal through its brilliant reflective surface, silver is classed amongst the precious metals. Indeed until the dawn of the 19th century it shared this status with gold alone. After gold, silver is the most malleable and ductile of metals which makes it an ideal vehicle for design and decoration. From about the fourth millennium BC, silver was used as ornamentation, but wrought silver vessels have only survived from between 2500 and 2000 BC. From about 800 BC until the early years of the 20th century, silver was also used as coin.

Silver is found only rarely as a native metal, but it is alloyed naturally with gold in Electrum and in ores, the principal of which is galena or lead sulphide. This ore was smelted and the silver was separated from the lead by the process of 'cupellation'. This technique, which was used throughout the Middle East and Greece as early as about 2000 BC, involves the lead/silver alloy being heated over bone ash, causing the lead to oxidize and run off through the ash leaving a deposit of pure silver. The resulting metal was considered too soft to work satisfactorily and was frequently alloyed with another metal, usually copper in varying proportions. In England the sterling standard used is 92.5% pure silver but standards of between 80% and 96% are not uncommon in Europe.

The main European silver-producing countries were Germany, Spain and Austro-Hungary, although in Antiquity much of the available silver was mined in Asia Minor, or from sources in Greece, while Spain served as the main source of supply for the Roman Empire. By the 16th century Austria was producing about half the total European supply, with Germany producing about half as much, or about 400,000 ounces. However, following the discovery of Potosi in Peru in 1533 the greater amount of silver used in Europe was imported from Central and South America. During the 19th century huge deposits were discovered in the United States, Canada and Australia and lesser quantities in India, Burma, Siberia and Japan so that by the turn of the 20th century Europe only provided one tenth of the world's output.

Making and working silver

THERE ARE two principal techniques of making silver artefacts, which were discovered in the third millennium BC and which remain virtually unchanged today, the only major innovation being the source of power. These techniques are casting and raising. In the first silver is melted and poured in liquid form into a prepared mould. On cooling it solidifies, shrinks a little and may be removed from the mould. Moulds may be made in many ways but the most frequent and simplest was by making an impression in fine sand (called 'sand casting') or by encasing a wax model in plaster or clay, and heating the plaster or clay to melt the wax which was then poured away and replaced by molten metal (called 'lost wax casting'). Whole vessels may be made in this fashion, or parts of vessels such as decorative details may be made and applied by solder to a larger piece.

In the second method, raising, a flat sheet of metal is hammered with a variety of hammers over various 'stakes' or anvils literally to raise the metal into vessel form. The hammering is done when the metal is cold but it has to be heated periodically and cooled ('annealing') to prevent the metal becoming brittle. A development of raising is the technique of 'spinning', introduced in the 19th century, which involves turning a flat disc of metal over a preformed 'chuck', a wood or metal model, which is rotated on a lathe. In addition, in common with other soft metals, silver can be drawn through a hole in a steel plate to form wire.

There are a variety of decorative techniques available to the silversmith. The most usual methods are embossing, which involves the metal being struck with a punch and stretched forwards from the back, and chasing, which is the reciprocal technique with the metal being worked from the front. In neither technique is any metal removed but merely pushed and stretched into decorative patterns. Silver may be decorated by engraving in which case the surface of the metal is cut away with a burin or sharp

☞ *right*

PAIR OF VASES AND COVERS

ENGLISH 1660s
These silver-gilt baluster vases and covers date from the reign of Charles II. Vases have always held an important place amongst displays of silverware.
Height: 33cm (13in)

steel tool.

Silver may also be decorated by the addition of other metals or metallic compounds. Filigree, strands of wire twisted into decorative patterns, or granulation, tiny pellets of metal, may be soldered to the surface. But the most common metal to be added to the surface of silver is gold, in the form of gilding. Until comparatively recently this was achieved by 'mercury' or 'fire' gilding. This requires an amalgam of gold and mercury being painted on to the surface of the silver, either overall, or in limited areas ('parcel gilding'), and heated to the point where the mercury evaporates and leaves the gold adhering to the silver. The process is exceedingly dangerous, mercury vapour being lethal, and was replaced in the 1840s by electroplating whereby gold was deposited by means of electrolysis.

Other forms of decoration include enamels – glass coloured with metallic oxides which can be applied in two ways. The technique of *cloisonné* requires that metal wires are soldered to the surface metal to separate the enamel colours whereas in *champlevé* the surface is cut away to form troughs into which the enamel is set. A further decorative addition might be *niello,* an alloy of copper, lead, silver and sulphur which is applied like champlevé enamel and provides a lustrous black surface. Both enamels and niello require firing in a kiln.

Silver has a unique place in the decorative arts. Not only was its value as wrought plate (the generic term for silver articles and not to be confused with plated wares) directly linked to the value of silver currency, it was also infinitely recyclable. Possession of silverware indicated both an owner's wealth, by its quantity, and his taste by the style of the pieces that he owned. Until the early 19th century the possession of antique or outmoded silver would have been considered eccentric, and as fashion changed so did the silver that a man possessed. Since the metal was expensive and the labour required to fashion it cheap, a position incidentally totally reversed today, many

☞ *above*

TANKARD

ENGLISH 1830
This tankard from the time of William IV was made by John Bridge of London to be the trophy

raced for in the King's Cup yachting race at Cowes in 1831.

commissions for new silver were paid for by the melting of old plate. Thus, not just wear and tear, but the continual process of refashioning makes silver that much rarer the further back in history one goes.

From antiquity to the Renaissance

BECAUSE OF its unique link between taste and wealth, silver was always intended for display as well as use. Homer describes the wealth of silver (and gold), used for display by the ancient Greek heroes and much survives from the Bronze Age cities of Greece and the Eastern Mediterranean, such as Mycenae and Knossos. While this tradition of the conspicuous display of silver does not have an entirely unbroken history, it runs until at least the mid-19th century. A rich man was expected to display his wealth and the principal way in which he did it was with silver.

There were two prime areas in a household where such displays were customary. The main one was in the dining room

where silver was displayed not only on the sideboard, or buffet, where many pieces had an ornamental rather than a functional purpose, but on the table where the functional aspect was, of course, much more important. Certainly from the Renaissance, and probably even from Classical times, the most significant pieces of plate on the sideboard were large dishes, ewers and basins, whose functional use in the ritual of hand-washing was made obsolete by the introduction of the fork in the 17th century. Vases were also important, together with a 'fountain', a vase-shaped vessel with a tap for water, and, at the base of the buffet, a cistern which served the dual purpose of chilling bottles and receiving the water from the fountain which stood above it.

The second setting for a display of plate was in the state bedroom, or its antechamber, where plate associated with the toilet was shown. It is perhaps not without significance that in both these rooms a rich man was at his most vulnerable, either eating or sleeping, and such displays of wealth, and in consequence power, were contrived as an antidote to these periods of weakness.

The habit of burying plate in tombs or to avoid discovery during the period of the barbarian invasions has resulted in the survival of a disproportionate amount of silver dating from the period between the time of Alexander the Great and the late Roman Empire (roughly from the 4th century BC to the 4th century AD). However most of what has survived is in the great museum collections of Europe and North America, the most notable being the Archeological Museum, Thessalonika, the British Museum, the Louvre, the Metropolitan Museum, New York and the Hermitage, Leningrad, and much of what appears on the market bears the stigma of illegal excavation and export.

Whilst accounts survive to give a mouth-watering idea of the riches of court life from the 4th to the 14th century, very little secular silver survives, although there is a certain amount of extant church metalwork, by no means all of it in precious metal. So far as can be judged from documents, two types of silver objects dominated in the so-called Dark Ages: the cup, of beaker form, and the *Hanap*, which was a shallow bowl. There was also the custom of mounting classical vessels in precious metals and the earliest to survive is preserved in the treasury of St Maurice d'Agaunne, Switzerland. Of early church plate to have survived the most remarkable are the altar frontal by the goldsmith Wolvinus in the mid-9th century in the church of San Ambrogio, Milan, and the cross of Lothair, in gold set with gems, in the cathedral at Aachen which dates from about the year 1,000 AD. Of surviving chalices the most famous is probably that from Ardagh in Ireland and now in the National Museum of Antiquities, Dublin.

From the mid-13th century the influence of the Gothic style is found in metalwork, but still the majority of extant pieces are for ecclesiastical use. One can only guess at the magnificence of court life from manuscripts and the handful of extant pieces. Fortunately two magnificent examples are on public display in Britain. The grandest, of enamelled gold, is the Royal Gold Cup made for Jean, duc de Berri, brother of Charles V of France about 1390 and now in the British Museum. The other, a cup and cover of silver-gilt set with translucent enamels, was made in Burgundy for the Merode family about 1400 and is in the Victoria and Albert Museum.

Other items of plate that would have adorned a table at this date were *nefs*, or models of boats designed to hold salt or spices, knives, forks and spoons, and salts, which in England attained great importance. Two splendid examples are the Huntsman salt of about 1400 at All Soul's College, Oxford and the salt of silver-gilt and crystal given by Bishop Fox to Corpus Christi College in the same university in 1494.

The largest single group of secular vessels to have survived are mazers. The name given to these silver mounted wooden bowls is derived from the High German word for spot, *masa,* since the

wood used in their manufacture is burr maple. Mazers usually have only a silver rim, and are frequently set with a print, or raised silver disc, in the centre. This is sometimes enamelled or set with a prophylactic stone such as crystal which was supposed to indicate the presence of poison.

The Gothic style was replaced by classicizing motifs during the period that we now call the Renaissance. Originating in Italy, the style rapidly spread throughout Europe, although it had been virtually abandoned in the purest form in its birthplace almost as soon as it had crossed the Alps. Once again the amount of surviving plate is very small, but it is apparent that so far as silver is concerned Classical ornament was soon imbued with another decorative style, the Mauresque, introduced from the East through Venice. As Italian craftsmen travelled north and as Italian engraved sources circulated in Germany, France and even England, or as Northern designers and craftsmen visited Italy, there emerged a curious compression of styles in Northern Europe where the Gothic style lingered into the 16th century, but was replaced by Mannerist ornament from the 1540s, giving very little scope for the absorption of pure Renaissance ideas.

During the 16th and 17th centuries national distinctions become blurred. Craftsmen and designers did not adhere to national boundaries, and in consequence one finds that the court goldsmith to the Medici in Florence was a Fleming Jacques Bylivelt; Hans Holbein moved from Switzerland to paint and design silver and jewellery for Henry VIII in London; and Benvenuto Cellini left Italy for the court of François I at Fontainebleau. Indeed Cellini is the most informative of all goldsmiths since he left an autobiography and a treatise on goldsmithing. For example, he tells of the salt now in the Kunsthistorisches Museum, Vienna, made for François I of France in 1543, which represents the 'Sea and the Earth seated' and a 'little temple of Ionic architecture . . . to contain the pepper'. It was however in the

North of Europe that Mannerism, the sophisticated reinterpretation of Classical forms, inspired some of the most outstanding examples of goldsmiths' work. The late John Hayward encapsulated the spirit of the age when he wrote, 'The more complex the form, the more recondite the Classical illusions, the more astute the philosophical programme upon which its ornament was based, the more worthy was a vessel of admiration.'

Northern European silverwork

THE PRINCIPAL centres of production and innovation were Nuremberg and Augsburg in Southern Germany and Antwerp in Flanders. Nuremberg was the home of arguably the greatest of all goldsmiths of the 16th century, Wenzel Jamnitzer (1535–85). Jamnitzer was not only technically superior to virtually all his contemporaries, he possessed a skill in design and inventiveness unparalleled in the history of the craft. Much of his work has been lost but amongst his greatest triumphs are the Merckel centrepiece in the Rijksmuseum, Amersterdam, bought by the Nuremberg City Corporation in 1549, the silver-gilt mounted trochus shell ewer of about 1570 in the Residenzmuseum, Munich, and a jewel casket now in the Green Vaults, Dresden, made in 1562. In Antwerp the names of the goldsmiths are less well known than those of the designers of silver, amongst whom the principal were Hans Vriedman de Vries, Adriaen Collaert and Erasmus Hornick, although the latter in fact lived in Nuremberg for the later part of his life.

So strong was the influence of Germany that at least one contemporary source states that in the early 17th century, 'the goldsmiths in London were nearly all Germans'. However, unlike the guilds of the German cities whose strict regulation of the craft led to the highest technical skills, the Goldsmiths' Company in London was primarily concerned with the standard of the silver used. In order to regulate this a series of identifying marks had been introduced, and since they were struck at Goldsmiths' Hall, they are known as hall-marks. From the 14th century in England goldsmiths were required to register a maker's or sponsor's mark, at first a device but later his initials. In the following century a system of date letters, changed each year, was introduced in order that the assay master responsible could be identified if a piece subsequently proved to be below standard. Early references seem to indicate that the standard mark was the leopard's head, but this was adopted by the London assay office following the introduction of the lion passant as the mark for sterling silver in 1544.

English silver in the 16th and 17th centuries

ENGLAND'S MOST significant contribution to the history of silver at this date is the development of the great salt. From its late Gothic form, the so-called 'hourglass', composed of one conical section inverted upon another, the standing salt became, in the 16th century, a Mannerist column of relatively broad section, with a depression at the top for the salt, and frequently with a cover supported on scrolled brackets. These salts were set on the right hand of the most important person at the table, and lesser salts of comparable but simpler form were placed amongst the cups and trenchers. This is the origin of the phrase 'below the salt', meaning someone of lowly origin.

Whilst much English silver dating from the 16th and early 17th centuries was melted to finance the Civil War, by far the most important group of English silver to have survived had already left England and is now preserved in the Armoury at the Kremlin in Moscow. Much of this plate formed gifts from English diplomats to the Tsars in the early 17th century, or was sold to them by merchants who bought the silver disposed of by Charles I in 1628 from the 'Great guilt Cubberd of

Estate'. The Kremlin collection gives a remarkable impression of Royal plate of the Tudor and Stuart courts. Most striking are the pair of flagons formed as leopards, over three feet high, made in London by an anonymous goldsmith in 1600.

Silversmiths in the Low Countries

DURING THE early years of the 17th century artistic impetus in silver moved to the Low Countries, and specifically to Utrecht where the brothers Adam (1569–1626) and Paul (1570–1613) van Vianen pioneered the transition from the Mannerist to the Auricular style. The style, which developed the scroll into complex relief forms reminiscent of the shape of the human ear, appears soon after 1610 when Paul returned to Flanders to work with his brother. The fluid contours of the plate that they produced were made possible by their extraordinary skill in the techniques of raising, embossing and chasing. Such was the fame of the family that Adam's son Christian (1600–1637) who continued to work in his father's style, became court goldsmith to Charles I of England. Sadly all has been lost apart from three pieces, a basin in the Victoria and Albert Museum, and a salver and a covered bowl both in the collection of the Duke of Northumberland, made during the period of Christian's employment in England.

17th Century French style

BY THE middle of the 17th century a new style had begun to emerge in France. This was the use of lush scrolling foliage, frequently embossed in high relief, to decorate broad surfaces of silver. A silver-gilt coffer of about 1645, apparently commissioned by Cardinal Mazarin, and now in the Louvre, is about the earliest example but the style finds full range in the magnificent vases, tables and toilet services of the reign of Charles II in

☞ *above*
TOILET SERVICE
ENGLISH 1675–6
A Charles II toilet service made by Jacob Nondendick and Robert

Cooper in London. The Restoration of the English monarchy brought with it new ideas of courtly wealth and ostentation.

England. In fact surviving French silver from the late 17th century is very rare, having been the subject of a great melt ordered by Louis XIV to help pay for the War of the Spanish Succession. The best evidence for the glories of French silver at this time is provided by illustrations in paintings and tapestries, and from English silver, much of which was made by Huguenot craftsmen who fled France following the removal of religious tolerance in 1685.

So far as England is concerned the great watershed in the history of silver is the Restoration of the Monarchy in 1660. The court of Charles II moved from France to London bringing with it all the ideas of courtly wealth and ostentation which were current at Versailles. It was there that the taste for silver furniture developed which soon spread rapidly throughout Europe. In England there are three important surviving suites, two comprising a table, a mirror, and a pair of candlestands, one at Knole in Kent and the other in the Royal Collection; the third, lacking its candlestands, is also at Windsor Castle. Several sets of andirons and fire furniture in silver survive, but sadly the 'great vases . . . tables, stands, chimney-furniture, sconces, branches, braseras (braziers) . . . all of massive silver and out of number' belonging to the Duchess of Portland, and Nell Gwyn's silver bed made by Jean-Gérard Coques, have disappeared.

Electroplating

DURING THE second quarter of the 19th century there were various experiments with electrolysis and electroplating. Several patents were bought up by the firm of Elkington & Co of Birmingham until by about 1846 they held a virtual monopoly. Unlike Old Sheffield Plate, where pieces were made from the plated sheet metal, items to be electroplated were first produced complete in base metal before plating. This means that certain elements could be cast, and there were no signs of the base metal showing through at the edges. In addition, instead of the base metal being copper, nickel alloys were also used and this yellow coloured metal can frequently be found showing through rubbed areas of silver plating.

English silver plate

THE FRENCH taste dominated table and sideboard plate at this period. Silver fountains, cisterns, dishes, ewers and basins, decorated with cast applied strap-

☞ *left*
WINE COOLERS
ENGLISH c.1710
This pair of magnificent wine coolers was made during the reign of Queen Anne. Wine coolers were a recent innovation at the time, enabling wine to be left on the dinner table for guests to help themselves.

work in the Régence taste after Jean Berain (1640–1711), abound in England but side by side this French style two other particularly English fashions in silver developed. In the 1680s the taste grew for silver flat-chased with chinoiserie figures, birds and foliage. Also found at the turn of the century is a taste for plain silver, devoid of all ornament but whose effect is enhanced by the play of light on the flat reflecting surfaces.

New pieces of plate emerge, again probably influenced by France. The grandest, and rarest, is the cadinet, a square of silver, usually gilt, with a box at one end. These curious pieces sat before monarchs and very grand nobles when they ate in state and held their napkin and bread, their knives, forks and spoons, and their salt. Only two have survived from the late 17th century and these are now in the Jewel House at the Tower of London. They were originally used for the coronation banquet of William and Mary in 1689.

Another more common form introduced at the end of the century was the single bottle wine cooler or ice pail, which could be set on the table for an individual to serve himself rather than having to summon a servant from the sideboard. The earliest English examples (1698) are at Chatsworth in Derbyshire, and a gold pair presented by Queen Anne to the first Duke of Marlborough is in the British Museum. However their use was still rare enough to cause comment at

Versailles in the 1730s.

Glasses were frequently cooled and rinsed at the sideboard, or more informally at the table in a vessel with a notched rim called a 'Monteith', after a fantastical Scot of the same name who wore a scallop-edged cloak. The form is first recorded in 1683, and frequently the rim detaches to allow the bowl to be used for punch. A particularly distinctive piece of plate, the two handled cup and cover, which appears to have been introduced from Holland, finds a place on the English sideboard at this date. Variously described as a porringer or caudle cup, it was probably not intended for use but merely for display. The form survives until the late 18th century by which time the squat, early shape had been converted into a Classical vase.

In addition the newly acquired habit of drinking tea and coffee led to the development of plate associated with them. The principals were of course the tea and coffee pots, but tea caddies, kettles, milk jugs and even cups and saucers in silver appear. However beer and wine cups which had been so popular earlier in the century completely disappear with the introduction of good glassware. By contrast, beer tankards are still made in silver today.

The great revival in the use of silver led to a shortage of coin which had been melted to form wrought plate. To inhibit this trend, Parliament raised the standard of the silver used for plate to 95.8% in 1697. The new standard, called New Sterling or Britannia standard, was that used in France, but the concomitant rise in the cost of plate led the goldsmiths to petition for the return of the old standard and from 1720 a choice of standards became available.

Rococo silver

IN FRANCE, once again, a new spirit of restlessness emerged to bring about the new style we now know as Rococo. Its greatest protagonist was a goldsmith born in Turin of French extraction, Juste

☞ *left*

CANDELABRA

ENGLISH *1744*

A pair of candelabra by John Le Sage, made in London during the reign of George II. They are designed after models of 1734 by Thomas Germain.

Aurele Meissonnier (1695–1750). Principally a chaser and designer, Meissonnier was admitted to the Paris guild of goldsmiths by Royal command but he preferred to style himself *Architecte*. He only appears to have marked one piece, a gold box made in Paris in 1728, but a pair of tureens bears his signature and a candelabrum closely follows his designs. All three were made between 1734 and 1738 for the Duke of Kingston. Much more prolific was Thomas Germain (1720–48), the French Royal goldsmith who espoused the rococo style and imbued it with an elegance unrivalled in silver at that date. His son, François-Thomas, continued in his father's style working not only for the French Court but also for the Portuguese and Russian monarchs.

However in England the most famous of the goldsmiths working in the rococo style was Paul de Lamerie (1688–1751). Of the French *petit noblesse*, de Lamerie arrived in London from Holland at the age of three. In 1703 he was apprenticed to another Huguenot, Pierre Platel, becoming free of the Goldsmiths' Company in 1713. He apparently had a considerable trade with Russia for he supplied two silver chandeliers, probably for the Empress Anna, which hang in the treasury of the Kremlin, and the same collection now possesses a large centrepiece commissioned by Count Brobinskoy in 1734. In 1726 de Lamerie was also involved in the trial of a Mr Dingley who

was accused of exporting unhallmarked silver to Russia, over 2,000 ounces of which was by de Lamerie. However, his best-known commission is the extraordinary ewer and basin made in 1741 for the Goldsmiths' Company itself. De Lamerie is the best known of all English goldsmiths, and while his fame is most deserved he was not alone in his adoption of the rococo style in silver. Nicholas Sprimont, a native of Liège, and better known as the founder of the Chelsea Porcelain Factory, worked as a silversmith in England from 1743 until 1749. His salts formed as shells and crayfish on a rock-work ground, derived from designs by Meissonnier and made in 1743 for Frederick, Prince of Wales, are still in the Royal Collection. Another goldsmith of distinction was George Wickes (*fl.* 1722–1759) whose work is made especially interesting by the survival of his firm's ledgers which detail his commissions. Apart from those from the Prince of Wales, which are in the Palladian taste, the most robust is a ewer and basin ordered by the City of Bristol for Judge John Scrope in 1735 and which shows the influence of the designs of the Frenchman Jacques Lajoue whose cartouches were published in Paris in the previous year.

Neo-classical silver

THE ROCOCO style was not universally popular and almost as soon as it had developed, it was being challenged by those who found the classical taste more appealing. However 18th century Neo-classical silver frequently borrows from mannerist sources rather than Classical. The impetus once again came from France, and the leading goldsmiths such as Nicholas Roettiers and Robert Joseph Auguste were quick to adopt the new style. Whilst their creations spread through Europe and were copied, in England the great entrepreneur and goldsmith Matthew Boulton wrote, 'Fashion hath much to do in these things, and as the present distinguishes itself by adopting the most elegant ornaments of the most refined Grecian artist . . . I am humbly copying their styles and making new combinations of old ornaments'. It is this last which is most important for the Greeks and Romans did not use tureens,

☞ *right*

CANDLESTICKS

ENGLISH *1757*

A fine set of four George II candlesticks, decorated with foliage, shells, scrolls and swags, and engraved with a crest, by Edward Wakelin. Their contemporary value is about £15,000 ($28,000).

coffee pots, candlesticks and the like, and so classical ornament was added to contemporary pieces.

Boulton also wrote of 'vase madness', and the vase became the principal feature of silver of the day. Several architects are known to have turned their hand to designing silver, notably Robert Adam, William Chambers and James Wyatt, and patrons such as the Dukes of Northumberland and Marlborough and Matthew Boulton himself commissioned their designs.

However, such men were considered by the end of the 18th century to have 'introduced too much neatness and prettiness' in design and in 1806 C. H. Tatham wrote that 'Massiveness, the principal characteristic of good Plate' had been replaced by 'light and insignificant forms . . . to the exclusion of all good ornament whatever'. Silversmiths and designers took a more archaeological approach to their plate and the man they looked to for inspiration was G. B. Piranesi, then engraving plates of the newly excavated marbles in Rome.

Silver and the Industrial Revolution
—

TECHNICAL DEVELOPMENTS in metalwork enabled silver plate to be produced much more cheaply. In the mid 18th century, Thomas Boulsover developed Old Sheffield Plate, a process whereby sheets of silver are fused onto an ingot of copper and passed through rolling mills until it reaches a thickness suitable for raising. It enabled craftsmen to produce pieces at a fraction of the cost of silver. Various new techniques introduced in the Industrial Revolution such as die-stamping made the process increasingly attractive commercially. Many of the techniques were also adopted by the goldsmiths of Sheffield and Birmingham.

In England the early 19th century was dominated by the Royal goldsmiths, Rundell, Bridge and Rundell, who had two workshops for their vast output, one at Lime Kiln Lane, Greenwich, run by Benjamin Smith, and the other at Dean Street, Soho, run by Paul Storr. With a design studio under the control of William Theed and employing John Flaxman, Thomas Stothard and Edward Hodges Baily, the firm adapted classical forms to contemporary use. John Flaxman's model of the Shield of Achilles and of the Theocritus Cup, both based on classical descriptions of heroic plate, date from this time.

The immensely confident style of silver produced by Rundells was in almost total contrast to the silver of the French Empire. There the firms of Biennais and Odiot were producing silver, frequently based on designs by Charles Percier, which achieves a lightness and elegance quite different from the solid 'Roman' English silver. Italy, the country where Napoleon's artistic influence was felt most strongly, followed France.

The Gothic revival
—

THE SECOND quarter of the 19th century was a period of reflection. The most dominant style in silver was the revived Rococo, championed by Paul Storr, free from the reins of Rundells, and by the firm of Robert Garrard. However, by 1830 the influence of the Gothic Revival was felt, with A. W. N. Pugin, who had worked for Rundells, designing silver, especially church plate in the Gothic style. He was by no means the first protagonist of the historicist movement in silver, for William Beckford had commissioned silver to decorate his houses at Fonthill and Bath derived from many earlier styles. However, Pugin's collaboration with the Birmingham firm of John Hardman & Co. led to some of the most spirited examples of Neo-Gothic plate. A more idiosyncratic version of historicism was provided by Edward Farrell who worked principally for the firm of Kensington Lewis.

The middle of the century is epitomized by the Great Exhibition of 1851 where plate of mediaeval, gothic, Renaissance and rococo taste prevailed although some Neo-classical silver was evident. The major goldsmiths at this date were Elington and Co. in Birmingham, Hunt and Roskell (successor to Paul Storr), Garrards and Hancocks. The antiquarian taste survived throughout the century, to such an extent that at the Paris Exhibition of 1900, the Goldsmiths and Silversmiths Company were exhibiting replicas of pieces in the Victoria and Albert Museum.

There was an inevitable move away from this somewhat sterile attitude and the increased use of mechanical aids in the production of silver. The influence of John Ruskin and William Morris led to the establishment of the Art Workers' Guild in 1884 and this spawned a number of Arts and Crafts goldsmiths at the close of the century. Without doubt the most famous is C. R. Ashbee (1863–1942) who began the School of Handicraft in London in 1888. A comparable body, the Birmingham Guild, was established two years later. The goldsmiths in these guilds and the commercial firms which aped them, such as Liberty and Co, were joined by a small body of artist-craftsmen who should be mentioned here; Alexander Fisher, Nelson Dawson, John Paul Cooper, Gilbert Marks and Omar Ramsden. This last had the habit of signing his work 'Omar Ramsden me fecit' to suggest a personal involvement in the manufacture. In fact he ran a relatively large workshop and is reputed to have given a hand-beaten finish to commercially manufactured plate that he bought in.

However, the Arts and Crafts movement fell to the onslaught of Modernism. Heralded by Dr Christopher Dresser's designs for silver and electron plate for Hukin and Heath in Sheffield in the 1870s, and by the Weine Werkstätte in Austria and Puiforcat in France, the movement in England is represented by the goldsmiths H. G. Murphy, Harold Stabler and the designer R. M. Y. Gleadowe. The emphasis was on plain polished surfaces, sometimes engraved, and clean crisp lines.

JEWELLERY
AND FANS

☞ *above*

JAR EARRINGS

FRENCH 1990

Supremely elegant swan earrings set with diamonds, coral,
sapphires and enamel, from the French jeweller Jar.

JEWELLERY

DAVID WARREN

Jewellery is by its very nature both expensive and ephemeral. Jewellery made from precious stones is often reset in new styles depending on fashion and it is therefore very unusual to find really old jewellery (that is pre-19th century) outside museums. 19th or 20th century jewellery however is accessible to today's collectors.

Women's rights, haute couture, travel, theatre, death and love are but a few of the forces to have influenced design and fashion in jewellery during the past two centuries. The opening of trade routes, advancements in technology, and the Industrial Revolution that began in the middle of the 18th century, were jointly responsible for expanding the jewellery market in which Britain and France were at the forefront. The dawning of 19th century Europe had arrived.

Ancient Egyptian, Classical Gothic and Renaissance epochs frequently inspired jewellery design of the 19th century. Neoclassical Empire style, with its swags and laurel wreaths applied to gem-set gold 'parures', marked the grandeur of Napoleon's Court (1804–1815). It was a style that became popular in England with the Prince Regent who, like Napoleon, had a passion for magnificent jewels.

Mourning jewellery

ONE VOGUE, revived from a 16th century tradition and activated by the Napoleonic wars at the turn of the 18th century, was mourning jewellery. Rings enamelled in black mourned those who had been married while white enamelling was reserved for the unmarried. Names, dates, compartments with plaited hair and inscriptions such as 'in memoriam' all served to preserve the memory of a loved one. Urns were a favourite motif, further expressing the wearer's despair. Death at sea was represented by women draped over anchors, while the height of morbid

☞ *above*

MOURNING BROOCH

ENGLISH c.1810

A typical diamond and enamel mourning brooch decorated with an urn.

☞ *above*

HEART-SHAPED LOCKET

ENGLISH c.1830

A ruby and diamond heart-shaped 'sweethearts' locket, the two larger stones symbolizing entwined hearts.

Victorian sentiment were parures constructed from the deceased's finely plaited hair. Remembrance jewels had become a fashionable status symbol.

Sentiment permeated throughout Victorian society and jewellery acted as a medium for it. Romantic love jewels of the first half of the 19th century counterbalanced the darker trends. Hearts encrusted with diamonds which were often entwined, lovers' knots, pairs of love birds, padlocks and keys were all popular symbols. So too were forget-me-not brooches, delicately enamelled in green and white as well as snakes with tails in their mouths signifying eternity. Less obvious were the cryptic messages spelled

by using the first letter of a gemstone so that Diamond, Emerald, Amethyst, Ruby, Emerald, Sapphire, Turquoise spelled 'dearest' and Amethyst, Moonstone, Opal, Ruby spelled 'amor'. By the middle of the 19th century this trend was dwindling and the death of Prince Albert in 1861 rendered such light hearted jewellery inappropriate.

Italian style

MEANWHILE, Italians were manufacturing micromosaic suites with images of classical architecture, mythology and horticulture. Naples was the centre of production for coral jewellery between 1830 and 1860 and the coral craze swept

☞ *above*

CORAL AND TURQUOISE BRACELET

ITALIAN c.1840

A white coral, turquoise and gold bracelet from Naples, with a Bacchanalian head and clenched fists.

☞ *below*

MICROMOSAIC BRACELET

ITALIAN c.1840

A micromosaic and gold bracelet depicting scenes from Rome: the Forum, the Temple of Vesta and the Coliseum.

throughout Europe, assisted by Napoleon's Italian campaign. Carved into bacchanalian scenes, winged cherubs, delicate flower sprays or simply left in its natural twig form, coral jewellery was at a peak of popularity by 1850. Soon after this, coral became vulgar and a fashion that had lasted several decades petered out.

☞ *top*

CASTELLANI SHELL CAMEO

ENGLISH *c.1850*

The gold and enamel ram's head mount for this Satyre shell cameo is typical of Pio Fortunato Castellani's Etruscan style.

☞ *above*

GUILIANO BROOCH

ENGLISH *c.1840*

A delicately enamelled and gem-set brooch by Carlo Guiliano, whose work was inspired by the Italian Renaissance.

Two Italian craftsmen worthy of note are Pio Fortunato Castellani and Carlo Guiliano. Castellani (1793–1865), who based himself in London, specialized in fine quality reproductions of Roman and Etruscan styles and caused a sensation with his designs at the Paris Exposition of 1862. His son Alessandro was a guest speaker in 1876 at the American Centennial Exposition where the explanation of his family's work sparked off an American Etruscan revival. Guiliano (1831–1895) who also worked in London, was inspired by the Renaissance style, producing jewels in polychrome enamels of intricate designs. Other important Italian exports included cameos in agate or more commonly shell and volcanic lava, all of which made ideal souvenirs for those returning from the Grand Tour, thus spreading their popularity.

Popular designs

TWO OF THE most regularly employed designs over the past 300 years have been sprays and ribbon bow brooches which over the same period of time have recurred frequently in haute couture. The spray was becoming more naturalistic by early 19th century and as jewellers' skills improved, designs became more complicated. The invention of the *en tremblant* mechanism, where sections of the spray were mounted on springs allowing flowerheads and buds to quiver gently, proved to be highly popular.

Topical subjects were often portrayed in jewellery and in 1834 the discovery of Halley's Comet caused great excitement. Lunar jewels abounded, in the form of crescents, stars, sunbursts and comets. These appeared predominantly in diamonds and most commonly as brooches, necklaces or tiaras.

While Europe had a centuries' old tradition of jewellery design, 19th century America was still a comparatively new country with little demand for sophisticated jewels. The American lust for extravagant jewellery was yet to come

☞ *top*

EN TREMBLANT BROOCH

ENGLISH *c.1840*

A diamond spray brooch with the flowerhead mounted en tremblant, using a spring mechanism which allowed it to quiver gently when moved.

☞ *above*

STAR BROOCH

ENGLISH *c.1840*

Jewellery designs were influenced by current events, such as the sighting of Halley's comet, which inspired many stellar creations such as this diamond star brooch.

and a definite air of sobriety reigned within their early designs.

Plain gold necklaces, lockets, rings, mourning brooches and patriotic commemorative items could all be bought at local general stores. The jeweller's shop was a later development. It was in fact silverware that was accepted as the premier status symbol in America up until the Civil War of 1861–65. Jewellery then took over, compounded by Tiffany's purchase in 1888 of one third of the sumptuous French Crown jewels.

The influx of gemstones

SIGNIFICANT discoveries of gems and minerals worldwide in the 19th century reduced manufacturers' prices to a more widely affordable level. They included sapphires from Kashmir, Australian opals, gold from California, green demantoid garnets from Russia and South African diamonds to name but a few. The Kimberley mine founded in 1871 was enormous, yielding unimaginable supplies of gem quality diamond. It was Cecil Rhodes' (1853–1902) eventual dominance over prospectors at Kimberley that gave rise to the Central Selling Organization, which through its virtual monopoly of the diamond market eventually stabilized prices.

This influx of raw materials undoubtedly hastened the production of jewellery manufacturers to feed the 19th century's demand for personal adornment. As a consequence jewellery production became more mechanized. This development was noted at the Great Exhibition of 1851 by the English writer and interior designer William Morris (1834–1896), who in 1856 founded the Arts and Crafts movement in reaction to contemporary mass manufacturing methods. The movement's return to traditional labour intensive skills was applied to jewellery, which was commonly made from plain or beaten silver. This less expensive metal was considered more in keeping with the simple aims of the movement, in the same way that enamel decoration took preference over precious stones. Images of the Holy Grail, maidens with flowing hair, peacock feathers, Viking long boats and Celtic designs were trademarks of William Morris's guild of handicrafts. It was the beginning of a truly inspirational period that would eventually break the dominant Victorian styles of bows, sprays, hearts, crescents and stars.

Art Nouveau jewellery

THE LAST QUARTER of the 19th century gave rise to a new art style with its origins firmly within the Arts and Crafts movement: Art Nouveau. The basis of Art Nouveau consisted of delicate flowing, bending lines that seem not to conform, beginning in parallel, converging,

☞ *above*

ART NOUVEAU BROOCH

FRENCH c.1880
An enamel, pearl and diamond brooch in the form of a poppy, typical of the sinuous plant forms adopted by many Art Nouveau designers.

☞ *below*

LALIQUE PENDANT

FRENCH c.1890
An enamel, pearl and diamond 'wings' pendant designed by René Lalique, the most influential of all French Art Nouveau jewellery designers.

☞ *right*

ARTS AND CRAFTS PENDANT

ENGLISH c.1860
A hand-crafted enamel, pearl and silver peacock pendant made in one of the Arts and Crafts movement workshops founded by William Morris in reaction to the mechanization of production.

contradicting each other and uniting. Horticulture and the female form lent themselves ideally to this new style and it was applied to most mediums including jewellery. Traditionalists regarded Art Nouveau as brash and vulgar, but despite this its popularity spread quickly throughout Europe and America finding particular favour in Paris, Vienna and Barcelona.

The French jeweller and craftsman, René Lalique (1860–1945), was undoubtedly the master goldsmith of this period. He created stunning and imaginative works of art using mixtures of precious and semi-precious stones, enamel and moulded glass, which was his favourite medium. One of his most significant works is housed at the Gulbenkian Museum in Lisbon, a huge predatory winged insect in the form of a stomacher (27.0 cm wide by 26.5 cm high). At first sight it resembles a dragonfly, but closer inspection reveals fearsome claws and from its hideous jaws extends the torso of a woman. In contrast to this nightmarish image, the woman is beautiful and supremely calm in what appears to be a state of metamorphosis. Lalique, who was so repulsed by 19th century industrial developments, created this symbolic work as the 20th century was about to begin. He may well have been expressing his future hopes for a more human society.

The American firms Tiffany and the Gorham Corporation travelled to Europe to gather design ideas, adapting them to their own market. Indeed it was Tiffany who at the Paris Exhibition of 1889 presented a series of richly enamelled Art Nouveau orchid brooches that in turn sparked off a revival of the use of enamel in Europe. In spite of the wide popularity of this new Art concept, traditional jewellery was thriving.

'The Garland Style'

FRENCH JEWELLERS, and in particular Cartier, introduced 'The Garland Style' that so befitted the turn-of-the-century 'Belle Epoque' years. They based their

☞ *above*

GARLAND STYLE EARRINGS

FRENCH c.1900
Diamond earrings in the Garland Style, which was introduced by French jewellers, particularly Cartier, at the turn of the century and which was based on the traditions of the Louis XIV style.

☞ *top*

BOW BROOCH

FRENCH c.1905
A Belle Epoque diamond bow brooch, with a platinum mount which creates a delicacy reminiscent of lace.

ideas on the grand tradition of Versailles and the Court of Louis XVI. Acanthus leaf scrolls, wreaths and quatrefoils on lattice-work structures, bound with ribbon bows and cupola tassels epitomized this fashion. Queen Alexandra, Mrs Cornelius Vanderbilt and Princess Marie Bonaparte were influential patrons of the garland style and undoubtedly consolidated its popularity.

A further reason for its success was the introduction of platinum to jewellery manufacture. This ductile, malleable precious white metal is remarkably strong. It allowed jewellers to create lace-like settings with the minimum of metal, achieving maximum delicacy and femininity. Platinum was first discovered by South American Indians, who considered it 'unripe gold' and of no value. The drawback with platinum has always been its very high melting point of 1772°C (some 700°C higher than gold), which for some decades proved too problematic for jewellers. However, in 1877, a more efficient jewellers' torch was invented, providing a flame intense enough to enable soldering. Cartier's great success with the Garland Style marked the beginning of the firm's position as world leaders of design that lasted for almost half a century.

The Cartier influence

UNDER THE directorship of Louis, Pierre and Jacques, the third generation to enter the business, the next 50 years would transform Cartier's name into a legend. A contributing factor to its success was the company's close links with haute couture and in particular the Englishman, Charles Frederick Worth (1825–1895). In 1845 Worth began his career in Paris, the centre of European fashion. He was one of the most dominant designers of the late 19th century, commissioned by Empress Eugenie, Princess Metternich and, to the disgust of his rivals, rich American hostesses. Cartier provided a range of items under the title of Boutique 'S', that included evening bags, compacts, belts and

buckles covered in silk brocade and set with gems that complimented the latest of Worth's designs. This successful collaboration with fashion provided Cartier with introductions to the international elite of Europe, America and Russia.

Art Deco jewellery

BY THE START of World War I, the popular Garland Style was beginning to wither. This was compounded by the unavailability of platinum which had a more important role to play in the production of explosives. A second influencing factor of the war was that women's clothing became more streamlined, tighter fitting and practical. This laid the foundations for the next important fashion, Art Deco. In the same way that America looked east towards Europe for inspiration, Europe through the centuries had often relied on the Middle and Far East for its inspiration. Images from Egypt, India, China and Japan epitomized the Deco style and were adapted in an angular and sometimes architectural way that was clean-cut and harmonious with 1920s dress requirements.

Colour was of the utmost importance,

being an integral part of this new design. Charles Jacqueau (1885–1968) was Cartier's chief designer at this time. His passion for the mystical East was reflected in his extraordinary jewellery designs that were imitated throughout Europe and America for nearly 20 years. Coincidentally, and of great good fortune for Cartier, Howard Carter discovered Tutankhamun's tomb in 1922. The world marvelled at the vibrantly coloured treasures that poured forth serving to underline and add impetus to Cartier's Deco designs.

☞ *above*

VAN CLEEF AND ARPELS BRACELET

FRENCH c.1925
An Art Deco diamond, ruby, emerald and sapphire bracelet by Van Cleef and Arpels, inspired by artefacts from the tomb of Tutankhamun, which was excavated at this time.

☞ *left*

SPRAY BROOCH

ENGLISH c.1940
A wartime adaptation of the spray brooch, consisting predominantly of semi-precious stones.

☞ *right*

ART DECO EARRINGS

FRENCH c.1920
Art Deco ruby and diamond earrings by Janesich, showing a strong Chinese influence.

The 1940s and 1950s

THE ONSLAUGHT of World War II brought Art Deco to a natural conclusion. Trade routes were closing, demand declining and many jewellers abandoned their work tools to take up arms. It was a time of economy and this was reflected in the shop windows of jewellers. Extravagant gems were no longer in evidence and patrons adjusted to colourful semi-precious and synthetic stones and a zealous use of gold. Most jewellery from the 1940s in Europe and America took its inspiration from machinery. This may partly have been owing to the intense

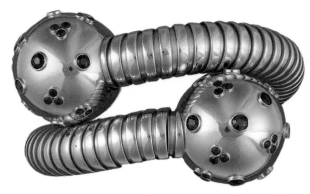

production of war machines that jewellers were temporarily caught up in. Caterpillar tracks, variations of stylized wheels and discs, screw threads, ball bearings and gas or hose pipes all found a place in 1940s' 'cocktail' jewellery.

The war altered far more than current jewellery designs. Forty years of French domination of the market came to a resounding halt as the Nazis invaded France, Belgium and the Netherlands. Jewellery manufacturers, retailers and diamond cutters alike fled to the relative safety of Britain and Switzerland, but more significantly to America. This great influx of expertise and the wealth of raw materials that the jewellers brought with them to America, was responsible for shifting the centre of the jewellery industry permanently away from Europe. For the first time America led the market.

In New York, one of Cartier's subsidiary branches that had been established in 1909, took on greater significance. Another important French firm, Van Cleef & Arpels decided to remain in New York after exhibiting at the World Fair of 1939. In 1940 the Parisian jewellery designer, Jean Schlumberger (1907–1987), also transferred there, ultimately amalgamating part of his company with Tiffany in 1956. One of many exciting young designers to settle in America was a Sicilian duke, Fulco di Verdura (1898–1978). He had worked with Coco Chanel in Paris before opening his own New York based business in September 1939.

The expanding wealth and opulence of American post-War society, helped by glamorous Hollywood images of Greta Garbo and Joan Crawford lavishly bejewelled, encouraged Americans to spend more money than ever before on jewel-

lery. This inspired the 1950s 'all diamond look'. Purveyor of the most valuable gemstones of the world and ideally located at his 5th Avenue premises, Harry Winston wooed the world's wealthy with his all-diamond jewellery. Simple bold designs set with large diamonds, often cut in marquise, rectangular, pear or triangular shapes were worn unashamedly by women of means.

At the same time European jewellery design was enjoying the input of established sculptors and artists such as Giacometti, Picasso and Braque, the latter experimenting with textured gold applied to cut mineral slabs. Salvador Dali, the great Spanish surrealist, created melting watches and pulsating ruby hearts.

*The antique
jewellery of the future*
———

THE TONE of the 1960s was altogether whimsical. Jungle animals by David Webb (1925–1975) in bright enamels and semi-precious stones were high fashion in New York. Cartier too produced many animal variations, including the popular ladybird in coral and black enamel, while seashells set with precious gems mounted in gold were Falco di Verdura's amusing offerings.

When Neil Armstrong stepped onto the moon in 1969, interest in lunar jewellery resurfaced, in the abstract style synonymous with the 1970s. Molecular and

BULGARI GOLD NECKLACE
ITALIAN 1980
Sophisticated but inexpensive, this gold necklace designed by Bulgari centres on a 4th century bronze coin with diamond detail.

☞ *above*
DAVID WEBB ZEBRA BRACELET
AMERICAN 1965
A zebra bracelet in diamond, ruby, enamel and gold, an example of the whimsical style of 1960s jewellery design, of which David Webb was a leading exponent.

☞ *above*
VERDURA EARRINGS
AMERICAN 1965
Seashell earrings studded with diamonds and mounted on gold by the designer Falco di Verdura.

☞ *above*
STAR BROOCH
ENGLISH 1970
The stylized seventies version of the star burst, in diamond and gold.

cellular structured jewels encouraged by scientific advancements and yellow gold with bark texturing or twig structures were typical of this decade.

Women now required jewellery of a more versatile nature, to wear by day or night, at any occasion. The travel explosion of the 1970s and 1980s found many people continually on the move, and preferring to travel with relatively inexpensive but sophisticated jewellery. The Italian firm, Bulgari, with a major outlet in New York, designed internationally acclaimed jewellery that met this demand. Simple rounded settings in warm 18 carat gold held cabochon-cut coloured gemstones. Antiquities in the form of coins and engraved gems were the focal point of chain link necklaces.

Today's jewellery could become the 'antiques' of the future. Inspired designers such as Graff (b. 1938) of London, and the Parisian, Joel Rosenthal (b. 1943), are the sort of names to watch, as continually rising costs force many other manufacturers to cut even more corners and quality falls firmly into second place.

FANS

SUSAN MAYOR

Although fans are as old as hot weather, the second half of the 17th century is where today's collectors might aspire to start their collections. In 1990 Christie's South Kensington sold a painted fan leaf showing Louis XIV celebrating the twentieth birthday of Le Grand Dauphin for £11,000 ($20,000). Rarely do more than two 17th century fans appear on the market each year, whereas hundreds of 18th century fans are sold.

There are various types of 17th century fan. Some are longer than many 18th century fans – about 12 inches. They are painted in bright bodycolour on dark kid with elaborate genre scenes – some very well painted – and most have brightly coloured flowers on the verso. They tend to have rather heavy, coarsely pierced sticks of ivory or tortoiseshell, and some leaves are slotted on to their sticks rather than stuck on to the leaf. Other types include rare *découpé* or cutwork fans resembling lace, or fans set with panes of painted mica.

Fans can be made from almost every conceivable material. They can be dated from the shape and carving of their sticks and guardsticks, and from the painting on the leaves or mounts. The painting can be

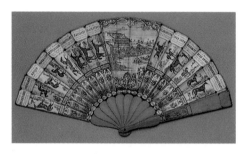

compared to contemporary portrait miniatures, watercolours and oil paintings, to give both date and country of origin. Dating the costume of the figures is also very helpful. To complicate matters, it is fairly common to find 18th century fans with a leaf from one country mounted in another. For instance, we know of fan leaves brought back from a Grand Tour in Italy to be mounted on sticks in England in the 1720s. The subject matter on fans varies considerably. From the beginning of the 18th century one tends to find classical and Biblical subjects, painted in Italy and Northern Europe and baroque in style. From the middle of the 18th century fans became rococo in style and pastoral subjects become predominant in French examples, painted as two or three shaped vignettes. Topographical subjects are more common

in Italy and England, while Dutch fans mainly have Biblical subjects. Also found from the third quarter of the 18th century are charming *trompe l'oeil* fans from England, Germany and Italy.

Very few 18th century fans were signed, although it is worth looking for pieces by the Swiss painter, Johannes Sultzer, who painted charming farming vignettes with straw-work peepholes in the 1780s.

From the first half of the 18th century one also finds lacquered brisé fans often called 'Vernis Martin'. These are a type of folding fan which does not have a separate leaf. This type of fan was again fashionable in about 1900, when pastiches of the earlier versions were produced.

Printed fans

PRINTED FANS, often commemorative, make an appearance from the 1720s onwards as fanmakers felt a necessity to expand their trade and produce cheaper pieces. Some of the English fans printed after the 1734 Copyright Act still have their publication lines with the name of the fanmaker, and/or engraver and his address and date of publication. Although printed fans were cheap at the time, they were ephemeral and are now much sought after. Some with rare and interesting subjects such as the 1727 coronation, the Battle of Colloden in 1745, and a New Game of Piquet in 1733 have fetched almost as much as comparable painted fans – about £2,000 ($3,750). Some subjects are amusing and entertaining, such as Conundrum fans. Most 18th century fans are etchings but all other types of prints do appear on fans: aquatints, stipple engravings (wooden brisé fans are often applied with stipple engravings in the 1780s), and even very rarely mezzotints or woodcuts. By the 19th century many fan leaves are printed – particularly in the 1830s to 1870s, when fan leaves were frequently hand-coloured lithographs, often pastiches of 18th century fans with pretty mother-of-pearl sticks. Chromolithographic fans appear in the 1860s to 1880s,

☞ *top*

RACING FAN

ENGLISH *19th c.*

A lithographic printed fan depicting winning horses and their jockeys. This process enabled fans to be mass produced and given away or sold cheaply by advertisers or promoters.

☞ *above*

LITHOGRAPHIC FAN

ENGLISH *c.1851*

A hand-coloured lithographic fan produced to promote and

commemorate the Great Exhibition of 1851, held in Hyde Park, London.

some printed on silk and linen. They make a fresh appearance in the early 20th century as amusing advertising fans for grand hotels, restaurants and scents. These were mainly French and are often designed by well-known decorative artists and illustrators such as Bernard de Monvel. Maquet was a prolific publisher of them.

The fans of the very early 19th century are mainly very small brise ones of ivory or horn. A few late 18th century and early 19th century brise fans were extremely well painted in the manner of Angelica Kauffmann and others. From the 1850s to 1890s some very fine lace fans were produced, with mainly Honiton, Brussels, Chantilly or Carrickmacross laces.

Many fans from the second half of the 19th century are signed but often by little-known decorative artists. However, some very fine fans were produced in the 1860s to 1890s – sometimes for the great international exhibitions – by artists such as A. Solde and Callamatta, who both worked for the great fanmaker Alexandre. J. Donzel painted some very fine fanleaves. Billotey, who also painted on glass, painted fine fan mounts on silk gauze of flowers and insects for the well-known fanmakers Duvelleroy. A number of traditionalist genre painters like Olivier de Penne in France and Richard Doyle in England painted mounts for fans, often for Royal Commissions. Compared with leaves by fan painters these are still very reasonable in price, unlike fans painted in the Art Nouveau style. In the 1890s Duvelleroy produced very fine double-sided fans depicting romantic subjects for the English market.

From the 18th century onwards fans often incorporated novelties. One finds mid-18th century double image fans, with three or four different scenes and when opened the wrong way, from right to left, a hidden scene is revealed. Some of the late 19th century Chinese fans of this type are painted with risqué images. There are also double-image brise fans from the 1820s. Novelties, however, went much further than this: articulated fans with vignettes set in the guardsticks, spy holes in the leaves, or handles carved to resemble objects; watches, spy-glasses and other objects set in the pivot of the fans; jewelled court fans; thermometers set in guardsticks; telescopic fans; fore-edge paintings and carvings; rare late 18th century French royalist fans with concealed portraits only visible when held to the light; fans carved to fold up as shapes such as shot-guns or bunches of flowers; parasol fans and collapsible fans.

Fans from outside Europe

MOST SURVIVING European fans are folding fans, with sticks. These were in fact introduced in the 17th century from the East where they had been held in high esteem, sometimes with leaves painted by distinguished artists. It is rare for the collector to find a mounted Chinese or Japanese fan from before the late 18th century but then fans and leaves of lesser artistry but great charm were made for export to the West. Exported paper leaves were similar in size and subject matter to European fans. From the late 18th century we find Cantonese carved ivory brise fans – about 11 inches in length, sometimes even of cockade shape (opening to 360 degrees). Like European fans they were smaller in the early 19th century, and the Chinese soon added tortoiseshell, mother-of-pearl, enamelled filigree metal, some gilt lacquered wood and sandalwood. Painted feather fans and handscreens also exist from this period. By the 1840s a new type of Chinese export fan appeared, painted with figures who were given applied silk clothes and painted ivory faces. One sometimes finds them with double or 'cabriolet' leaves – so called after the 18th century French carriage, as they look like spokes of a wheel. By the 1870s some leaves are asymmetrical.

From Japan the collector can find fine ivory brise fans lacquered and decorated with Shibayama work dating from the 1880s. These can fetch about £3,000 ($5,500). Folding fans with watercolour landscapes can also be found with Shibayama-work sticks, but these are far less common. Very sought-after are the War fans – folding fans with wrought iron sticks that were made for signalling in battle.

Most other cultures produced fans: they were useful for winnowing grain and fanning the fires. As yet only a fan and fan handle from Rarotonga in the South Pacific have fetched big money, going for £38,500 ($71,200) in 1979. They were the only two pieces of carving to survive from an island that was famed for the splendour and quality of its woodcarving. Other ethnographic fans abound and they are therefore fairly cheap. These are mainly handscreens, the most commonly found being: rigid hide ones from North and West Africa, beech bark and feather fans from the Huron Indians in North America (those decorated with quills are more sought-after), feathers mounted with humming birds from Brazil, and West Indian folding fans of pressed ferns. Once Christie's sold a fine pair of 18th century Indian handscreens of plaited ivory for over £1,000 ($1,850). We find raffia and straw-work fans from India and also from Italy.

It has only been possible here to skim through the many types of fan. The brief bibliography at the back of the book should help fill in gaps, but yet I still keep on finding new types of fan.

T E X T I L E S

EMBROIDERED PICTURE

ENGLISH c.1700

A typical subject for an embroidered picture, this depicts
Erminia mourning Tancred; worked in coloured silks.

TEXTILES
....
DIANA FOWLE

Tapestry

NEARLY EVERY textile except felt is produced by weaving, the interlinking of the warp and weft thread on a loom. However, some are patterned during this process and some are decorated afterwards either by a needle, as in embroidery, or by painting or printing. Tapestries are perhaps the best known of the woven textiles. Technically the term tapestry describes the weaving process as well as the actual hanging: the pattern is worked during weaving by the weft and not embroidered by a needle. Tapestries are normally large scale wall hangings and are composed of coloured wool or silk wefts and undyed linen warps.

Tapestry weaving is a very old process. The first recorded tapestry fragment was found in Egypt and has an inscription dating it to circa 1503–1449BC. However it was not until the 13th century AD that tapestry weaving seems to have become a European industry. Paris and the Low Countries, in particular Arras, were important centres of production. The

industry must have been stimulated by the growth in demand from an increasingly wealthy aristocracy who required tapestries to decorate their castles and demonstrate their wealth. Knowledge brought back from the Crusades may also have contributed. Tapestries were very practical items; they could be relatively easily transported and re-hung in each castle visited by an itinerant court to give colour and warmth.

Medieval designs

THE STYLISTIC development of tapestries closely follows that of paintings. Early tapestries are flat in feel revealing the Gothic style's pleasure in surface patterning. There is little spatial recession and the figures seem to be piled vertically on top of each other, producing a crowded wall of colour. The weavers rendered each detail with great care; it is possible to date tapestries by examining the details of the costume. The scenes are normally taken from contemporary courtly romances, mythology or the Old Testament. Hunt-

ing and processional scenes were also popular, for example, the Devonshire Hunting Tapestries, woven in Burgundy in circa 1450, now at the Victoria and Albert Museum in London. Tapestries without figures were also produced at this period; the millefleur tapestries are particularly attractive as they depict fields of flowering plants.

Later tapestries

BY THE 16th century the effects of the Renaissance were beginning to be felt in tapestry design. This change was underlined by the Raphael cartoons, which were produced by the artist for Pope Leo X in 1515 and were woven in Brussels. The cartoons depict the Acts of the Apostles, with real figures in three dimensional receding landscapes. The

☞ *below*
TAPESTRY
SWISS c.1430–44
*A panel from a tapestry
from Basel, woven with
gentlefolk, beasts and
wildmen.*

skyline has been lowered producing an impression of well ordered rational space. These developments in the rendering of perspective continued throughout the century, as did the gradual increase in the colour range used; by the 18th century as many as three hundred different dyes were used in tapestries so that realistic shading could be achieved.

Similarly, 17th century tapestries are baroque in feel. They show large scale, grandiose subjects with figures dressed in costly fabrics with elaborate details. During the 17th century Brussels continued to remain a tapestry centre; however workshops in both England and France became serious rivals. The Mortlake workshop in London was set up under James I's patronage in 1619 and produced many large sets. In the second

☞ *right*
GOBELINS TAPESTRY
FRENCH Early 18th c.
A tapestry woven with the figure of Flora and attendants, from the famous Gobelins factory set up by Colbert.

☞ *below*
RAISED WORK CASKET
ENGLISH c.1660
A delightful embroidered work casket, with the embroidered purse, pencase and silk bookmark found in the casket. The purse features the name 'Jean Morris' and the date.

half of the century France began to rival Mortlake after the creation of the Gobelins and Beauvais workshops by Colbert for Louis XIV; the production at Aubusson was also re-organized.

The Gobelins was the Crown's personal factory, directed by the artist Charles Le Brun (1619–90), who produced many tapestry designs including 'the Royal Palaces', important tapestries intended to increase the Sun King's prestige. Beauvais and Aubusson were smaller centres producing less grandiose tapestries for private clients. They really came into their own during the 18th century, producing elegant rococo subject matters, some designed by the artists Boucher and Oudry. Chinoiseries and light-hearted romantic subjects were popular; for example the Love of the Gods and Don Quixote.

English weavers from Soho were also producing this type of tapestry during the 18th century, although not on the same scale as France. John Vanderbanke and Joshua Morris were two of the best known weavers of this period. Morris produced colourful pieces often with decorative sprays of flowers and exotic parrots; Vanderbanke produced a famous set of Chinoiserie scenes.

The Gothic revival

BY THE END of the 18th century the fashion for tapestries had virtually disappeared and it was not until the Gothic revival that they once again became popular. The Arts and Crafts movement was also influential in this as it encouraged people to re-examine the old textile crafts. William Morris (1834–96) established a tapestry workshop at Merton Abbey where extremely successful re-interpretations of earlier tapestries, such as millefleurs and verdures, were produced, as well as figurative tapestries.

Embroidery

WILLIAM MORRIS also produced other types of decorative textiles, in particular printed and embroidered hangings. Embroidery has been used for furnishings for a long time. Although it requires much skill it is easier to produce domestically than a tapestry and is cheaper. Since the late 16th century well-to-do schoolgirls were taught embroidery. They practised various stitches and recorded new patterns on their samplers. In the 16th and 17th century these took the form of long narrow strips of cloth, normally of linen, worked in a random manner as a form of reference which would serve to remind the embroiderer of previous works. Some are dated and worked with the embroiderer's name and age.

By the late 17th century samplers had lost much of their practical value and came to be admired for their decorative appeal. They were often framed and were seen as a type of embroidered picture showing off the skill of the worker. Gradually the design of samplers became standardized and by the late 18th/early 19th century, the period from which most samplers on the market today come, they follow a set pattern. This usually consists of a religious verse, with spot motifs of flowers, birds, animals and architectural features below, the whole design framed

☞ *above*

LONG SAMPLER

ENGLISH *Early 17th c.*
An early sampler embroidered with coloured silks and metal threads, embellished with seed pearls and spangles.

☞ *above*

FORMAL SAMPLER

AMERICAN *1812*
By the 19th century, samplers took on a set pattern, and were often 'signed' as with this American example, worked in coloured silks.

by a floral border. Most samplers are worked in coloured silks; however by the mid-19th century wools became more common. Samplers dating from later than circa 1850 are rarely seen.

Another form of popular embroidery was the needlework picture. Although there are earlier examples, it was not until the 17th century that they seem to have become widespread. At this period they were normally worked in coloured wools highlighted with silks, or silk on silk, and often depict religious or mythological subjects. English embroidery from this period is particularly attractive as it is often worked with strange details such as carefully observed insects and animals. These were copied from pattern books or from herbals full of botanical drawings. Many of these details are worked in raised or stump work: the technique by which details are padded and so stand above the surface of the ground. Raised work is found in some earlier embroidery, but it was particularly widespread during the third quarter 17th century in England. It

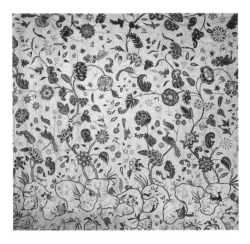

is also found on caskets dating from this period.

Once the needlewoman had finished her sampler and embroidered picture she often progressed to a needlework casket. These were boxes measuring about 10 inches square with the outsides covered with embroidery and usually with two doors at the front opening to reveal small drawers, sometimes with secret compartments at the back. The top may sometimes open to show another compartment, often with a mirror and lined with silk. They were used to store special treasures such as jewellery, lace and letters.

Although the vogue for needlework caskets had died out by the 18th century, embroidered pictures were still being produced, if not in such large numbers. Pastoral and chinoiserie subjects were popular as were urns of flowers, in particular tulips and carnations. By the end of the 18th century embroidered pictures became much lighter in feel. They were often worked on an ivory silk ground which was left visible as the background, and were usually worked in silks rather than wools. Facial and other details were sometimes painted rather than embroidered on to the ground. Flower pictures were still popular as were subjects derived from popular prints depicting Romantic landscapes and stories. Hairwork pictures, embroidered pictures worked in black and brown silks, were also produced at this period. They were intended to give the impression of an engraving.

Berlin woolwork

By the second quarter of the 19th century the craze for Berlin woolwork began to dominate contemporary needlework. This was a type of embroidery worked on a wide meshed canvas (rather than the finer woven linen) often in cross stitch in wools. The wools were dyed in Berlin and the patterns, printed on squared paper, were produced

there. Many embroidered pictures, fire screens and cushions were produced using this technique. They are characterized by the bright colours of the wools, sometimes highlighted with beads or in plush stitch. The subjects are often of medieval scenes, for example 'Bolton Abbey in the Olden Times' after Landseer, or of flower arrangements typified by lush three dimensional flowers; arum lilies and large cabbage roses seem to have been favourites, as were parrots and spaniels.

Embroidered furnishings

THE AMATEUR needlewoman also turned her hand to more practical domestic objects, in particular furnishings. In the 18th century many chair backs and seats were embroidered by amateur and professional alike. They were usually in tent stitch on a linen ground and show subjects similar to those in embroidered pictures; some have figurative scenes worked in petit point within a gros point border of scrolling flowers and strap work. Cushion covers were also popular as were large coverings for tables, known as table carpets. These are normally characterized by a non-directional central panel framed

by a border which was intended to hang round the edge of the table. These were popular during the 16th and 17th century and were sometimes worked with the family coat of arms.

The other important domestic furnishings were bed hangings and covers. The four poster bed required several pelmets and curtains which were often elaborately decorated. During the 17th and 18th century crewelwork was popular for bed furnishings. This was wool embroidery on a linen tabby or cloth weave ground.

Quilting

IT WAS NOT until the 19th century that the patchwork quilt became widespread. A quilt is a very practical way of providing a warm covering as it is composed of two layers of material sandwiching a layer of wadding, often wool; the three layers are sewn together with decorative patterns. The term 'patchwork' refers to the top cover, which was composed of scraps or patches of material joined together in

☞ *left*

EMBROIDERED CHAIRBACK
ENGLISH *Early 18th c.*
Furnishings were
embroidered by amateurs
and professionals alike,
usually in tent stitch on a
linen ground. This
chairback has a typical
pastoral scene worked in
coloured wools and silks.

☞ *top*

CREWELWORK HANGING
ENGLISH *Late 18th c.*
Bed hangings were often
carefully embroidered in
coloured wools, as this
one, with bed covers in
similar patterns.

elaborate designs to form a complete cover. This economical bed covering was popular in North America where many different and often dramatic designs were produced.

Collecting tapestries and needlework

PRICES FOR tapestries vary greatly depending on condition, subject matter, age and whether the price is complete or merely a cut down section. Very early tapestries rarely come on the market and attract very high prices; even good 18th century tapestries may reach six figures at auction, but a small fragment in poor condition might only fetch £1,000 ($1,850).

Antique needlework can also command high prices, 16th and 17th century samplers could reach thousands of pounds at auction, but attractive 19th century samplers can be obtained for a few hundred. Embroidered caskets are particularly sought after; the one illustrated fetched the exceptional price of £75,000 ($13,800) in 1990, but others could be purchased for around £5,000 ($9,250).

Quilts are now among the most collectible items in the textile world, particularly in the United States. In Britain they might fetch between £50–£1,000, but in the States, quilts fetch thousands of dollars.

Printed fabrics

PATCHWORK QUILTS are mainly composed of scraps of printed cotton dress material. Printed cotton was popular for both dress and furnishing fabrics from the early 18th century onwards. Originally printed and painted cottons, or chintzes, came from India where the process of dyeing clothes with permanent bright colours had been known since at least the 17th century. These Indian cottons were highly valued in the West as their exotic designs and strong colourfast dyes were not available in Europe. They were used as bed hangings, covers and also for dress

☞ *right*
PATCHWORK QUILT
ENGLISH *c.1840*
Patchwork quilts were usually made up of printed cottons, so old quilts are a good source for researching early print patterns. This quilt has a central chintz panel commemorating the coronation of Queen Victoria.

fabrics. It was not until 1752 that a method for producing high quality printed cottons was available in Europe with the invention of copper plate printing by Francis Nixon in Ireland, which substituted the old block printing method. The most famous copper-printed cottons were produced at the Jouy factory in France founded by C. P. Oberkampf in 1760, and are sometimes known as *toile de Jouy*. They are typified by 'islands' of design printed in monochrome colours against a natural ground; the designs often show classical landscapes, Chinoiseries scenes or even contemporary stories such as Robinson Crusoe. These cottons were produced in other centres in France, Alsace and England.

Smaller scale printed cottons were produced for dress rather than furnishing fabrics. The 18th century cottons often show delicate garlands of flowers running across a pale ground, the flowers showing Oriental influence. Gradually the designs become smaller and by the early 19th century are often against a dark ground. Motifs were taken from shawls, abstract and geometric designs and flowers. Printed cottons were produced throughout the 19th century on a large scale and it is really the late 18th and early 19th century European cottons that are most interesting for the collector.

Silk

THE LATE 18th century fashion for printed cotton dress fabrics seriously damaged the silk industry. Previously the finest costume had been made from elaborate figured silks, brocades and damasks. These were woven on a drawloom by skilled weavers copying a pattern produced by designers such as Philippe De Lassalle or Anna Maria Garthwaite. Lyon in Southern France was the most important centre of production and her designers led the silk fashion, creating new patterns for each year. In the 18th century it was the pattern of the fabric, rather than the cut of the clothes that counted among the fashion conscious. Silk designs changed regularly and followed a clear trend. Early in the century bizarre silks with strange abstract patterns were popular; these were followed by lace pattern silks, then silks with lush naturalistic motifs and by the end of the 18th century silks with rows of meandering ribbons or garlands were popular: these eventually developed into a neo-classical stripe. Fashions in furnishing silks changed more slowly; the large scale damasks with formalized flowering plants dominated this period's upholstery. Other woven fabrics such as velvet were also popular.

LACE, SHAWLS AND COSTUME

PATRICIA FROST

Lace

LACE-MAKING has a long history, the simplest techniques and oldest known laces consisting of motifs darned on to a knotted or woven net (lacis). The most common are knotted filet and then woven ground Buratto. They are known to have origins in medieval times and have remained largely in the same format into the 20th century. Dating these laces is extremely difficult. Right from the start patterns for lace were recorded in books, with needle lace patterns pre-dating bobbin lace patterns by 50 years. The first needle patterns were published in Switzerland in 1524.

Other early laces from Italy arose from the need to decorate the newly visible line partlets and shirts. Seams were joined by plaited silk stitches and small holes were cut into the fabric and finished with either self or brightly coloured silks (cutwork or Punto Tagliato). Another form of decoration known as drawn thread work or Punto Tirato was formed by pulling bunches of threads together to form holes. The holes thus formed by cutwork became larger and larger, leading to decorative needlework infilling based on the original threads of the ground. This is known as Reticella. Patterns are necessarily geometric and angular. The next development in the late 16th century was to discard the linen fabric and pin thread to a parchment pattern on a pillow. In this way curved lines could be formed, with a buttonhole pattern built up on them. This lace is known as Punto in Aria, literally, stitches in the air. It was used to trim linen and the newly fashionable ruff.

European lace-making centres

THE MOST important trading cities in the late 16th and early 17th centuries were the centres of the lace industry. Venice specialized in needlelaces of creamy white fine linen thread. Typically it has a large padded outline to the damask-like floral patterns, often edged with loops (picots). This type of lace was designed to lie flat and was therefore perfectly suited to the new fashion for deep cuffs and cape-like collars known as 'falling bands'. This lace is known as Gros Point de Venise, with a small scale variant known as Point de Neige, and a flat variant known as Coraline or Point Plat. Many of the motifs of these laces have been reassembled in the 19th century to form crescent-shaped collars.

Another needle lace of distinction arose as a result of royal patronage of Louis XIV under the direction of Colbert, his brilliant finance minister. In order to stem the flow of capital abroad to buy Italian and Flemish braids and laces, the French court were ordered to wear only French laces. The towns of Alençon and Argentan benefited enormously from this monopoly. Leading artists of the day submitted designs, resulting in a superb quality dramatic needle lace characterized by a ground of hexagonal links or 'brides' worked with picots. It was occasionally completely flat but usually had raised padded outlines and was known as Point de France. By the turn of the century Alençon and Argentan were diverging, with Alençon retaining a hexagonal, twisted ground and Argentan developing a mesh encased in buttonhole stitching. A further rare variant is Argentella, with a ground of hexagon-within-hexagon, like a spider's web. Although these three laces

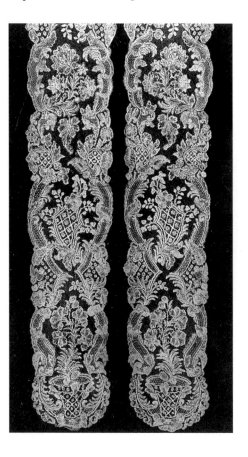

☞ *above*
BRUSSELS LACE
FLEMISH 1730–40
A fine example of 18th century bobbin lace from Brussels. The patterns were sometimes pictorial but more often featured plant motifs.

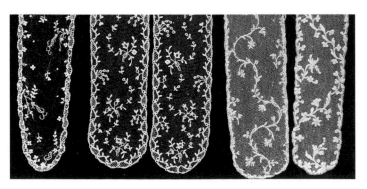

☞ *left*
BRUSSELS AND VALENCIENNES LACE
FLEMISH/FRENCH Late 18th c.
Lace lappets were a headdress feature at this time. Valenciennes lace is made in one piece. Brussels lace flowers are made separately.

share a common vocabulary, they are told apart by the different grounds. Alencon in addition often still has a horse hair stiffening for the outlines.

Valenciennes lace owes much to France but also to Flanders. As it is made in one piece on the pillow, unlike Brussels bobbin lace where the flowers are made separately from both the ground and raised work, it is technically very complex and demanding. It was well established in the 17th century but like many laces reached a high point in the early 18th century with the popular demand for lappets and caps. A well-dressed woman typically wore a fine lace cap with matching lappets, which were ribbon like streamers falling either side of her head. They were fashionable from the turn of the century until the French Revolution, when wearing lace was seen as a very aristocratic and therefore foolhardy activity.

Flanders had an advantage over other lacemakers in Europe in having the damp climate best suited to spinning flax. The finest linen thread was widely exported to England and Italy. Brussels lace used it to advantage. In the 17th century the town produced a variety of bobbin and needle laces, sometimes pictorial but more commonly with plant motifs, with the beginning of the characteristic bunched thread outline. The ground used in bobbin laces is typically a Droschel ground. 19th century Brussels lace whether bobbin or needle shares the common vocabulary of fat roses with serrated leaves with raised veining. The needle lace is known as Point de Gaze.

Mechlin laces are characterized by an untwisted flax thread outlining the motifs, known as the cordonet. This lace can be pictorial in style but is more usually floral closely echoing contemporary silk patterns.

English lace

ENGLAND WAS an important consumer and producer of laces. Home-grown laces include Honiton, produced in Devon, helped by the influx of protestant crafts-men fleeing various persecutions on the continent. It is thought to have been made in the 17th century, but research is still in progress to identify surviving pieces as Honiton. By the 19th century a typical piece would probably include a rose, a shamrock and a thistle and would have crosshatched centres to flowers.

Much lace was produced in the East Midlands in Buckinghamshire. An indication of how large an industry existed is given by the large numbers of turned bone bobbins in circulation. Hollie Point is a particularly charming English speciality – although samplers also exist. The pattern, typically of a lamb or pot of flowers, is formed by gaps in a mesh of button hole stitches. Rare pieces are dated.

With the widespread adoption of machine laces towards the middle of the 19th century, laces became much more standardized throughout Europe and the strong regional flavour of hand made laces was lost. They could not compete with the quantities or prices demanded. A few peasant communities still produce hand laces, but as an industry, it began a decline after the French Revolution.

Shawls

KASHMIR SHAWL weaving techniques are very similar to those of tapestry weaving, with the weaver working with small shuttles following the instructions of a second man. The special quality of Kashmir shawls lies in the use of goat down, harvested in the spring in the Himalayas. In spring, the Kashmir goat, *Capra hircus,* sheds its winter down by rubbing against thorn bushes. The hairs are carefully sorted and spun. Attempts to farm this goat have been unsuccessful as the goats fail to produce down unless temperatures match those in the Himalayas.

Kashmir shawls were certainly being imported into Europe by the 17th century, and can still be acquired, although whole shawls are now extremly rare. By its nature, the fine wool of the field is easily damaged by tearing or parasites. 17th century shawls are very simple, composed of a monochrome field with both ends woven with bands of elegant flowering shrubs usually based on indigenous flowers, such as the poppy or iris. This floral border does not usually exceed 12 in in depth.

During the 18th century, motifs became more stylized and the naturalistic flowers make way for floral mosaics usually perched on a stylized urn. At the same time, striped and moon shawls (with a central medallion and four corner medallions) were also being woven, mainly for export to Arabia.

By the beginning of the 19th century, a typical shawl would have end borders woven with approximately eight cones of about 12 in high, usually composed of a myriad of smaller flowers forming a bush. As the century progresses, these bushes begin to tilt at the tip until by mid-century they are the typical Paisley cone shape so familiar to western eyes. By 1820 the ground between the cones is beginning to be filled with stray flowers and by 1830 the cones are indicated only by reserves of the ground. The woven borders begin then to fill the whole field partly as a response to European demand for more Oriental motifs.

A simple method of spotting early shawls is based on the fact that the taxation system current in the mid-19th century allowed tax collectors to cut shawl fragments from the loom as soon as possible to avoid the possibility of a weaver dying with unpaid taxes owing. Skillful embroiderers later sewed the fragments together.

The Indian market catered not only for indigenous demand but was skillful in supplying Europe with designs especially tailored to suit European taste. Agents from France and England dictated patterns and exported shawls to meet the demand for this perfect accessory to the Grecian modes then prevalent. The Empress Josephine is said to have owned 60 Kashmir shawls, some costing as much as 12,000 Francs.

European shawl weaving

PARALLEL to the Indian industry, the French, English and Austrians began to weave copies of Indian shawls. The main difference between Kashmir and European shawls is one of technique – European shawls are woven on a Jacquard loom, leaving floating wefts on the reverse, which are usually clipped to a rough surface. All threads run parallel to the shawl ends. On the reverse of Indian shawls, threads run in all directions from one area of colour to the next.

One of the earliest shawl manufacturers in France was Guillaume Ternaux (1763–1833), producing shawls with marked European motifs. He considered the Indian motifs 'barbarous'. Useful documents survive from the Parisian *Expositions Universelles* which awarded medals for the best shawls. The most important makers wove their signatures into the shawl ends or central medallions. An especially spectacular shawl was produced in 1839 after a design by Amadée Couder. It was called Nou Rouz and was woven by Gaussen & Cie. It depicts the Arabian New Year Ceremony, including elephants, elaborate temples and a procession around the edge of the shawl. An important archive of designs by Anthony Berrus is preserved in the Musée des Arts Decoratifs in Paris.

Nineteenth century shawls

DATING EUROPEAN shawls of the first half of the century can be done by comparing Indian patterns. The field is generally monochrome with the shawl ends woven with cones. In 1837 a relatively short-lived fashion for 'turnover' shawls bloomed. These were sewn together in such a way that when folded diagonally both borders showed right side up. Towards the middle of the century shawls became smaller and sometimes square with very narrow borders. Until the second quarter of the century narrow ribbon borders were sewn on the length

of the shawl. After this time they are woven as a piece with the shawl. The shawl fields gradually gave way until in the 1860s the whole shawl was covered with cones with only a residual central medallion. Most shawls of this date are approximately 170in × 66in. The end of the shawl as an important fashion accessory came with the demise of the crinoline. While these remained, the shawl was the ideal, if not the only practical outer garment to wear, as coats fitted only with difficulty over such large skirts. With the 1870s and the introduction of slimmer silhouettes, the days of the shawl were numbered. They continued to be given as wedding presents to wealthy brides, but were no longer worn. This is partly the reason why so many of the late 1860s survive in such good condition.

Men's costume

SEVENTEENTH century men's costume is really only found in museums, although occasional pieces do turn up. 18th century costume, however, is relatively plentiful. Throughout the century men's costume was basically composed of the suit, comprising breeches, waistcoat and coat. Fabrics, trimming and embroidery however changed with the fashion. The quality

of cloth and trimming were indicators of status.

At the beginning of the century coats reached well below the knee, almost completely concealing the very roomy breeches. They stopped above the knee until the 1730s and were worn with stockings rolled over them. They were often of the same fabric as the coat. The coat was collarless and with stiffened side pleats echoing the shape of ladies' panniers. Cuffs are flared and deep almost to the elbow (boot cuffs). Waistcoats were often sleeved and could be of contrasting fabric.

Formal wear sports virtuosi embroid-

ery, particularly well done in France in
the 1770s and 1780s. Perhaps the visual
splendour of these suits has led them to be
preserved in greater numbers. The last
two decades of the 18th century saw
changes in fashion epitomized by the
Incroyable, with his tight fitting short coat
with high collar, dazzling waistcoats and
raffish appearance.

The early 19th century saw the coat
being cut back at the front and the introduction of a waist seam about 1820.
Trousers make their first appearance with
the variation strapped under the foot
known as Cossack trousers. Surviving
men's dress from the 1840s and 1850s is
rare as it was worn out in service. Late
19th century men's wear is comparatively
common, but very standardized, and the
flair of the early part of the century is rare.

Women's costume

VIRTUALLY ALL costume pre-dating the
17th century is now in the possession of
museums and collections. Even 17th century costume is so rare as to command
five figure sums at auction. Little has survived, partly because of the early 17th
century fashion popular until the 1630s
for decorative slashing of costly brocades,

TEXTILES
....
Encyclopedia of Antiques

☞ *left*

SACKBACK DRESS

ENGLISH *Late 18th c.*
*A sackback dress in red
and yellow striped silk.
Because they used so much
material dresses like this
were often remodelled.*

which weakened the fabric. Several examples survive of the later fashion of embroidered linen bodices, elaborately worked with scrolling foliage, birds and insects. An exception to the scarcity of 17th century costume is the number of fine linen shirts and chemises.

It is far more common to find 18th century costume, of which far more has survived, if rarely unaltered. Women's costume can be divided roughly into two basic shapes, both being worn over stays, rather than having boned bodices. One shape developed from the T-shaped nightgown, an informal robe of the late 17th century. This evolved into the loose-bodied 'sack' dress, or *robe à la française*. This could be open at the front, worn with a triangular stomacher, usually embroidered (of which many have survived), or closed (few have survived). Worn over a petticoat, the back was pleated between the shoulder blades to form the elegant sweeping silhouette portrayed with such charm by Watteau in the 1720s. These dresses required vast lengths of material and were therefore immensely expensive. Both these factors meant that daughters were likely to re-cycle such expensive fabrics, especially since the original shape involved very little cutting.

The second basic shape evolved from the mantua of the 1690s – a robe pleated to the waist, with a train for formal occasions, but without one for everyday use. The characteristic of a mantua is the elaborate pinning of the skirts to the waistline. Both these types of robe were suited to showing off the large 'ramping' designs of the first decades of the century, both brocaded and embroidered. Both types of dress were worn over hoops, round at the beginning of the century, then oval and at their widest in the 1730s. The close-fitting mantua continued to be worn with panniers for court dress until the 1780s, although the pinned train seems to have been replaced by a vestigial flap from waist to hem in the late 1740s and early 1750s.

18th century robes are dated by various means – the silk used can usually be accurately placed by its design – and then also by the accessories, trimming and sleeves. The basic shape does not alter greatly until the 1780s. It is worth noting the changing shape of sleeves, with deep wide cuffs in the 1720s, a tighter and narrow cuffed sleeve in the 1730s, deepening in the 1740s, leading to wing cuffs of the 1750s. It is common to find robes of early 18th century silk with late 18th century cut. Early unaltered examples are extremely rare and avidly sought after by museums and collectors.

The late 18th century saw the first radical change in dress structure, as portrayed so successfully by Gainsborough. The waistline rose, the tight bodices with a characteristic diamond-shaped panel at the back. Small jackets, known as Spencers, became popular. Hoops disappear. The new striped lightweight silks by their nature are frailer and less likely to survive. Dark ground printed cottons are extremely popular in these last years of the century.

The nineteenth century

EARLY 19TH century dress was heavily influenced by the taste for Grecian culture. White was the most fashionable colour, with dresses having a high waistline reaching its highest point just below the bust by 1815. It reaches a more natural position in the late 1820s. New fabrics for these figure-hugging fashions include fine Indian muslins, often worn with expensive Kashmir shawls. In the first decade dresses are trained. Sleeves become more exaggeratedly leg of mutton and are at their widest in 1830. In the 1840s the sleeves are tighter fitting and curved, severely restricting movement of the shoulders.

The waistline dips to a V-shape from the late 1820s onward to a pronounced 'V' in the early 1840s. Fabrics are predominantly heavy wools and silks. The 1850s see skirts made of lighter silks, and sleeves form bell shapes. The skirts are puffed out by heavy layers of petticoats, soon to be replaced by horsehair petticoats (crinolines) which gave women more freedom of movement. The fashions of the 1860s exaggerated these features, with skirts billowing behind and sleeves being pendulous. By the 1870s, the skirt is being pulled to the back and bodices are tighter and longer to emphasize the curve of the back, underlined by the bustle. This marked slimming of the silhouette continues in the 1880s, with a profusion of trimmings and exotic feathers. The Naughty Nineties see exaggerated puffed sleeves until 1895 when they deflate as quickly, with the skirt mirroring this movement to balance the silhouette.

The use of the Couturier

THE MID-19TH century saw the emergence of the Couturier, beginning with Charles Worth in Paris in 1858, creating dresses for Empress Eugenie and the courts of Europe. Early in the 20th century two names stand out from the mainstream – Poiret and Fortuny. Poiret's creations were heavily influenced by Bakst's Ballet Russe designs and by his love of oriental fabrics and fashions. His designs were probably the first to be worn without corsets. Mariono Fortuny, working in Venice, created his patent silk 'Delphos' dresses, the secret of whose pleating has never been discovered. His stencilled velvets after 15th and 16th century models are masterpieces and are widely collected. Coco Chanel (1883–1971) also contributed to the freeing of the female form by the use of cuts from the world of sport and the golf course.

Paris has always been the centre of the *haute couture* industry. Patou, Paquin, Vionnet and Lanvin all worked here, with Schiaparelli's surrealist creations standing out from the crowd. Later, Dior and Balenciaga must also be mentioned. The influential New Look of the late 1940s made a break with pre-war fashion. Balenciaga's contribution to women's fashion is of prime importance. His masterly cutting created a sculptured look and flights of fancy which remain immensely important as inspiration today.

PAINTINGS

☞ *above*

THOMAS MORAN

MIST IN THE CANYON

AMERICAN Late 19th c.

*Moran's stunning visions of the extremes that the land had
to offer were initially received with disbelief by Eastern
audiences. Today, viewers relish his tinted mists and other-
worldly interpretations of the West. This painting sold for
$385,000 in 1990.*

OIL PAINTINGS
....
JEREMY HOWARD

Painting is one of the oldest and most venerable of the arts. Since the Renaissance it has enjoyed the status, along with sculpture and architecture, of 'fine' as opposed to 'applied' art. This distinction, which certainly would not be recognized in China and Japan, where ceramic art enjoys the degree of veneration we reserve for pictures, has meant that all too often we forget that painting is also a craft, and a very difficult craft at that. We also ignore the fact that pictures were often painted for very practical reasons. Thus, for example, some of the earliest paintings on canvas were commissioned as banner paintings for ceremonial occasions. It was cheaper to paint a banner than to embroider it, and therefore the whole tradition of painting on canvas, which has produced some of the most sublime manifestations of human genius, began in a very humble way.

Equally, up until the end of the 15th century painters were regarded as craftsmen on more or less the same footing as goldsmiths. Indeed, many of the architects and painters of the Italian Renaissance received their first training as goldsmiths. The great altarpieces which adorned the Italian churches were collaborative efforts involving a team of craftsmen, of whom the carpenter who made the frame was generally paid more money than the painter who decorated it. Since the lines of the composition of a medieval painting had to be carefully planned before work began, and the gold background was applied before the painted figures, there was very little scope for spontaneous strokes of genius by the painter. The whole notion of artistic individualism was also held in check by a highly organized guild system which was only gradually replaced with the growth of the art academies in the late 17th century in France. This happened even later in England – in as late as the 18th century, for example, Hogarth spent his early years employed in decorative work for a

☞ *above*

JACOPO DI CIONE

VIRGIN AND CHILD

ITALIAN Late 14th c.
162 × 58cm (63½ × 22¾in)
Tempera and gold on a
shaped panel, this

remarkable transitional
painting is still in the
Gothic tradition, but the
strongly recessed floorline
points forward to the
developments of the
Florentine Renaissance.

silversmith.

Painting can be divided into two basic categories: mural painting and easel painting. While one cannot ignore mural painting in any history of Western art – some of its greatest achievements, such as Michelangelo's Sistene Chapel ceiling, fall into this category – for obvious reasons the collector will be primarily concerned with the category of movable easel painting.

The earliest easel paintings (though easel is a somewhat anachronistic term at this period) were altarpieces. The most important were large and highly complex works of art, but the collector may also encounter smaller-scale paintings, such as the diptyches which were painted for private devotion and were designed to be portable. Many of the large altarpieces were removed from their positions of prominence in Italian churches around the time of the Council of Trent in the second half of the 16th century as a response to a fundamental change in liturgical practices, and were often transferred to side chapels or refectories. Then in the 18th century many of them were dismembered by the unscrupulous and sold to tourists. This explains why there are so few intact altarpieces and why fragments frequently come up for sale at auction.

Early Italian altarpieces were invariably painted on a wood support covered in gesso (a mixture of size and plaster of Paris) over a ground colour of a greenish substance known as *terre verte*. The medium used at this period was tempera, not oil paint, the distinction being that in tempera painting the pigments are suspended in egg rather than linseed oil, and water is used as a solvent. The most important artistic centres in Italy in the late Middle Ages were Siena, where in the late 13th century Duccio (active 1278–1318/19) founded a great school of painting whose principal masters were to be Simoni Martini and the Brothers Lorenzetti, and Florence, where at the same moment Giotto's work was to be the basis of the main tradition of Western European painting. Sienese painting is characterized by great grace and lyricism, but the achievement of Giotto (c. 1267–1337) was that he managed to break away from the flat Byzantine style and invest painting with a new realism and sense of three-dimensional space. The discovery of perspective itself did not come about until later in the 15th century, although naïve attempts at suggesting recession can be found in 14th century Italian painting, and it was not until the time of Masaccio in the 1420s that the lessons of Giotto seem to have been adopted into the mainstream of Florentine painting.

Meanwhile, in Northern Europe a flourishing school of painting centred on Bruges, Antwerp and Ghent produced such masterpieces of realism as Jan Van Eyck's 'Marriage of the Arnolfini' (1434) and the intense spirituality of his altar-piece, 'The Adoration of the Mystic Lamb' (1432). It was a Flemish artist, Van Eyck (d. 1441), who was credited by Vasari with the invention of oil painting. According to his account, the Sicilian painter Antonello da Messina saw some paintings by Van Eyck in Naples, went to study in Flanders and then on settling in Venice transmitted the secret of the new medium into Italian painting. The reality is rather more prosaic, because some form of oil painting had been practised from as early as the 12th century, but it was Van Eyck's mastery of the new medium which ensured its ready adoption south of the Alps.

Portraiture

ONE OF THE most revolutionary developments of the Renaissance lay in the realms of portraiture. In the Middle Ages portraits tended to be rather generalized and hieratic, but the interest in antiquity

☞ *right*
**LUCAS CRANACH I
PORTRAIT OF JOHANN
FRIEDRICH, LATER
KURFÜRST HERZOG VON
SACHSEN**
*GERMAN Early 16th c.
A panel forming part of a
diptych showing portraits
of Kurfürst Herzon von
Sachsen and his son.
Cranach's portraits
indicate the very high
level which the portrait
tradition attained in
Germany at this time.*

☞ *below*
**SANDRO BOTTICELLI
PORTRAIT OF GIOVANNI DI
PIERFRANCESCO DE'
MEDICI**
*ITALIAN Late 15th c.
58 × 39cm (23 × 15½in)
A tempera portrait of a
member of Florence's most
powerful Renaissance
family, it was sold at
auction in 1982 for
£810,000 ($1,490,000).*

in the Renaissance led to a rediscovery of Roman portrait sculpture, and the sculpture and painting of the 15th century in Italy, particularly in Florence, became highly realistic. This new psychological realism is also found in Flemish painting of the period, particularly the donor figures in religious paintings, who are often portrayed with an almost comic candour. As well as oil painting Antonello da Messina (*c.* 1430–79) introduced some of the lessons of Flemish realism into Venetian painting. Subsequently a convention developed of painting bust-length portraits, the most distinguished practitioner being probably Giovanni Bellini (*c.* 1430–1516). This North Italian tradition of portraiture continued in the 16th century in the work of Titian (*c.* 1485–1576), and also in the more provincial schools such as Bergamo and Brescia, as for example in the work of Moretto da Brescia and Moroni; the latter is one of the first artists to have specialized almost exclusively in

portraiture. Meanwhile, in Germany Albrecht Dürer (1471–1528) and Hans Holbein (1497/8–1543) gave a new intensity to the Northern European portrait tradition, Dürer in his marvellously observed self-portraits and Holbein in his portraits of the Tudor court.

Titian's influence was felt most clearly in the 17th century by Rubens and Van Dyck in Flanders and Velazquez in Spain. In his portrait of Charles V at Muhlberg (1548) Titian had developed a new convention of the equestrian portrait, which was to be emulated most notably by Van Dyck in his famous portraits of King Charles I on horseback. A further innovation pioneered by Titian, dating from his early portrait of 'The Young Man with a Glove', was the pose of aristocratic nonchalance (the Italian word, derived from Castiglione's 'Book of the Courtier', was *sprezzatura*) which became almost a cliché of portraiture from Van Dyck to John Singer Sargent.

In Holland a more bourgeois system of patronage meant that the conventions of the Grand Manner did not really take root. Although there is bravura to be found in the work of Frans Hals (see in particular his famous 'Laughing Cavalier' of 1624), the prevailing tone was one of sober realism, as is evident in the portraits of the Rembrandt School. Van Dyck's arrival in England in the 1630s determined the future course of portrait painting for the next two centuries. Although Van Dyck (1599–1641) left few immediate followers other than the accomplished but more prosaic William Dobson, his example was consciously emulated in the 18th century by Sir Joshua Reynolds, who not only borrowed poses from Van Dyck but even dressed many of his sitters in Van Dyck costume. Meanwhile, Reynold's arch rival Gainsborough adopted Van Dyck's feathery brushwork and his unrivalled talent for capturing the textures of silk and satin.

Running at variance to the Van Dyck tradition in English portraiture was the more earthy, realistic and essentially middle-class style of portraiture of William Hogarth (1697–1764). Hogarth was the first native English portrait painter of any real moment to emerge for over 100 years. English portrait painting in the 17th century had been dominated by a stream of foreigners, first Van Dyck, then at the time of the Restoration Sir Peter Lely, and during Queen Anne's reign, the German artist, Sir Godfrey Kneller. The English demand for portraiture seemed to be insatiable, whether it was for portraits of themselves or their dogs and horses. In order to fulfil this demand, both Lely and Kneller were helped by numerous assistants who specialized in painting the draperies or backgrounds so that the master himself would often do no more than paint the face and hands. Some of these drapery painters were accomplished artists in their own right – the great French portrait painter, Largillière, for example, worked for a time as a drapery painter for Lely.

Portraits even became fashionable as a

form of interior decoration hung in sets. Lely, for example, painted a series of female portraits at Hampton Court, known as the Windsor Beauties (many of these beauties were, in fact, the mistresses of Charles II) and Sir Godfrey Kneller followed suit with his series, the Hampton Court Beauties. The logical extension of this idea of painting series of portraits was to group them all together in one picture, and so at the beginning of the 18th century a type of convivial group portrait develops which became known as the conversation piece. One of the finest earliest examples is Hogarth's 'The Graham Family'.

Hogarth was professedly anti-French but ironically took many of his artistic ideas from France, and the convention of the conversation piece almost certainly developed at first in France as a reaction to the more formal tradition of court portraiture which had obtained under Louis XIV. The sitters are very much on parade in the portraits of Largillière and Rigaud, but during the period of Louis XV's regency a new sense of lightness of touch comes into French painting, a delight in intimate portraits in interiors found in the work of De Troy, and above all in Boucher (1703–70). Even when painting grand sitters such as Madame de

☞ *top*

NICOLAS DE LARGILLIERE
PORTRAIT OF A
GENTLEMAN
FRENCH *Late 17th c.*
137 × 101cm (54 × 40in)
Oil on canvas, this is a
bravura example of
Largillière's dashing
Baroque style of
portraiture.

☞ *left*

SIR ANTHONY VAN DYCK
PORTRAIT OF SIR THOMAS
HANMER
ENGLISH *Early 17th c.*
Van Dyck pioneered a
style of portraiture, both
grandiose and relaxed,
which was to dominate
English painting for more
than 200 years. This
painting was accepted by
the British Treasury in
lieu of taxes in 1987.

Pompadour, Boucher cannot resist including details of the furniture and the pleasing jumble of objects on her side table. This delight in the depiction of interiors is also to be found in the work of Johann Zoffany, a German artist who became the greatest master in England of the conversation piece.

In the 18th century two strains run through the history of portraiture. The first is the 'paint me warts and all' tradition of realism found in the work of Dürer and many of the greatest Renaissance masters, in Hogarth in the 18th century, and subsequently right through to Lucien Freud today. The second tradition assumes that the function of the artist is to flatter the sitter. This is the tradition of

the so-called Grand Manner which was developed by Titian and Van Dyck. It is found in the work of Sir Joshua Reynolds, who plundered antiquity for suitable poses in order to aggrandize his English aristocratic sitters, and also notably in the work of the leading portrait painter of the English Grand Tourists, Pompeo Batoni. The Grand Manner culminates in the work of John Singer Sargent (1856–1925), who deliberately harked back to Reynolds for many of his most successful compositions. The Edwardian era, however, was the swan song of the Grand Manner, and many of the most talented artists working in the shadow of Sargent, such as Sir William Orpen and Glyn Philpot, turned to a more realistic style of portraiture later

in their careers. The 20th century has on the whole seen the triumph of the realistic school in portraiture, and Pietro Annigoni may perhaps prove to have been last exponent of a more courtly tradition.

Landscape

LANDSCAPE PAINTING is found sporadically from earliest times – a delight in the countryside, for example, is evident in Roman frescoes; but landscape as a separate genre of painting emerges surprisingly late in Western art. The reasons for this were partly to do with patronage: throughout the Middle Ages and early Renaissance the most important commis-

Joachim Patenier (*c*. 1485–1524) and Paul Bril (1554–1626) were among the pioneers of the new genre, Bril also being the first Northern landscape painter to bring the new art to Italy. His example was followed by Adam Elsheimer, a painter from Frankfurt who settled in Rome in the first decade of the 17th century and whose example was to be enormously influential on Rubens and Claude Lorraine.

In the 17th century three separate strains in the landscape tradition can be identified. The first was that of the heroic landscape, pioneered by Annibale Carracci and Domenichino, and taken up by three French artists who spent their working life in Rome – Claude Lorraine, Nicholas Poussin and Gaspard Dughet. By way of contrast to the calmly classical compositions of these masters, the Neapolitan painter Salvator Rosa developed a highly personal type of heroic landscape which was at once savage and sublime. At the opposite end of the scale were the more realistic and homely landscapes of the Dutch School, as exemplified by the Ruisdaels, Hobbema and Van Goyen. The middle ground between these two strains was occupied by a school of Dutch painters of which Cuyp, Pynacker, Both and Berchem were the leading exponents.

☞ *opposite*

**JOHANN ZOFFANY R.A.
GROUP PORTRAIT OF THE
FAMILY OF LORD
WILLOUGHBY DE BROKE**
ENGLISH Late 18th c.
100 × 125cm (50 × 40in)
Zoffany was a master of the 'conversation piece', the hallmark of which was informality. His detailed interiors give a vivid insight into life in Georgian England.

☞ *left*

**POMPEO BATONI
PORTRAIT OF SIR HENRY
WATKIN DASHWOOD ON
HIS GRAND TOUR**
ITALIAN Late 18th c.
98 × 74cm (38½ × 29in)
Batoni was the most fashionable portrait painter in Rome.

☞ *below*

**CLAUDE LORRAINE
PASTORAL LANDSCAPE
WITH RUINS**
FRENCH Mid 17th c.
*98 × 148.5cm
(38½ × 58½in)*
An important work by the leading classical landscape painter of the 17th century.

sions tended to be for religious paintings where landscape performed merely an ancillary function. But there was also an element of artistic snobbery. Landscape was considered to be a rather lowly genre of painting because it was thought to appeal primarily to the senses rather than to the intellect. Around the time that an independent tradition of landscape painting was emerging in the Netherlands, Michelangelo wrote to a friend: 'They paint in Flanders only to deceive the external eye . . . trees . . . bridges and rivers, which they call landscapes . . . in truth done without reason, without symmetry or proportion, without care in selecting or rejecting.' One of the reasons why the landscape tradition seems to have taken root in that part of Europe was that the effect of Reformation deprived artists of their principal source of patronage, the Church, and they therefore started to paint pictures which would appeal to a secular audience.

☞ *left*
JAN BAPTIST WEENIX
A BEGGAR BOY IN AN
IMAGINARY LANDSCAPE
DUTCH Mid 17th c.
78.5 × 61cm (31 × 24in)
Weenix was one of many
Dutch artists who settled
in Rome and excelled in
landscape and in low life,
or genre scenes, gaining
the nickname
'Bomboccianti'.

Their realism was modified by experiences of Italy and Italian-based painters, and their landscapes are consequently suffused with a golden light which owes much to Claude Lorraine. This school was very popular with English collectors in the 18th century.

In France the stern landscape tradition of the 17th century gives way to a whimsical approach in the following century, when Boucher, Fragonard and Hubert Robert painted landscapes in a magical never-never land.

A dramatic contrast to these poetic confections were the more-or-less contemporary, but far more pragmatic townscapes of Canaletto (1697–1768) and the Venetian *vedutisti*. Canaletto's works were thought to be so life-like that many people considered he must have used a 'camera obscura' (a box with a peep-hole and a system of mirrors which transmitted an image onto a piece of frosted glass), although in reality he took so many liberties with Venetian topography that this theory is no longer generally accepted. The impact of Canaletto's visit to England in 1746 was to be highly influential on English painting. Samuel Scott, William Marlow, and two rather shadowy figures, William James and John or Joseph Paul, who may in fact be inventions of the auctioneers, were among his followers. Meanwhile, the Claudian tradition of heroic landscape

was pursued by Richard Wilson, and at the beginning of the 19th century John Constable and the painters of the Norwich School discovered in Dutch 17th century landscape painting, in particular Hobbema, a potent source of inspiration.

Classical landscape died hard in French art, largely because of the strength of the academic tradition. Pierre-Henri de Valenciennes (1750–1819) was the high priest of the Neo-classical French school of landscape painting, although he anticipated by almost 100 years the achievements of the Impressionists in his oil-on-paper sketches done from nature in the Roman campagna. One painter who was strongly influenced by Valenciennes was Corot. The Barbizon School of painters not only found sources of inspiration in Dutch painting but were also pioneers of the *plein air* approach to painting. Meanwhile in England the ageing Turner was moving in the last 20 years of his life towards an abstraction and a sense of pure colour

☞ *opposite above*
CANALETTO
VIEW OF THE GRAND CANAL
VENETIAN Early 18th c.
Canaletto was the greatest
18th century master of the
veduta or topographical
view painting. His visit
to England in the 1740s
had an important impact
on British landscape
painting.

☞ *left*
FRANCOIS BOUCHER
LANDSCAPE
FRENCH Mid 18th c.
Boucher was the dominant
artistic personality of the
Louis XV period: his
influence extended to
tapestry, porcelain and all
the decorative arts.

☞ *left*
**JOHN CONSTABLE
LANDSCAPE WITH
FLATFORD MILL**
ENGLISH c.1825
*The first of five paintings
of Flatford Lock by
Constable, one of
England's best known
landscape painters. His
more homely brand of
Romanticism was greatly
admired in France and
influenced the Barbizon
School there.*

☞ *left*
CLAUDE MONET
LE PONT DU CHEMIN DE
FER À ARGENTEUIL
FRENCH Late 19th c.
Monet is regarded as the
archtetypal Impressionist
painter as he never
wavered from the ideals of
the movement throughout
his life. One of his
paintings, 'Impression:
Sunrise', even gave the
movement its name.

☞ *below*
JAN WEENIX
STILL LIFE WITH DEAD
HARE
DUTCH Late 17th c.
An exquisite example of
the hunting still life.

which was to be highly influential on the work of Monet.

Ironically, as with so many art historical terms, Impressionism was first coined as a term of abuse. Reviled by the establishment – 'this is the painting of democrats, of men who don't change their linen', wrote Comte de Nieuwerkerke – the Impressionists are now the most popular and sought after (and most expensive) landscape painters of all time.

Still Life

IF LANDSCAPE occupied a fairly lowly position in the artistic hierarchy, still life, in the opinion of most academicians, was the lowliest of the genres. Like so many areas of painting, it did not really evolve as a separate category until the 17th century. The changing nature of patronage in the Netherlands then and the increasing specialization of studio practice encouraged certain artists not only to specialize in still life, but even to take certain types of still life as a sub-speciality. One thus has a situation where a painter such as Jan Leemans painted little else but still lives of birdcages, and where specialists in flower painting such as Jan Breughel the Younger

or Daniel Seghers would collaborate with a specialist in *trompe l'œil* marble painting such as Erasmus Quellinus, or a specialist in figure subjects such as Hendrick Van Balen.

Certain categories of the genre have fallen out of favour in modern times. These include those with dead game, of which Rubens' assistant Frans Snyders and the painter Jan Weenix (1642–1719) were probably the leading exponents, and a special category known as the vanitas still life, which included examples of memento mori such as skulls and candles

in order to emphasize the transience of human life, together with the banqueting still lives, or 'Pronkstilleben'. The most popular category though, then and now, was probably the flower and fruit still life, which reached a peak of perfection in the Netherlands in the 17th century which has never since been attained. Leading exponents were Jan Van Huysum, Van Os and the painters of the Bosschaert dynasty.

Outside the Netherlands the tradition of still life painting was particularly strong in Spain where a type known as *bodegones* (a sort of kitchen still life with figures) became popular, particularly in Seville, as can be seen in the early paintings of Velázquez (1599–1660). Spanish still lives of the 17th century are marked by their austerity and their very strong sense of texture and form, and the tradition continued into the next century in the work of Melendez. In Italy the still life was strongest in Naples, which was under the rule of the Spanish viceroys in the 17th century; Michelangelo Merisi de Caravaggio (1571–1616), who was such a major influence on Neapolitan painting, was also a still life painter of genius. In France only Chardin in the 18th century and Fantin Latour in the 19th century can be said to have painted still lives of the

☞ *left*

WILLEM CLAESZ HEDA
STILL LIFE WITH BANQUET
AND OYSTERS
DUTCH c.1625
The Dutch were famous
not only for their flower
and fruit pieces but also
for their Pronkstilleben,
or breakfast pieces.
Willem Claesz Heda was
one of the most
distinguished exponents of
the genre which developed
particularly in Haarlem
and Amsterdam in the
1620s.

☞ *left*

HENRI FANTIN-LATOUR
STILL LIFE WITH FLOWERS
AND FRUIT
FRENCH 1876
This painting belonged to
Edwin Edwards who was
the artist's English agent.
Fantin-Latour's still
lives of flowers were
enormously popular with
collectors then as now.

which is why one of the first things that an expert does when he looks at a picture is to turn it over and inspect the back! If it is wood then the type of wood may give a clue as to the painting's country of origin, which may not always be self-evident merely from stylistic analysis. As a general rule, oak was used in Northern Europe, whereas soft woods such as poplar were favoured south of the Alps. Other clues may be given, if the picture is on canvas, by far the most common surface, by the type of canvas used. Venetian canvases, for example, have a characteristic herringbone pattern, which one can observe in the surface of paintings by Tintoretto. Neapolitan canvases, on the other hand, tend to be of a coarse open weave akin to sacking, as one can see if one scrutinizes paintings by Mattia Preti (1613–99). Flemish canvases on the whole tend to be of much finer weave, as one would expect, given Flanders' importance for centuries as the centre of the cloth trade, and a number of early Flemish pictures are painted on linen.

Examination of the back of the picture will also throw up other clues such as the nature of the stretcher: collectors' marks, seals or labels, or even the tell-tale Christie's stencil mark (two letters followed by three digits). It will also tell you whether the picture has been relined or not, that is, transferred onto a new backing canvas. This process should not always be regarded with suspicion since most paintings have to be relined every 100 years or so in order to prevent flaking. But a new lining may cover a multitude of sins, such as holes and tears, and should therefore alert

very first rank, while in England, where the tradition has never been very strong, the painting of flowers and fruits has tended to be reserved as a polite occupation for young ladies.

Looking at a painting

THE ART OF appraising a picture requires not only considerable knowledge of the history of styles but also an understanding of the basic techniques and materials. Whether oil or tempera based, a painting will have a support which can be made of wood or metal or canvas, onto which is laid a ground, the principal layers of paint, and finally a varnish which may incorporate glazes, whether transparent or semi-opaque (a scumble glaze), and which alter the colour values of the pigments beneath.

The support will tell the collector a great deal about the history of the picture,

☞ *left*
MATTIA PRETI
ST HELEN (DETAIL)
ITALIAN Mid 17th c.
*This detail of a fine
painting by the
Neapolitan Baroque artist
Preti shows the coarsely
woven canvas
characteristic of the
Neapolitan School. The
creamy handling of paint
and the red shadowing*
round the tips of the
fingers are the hallmarks
of Preti's technique.

you to possible damage when inspecting
the front of the picture.

The condition of a painting is not easy
for a layman to assess, but certain modern
gadgets, such as ultra-violet lamps, help
to detect the presence of recent over-
painting by a restorer. Attention also
should be paid to areas such as the sky
where thinness often develops, and to the
foliage of trees, which is particularly sus-
ceptible to the vagaries of time and mis-
guided restorers. When examining the
front of the picture you should also look
out for *pentimenti,* the tell-tale signs of
where the painter has changed his mind,
which are usually a guarantee that the
painting is autograph work and not a
copy. The final criterion, though, in
assessing a picture is quality, and a sense
of this can only be acquired by years of
attentive looking.

☞ *right*
TINTORETTO
PLATO (DETAIL)
ITALIAN Late 16th c.
*This shows evidence of
pentimento – the artist has
painted over the original
rendering which is
beginning to show – a
good sign of age and
authenticity.*

DRAWINGS
....
JEREMY HOWARD

Drawings provide one of the most challenging and rewarding areas for the collector. Challenging because unlike silver and porcelain there are no factory marks or hallmarks to guide you and because, at any rate before the 18th century, drawings were rarely signed. Rewarding because drawings provide greater variety than any other sphere of collecting and an unrivalled sense of intimacy with the creative processes of the artist.

Early drawings
—

THE ORIGINS of drawing are shrouded in the mists of time, but for practical purposes may be said to begin in the medieval monasteries. The art of illuminating manuscripts reached such a high point in the late Middle Ages that the major artistic developments north of the Alps may be said to have taken place in the field of illustration, rather than panel or wall painting. And this persisted remarkably late in Northern Europe. Artists such as Jean Fouquet were first and foremost illustrators and a feeling for landscape can be seen developing in the vignettes to Books of Hours before land-scape makes its appearance as an independent art form in easel painting. However, it was not until the 15th century in Italy that drawing began to play a central role in all areas of artistic activity. The reasons for this were partly practical. Until around the middle of the 15th century paper was not available in large supply and the alternatives, vellum or parchment, were too expensive to be used merely for roughing out ideas. In the early 15th century the assistants in an Italian artist's studio would sketch out ideas with a metal point on prepared wooden slates which were then wiped clean after use, which is why there are so few surviving preparatory drawings from the period. Vellum was reserved for presentation drawings or for the workshop's model books, in which studies of draperies, of animals, and of exotic figures were recorded, or they were then incorporated as part of the stock-in-trade of early Renaissance compositions.

As paper became cheaper and more plentiful, these stock images were replaced by studies from life and drawing became more empirical. Artists were encouraged to study anatomy, and life drawing, both from the nude and clothed model, became *de rigueur*. As Leon Battista Alberti wrote, 'For a clothed figure we must first draw the naked body and then cover it with clothes.' Careful drapery studies were then made either from the living model or, in the case of more complicated poses which could not be held by a studio assistant, a length of fabric was dipped in plaster and set up for study over an articulated and jointed wooden model These drapery studies reached their highest point in the work of Leonardo da Vinci (1452–1519).

Drawing became the essential medium of communication between the master and his assistants and the artist and his patron in the 16th century. On being given a commission, the usual sequence was as follows: first, the artist sketched out a rough idea which was known as the '*primo pensiero*'. Next, detailed studies were taken from life, the assistants or '*garzone*' being used to pose for the various figures in the composition. Studies of drapery and of the heads and hands of the principal figures would then be made. Where exotic figures or animals were to be incorporated, these were often copied from the studio pattern books. These elements were then assembled and a more finished drawing was provided for presentation to the client before work began on the preparation for painting. This drawing would be highly detailed, and since it often had the status of a legal contract, would normally be on a high-quality support such as parchment or vellum.

☞ *left*
NICOLÒ DI GIACOMO DA BOLOGNA
ITALIAN 17 × 15.5cm (6⅝ × 6⅛in) Between 1351 and 1403
This historiated initial P has been cut from an antiphonary, and is on vellum.

☞ *above*
FEDERICO BAROCCI THE MADONNA DEL POPOLO
ITALIAN Late 16th c. 55 × 38cm (21½ × 15in) This drawing, which is a study for an altarpiece for a church in Arezzo, has been lightly squared for transfer in black and red chalk.

Once the client's approval had been given, drawings would be squared up for transfer on to canvas or, in the case of fresco, on to a wall. Squaring up involved drawing a grid which then enabled the composition to be blown up into life-sized cartoons, a famous example of which is the Leonardo cartoon in London's National Gallery. These cartoons, generally drawn in charcoal on a rather coarse paper, were placed against the wall and the design was transferred on to the plaster by pricking through the outlines of the cartoon and then joining up the dots on the wall in a red chalk drawing known as *sinopia*. The wall was then covered with a final thin layer of plaster in preparation for the fresco painting. This method was to remain the standard practice in Italian studios for over three centuries.

Drawing comes of age

IF THE basic work methods changed little from the end of the 15th century, there was a fundamental shift early in the 16th century in the attitude towards draughtsmanship. With the advent of the movement known as Mannerism, drawings ceased to be merely functional and virtuoso draughtsmanship became an end in itself. This change of attitude coincided with the formation of the first academies of drawing founded in the mid-16th century in Florence and Bologna and the formation of the first important collections of drawings, the most notable of which was that assembled by Giorgio Vasari (1511–74). The care he took in the presentation of his 'Libro dei desegni' reflects the new importance given to drawings as works of art in their own right.

North of the Alps, a lively tradition of portrait drawing developed in France in the work of François Clouet (*c*.1510–72), and in Germany in the work of Hans Holbein (1497/8–1543). German draughtsmanship of the period showed a curious mixture of innovation and conservatism.

☞ *left*
GIORGIO VASARI
PAGE FROM LIBRO
DE'DISEGNI
ITALIAN Mid-16th c.
57 × 46cm (22½ × 18¾in)
The putto and altarpiece study are by Raffaellino del Garbo, and the angels and metalpoint studies by Filippino Lippi. The elaborate presentation shows the importance Vasari attached to his collection of drawings.

☞ *below*
PIETRO BERRETTINI,
CALLED PIETRO DA
CORTONA
STUDY OF A HEAD
ITALIAN Mid-17th c.
242 × 193cm (95¼ × 76in)
Pietro da Cortona was best known for his mural paintings, and this drawing is a preparatory study for a fresco.

In the work of Albrecht Dürer (1471–1528) we find the earliest landscape watercolours in Western art, but at the same time the Gothic style, and with it the old-fashioned techniques of silver point, survived well into the 16th century. The invention of printing allowed the dissemination of Mannerist ideas throughout Europe, and Michelangelo's drawings, through the engravings of Raimondi, entered into the stock repertoire of Northern artists.

When in the 1580s reaction to the Mannerist style set in in Italy, it was centred on Bologna where the Carracci moved away from the coutured stylishness of Mannerist draughtsmanship towards a greater naturalism and a sense of solid form. This had two important implications: the first was the revival of life drawing, and the second was the birth of landscape sketching from nature, which we find most noticeably in the drawings of Domenichino (1584–1641). Drawing again became a medium for working out ideas on paper, allowing the artist to

change his mind, and a more tonal approach is apparent in the drawings of the sculptor Gianlorenzo Bernini (1598–1660) and Guercino (1591–1666), where the forms are modelled more sculpturally and the play of light, rather than outline, determines form. In Genoa the Flemish influence of Van Dyck and Rubens led to

certain pioneering experiments, such as Castiglione's use of the oil sketch on paper, and in Naples the broken lines and zig-zag rhythms of the drawings of Ribera and Luca Giordano were to have a powerful influence on Fragonard in the following century.

In the Low Countries the late survival of Mannerism centred on Haarlem gave way to an emergent landscape tradition in the drawings of Roelandt Savery (c.1576–1639) and Paul Bril (1554–1626) who used a form of aerial perspective by putting the warmer tones – the brown washes – in the foreground, and using blue washes in the background of their compositions. This landscape tradition was continued by the Northern artists who settled in Rome in the 17th century, most notably Claude Lorraine and Nicolas Poussin.

In the 18th century France began to rival Italy as the artistic centre of Europe, although the continuing importance of Venice is attested by the brilliant draughtsmanship of the Tiepolos, and the sparkling evocation of the Venetian lagoons in the drawings of Francesco Guardi (1712–93) and Antonio Canaletto (1697–1768) are greatly sought after by collectors. The most important artist of the early 18th century in France was Jean-Antoine Watteau (1684–1721), whose technique of using either two crayons (red and black) or three crayons (red, black and white), was to be much emulated. Watteau's drawings are nearly all studies from life – *aides-de-memoire* for his paintings – but such was the enthusiasm of the French collectors such as Watteau's patron, Pierre Crozat, that artists began to produce drawings in large numbers, specifically with a view to sale. These were often elaborately presented in the characteristic *eau-de-nil* mounts of the period, and such was the popularity of the red chalk drawings of Boucher, Fragonard and Hubert Robert that a crayon manner method of engraving was invented which enabled highly deceptive reproductions to be produced.

The 18th century in France also witnessed the development of the pastel, which became particularly popular for portraiture. In the hands of Chardin, Perroneau and, above all, Maurice-Quentin de la Tour (1704–88) it reached such a level of accomplishment that some members of the French Academy were fearful lest pastels should threaten the future of oil painting. But a reaction to the frivolous world of the *ancien régime* set in with the French Revolution, as is reflected in the increasingly cool style of draughtsman-

☞ *above*
JEAN-AUGUSTE-DOMINIQUE INGRES PORTRAIT OF THE HONOURABLE MRS FLEETWOOD PELLEW FRENCH Mid-19th c. *29 × 22cm (11½ × 8¾in) Ingres believed that* drawing was the 'probity of art' and achieved his effects with great economy of line. This work was sold at auction in 1985 for £226,000 ($418,100).

ship which one associates with the Neo-classical movement. The greatest Neo-classical draughtsman was undoubtedly Jean-Auguste-Dominique Ingres (1780–1867) whose marvellous portrait drawings executed in Rome in the 1820s show what can be achieved through the use of line with very little recourse to shadowing. At the opposite end of the pole were the dashingly romantic drawings of Géricault and Delacroix. As the 19th century wore on a number of revivalist movements, beginning with the German Nazarene Brotherhood and continuing with the Pre-Raphaelites in England, encouraged a return to the techniques of draughtsmanship of the late Middle Ages. This in turn was followed by the Victorian 'High

Renaissance' artists, such as Lord Leighton (1830–96) and George Frederick Watts (1817–1904), who revived the art of fresco painting and with it some of the old studio practices of the Renaissance.

Master drawings – techniques and materials

ALTHOUGH PAPER was manufactured in China from the 2nd century onwards, it was not readily available in Europe until the early 15th century. Medieval and Renaissance drawings were generally executed on either parchment or vellum, materials made from animal skins. Vellum was the more expensive material and was made from the skins from calves, lambs or young goats. The surfaces of the skins were rubbed with pumice, ground bone or chalk, and in order to prepare the vellum for metal point drawing, it was then generally coated with a preparation of lead oxide and ground bonemeal. After about 1450 vellum and parchment were largely superseded by paper in Italy except for legal documents, model books and highly finished drawings made for presentation, although it survived well into the following century north of the Alps. Use of vellum was briefly revived in the 19th century by the Arts and Crafts movement, for example in the designs of C. R. Ashbee.

Paper first appeared in Europe in the 12th century but was not readily available until after 1400. Until the 19th century, artist's paper was made from pulped rags, and came in two basic types, laid paper and wove paper. Laid paper was made by dipping a grid consisting of fine meshed horizontal wires and wider spaced vertical wires into a mould containing liquid pulp. In laid paper these vertical lines are easily discernible by holding the paper up to the light. Wove paper, which did not become available until the early 19th century, was manufactured by dipping a much finer-meshed grid into the pulp, which gave the appearance of a woven fabric.

During the early Renaissance coloured

☞ *above*
JOST AMMAN
HEAD OF A BEARDED MAN
GERMAN *Late 16th c.*
15.5 × 11.5cm (6 × 4½in)
The spiky and lively use
of line, and the chiaroscuro

technique, are
characteristic of the
German 16th century
draughtsmanship, where
the Gothic tradition
survived much later than
in Italy.

papers became fashionable, particularly for metal point drawing. The Venetians were among the first to import blue paper known as '*carta assura*' and shades of grey and fawn were also popular in northern Italy. The first paper-making machine was not invented until 1799 and it was not until the 1840s that wood pulp was introduced into paper manufacture, but it was never very suitable for artist's paper owing to its tendency to turn brown when exposed to light. In the late 19th century Oriental papers derived from bamboo and rice paper became popular, coinciding with the vogue for Japanese prints, and were favoured by artists such as Whistler and Burne-Jones.

Metal point

METAL POINT was used from the Middle Ages until the second half of the 15th century in Italy and later north of the Alps. A two-ended stylus made of silver, gold or some base metal such as lead was used on a prepared ground, and left a

deposit on the skin of the support. The technique was particularly appropriate for fine work, but it allowed artists little flexibility and was therefore ill-adapted to preliminary sketching. It was largely superseded in the 15th century in Italy by other media, and lead point was replaced entirely with the invention of cased pencils in the mid 16th century. However, silver point enjoyed a brief revival in the late 19th century in England and was used by artists such as Lord Leighton, William Strang and Alphonse Legros. Kits were manufactured by Winsor and Newton from the 1890s until after the First World War.

Pen and Ink

TWO TYPES of pen were used in the Renaissance, the reed pen and the quill pen. Quill pens gave greater flexibility but reed produced a more powerful effect, and hence was favoured by, for example, Van Gogh and Rowlandson. Metal nibs were recorded in the 16th century but were not widely used for drawing until the 19th century. The ink most commonly used in the Italian Renaissance was iron gall ink which had the disadvantage that the gallic acid tends to eat into the paper and the ink turns from black to brown with age. A more satisfactory ink was carbon ink derived from soot, as it did not turn brown or fade, or bistre, which was also derived from soot but was more browny-yellow in colour – it was favoured by Tiepolo. Sepia, a brownish ink derived from cuttlefish, was the last to be adapted by artists. Inks can provide important clues for dating; for example, bistre and carbon inks were not generally in use until the 16th century and sepia did not appear as a drawing medium until the 18th century.

Chalks, Charcoal and Pastel

THE PRINCIPAL chalks used by artists were black chalk and red chalk, although

white chalk became popular, used in conjunction with the other two, in the 18th century. Black chalk was little used before the end of the 15th century but then became extremely popular. Red chalk, also known as sanguine, appeared later than black chalk, Leonardo being the first major artist to use it. It was particularly favoured also by the Carracci School and was also very popular in the 18th century when it was imitated in crayon manner prints.

Charcoal was the preferred medium for sketching large-scale mural compositions in free hand from the time of the Greeks and the Romans, although not widely used on drawing paper until the 16th century. The ease with which it can be erased made it a popular medium for preliminary sketches.

The closest drawing medium to painting is pastel, which has been called a dry form of painting. It consists of sticks of variously coloured powdered pigments mixed with white. Although found in the 17th century, pastel did not become widely popular until the 18th century, first in Venice with Rosalba Carriera, and later in France and in England. Pastel was also favoured by Degas in the 19th century.

Watermarks and collectors' marks

ONE OF of the first things a connoisseur does when appraising a drawing is to hold it up to the light. This gives him important information about the nature of the paper and the watermarks, as well as revealing the presence of any restoration. In the case of English 18th century paper, dating is normally very easy since the date will normally be given underneath the paper manufacturer's name. When it comes to Old Master drawings, the watermarks for most of them can be identified by consulting Bricquet's dictionary, *Les Filigraines*. On the face of the drawing, normally in the bottom left or right hand corner, there will often be a collector's mark, normally a stamped monogram, which may give an important clue to the drawing's provenance. Peter Lely's or Sir Thomas Lawrence's collectors' marks, for example, are generally a good indication of quality. An extensive list of these marks can be found in Lugt's monumental *Les marques de collections des dessins et d'estampes*.

Copies, reproductions and forgeries

COPYING HAS a long and distinguished ancestry and only an intimate knowledge of the work of an artist makes it possible to distinguish between his hand and that of a good studio copyist. Faking has an almost equally long ancestry, although it did not become generally current until the 18th century, spurred by the popularity of 17th century drawings, in particular those of Guercino. The drawings of Francesco Guardi have also proved particularly liable to the attentions of the counterfeiter.

The collector should also be aware of reproductions. In the 18th century various techniques of engraving were developed, which produced highly successful imitations of drawings, among them crayon manner and soft ground etching. Here, the presence of a plate mark will sometimes give them away. More dangerous still are the various photomechanical processes developed in the second half of the 19th century, especially Frederick Hollyer's platino-type reproductions of Burne-Jones' drawings and of Old Master drawings. Photographic reproductions can be detected by holding the paper in a raking light when the surface will show a slight glitter, caused by the photographic salts. A final recourse is careful inspection with a fingertip or an eraser, preferably to the edge of the drawing, but this is not generally recommended, as it damages the work.

Although knowledge of the various media and inspection of such indicators as watermarks and collectors' marks is helpful, the ultimate test is that of quality

☞ *above*

FRANCOIS BOUCHER
VENUS AND CUPID
FRENCH 1759
36 × 25.5cm (14 × 10in)
During the 1750s Boucher created a number of highly finished drawings which were keenly sought after by private collectors. This is a particularly fine example.

☞ *below*

CIRCLE OF BOUCHER
LA SULTANE LISANT
FRENCH Mid-18th c.
26.5 × 32 cm (10½ × 12½ in)
The drawing is inscribed on the reverse 'To Mr Dingley'. Robert Dingley was a member of the Society of Dilettanti and a notable drawings collector.

since forensic evidence alone will not help the connoisseur to distinguish between a studio copy and an autograph work of the artist. A couple of examples will demonstrate how one can set about developing this eye for quality. Two drawings on this page, one by the great French master, François Boucher, the other by an unknown artist working in his studio. In the case of the drawing by the unknown artist, the sheet passes most of the criteria on the check list. The paper is 18th century and the use of the three coloured chalks is highly characteristic of Boucher. The drawing is connected to and probably a preliminary study for an engraving which appeared in a book published in the 1740s. There is even a tantalizing inscription on the back which identifies the name of the collector to whom the drawing once belonged, an 18th century Englishman who had a distinguished collection of Old Master drawings. What is lacking, though, is the sense of volume and fluency that is apparent in the other illustration. The line is somewhat hard and hesitant and the fingertips do not taper to the same extent. Although doubtless a very pretty and interesting 18th century example, this drawing is considered to be one of three known copies of a lost work by Boucher.

WATERCOLOURS
....
JEREMY HOWARD

In origin watercolours are not really a separate category but a branch of drawing. However, for various historical and geographical reasons, the art of watercolour developed along independent lines, particularly in England, and so we are justified in treating it as a more or less autonomous art form with its own distinct conventions.

Technically speaking the term watercolour is somewhat misleading since the medium is in fact gum-based, rather than water-based. Whereas in an oil painting the pigments are bound to each other with linseed or other oil, in watercolour painting pigments are bound with gum arabic, a substance obtained from the acacia tree. The water is used as a solvent in the same way that turpentine is used in oil painting. Whereas oil paint takes many hours to dry, watercolour is a much faster-drying medium, which makes it particularly suitable for catching fleeting atmospheric effects but which allows little possibility for correcting errors, and makes it hard for the artist to change his mind.

The peculiar beauty of watercolour lies in its translucent effects, which allow colour washes to be laid on top of each other, and the whiteness of the paper to shine through. A form of watercolour, much favoured on the continent by artists such as Marco Ricci, but shunned by most English practitioners, is called gouache or body colour, where Chinese White is mixed with the pigment, rendering it opaque rather than translucent and giving it an effect more akin to oil painting.

The watercolour tradition in England begins with portrait miniatures, which were the most important vehicle of artistic expression at the Tudor Court. The most famous of the Elizabethan 'limners', as the miniaturists were called, was Nicholas Hilliard (1547–1619). The tradition was continued in the 17th century in the work of Isaac and Peter Oliver and, most notably, Samuel Cooper (1609–72), whose famous 'warts and all' miniature of Oliver Cromwell has passed into the history books. The Golden Age of the English miniature ends with the death of Cooper but a lively tradition of portrait drawing continues under the Restoration in the drawings of Lely and Kneller, and Jonathan Richardson in the following century. Portrait drawings enjoyed something of a Renaissance in the Regency period, most notably in the work of Lawrence, Henry Edridge and John Downman, and into the Victorian era in the work of George Richmond.

During the 18th century pastels were a favoured medium for portraiture. The technique of pastel drawing originated in Italy and was greatly popularized by the Venetian pastellist Rosalba Carriera who visited Paris in 1720. Her '*sfumato*' technique was much admired by English pastellists in the mid-18th century, such as Francis Cotes. Cotes' pupil John Russell was the most talented pastellist of the Regency era, developing a technique of deliberately smudging his pastels to sweeten the outlines. In Ireland a flourishing school of pastellists grew up in Dublin at the Academy schools where oil painting was not taught; the most distinguished Irish practitioner was Hugh Douglas Hamilton.

Landscape and topography
~

THE MAINSTREAM tradition in English watercolours is the landscape tradition which first developed in the 17th century. As with most developments in English art, landscape painting in watercolour grew out of an essentially practical activity – topography – and, right into the 19th century it retained a connection with the skills of map-making and surveying. Thomas Sandby, for example, brother of the more famous Paul Sandby and one of the more distinguished topographical painters of the second half of the 18th century, was an instructor in military surveying at Woolwich.

However, ironically the founders of the English topographical tradition were all foreigners. Wenceslaus Hollar was the first of these, a Bohemian artist who arrived in England in the entourage of the Earl of Arundel in the 1630s. He was followed by the Flemish artists Jan Kip and Leonard Knyff, who both published bird's eye views of the English landscape. Both these artists were essentially cartographers, but one native English watercolourist who was strongly influenced by Hollar, Francis Place (1647–1728), produced a number of watercolour drawings which have earned him some claim to the title of father of the English school of landscape painting. In Van Dyck's watercolours of the 1630s we find for the first time a feeling for poetic landscape, but these rare watercolours, done for his own pleasure, did not exercise a very strong influence on the English tradition.

In the 18th century the topographical watercolour was given further impetus by the visit of Canaletto in 1746, whose most notable English followers were Samuel Scott. Paul Sandby (1730/1–1809), another follower of Canaletto, used a mixed technique of gouache and watercolour in emulation of another Venetian painter, Marco Ricci, and is best known for his views around Windsor. Other notable topographical artists were Thomas Malton senior, who wrote a treatise on perspective in 1775, and Edward Dayes, who taught Thomas Girtin and was a strong influence on the young Turner. A ready market for topographical watercolours grew up at the end of the 18th century, spurred by the fashionable antiquarianism and the impact of the French wars which effectively prevented English travellers from visiting the Continent and encouraged domestic tourism in its place.

A reaction against what was known as the tinted drawing, the carefully washed outlined drawings of Dayes and Malton, was inevitable. It came about partly as a result of technical experimentalism, and partly in response to the burgeoning Romantic movement. A theoretical basis for this reaction was provided in the 1790s by the cult of the picturesque, formulated in the writings of the Reverend William Gilpin, Uvedale Price and Richard Payne-Knight, and lampooned in Jane Austen's novel *Northanger Abbey*.

This reaction was essentially an attempt to apply theories of picture-making derived from Claude Lorraine, Gaspard Dughet and Salvator Rosa to landscape composition. It had an important effect on the public perception of the twin arts of watercolour painting and landscape gardening, but as far as the practitioners were concerned did little more than echo the responses of successive English artists who had visited Italy in the second half of the 18th century. The first of these was Alexander Cozens (1717–86), who developed a highly individual technique of sepia wash drawing, using a system of apparently haphazard ink blots. This earned him considerable ridicule and the nickname 'Sir Dirty Didgit', but he was an influential drawing master who did much to liberate watercolour from the straitjacket of topography. Another great innovator was Thomas Gainsborough (1727–88). He used a similarly experimental technique of chalk drawing rubbed with white lead, which was then dipped in skimmed milk and finished off with watercolour.

The picturesque experiments of Alexander Cozens bore remarkable fruit in the work of his son, J. R. Cozens (1752–97). He was greatly admired, not only by Constable who called him the 'greatest genius that ever touched landscape', but also by Turner and Girtin who, as young men, were employed by a benevolent amateur, Dr Thomas Munro, to copy the Cozens watercolours in his collection. Both artists had been trained in the 18th century topographical tradition where the outlines of a watercolour were neatly inked out and coloured washes then laid in. The impact of Cozens' example was

☞ *left*

**THOMAS GAINSBOROUGH
LANDSCAPE WITH CATTLE
WATERING**

ENGLISH 1770s
This is a typical example of Gainsborough's pioneering technique of experimenting with chalk rubbed with white lead and dipped in skimmed milk, before being painted over in watercolour.

☞ *left*

**JOHN ROBERT COZENS
A VIEW FROM SIR WILLIAM
HAMILTON'S VILLA AT
PORTICI**

ENGLISH Late 18th c.
The hazy blue tonality is highly characteristic.

☞ *below*

**THOMAS GIRTIN
VIEW OF THE VILLAGE OF
JEDBURGH**

ENGLISH 1800
The artist has omitted the ruined abbey of Jedburgh and has deliberately played down the picturesque qualities of the scene.

revolutionary. Of the two, Thomas Girtin (1755–1802) was the first to break away from 'the neat precision of Malton and his school' and he pioneered a technique of rendering landscape with a loaded brush on a rough cartridge paper which was surprisingly expressive, capturing the effects of light and atmosphere. The watercolours he executed in the last three years of his short life are among the high points in the history of watercolour painting and, after his death from tuberculosis at the age of 27, Turner remarked 'if poor Tom had lived, I would have starved'.

In the late 1790s Turner himself began to move away from his early Edward Dayes manner, but, despite the increasing freedom of handling, Turner's watercolours never quite lost sight of their origins in the topographical tradition. This is shown in the series of watercolours of the harbours of England and the Continental tours, the first in 1817, which were recorded in watercolour and subsequently engraved. Towards the end of his life, though, some of Turner's watercolours became almost abstract colour notes which have been seen as foreshadowing Impressionism.

This movement towards pure colour and almost abstract form was paralleled in the work of the leading artist of the Norwich School, John Sell Cotman (1782–1842), particularly in his Yorkshire landscapes of the area around the River Greta, Peter de Wint (1784–1849), whose wash technique almost entirely abandons the use of line, and David Cox (1783–1859). At the same time a much more mystical approach to landscape was demonstrated by Samuel Palmer (1805–

81) and his group of followers, George Richmond, Edward Calvert and Francis Oliver Finch, who became known as the Shoreham 'Ancients'. Meanwhile, the topographical tradition was continued in the work of Samuel Prout and William Callow, who recorded the Gothic architecture of Continental Europe, with loving, if rather prosaic, industry. The reopening of Europe after the Napoleonic Wars encouraged a fruitful interchange between French and English artists in the 1820s and 1830s. English artists, such as Richard Parkes Bonington, Thomas Shotter Boys and William Wyld, spent much of their working lives in France, and the success of the English exhibitors at the 1824 Paris salon encouraged a great admiration in France for the English Romantic landscape painters. The French regarded watercolour as an English

novelty, and among those who eagerly adopted the medium were Paul Huet, Eugène Lami, Eugène Isabey and, most famously Eugène Delacroix.

In the 1840s the formation of the Pre-Raphaelite Brotherhood and its championship by Ruskin had important implications for the English watercolour. Both Ruskin and the Pre-Raphaelites favoured a meticulous technique and an almost photographic intensity of vision which was emulated by watercolourists like William Henry ('Bird's nest') Hunt. Hunt developed a technique of painting his watercolours of flowers and fruit over a ground of Chinese white which gave a particular enamel brilliance to the colours. Ruskin's enthusiasm for Turner found pictorial expression in the watercolours of Albert Goodwin and Hercules Brabazon, while his more dubious encouragement of

☞ *above*

JOSEPH MALLORD WILLIAM TURNER

A STUDY OF SEA AND SKY THOUGHT TO BE MARGATE

ENGLISH 1844

22 × 33cm (8¾ × 13in)

This drawing was made on a leaf of one of the paper covered 'roll' sketchbooks favoured by Turner as they were portable, yet had relatively large pages.

☞ *below*

WILLIAM HENRY HUNT BIRD'S NEST WITH WHITE ROSES

ENGLISH Mid-19th c.

7.5 × 9.5cm (3 × 3¾in)

☞ *opposite*

HERCULES BRABAZON BRABAZON

VIEW OF THE CHURCH OF SANTA MARIA DELLA SALUTE, VENICE

ENGLISH

17 × 22.5cm (6¾ × 9in)

Kate Greenaway helped the success of a whole school of pretty but sentimental watercolourists, among them Miles Birket Foster and Helen Allingham, who have been nicknamed the 'Hollyhock School'. In general the availability of a wide range of new pigments and increasing use of bodycolour in the second half of the 19th century favoured technical virtuosity, rather than imagination. There were a large number of technically accomplished watercolourists but no watercolourist of major stature emerged after the death of Turner in 1851.

However, the late 19th century did see the development of a distinctively American school of watercolourists, most notably Winslow Homer (1836–1910), and two expatriate Americans working in Europe, John Singer Sargent (1856–1925) and James McNeill Whistler (1834–1903), showed how splendidly watercolour could rise to the challenge of Impressionism. In the 20th century the influence of the golden age of watercolour has been felt in the works of John and Paul Nash, which owe something to the example of Francis Towne, and the Neo-Romantics, Graham Sutherland and John Piper, paid an eloquent tribute to Samuel Palmer by demonstrating how the vocabulary of the romantic watercolour can be adapted to the themes of the present century.

Materials and media

As a general rule, the earlier the watercolour, the simpler the technique. Many 17th century watercolours are just brown wash drawings in the Dutch-Flemish manner. Towards the end of the 18th century the availability of commercially manufactured colours, first in cakes and later in tubes, supplied by stationers such as Reeves and Ackermann, and in the early 19th century the introduction of a wide range of new pigments, made for greater technical complexity and a wider palette.

Artist's paper in England was generally of rather poor quality in the 17th century. Brown and blue paper were often used (the blue paper was used for wrapping sugar) as being cheaper than white paper since white paper of any quality had to be imported. In the 18th century the founding of, in particular, Whatman's Turkey Mill, meant that high-quality white paper was more readily available, which was widely exported. Whatman paper, generally being dated, gives an important clue to the period of a drawing.

Reproductions and copies

The connoisseurship of English watercolours is complicated by the fact that although there are few early forgeries, copying was extensively practised. Drawing masters would give pupils their watercolours to copy and Ackermann's Repository of Arts even had a lending library service to members, providing that the value of the watercolours borrowed did not exceed the annual subscription. There are thus a substantial number of copies by amateurs dating from the end of the 18th century. Even more problematic is to distinguish between the work of two professional artists working in the same manner, such as Gainsborough and Gainsborough Dupont, Francis Towne and John White Abbott. Rowlandson and Gainsborough were both forged in their own lifetime, but in general it was not until the 20th century that watercolours were sufficiently prized to attract the attentions of the forger, most notoriously Tom Keating who faked a large number of Samuel Palmers.

Advice to the collector

Prices of the very best English watercolours are now into the several hundred thousand pound bracket, but work of quality can still be found for a relatively modest outlay if one collects in an unfashionable area. Unfortunately, Victorian watercolours, which until ten years ago offered an attractive route into collecting, being cheap, plentiful and almost invariably signed, have now become very expensive, and 18th century watercolours by Joseph Farington, Thomas Hearne and other masters of the tinted drawing represent a much better buy. As a general tip, figure drawing tends to be much cheaper than landscape. The collector should be even more aware than with Old Master drawings of the condition of watercolours, since they are very prone to fading and this can radically affect their resale value.

AMERICAN
IMPRESSIONISTS
LAUREN RABB

The influences of French Impressionism were not immediately felt in America, primarily because in the latter part of the 19th century America was still a provincial country and not yet able to provide much serious study of art. Young artists in America were trained as draughtsmen, and completed their studies by travelling abroad. In Paris they attended the Academies, where the traditional methods of painting were still taught and their initial training as draughtsmen was reinforced. Americans quickly came in contact with the French *avant garde,* however, and began to adopt some of the new techniques and theories. It is interesting to note that despite their contact with the French Impressionists, American artists never completely abandoned their academic backgrounds. Instead they blended the two schools together to develop their own individualized style. In general, form and line were maintained, as Americans insisted on the integrity of the object; but the bolder palette of the Impressionists and a looser brushstroke were accepted.

Americans also differed from the French in their interpretation of subject matter. The French worked to produce spontaneous, literal, objective views of nature; figures placed in their paintings were there for the sake of recording an actual scene, and no concern was given to evoking a personality in the sitter. American Impressionists celebrated the human figure, did not dissolve the lines of animate objects, and often used figures to create a sense of nostalgia or a pastoral quality where 'all is right with the world'. As the critic William Downes said of these figurative paintings in 1911, 'It is a holiday world, in which nothing ugly or harsh enters, but all the elements combine to produce an impression of natural joy of living.' The beauty of American Impressionist paintings has tremendous appeal to collectors.

The first American Impressionists worked mostly abroad. Mary Cassatt, (1845–1926) perhaps the most important of these, became friends with Edgar Degas in 1874 and basically remained in France the rest of her life. She was instrumental, however, in persuading her American friends to collect the French Impressionists, thereby introducing these artists to the United States. John Singer Sargent became famous for his portraits, but his landscapes are celebrations of the new Impressionist freedom of style. James Abbott McNeill Whistler, another expatriate, experimented tremendously with Impressionism and its aesthetic implications. And Theodore Robinson, another early American Impressionist, spent most of his career abroad, and was one of the first generation of American artists who 'discovered' the French Impressionist Claude Monet's Giverny countryside and made it his home. Theodore Robinson died young however; had he lived, he would undoubtedly have been a member of the 'Ten American Painters'.

The 'Ten American Painters'
—

AMERICANS BACK home were officially introduced to American Impressionism by the first exhibition of the 'Ten' held on 31 March 1898 at Durand-Ruel in New York. These ten artists had all studied abroad, and were united by a dissatisfaction with the Society of American Artists, then the predominant institute of American art – a point which links them spiritually with the original French Impressionists who organized their exhibitions in protest against the Paris Salon. The 'Ten' created the group not so much to champion Impressionism as to escape the conservatism of the Society. The Ten American Painters were artists mainly from New York and Boston: Frederick

☞ *top*
FREDERICK CHILDE
HASSAM
IN THE GARDEN
AMERICAN 1889
45.5 × 27cm (18 × 10¾in)
This painting is signed
and inscribed 'Paris' on
the lower left side. He
studied in Paris in the
1880s, where he
discovered Impressionism.

☞ *above*
FRANK WESTON BENSON
CHILD IN SUNLIGHT
AMERICAN Early 20th c.
Frank Benson was one of
the original Ten
American Painters. This
painting sold in New
York for $82,500
in 1984.

Childe Hassam, J. Alden Weir, John Twachtman, Willard Metcalf, Edmund Tarbell, Frank Benson, Joseph De Camp, Thomas Dewing, Edward Simmons and Robert Reid. (Winslow Homer, who never considered himself an Impressionist, was invited to join, but declined.) When Twachtman died in 1902 his place was taken by William Merritt Chase. All of their lives bridged the 19th and 20th centuries: in fact Dewing and Tarbell died in 1938, and Frank Benson lived on till 1951. They were all committed to the Impressionist aesthetic, although in practice each artist differed greatly, and over the course of the next twenty years they continued to exhibit annually in New York and often in Boston. Their influence on American art was far-reaching and profound.

Although the 'Ten' did not increase their ranks, many other, more informal, groups of American Impressionists were formed around the country, and it was not long until Impressionism was the predominate style of painting in America. Significant schools of Impressionism developed in New Hope, Pennsylvania, Old Lyme, Connecticut, Woodstock, New York, and in the midwest. Abroad, many American artists continued to follow Claude Monet to the provinces of Brittany and Normandy, where groups such as 'The Giverny Group', which included Frederick Carl Frieseke and Richard Miller, were formed.

Although American Impressionism changed the course of American art forever, it soon became outmoded itself, and new movements inspired the next generation of artists. As American art moved from the 'holiday world' of the Impressionists to the urban realism of the 'Ashcan School', or the abstract geometry of modernism, Impressionism gradually lost its dominance not only among artists but among collectors as well. During the 1970s a few foresighted collectors began quietly amassing American Impressionist collections, but it was not until the 1980s that American collectors significantly rediscovered Impressionism, and in that decade prices skyrocketed. Paintings that

☞ *left*
FREDERICK CARL FRIESEKE
LILIES
AMERICAN 1911–12
64.5 × 81cm (25½ × 32in)
Frieseke was one of the 'Giverny Group' of expatriate American Impressionist painters working in France.

a decade before could have been purchased for $10,000 or $15,000 were suddenly worth ten times that much, or more.

Due to its long inactivity, the market for American Impressionism began the 1980s with a huge supply of high-quality paintings. Except for Sargent and Whistler, whose best works have long been in museum collections, excellent examples of works by Mary Cassatt, Winslow Homer, and all members of the 'Ten' were plentiful. As the years progressed, and the demand for paintings increased, the best examples of these artists became rare, sending prices soaring. For example, between November 1989 and June 1990 the only three Cassatt oil paintings to come up at public auction all broke the million dollar mark. A decade earlier they might have been worth $50,000–$100,000. In December of 1989 a Hassam entitled 'The Fourth of July' sold at Christie's for $2.9 million, setting the record for that artist, and even his watercolours have made as much as $900,000 at auction.

Collectors soon discovered the regional schools of American Impressionism, which remain more affordable than the 'Ten' and their circle. Artists such as Daniel Garber and Edward Redfield of the New Hope School are selling for over $100,000, but in general the artists of schools such as Woodstock and Old Lyme are still under $100,000, and good ex-

amples are still available. The prices for some Giverny artists, however, such as Frederick Frieseke and Richard Miller, have reached upwards of $500,000 at auction.

As the recession of the 1990s affects the American pocketbook, prices are expected to come down some, but this is seen as an adjustment of the market, and certainly not a decline in popularity for these artists and their paintings, which remain very much in demand. Although the American Impressionists will probably always be priced well below their French counterparts, they will still be out of reach for many antique collectors.

☞ *above*
ROBERT HENRI
AT JOINVILLE
AMERICAN c.1890
Robert Henri studied in Paris in the 1890s where he was particularly
influenced by Manet. This painting was sold in New York in 1987 for $462,000.

19TH CENTURY AMERICAN LANDSCAPE

HOWARD REHS

The Hudson River School

THE NAME 'Hudson River School' was coined to group together a large number of American landscape artists who were working between 1825 and 1875. These artists spanned several of the most important periods in American history, painting through the Jacksonian Era, Civil War, Secession and the Abolition of Slavery. They were contemporaries of such important writers as Irving, Cooper, Emerson, Thoreau, Whitman, Melville and Stowe and were not only familiar with the works of these authors, but at times heavily influenced by them.

An outgrowth of the Romantic movement, the Hudson River School was the first native school of painting in the United States. The school was strongly nationalistic in both its celebration of the natural beauty of American landscape and in the desire of its artists to become independent of European schools of painting. The name, applied retrospectively, refers more to an attitude and style (showing the American wilderness in all its glory and detail) that these artists favoured rather than to a specific geographical location that they painted; though it is true that many of the older members drew inspiration from the Catskill region north of New York City, through which the Hudson River flows.

One important note to keep in mind is that like many other areas of American art, the Hudson River School was almost totally forgotten during the first half of the 20th century. It was not until the late 1960s that dealers and collectors began to re-evaluate and collect their work.

The School took root in 1825 when John Trumbull, Wiliam Dunlap and Asher Brown Durand first saw the work of Thomas Cole (1801–1848) – the British born artist who is credited with its founding. Cole's early landscapes were spon-

taneous, capturing the boldness and majesty of the American wilderness. However, he could never completely give up his need to create large allegorical works; producing many important paintings in this vein including his famous series: 'The Course of Empire' (now in The New York Historical Society) and 'Voyage of Life' (now in Munson Williams Proctor Institute). Today, the collector seems to favour both of Cole's styles equally – this is evidenced by the two important paintings by the artist that have sold in recent years: his 'View of Boston' which sold for $990,000 in 1984 and his

'Last of the Mohicans' which sold for $1,045,000 in 1988.

After Cole's death in 1848, Asher B. Durand (1796–1886) emerged as the central figure of the movement. Durand's work was more lasting in the scope of American Art and his aptitude for detailed, realistic scenes, influenced by John Ruskin's 'Truth to Nature' philosophy, made him very popular with an America that needed an escape from its growing cities. Durand glorified the American landscape with his ability to express Nature convincingly in all its forms. His

belief in open-air oil sketching allowed him and his followers to study and record, in colour, the true effects of sunlight on the landscape. However, like Cole, Durand's choice of colours was somewhat limited – preferring shades of green and brown. This has had a marked effect on the value of Durand's work – though not many important examples have come up for public sale in recent years. His large scale 'Mountain Stream' was sold in 1987 for $270,000, a far cry from the lofty sums paid for works by Cole and some of his more celebrated followers.

John W. Casilear and John F. Kensett travelled to Europe to study with Asher B. Durand in 1840. Casilear returned to the States with Durand in 1841 and returned to his earlier profession of engraving. This shift to engraving curtailed his

above
THOMAS COLE
LAST OF THE MOHICANS
AMERICAN Early 19th c.
The British born artist Thomas Cole's spontaneous landscape paintings helped found the Hudson River School. This famous painting was sold for over a million dollars in 1988.

right
FITZ HUGH LANE
THE ANNISQUAM RIVER LOOKING TOWARD IPSWICH BAY
AMERICAN Mid 19th c. Fitz Hugh Lane is considered the leading member of the movement known as 'Luminism'. His work typifies the movement's characteristic concentral on depicting sun-bathed landscapes.

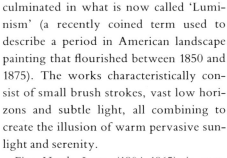

☞ *left*
**WILLIAM LOUIS SONNTAG
AND ARTHUR FITZWILLIAM
TAIT
SUMMER MORNING, N.H.**
AMERICAN Mid 19th c.
51 × 76cm (20 × 30in)
*An interesting and rare
example of the
collaborative efforts of
these two artists.*

painting output and has resulted in a negative effect in the price level of his works today. Kensett remained in Europe to study the Masters, returning to America in 1847.

Jasper F. Cropsey (1823–1900), one of the School's youngest members, was a faithful practitioner of its ideals and a staunch advocate of direct study from nature. Cropsey received greatest acclaim for his paintings of autumn which today are still highly sought after. Recently a beautiful example of an autumnal work, entitled 'Indian Summer on the Delaware River' (painted in 1862) was sold for $190,000. These works, with their vibrant colours, capture both nature's delicacy and majesty.

During this period many other artists began working in styles closely aligned with the ideals of Thomas Cole. Included in this group are: Sanford R. Gifford, Worthington Whittredge, David Johnson, William Louis Sonntag, George H. Durrie, Martin Johnson Heade and Frederic E. Church. Some of these artists continued painting, throughout their careers, in the 'Hudson River' style, while others began to experiment with new ways of depicting the American landscape.

'Luminism'
~

By 1850 the natural progression of the intense interest in landscape and sunlight culminated in what is now called 'Luminism' (a recently coined term used to describe a period in American landscape painting that flourished between 1850 and 1875). The works characteristically consist of small brush strokes, vast low horizons and subtle light, all combining to create the illusion of warm pervasive sunlight and serenity.

Fitz Hugh Lane (1804–1865) is considered, by most, to be the leading member of this movement. Lane spent the first half of his artistic career in Boston working as a lithographer. His love of painting soon won out over the more mundane rigours of lithography and by the early 1840s he had become known as a painter in oils. In the late 1840s he moved to Gloucester, Mass. (his birthplace) where he painted full time in the Luminist style. Today it is rare to find Lane's large Luminist works for sale (many are in public and private collections). However, recently two nice but far from important examples were offered at public auction: 'The Annisquam River Looking Toward Ipswich Bay' (from 1848) which sold in 1989 for $825,000 and 'Camden Mountains from the South Entrance to Harbor' (n.d.) which brought $770,000 in 1988.

This new style of painting was also being explored and expanded on by Martin Johnson Heade (1879–1904). Heade began as a portrait and genre artist but, by the 1850s he turned to painting landscapes. These early works show an affinity towards the Hudson River ideals, but by the 1860s Luminist traits began to show through and would be of utmost importance from then on. Heade's most noted works in the Luminist style were his marsh scenes, done at different times of the day and painted on long narrow canvases. It is interesting to note that though his marsh scenes (which can command prices in excess of $500,000) really capture the very essence of Luminism, it is one of his paintings of 'Hummingbirds and Orchids' that holds the record for a painting by Heade sold at public auction – selling for $1.9 million in 1987.

By the late 1850s John F. Kensett and Sanford R. Gifford (1823–1886) had also made the transition from the Hudson River ideals to Luminism, favouring more horizontal views with a feeling of infinite space. These scenes became open and detailed – topographically correct – yet with a light and stillness that placed them well within the Luminist movement. Presently it is their Luminist works that are most highly sought after and can command prices in excess of $500,000.

In the late 1860s, with the close of the Civil War, the whole continent became available to the American artist. The prevailing mood was one of patriotism and heroism, and with the expansion of American territories westward, artists found new subjects in the yet untouched frontiers.

One of the most important artists of the period was Frederic Edwin Church (1826–1900). The only true student of Thomas Cole – studying with him in the mid 1840s – Church never became a Luminist in the pure sense of the word; however, his monumental painting entitled 'Niagara' (of 1857) with its large horizontal format had a great impact on the works of Heade and Gifford. Church favoured large canvases and painted scenes of places as far south as the Andes and as far north as the Arctic. It was Church's brilliant arrangement of colour – used to create his effulgent sunrises and sunsets – that was to have a profound effect on the Luminists. In recent years it has been the works of Church that have captured the passion of the American collector – with 'The Icebergs', his monumental view of the Arctic, selling for $2.75 million in 1979 (then a record for any American painting selling at auction) and more recently his 'Home by the Lake (Scene in the Catskill Mountains)' selling in 1989 for a record $8.25 million.

There were many artists whose work touched on the ideas and ideals of the Luminist movement, the most notable of whom are Bierstadt and Whittredge. Albert Bierstadt (1830–1902), Church's chief rival, was mainly noted for his grand scale Western landscapes done with meticulous draftsmanship. Even though many of his compositions hark back to the ideas of the Hudson River School, his effects of light are pure Luminism. The twilight dusk scenes of Worthington Whittredge (1820–1910) capture the Luminist light of both night and day simultaneously, creating the silent and eerie feeling of a vast vacant region. His well known series of works done on the beaches of Newport, Rhode Island were also painted in the Luminist style. It was Whittredge's painting 'Second Beach, Newport' that sold at public auction for a record $1.87 million in 1989. Other artists of the period include William Bradford, Alfred T. Bricher, William Trost Richards and Francis A. Silva all of whom favoured views of the sea and whose works, at times, would capture the very essence of Luminism.

☞ *left*

MARTIN JOHNSON HEADE ORCHIDS AND HUMMINGBIRDS IN A BRAZILIAN JUNGLE
AMERICAN 1871–2
43 × 53 cm (17 × 21 in)
Although it is Heade's landscapes which really capture the essence of Luminism, it is this painting which holds the record price for a Heade painting sold at auction – $1.9 million (c. £1 million) in 1987.

Collecting American landscape artists

It is interesting to examine the fluctuating popularity of the 19th century American landscape artists. For the first half of the 19th century the Hudson River School dominated the art scene. They founded and controlled the National Academy of Design, placing many of their members in key positions. Their paintings were highly sought after and commanded impressive prices. By the mid 1860s the first New York Galleries had opened – showing works by European artists, resulting in a fall in the demand for Hudson River School works. A renewed interest evolved with the Luminist artists, but by 1875 their demand had peaked.

For the next 80 years many of the works by these artists found their way into storage rooms, basements and attics. It was not till the 1960s that a serious re-examination of the School began and prices started to rise. Even so, during the late 60s and early 70s, exceptional paintings by many of these artists could have been purchased for under $20,000. Today works by these artists can command prices in excess of $1 million. This is not to say that there are not still works by many that can be had for more affordable prices. Thomas Cole's pen and ink entitled 'Narcissus' sold for $16,500 in 1990; Jasper F. Cropsey's small 'Autumn on the Delaware River' sold for $14,300 in 1989 and many of his works can be purchased for under $50,000. Works by William L. Sonntag, David Johnson, Sanford R. Gifford, John F. Kensett and Worthington Whittredge can regularly be found for under $40,000. Some still lives by Martin J. Heade can be purchased for under $50,000 and even works by Lane, Church and Bierstadt can still be acquired at modest prices – e.g. Lane's 'Sunset after Storm' – $33,000 in 1989.

ART OF THE AMERICAN WEST

ROBYN G. PETERSON

Spanning nearly two centuries, American Western art is a stylistically diverse genre with its sources in the myths and history of the North American frontier. Western art has served in turn as a catalyst in the evolution of American popular culture. Today, prices commanded for Western works reflect the growing popularity of this branch of American art.

The earliest artists

MANY OF THE first artists to paint the West accompanied expeditions sponsored by adventurous European noblemen or the United States government. The first wave of artists in the 1820s included Samuel Seymour (c.1775–1823) and Titian Ramsay Peale (1799–1885), both skilled watercolourists. They provided Eastern and European viewers with the first glimpses of the Rocky Mountains. Today these rare works are precious historical documents as well as art objects.

The 1830s and 1840s saw the arrival of George Catlin (1796–1872), Karl Bodmer (1809–1893), and Alfred Jacob Miller (1810–1874). Catlin's charming style is tempered by the urgent need he felt to document the Native Americans before the inevitable wave of change overtook them. In his exquisite watercolours, Bodmer was the first to render Native Americans with ethnographic accuracy. Miller was the only artist to provide visual documentation of the fur trade, employing a wispy, Romantic style of great sophistication.

Seth Eastman, John Mix Stanley, Rudolph Friedrich Kurz, William de la Montagne Cary, and Peter Rindisbacher were also among the first generations to record the frontier and its native inhabitants. Each artist's work honed the evolving public conception of the West, a process that melded fact and fiction into an inseparable whole.

The land became a national symbol of wealth, majesty, and dominion. Landscape artists, including Albert Bierstadt (1830–1902) and Thomas Moran (1837–1926), created exhilarating, epic visions reflecting the 19th century American's convictions about the origins and destiny of his nation. Trained in Europe, Bierstadt and Moran had been influenced by international movements such as Romanticism and Realism, as well as the burgeoning spirit of scientific discovery.

The Native American also continued to be a favoured subject. The work of Henry F. Farny (1847–1916) – serene and intimate in scale – exemplifies a continuing desire on the part of many artists to depict the Native American accurately, a trend that existed alongside more popular and sensationalized interpretations.

Scores of other artists portrayed the land and people in topographical and naïve

☞ *left*

ALBERT BIERSTADT
SUNSET IN THE ROCKIES
AMERICAN Late 19th c.
Extremely popular in his day, Bierstadt was virtually eclipsed in the early 20th century before 'rediscovery' in the 1970s and 1980s. Major works are valued in the millions, but small oils in the $20,000 to $40,000 range reach the market fairly regularly.

styles suggesting a minimum of artistic training. Hasty sketches documenting geological wonders, unusual animals, or tribal leaders were produced in response to growing public demand for images of the West.

Artists in the Southwest

LATE IN the 19th century, the South-west became a mecca for American artists. Many of the country's most innovative artists visited the area – among them Marsden Hartley, Robert Henri and Stuart Davis – but the artists whose work

☞ *left*

GEORGE CATLIN
THE MANDAN INDIANS
AMERICAN 1871
45.5 × 63cm (18 × 24⅝in)
Catlin produced hundreds of works that focus on the costumes and customs of the native tribes he encountered. A 'family snapshot' quality in group portraits is typical of his style. Today, the work of all the early explorer-artists is comparatively rare.

above

HENRY F. FARNY

ON THE TRAIL IN WINTER

AMERICAN 1894

40 × 27.5cm

(15¾ × 10⅞in)

Unlike the artists who tended to portray Native Americans exclusively in scenes of conflict with whites, Farny's thoughtful depictions were sympathetic and ethnographically authentic.

is most intimately associated with the Southwest are those who came to stay. The most renowned of these formed groups known as the Taos Society of Artists, founded in 1912 in Taos, New Mexico, and Los Cinco Pintores, based in Santa Fe, New Mexico.

The artists of the Taos Society strove to create a distinctively American art. Their work ranges from the romantic staginess of E. Irving Couse through the dignified portraiture of Joseph Henry Sharp to the restrained modernism of Ernest Blumenschein and Victor Higgins. These artists provide sympathetic interpretations of individual Native Americans, native ceremony, and the steady calm of daily pursuits.

In the early 1920s, Fremont Ellis, Willard Nash, Wladyslaw (or Walter) Mruk, Jozef Bakos and Will Shuster formed the out-spoken, unconventional and populist group, Los Cinco Pintores. Their work ranges from the traditional style favoured by Shuster through the modified Impressionism of Fremont Ellis to the radical abstractions of the theorist of the group, Nash.

Other artists among the many whose work, in whole or in part, has been inextricably bound to the Southwest include John Sloan, the Cubist-influenced Andrew Dasburg, and the ever popular Georgia O'Keeffe.

Fact and fantasy in the 20th century

THE MYTH of the West developed quickly, fostered by a group of artists which arose to give shape to the identity that Americans were creating for themselves. Through illustrations for popular novels, magazines, and posters, artists like Harvey T. Dunn, W. H. D. Koerner, Norman Rockwell, Frank Schoonover, Charles Schreyvogel and N. C. Wyeth catered to demands for the sentimental and the sensational, helping to form the stereotype of the Wild West that many Americans still cherish.

Illustrators expressed the character of the West less by the native inhabitants and more by a new symbol for the unfettered, adventurous spirit – the cowboy. The cowboy eventually became as rigidly stereotyped in art and in the popular imagination as the Native American.

The most renowned Western artists, and the two whose work has gained steadily in value since their own day, are Charles M. Russell (1864–1926) and Frederic S. Remington (1861–1909). They stem from the tradition of popular illustration. Russell's narrative imagery expresses an empathy for other creatures and a sense of humour both gentle and boisterous. Remington is the most widely known and influential of all the artists of the American West. His career was marked by dramatic artistic development, in work ranging from large canvases, heavy with narrative detail, to nocturnal scenes. His mastery of the depiction of dramatic tension is most evident in his bronzes.

The contemporary Western experience is qualitatively different from the West of the 19th and early 20th centuries that spawned the popular culture of the American West.

Collecting American Western art

IMPORTANT works in this field are mainly handled by the major auction houses and there are several specialist galleries in New York City and the Southwest. Exclusively Western-oriented auctions are also held in the United States, such as one that is held every Spring in Great Falls, Montana, but the chances of finding important work by the historic painters is slim at these auctions.

Minor work by some artists could be obtained for prices to suit the average pocket: prints by some of the Santa Fe artists can be obtained for a few hundred dollars. At the other end of the scale, $1,000,000 will not be enough to purchase the best work by Moran or Remington.

above

FREDERIC S. REMINGTON

THE CHEYENNE

AMERICAN 1901

50 × 59.5cm

(19¾ × 23½in)

Remington's successes in bronze redefined the limits of the medium.

Involved with every detail of the casting process, Remington often made minor alterations to individual castings; thus, the examples from a single edition may not be identical.

ENGLISH PORTRAIT MINIATURES

CLAUDIA HILL

The word miniature nowadays implies any small object, but it has altered its meaning over the ages. It actually derives from the Latin word 'minium', meaning red lead, or vermillion, the pigment used to paint initial letters on the illuminated manuscripts of the middle ages. The verb 'miniare' denotes the process, and the person who did this work was called a 'miniator'. Thus the word originally described a process and not the object.

In terms of painting a miniature is a portrait or scene which reflects its technical descendance from the art of book illumination. The paintings are usually executed on a small scale, although many are larger than small oil paintings. Miniatures can be painted in any medium, such as watercolour, oil, enamel or plumbago, and whilst the earliest examples are painted on vellum, those of the 18th and 19th century are on ivory.

The miniature portrait originated in the early years of the 16th century, through the union of two separate streams of tradition, one being the illuminated manuscript, the other that of the portrait medal. Technically the miniature portrait had its origins in the Ghent-Bruges school of illuminators. Before printing was invented, manuscripts were illustrated by the medieval limner. The limner drew with exquisite finesse using transparent watercolours and opaque body-colours; both the materials and the delicacy of handling were adopted by the first masters of the portrait miniature. It was not until the time of Henry VIII, however, that any effort was made to paint portraits of living persons.

The medal, on the other hand, was a Renaissance revival of an antique art; and the great medallists did try and capture the true likeness of the sitter. They were modelled with great care and were designed to be worn by the recipient. They were housed in small circular containers covered with glass, not dissimilar to those used by the earliest painters of miniatures. From the medal the portrait miniature took its circular form, its size, and its meticulous analysis of the contours and forms of the sitter's face.

Miniatures fall into two types, the portrait miniature and cabinet miniature. The former is usually circular or oval, being commissioned as a memento of a loved one and worn as a piece of jewellery. The latter is generally square or rectangular in shape and was designed to sit on top of furniture or to hang on a wall.

Early portrait miniatures

THE EARLIEST separate portrait miniature is believed to be Jean Fouquet's self-portrait in enamel, painted circa 1460. The substance used for enamelling is a combination of a simple flux which contains proportions of silica, nitrate of potash and powdered glass, together with different metallic oxides which, when mixed together, produce a variety of colours, and this compound has to be placed on a metal surface. Fouquet's enamel is an isolated example, for the art of enamelling did not flourish until the 17th century.

In England the miniature as a detached small portrait in watercolour emerged during the reign of Henry VIII, circa 1520. It was formerly believed that Hans Holbein (1497/8–1543) was the leader in this field, but it is now known that Lucas Hornebolte (1490/5–1544), a Flemish illuminator and miniaturist, taught Holbein the art of limning.

All the 16th century miniatures, except those in oil, were painted on vellum, and the skin, being of the thinnest possible kind, was stuck onto cardboard; playing cards were usually used for the backing as they provided the strongest support. The artists ground down their own colours,

which were mixed before use with a solution of powdered gum arabic, to which sugar was often added, and the mixture dissolved by hot water. This produced clear opaque colours, which maintain their brilliance even today. More often than not, the backgrounds of 16th century miniatures were of a uniform copper blue, frequently adorned with an inscription about the date and sitter's age, or a motto, executed in gold leaf.

☞ *above*
NICHOLAS HILLIARD
A GENTLEMAN
ENGLISH
Height: 5.5cm (2⅛in)
This portrait is thought to be of George Clifford, 3rd Earl of Cumberland. The blue background is very *typical of the miniatures of the 16th and early 17th century, as is the elaborate gold inscription in the background.*

The earliest portraits by Hornebolte and Holbein were circular, but by the end of the 16th century Nicholas Hilliard (1547–1619), the first great English miniature portraitist, made the oval popular. Hilliard, limner and goldsmith to Queen Elizabeth and King James I of England, detailed the elaborate dress of the court with extraordinary skill. He continued to use a blue background but he attempted to relieve its monotony by innovations such as the introduction of a crimson curtain. He also painted rectangular miniatures, painted against a landscape or the interior of a room. He preferred modelling with line and delicate flesh tints. He encouraged the use of gold leaf and gem-like colours to give a rich and precious effect. His work is highly sought after, and as they are quite rare, his miniatures can command prices up to £75,000 ($140,000).

Hilliard had many pupils, the most notable being Isaac Oliver (1556–1617), who continued in the tradition and style set by Hilliard, but whose work was artistically more advanced. Oliver's features are better modelled and the characters were portrayed with more insight. Hints of the potential decay of historical limning in England are already evident in Oliver's practice, for at the turn of the 17th century James I and other noble

patrons began to show a preference for small limned copies of prized Old Master oil paintings, rather than for original compositions.

Artists of the 17th century such as John Hoskins (d. 1664/5), and his nephew Samuel Cooper (1609–1672) were particularly influenced by Anthony van Dyck, the Flemish artist working at the court of Charles I. They abandoned the traditional colour schemes and brushwork in favour of a palette and technique related more to those of oil painting, and by so doing, produced works of a new depth and vitality.

Cooper had the reputation of being the leading miniature painter of his age. He was so highly regarded that he was patronized by Charles II and his court as well as by Oliver Cromwell and members of the Commonwealth. He was a great innovator in the field of miniature painting. He abandoned the detailed jewel-like approach of his predecessors and painted instead with a broader and freer style. He generally rendered his flesh tint in a warm reddish brown tone, in place of the pink over white hitherto used in the English school of limners. While limners of the 16th century had shown their subject in an even, direct light, Cooper explored the effects of indirect illumination and shadow which emphasized the individual characteristics of the sitter. He usually signed with the initials SC in separate letters or monogram followed by a date. His work is sought after and one could expect to pay in the region of £10,000–35,000 ($18,500–65,000) depending on the quality, condition and provenance.

Many of the miniaturists working during the the 17th century were greatly influenced by Cooper. As a result the ornate inscriptions which are so typical of the backgrounds of Elizabethan miniatures were replaced with simple block signatures, frequently dated, and more subdued colouring with the occasional cloud being introduced. By the end of the century a form of stippling or dotting was introduced in shading the face and sometimes the backgrounds, a technique first used on the Continent.

Enamelling

THE 17TH century also saw a major development in the art of enamelling. Up till then, enamel portraits had been created by painting directly in enamel, and a metal division had been necessary to keep the colours from running into each other. Jean Toutin (1578–1644), a French goldsmith, discovered the method of applying colours onto a thin ground of previously fired white enamel, which enabled the portrait to be re-fired without damaging the tints. This allowed opaque colours to be laid onto the enamel ground in the same way that watercolour could be laid upon vellum.

With this discovery, a school of enamellers emerged. The Swiss artist Jean Petitot (1607–91) first introduced the art of enamel painting into Britain, having learnt the art from Jean Toutin (1578–1644) and the Swede Jacques Bordier (1616–84). Petitot was employed by Charles I to make rings and jewellery and to paint enamel portraits of most of the principal persons of the Court. His portraits are marvels of expression, drawing and force. He discovered a greater range of colours, which led to the independent development of enamel portraits.

The art of enamelling portraits was not firmly established in England, however, until the time of the Restoration, when the activity of the Swedish miniaturist Charles Boit (1662-1727) in London encouraged a new interest. He came to England in 1687, and for many years after his arrival court patronage was disposed to favour enamel painting. In 1696 his abilities were recognized by William III, who appointed him Court Enamellist, the first time such an appointment had been made in England. Technically Boit's enamels are excellent and are often pink and yellow in colouring.

Boit taught Christian Frederick Zincke (1683/4–1767), who came to England in 1706 and was in great demand. His enamels are not quite as smooth as Boit's and often a red stippling can be observed on the face. One great difference between the two artists is that Zincke's enamels almost always have a smooth enamelled back to the miniature, whilst Boit's tends to be rough. One feature that distinguishes him from most other enamellists is that he did insist on making his enamels from life. There are many examples of his work around today, which perhaps accounts for the modest price that his works achieve at auction, ranging from as little as £600 up to £3,000 for the better quality examples ($1,000–5,500).

Plumbago miniatures

DURING THE latter part of the 17th century plumbago miniatures and drawings were introduced and remained in vogue till about 1720. These are finished drawings, executed with a sharp piece of graphite or black lead. The word is derived from the Latin *plumbum* or graphite, a pure mineral, unlike the lead in the modern pencil which is mixed with clay. The portraits were executed on vellum and on paper, and were not usually stuck on to a support, as in the case of miniatures painted in watercolour.

There were several artists working in plumbago in England during the late 17th century, the most notable being David Loggan (1633–1697), Thomas Forster (b. 1677) and Robert White (1645–1703). Characteristic of these plumbagos is their extreme attention to detail, particularly that of the sitter's costume. Most of them were in monochrome, but occasionally washes of grey or sepia were introduced.

Ivory based miniatures

At the turn of the 18th century a major development took place which greatly affected the history of miniature painting. Rosalba Carriera (1675–1757), an Italian miniaturist, discovered that pieces of ivory or bone made a good base on which to paint instead of vellum, providing greater luminosity through watercolours.

The first artist in England to use ivory as a base was Bernard Lens (1682–1740). Although he painted on a new material he used it in an old-fashioned way, for in order to obtain a luminous effect the colours had to be transparent, and Lens only used a few touches of transparent paint on the flesh. However, his work must still have seemed remarkably fresh in comparison with his contemporaries like Peter Cross and Benjamin Arlaud, who still worked on vellum.

'The modest school'

By the middle of the 18th century, there emerged what has now been classified as the 'modest school' of miniaturists, who flourished between 1740–70. In keeping with the spirit of the day, the miniatures of this period reflect a break from the ostentations of the Baroque age. This lack of pretension is reflected not only in the way the sitter's appearance and character are presented, but even in the size of the miniature, which would be about 30–40 mm (1¼–1½ in) high. This small format made them most suitable to be worn as jewellery, either set in rings, bracelets or to be worn in a locket around the neck. Though they are by minor artists, the miniatures of this period are charming and very accessible today. By concentrating on a small scale, they mastered some of the technical difficulties of working with watercolour on ivory and paved the way for many of the more notable masters of the end of the century.

It is sometimes difficult to discriminate between individual styles of this period by the very nature of the size and modest approach to the portrait. Fortunately a sufficient number are signed enabling the collector to recognize them. An influential artist of the modest school was Gervase Spencer (d. 1763). His miniatures bear the initials G.S. and are dated between 1745 and 1761. He practised both in enamel and on ivory, as did many of his contemporaries. However, the balance of preference was slowly tipping away from enamels, which reflects the taste of the patrons of the period.

Nathaniel Hone (1718–1784) is one of a number of Irish artists who made an important contribution to British miniature painting. He was a prolific artist and many of his examples are available today in the sale rooms. His sense of colour shows to advantage in his best miniatures. His sitters appear to be fuller blooded and of more sanguine temperament than those of Spencer's. His miniatures are signed with a monogram NH and are dated between 1750 and 1770.

Caution must be sounded here for confusion can arise if one relies solely on monograms and initials as a guide to the artist. Several artists of this time had the same initials and signed their work

accordingly, for instance Samuel Cotes and Samuel Collins. A careful examination of the two reveals that the former used opaque colours to touch up the hair and lace or cravats worn by the sitter. In addition Cotes's miniatures became larger in format as his career progressed.

The heyday of miniature painting

By the end of the century ivory was the most popular base for miniatures, and although it had been in use for some time, it was Richard Cosway (1742–1821) who first discovered its true potential. His early works are often small with plain backgrounds in keeping with those of his contemporaries, but as larger ivories became popular, circa 1785, so his style developed. He learnt that by floating transparent pigments on to the ivory, one could leave the material itself to suggest the light. Instead of painting the hair in definite lines he adopted the method of painting in soft masses. He also introduced a background of blue clouds, and the use of Antwerp blue is very typical of him. Occasionally he signed his works in full on the reverse, but rarely on the front. His miniatures are plentiful and there is scarcely an important collection without some examples of his work. Whilst examples from his early career are still affordable to the collector, being priced at around £400–800 ($750–1,500) his later more brilliant creations can command prices in the region of £15,000 ($27,500).

Jeremiah Meyer (1735–1789), a contemporary of Cosway and founder member of the Royal Academy, produced a large number of miniatures, but surprisingly his are quite rare today. As his work is rarely signed, it may go unrecognized, but his work can be identified by studying the treatment of the sitter's face. The mouth, nose and eyes are slightly angular-looking, in comparison with Cosway's more lucid approach. His backgrounds are usually soft, pale and uniform in colour as opposed to Cosway's cloud effect.

Richard Crosse also used the linear approach, and like Meyer, gives prominence to the mouth in his drawings; but his system of colouring is quite individual. His small portraits always seem to be pervaded by a greenish blue tint. His touch is soft and he draws the hair finely. Between 1777 and 1780 he produced about one hundred miniatures a year. This extensive practice is evidence of the increasing patronage for miniatures at the time.

Arguably the most sought after artist of this period is John Smart (1742/3–1811). The identification of his work is helped by the practice he formed at the very outset of his career of adding his signature of a cursive 'J.S.' and date. Between 1785–95 he visited India; miniatures done during this time are easily recognizable for he added a capital I after his signature.

Unlike many miniaturists his style and technique were fully developed at the beginning of his career. He favoured a background of uniform grey buff colour and used a red brick colour for the complexion. The eyelashes are so carefully drawn that one can sometimes count each individual one. A trait that is typical of his miniatures is the way in which he drew lines under the eyes and even crow's feet if they were present – he did not flatter his sitters. Perhaps one of the reasons his work achieves such a high reputation today, besides being very attractive and beautifully executed, is that the details of the costume are painted in flat body-colour and consequently have not faded.

His work is plentiful today, and whilst many of his miniatures are beyond the pocket of the small collector, there are a number of his watercolour and pencil sketches available which can be purchased for around £1,000. These sketches, which Smart probably kept in case repetitions were required, are works of art in themselves, and are the same size as the miniatures for which they were intended.

Another artist of considerable ability was George Engleheart (1750–1829), whose miniatures have the impression of solidity and strength. Regrettably many of his works have been exposed to light causing the greens and carmines to fade. Nevertheless, his work is desirable, particularly those he painted after 1780, which are about 75 mm (3 in) in height and signed with a cursive E on the front and, occa-

sionally, in full with an address and date on the reverse. Characteristics of his miniatures from this period are the linear massing of hair, diagonal grey strokes at the corner of the mouth and zigzag outlining of the drapery in opaque white. He favoured the use of blue backgrounds drawn in diagonal strokes. He excelled in painting women and children and often portrayed them wearing large straw hats entwined with bows and ribbons.

After 1800 Engleheart often used the rectangular format in place of the oval one: these examples are usually signed with a G.E. The rectangle had been used sporadically in the past but it was not until the 19th century that it became more popular. Engleheart's fee books from 1775–1813 are an astounding record of industry and indicate the prolific patronage which he had. It is known that he could produce up to 228 miniatures in a year. This vast quantity is indicative of the great demand for miniature portraits at the end of the 18th century.

There are many lesser but, none the less, excellent artists who took up miniature painting at this time. One such artist whose work is plentiful is Andrew Plimer. His earlier works, of the years between 1785 and 1789, are signed AP and dated, but lack the brilliance of his later work by which he has become known.

Samuel Shelley (1750/56–1808) was another late 18th century artist of considerable ability, and his work is easily distinguishable once his style and technique have been examined. His miniatures, particularly those of young ladies, possess great charm and his draughtsmanship was good. Characteristics of his work are a yellowish green flesh tint, and the enlargement of the pupil of the eye. Occasionally the miniatures are signed SS on the front, but more frequently, the signature is 'Sam Shelley' on the reverse, followed by his address.

The enamel miniature was being continued in the second half of the 18th century by artists such as Henry Spicer (1743–1804), a pupil of Gervase Spencer, and by Johann Heinrich Hurter (1734–

1799). The latter was a good enameller and his work is pleasing and has a softer effect than that of many other artists.

19th century miniaturists

ANDREW ROBERTSON (1777–1845) at one time also intended to make a series of copies of Old Masters, but he changed course to that of miniature portraits from life. In place of the attractive but rather frivolous paintings of Cosway and other 18th century miniaturists, 19th century patrons were looking for more solid and richly painted portraits executed on a larger scale and more like the oil paintings and watercolours that were becoming so popular at this period. Robertson also felt that miniatures ought to be oil paintings on a small scale, and his style reflected the change in public taste. He therefore endorsed the movement towards the larger rectangular format.

By 1814 Robertson met with such success that he employed Sir William

Charles Ross (1794/5–1860) as his assistant to help paint in the backgrounds of his miniatures. Once Ross became known he too became a prolific artist in his own right, and he was appointed in 1837 as Queen Victoria's miniature painter. His

miniatures are well designed and show an accuracy of draughtsmanship in rich colours. He had a great ability to paint full-length figures on ivory and compose them into charming pictures.

The demand for larger portraits, designed more for displaying on the top of furniture or for hanging, meant that miniatures lost the intimacy that they had hitherto possessed. These larger portraits, good though many of them are, could not defend themselves against the cheaper method of photography.

Collecting miniatures

THERE ARE certain subjects which prove to be especially popular today judging by the prices they reach at auction, namely examples of pretty ladies, children, soldiers or historical figures.

Collectors should not be swayed by fashion or taste for these fluctuate, but it is advisable to buy what appeals and try to obtain those that are in good condition. Damaged miniatures, especially those on ivory, are difficult to repair satisfactorily. It is important to remember, however, that whether a miniature is set in a jewelled locket or in a simple frame, it is the quality of the painting that matters, regardless of the period in which it was painted.

Needless to say there are forgeries around. The most obvious type are those which are housed in ivory frames, made of old piano keys. These were made on the Continent at the end of the 19th century, and indeed are still being produced today. They have old paper from French or German books pasted on the back and are often signed with the names or initials of well-known painters, such as Reynolds or Gainsborough, and miniaturists such as Cosway, or Engleheart. Another form of forgery is to overpaint a photograph which is then offered as a genuine miniature. During the late 19th century when photography became popular, studios employed artists to hand-tint photographs. The result was a coloured likeness, but not a true portrait miniature.

right
ANDREW ROBERTSON
PRINCESS AMELIA
ENGLISH *1810*
Height: 10.7cm (4¼in)
Robertson has imitated the qualities of oil painting in this rectangular miniature on ivory. Robertson spent time at Windsor making portraits of the King's daughters in 1807: following Princess Amelia's death in 1810 he was called upon to make posthumous copies.

left
JOHANN HEINRICH
HURTER
MRS MARY NESBITT
ENGLISH *1783*
Height: 5.7cm (2¼in)
The decorative copy based on a portrait by Sir Joshua Reynolds is representative of the types of copy in enamel that were being produced at the end of the 18th century.

PICTURE FRAMES
···
JAMES BRUCE GARDYNE

Only in the last five to ten years has the art world shown an interest and desire for knowledge in a hitherto virtually unknown field. The picture frame has always been an integral part of the visual impact of the painting, yet has been continually neglected as an object in its own right. But the late 1980s saw a change in attitude which has resulted in a more educated approach, with museums even devoting single exhibitions to this unique art-form. Frames are now available to the discerning collector through specialist auctions devoted entirely to frames and from specialist dealers.

It is generally accepted that the origins of the picture frame as we know it today are in Renaissance Italy. The 15th century saw a change in the siting of paintings; instead of being a fixed part of the wall they could be a more moveable object requiring both a protective and structural support. As many of these pictures were housed in churches, it was not surprising that the earliest frames were derived from architectural elements, resembling window and door designs or even church façades, consistent with both their present surroundings and past forms.

By the beginning of the 16th century the frame had lost most of its architectural components and had been reduced to a plain structure made up of four flat panels of wood, the basis of the frame as we know it today. This structure was known as the *Cassetta*. Its basic format was adhered to throughout Italy during the 16th and 17th centuries, although the gilding and painted decoration varied from region to region. In Venice, for example, expensive materials such as marble and tortoiseshell were imitated through the skilful use of paint.

Later, the flat profile of the Cassetta was to develop into a distinctive baroque manner with complex sweeping silhouettes and pierced fruit and foliate carving. In Florence the 'Leaf' frame variation had a curved, graceful, almost sculptural, outline with carved scrolls and foliage.

☞ *left*
CASSETTA FRAME
ITALIAN Late 16th c.
A carved, gilded and painted Cassetta frame with characteristic flat panels, sold in 1990 for £7,500 ($13,800).

☞ *above*
CARVED FRAME
ITALIAN 17th c.
A carved, gilded and marbled frame, sold in 1990 for £7,000 ($12,950).

French and Spanish frames
—

UP TO the end of the 17th century the most influential centres of frame-making were in Italy, but slowly there was a gradual geographical shift, so that by the early 18th century French craftsmen had come to dominate the art. Louis XIII (1601–43) frames were characterized by a strict rectangular format with a tight bonding of decoration that did not interfere with the profile. If one takes this period to be the starting point of a sustained period of French frame manufacturing, one then sees a gradual progression through the Louis XIV (1653–1715) style, with corner and centre decorations but still retaining strictly defined boundaries to the French Regency period (1715–23), where the corners and centre motifs come to dominate the frame, resulting in pierced scrolling tendrils and ribbons, with an ornamental silhouette.

The culmination of this process of increasing elaboration came during the reign of Louis XV (1723–74), when an abundance of naturalistic carving breaks the rectangular boundaries, forming flowing curved lines that produced an overwhelming sensation of movement. This was later to subside into a formal simplistic style during the time of Louis XVI (1774–92).

The Spanish frames of the 16th and 17th centuries were influenced by those in Italy, which was understandable, considering the historical and political links between the two nations. Although more decorative and less subtle than their Italian counterparts they stuck to the basic flat Cassetta form, but adorned the centres and corners with high relief ornamentation, producing a rather naive but decorative result. This tendency towards heavy decoration gave the frames a three-dimensional quality that was sometimes lacking in their Italian counterparts. Whilst incorporating many similar aspects of design, it would be inconceivable for a Roman or Venetian frame to have an acanthus cresting that virtually protrudes at right-angles to the rest of the frame, or distinctive cut

CARVED FRAME

FRENCH Early 18th c.
A French Regency carved
and gilded frame, sold in
1989 for £6,000
($11,000).

☞ *above*

CARVED FRAME

SPANISH 17th c.
A carved and gilded frame
with distinctive Spanish
cut corners, which sold in
1990 for £8,500
($15,700).

corners. Yet these are a hallmark of the Spanish 17th century frame.

Frame-makers in the following century were not to attain the same level of imagination, and consequently designs were to change little in concept except to become heavier and more static in appearance.

The greater plainness of Dutch and English frames

IN COMPARISON to most European countries, the Dutch frames of the 17th century adhered to two basic designs, which were to remain the dominant formulas for the next two centuries. The most common form was the black or ebonized frame whose decoration lay in a shallow surface carving which produced a basketweave or ripple effect, by contrasting light and shadow across differing levels of moulding. A simpler although more expensive way to achieve a similar effect was to decorate the frame with a tortoiseshell veneer.

An alternative to the ebonized or tortoiseshell frame in the first quarter of the 17th century was the 'Lutma'. It incorporated a relief-like form with swags of flowers, putti and stylized heads running from a cresting top to the base of the frame. This was later to give rise to a similar design in England during the second half of the 17th century, called the 'Sunderland' frame.

In England, frames like other artforms of the period were influenced by ideas from the Continent. Whilst the 'Lely' frame was inspired by the Venetian panel frame, the 'Carlo Maratta', named after the artist, was a variant of the 'Salvator Rosa' frame, characterized by its distinct profile and applied bands of ornament. Later the 'Swept' frame was to have its origins in the curvilinear profiles of the Louis XV frames.

English 18th century furniture was dominated by Thomas Chippendale (1709–79) whose brand of fantasy mixed with French and Chinese motifs produced rich elaborate ornamental structures including picture frames. By the mid-1700s the English neo-classical style created harsh outlines decorated with Vitruvian scrolls, volutes and egg-and-dart running patterns.

Throughout England and the Continent the 19th century was dominated by the composition frame, which enabled earlier styles to be reproduced in vast inexpensive quantities, relying first on classical then gothic and finally baroque motifs. The age of the individual frame-maker and skilled craftsman had finally passed and its effect would only be recreated in plaster.

From its Renaissance, architecturally induced origins, through the flat surround of the *Cassetta* and culminating in the rhythmic proportions and profiles of the French 18th century, the frame had always been an important, if secondary component, to the painting as a whole. Consequently, it is worth remembering in the age of ever increasing prices and multi-million pound records, that the cost of making a frame was often higher than that of the commissioned picture itself.

☞ *above*

NEOCLASSICAL FRAME

ENGLISH 18th c.
A George II Kentian
carved and gilded
architectural tabernacle
frame. This example sold
in 1989 for £30,000 – the
world record for a frame.

EUROPEAN
SCULPTURE

IONA BONHAM-CARTER

☞ *above*

GIAMBOLOGNA

RAPE OF A SABINE

ITALIAN Late 16th c.

Giambologna's highly finished bronzes in the Mannerist
style were immensely influential in his own lifetime and
later.

The field of European sculpture is a richly varied and expansive domain of antique collecting. Unlike the more utilitarian areas, such as furniture and carpets, the acquisition of sculpture has primarily been a luxury.

The Middle Ages

DURING THE Middle Ages the Church was the main patron of sculpture. Churches were decorated not only with stained glass and frescoes, but also with richly coloured and gilded wood sculpture, finely wrought metalwork, enamels and reliquaries; to all the church goers of the day the atmosphere created by such surroundings would have been heavenly, and many of the works of art would have been narrative and consequently instructive to the illiterate majority.

The medieval and gothic sculptures and works of art of exceptional craftsmanship which survived the vicissitudes of centuries of anarchy and religious turmoil are now mostly to be found in museums, and sometimes in church treasuries. When an important medieval enamel or ivory comes up for sale, the competition from museums and specialized private collectors is fierce. An example of this was seen at Sotheby's in the late 1970s, when the collection of Robert von Hirsch came under the hammer; two enamels fetched over £1 million each.

The main workshops of enamels were in Limoges in France in the 12th and 13th centuries, where the art of enamelling became a highly sophisticated production. One can still purchase a 13th century Limoges enamel cross for £3,000–5,000 ($5,500–9,250) although a complete reliquary casket would fetch closer to £200,000. The rarer, and often finer, 12th century enamels from the Mosan region seldom appear on the market, and can make up to £500,000 (nearly a million dollars) for a well-preserved small plaque. Italy and Spain also produced fine translucent enamels in the 14th and 15th centuries, many of which adorned silver-gilt

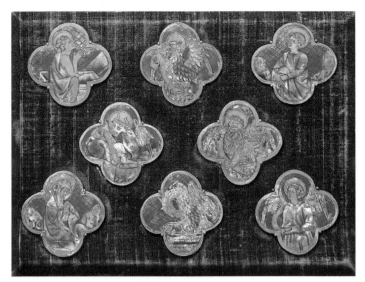

☞ *left*
TRANSLUCENT ENAMEL QUATREFOILS
SPANISH Late 14th c.
A set of eight enamel quatrefoils that probably decorated church plate. The Church was the major patron for medieval works of art.

☞ *left*
CARVED SANDSTONE FIGURES
ENGLISH 13th c.
These large carved figures from the city gates of the cathedral town of Hereford depict seated knights. They were sold at auction for £26,000 ($48,000) each.

church plate. These can still be found on the market, and bearing in mind their early date and fine quality are relatively inexpensive, as one sees from the eight plaques sold at Christie's in December 1988 for £19,000 ($35,000).

Due to the perishable nature of wood, not many examples of early wood sculpture of high quality have survived. However, unlike the specialized skills required for enamel work, wood sculpture necessitated simpler talents and could therefore be carved locally. Examples of these provincial works also appear on the art market. On the other hand, medieval stone sculpture survives with greater ease, and

is often still in situ decorating the exterior of cathedrals for example. Secular stone carving of this date is rarer, but interesting examples sometimes surface. A pair of 13th century sandstone figures of knights from the city gates of Hereford were sold for £26,000 ($48,000) each.

The Renaissance and Early Modern period

WITH THE growth of the wealthy merchant classes in the 14th and 15th centuries, the demand for secular art increased, though the burghers also

commissioned religious sculpture, but of a size more suited to their homes rather than to an abbey. In July 1990 Christie's sold a charming miniature house altar which illustrates this type of commission for £48,000 ($88,000). The wings were painted on both sides with figures of saints, while the central enclosure contained three carved coloured and giltwood figures.

Italy had long had both a powerful church, and a society of wealthy merchants, whose commissions in the field of sculpture gradually came to influence their northern counterparts. An outstanding example of early Italian sculpture to come on the market recently was a marble relief of the Virgin and Child attributed to the Master of the Marble Madonnas, dated to the second half of the 15th century and sold for £280,000 ($500,000) at Christie's in April 1988. This type of sculpture illustrates the close correspondence between the ecclesiastical and secular patrons of the early Renaissance, but is most likely to have been commissioned by a merchant to be placed either in his home or in a church he patronized.

The invention of printing had an immense effect on the production, in particular, of enamels, stained glass and marble, wood or ivory reliefs. A craftsman did not himself have to 'invent' a composition. He could enamel a plaque or carve a relief using as his inspiration a woodcut or engraving. An interesting example of this is a series of four early 16th century Limoges enamels sold at Christie's in April 1991, by the Master of the Aeneid Enamels. These plaques, which glow with vibrant colours heightened with gilding, and illustrate scenes from Virgil's *Aeneid,* would have adorned the walls of a magnificent study, set like jewels within wood panelling. A large wooden relief from an altarpiece, dating from the early 16th century, by the Swabian sculptor Niclaus Weckmann the Elder, was sold at Christie's in 1989 for a record price of £240,000 ($444,000). The composition of this relief probably also derives from a contemporary engraving.

☞ *opposite page, top*
**MINIATURE WOODEN
HOUSE ALTAR**
GERMAN *c.1500*
*The wealthy merchant
classes began to patronize
the arts in the Renaissance
period, commissioning
domestic devotional
objects such as this painted
and gilded house altar
from the Middle Rhine
area of Germany.*

☞ *opposite page, bottom*
**MASTER OF THE MARBLE
MADONNAS
RELIEF OF THE VIRGIN AND
CHILD**
ITALIAN *15th c.*
*Italian sculptors of the
Renaissance produced
exceptionally fine work,
influencing their northern
counterparts in this as in
so much else. It is easy to
see why the sculptor
known as the 'Master of
the Marble Madonnas'
was so called.*

☞ *right*
**NICLAUS WECKMANN THE
ELDER
CARVED ALTAR WING**
GERMAN *Early 16th c.*
*Niclaus Weckmann the
Elder carved this Swabian
alter wing with a
depiction of the Adoration
of the Magi.*

☞ *left*
GIAMBOLOGNA
A REARING HORSE
ITALIAN Late 16th c.
This vital bronze model
was cast from a model by
Giambologna by one of
his pupils, Antonio
Susini.

☞ *below*
BARTHELEMY PRIEUR
KING HENRI IV AND QUEEN
MARIE DE MEDICI
FRENCH Early 17th c.
A magnificent pair of
large bronze statuettes
depicting the King and
Queen of France as
classical figures.

Secular art in the 16th and 17th centuries

~

Wɪᴛʜ ᴛʜᴇ advent of Humanism in the 16th and 17th centuries the great princes acquired important collections of secular art, including curiosities, such as ostrich eggs, coconuts and nautilus shells, which were mounted in silver or copper gilt, with enamels and jewels, and placed in special cabinets of works of art. In 1984 Christie's sold one of these luxury items, a large and elaborately carved ivory 17th century German work of art comprising a clock, for £780,000 (nearly $1.5 million).

The presence in one place of many prominent artists of different nationalities created a distinctive style particular to an area. This was the case in Prague, where Rudolph II (1552–1612) attracted to his court many of the great artists of the time. Similarly, a particular style was generated by the fusion of major sculptors working for François I at Fontainebleau. However, the diplomatic exchange of prized works of art took place between the different European courts, thus disseminating styles. For example, the work of the celebrated mannerist sculptor Giambologna, who worked for the Medici in Florence, influenced both the French and German courts through the portable medium of the small, highly finished bronze. In 1989 Christie's sold a bronze 'Rape of a Sabine' by Giambologna, possibly intended for Rudolph II or the Ruling Prince of Liechtenstein, for £2.5 million ($4.6 million).

☞ *left*

MASSIMILIANO SOLDANI-BENZI

BUST OF A YOUNG FAUN

ITALIAN 18th c.
A bronze head attributed to Soldani-Benzi, one of a number of Italian artists following the Giambologna tradition of high finish and reddish-gold patination.

The bronzes produced by Giambologna's close assistants such as Antonio Susini, are also highly prized. France, too, had highly prized court sculptors such as Barthélémy Prieur who worked for Henri IV and Marie de Medici. A magnificent pair of large portrait bronzes by him of these monarchs portrayed as classical gods was sold by Christie's in Monte Carlo in 1985 for £850,000 ($1.5 million).

The Baroque age

BAROQUE SCULPTURE of the late 17th and 18th centuries was most prominent in Italy and Germany. In Germany and Austria in particular, the Baroque style was used to ravishing effect as decoration in churches, and also in the palaces and libraries built by the nobility. Baroque sculpture is still relatively inexpensive today, possibly because of its high religious content and flamboyant style, but much depends on the medium used, whether ivory, wood, bronze or stone. An interesting example of this association of Christianity and elaborate adornment is a lavish house altar in ivory, bone, silver, gilt copper and wood sold at Christie's in April 1991. It is a rare and splendid work of art of the typically Baroque taste for precious mixed media in objects of private devotion.

☞ *left*

JOHANN ANDREAS THELOT

HOUSE ALTAR

GERMAN Early 18th c.
The baroque style was applied to devotional objects in the southern Catholic areas of Germany, as seen in this lavish house altar incorporating a variety of precious materials.

With the 18th century and the settled monarchy in England, the English patronage of sculpture became established, partly as a result of the taste for the Grand Tour through which their horizons and knowledge of the arts was widened. As a result of these continental travels, the English patronized the artists of Italy and France, and brought their acquisitions home to grace their elegant mansions. Artists such as Massimiliano Soldani-Benzi of Florence received commissions for bronze reductions of celebrated sculptures from both English travellers and European royalty, such as the Prince of Liechtenstein. His bronzes follow the Giambologna tradition of high finish and glowing, reddish gold patination.

☞ *right*

THE KISS OF VICTORY
SIR ALFRED GILBERT
ENGLISH *Late 19th c.*
This bronze group
typifies the freer and less
academic style of the small
group of late 19th century
English sculptors whose
movement was known as
the New Sculpture.

The 18th and 19th centuries
~

TOWARDS THE the end of the 18th century, the production of Grand Tour bronzes, often based on Antique Roman originals, had reached its zenith of industry. In Rome the Zoffoli and the Righetti workshops specialized in this commodity, executing small bronzes. These bronzes are still relatively inexpensive at auction, and can be acquired for as little as £3,000–5,000 ($5,500–9,250). The 18th century also saw the enriching of English sculpture by the influx of foreign sculptors, particularly Huguenots and Flemings, who sought the stability and prosperity of English patrons. The art of portraiture, mainly in marble, was revived and it became *de rigueur* for an Englishman of culture to have his bust done by one of the fashionable foreign sculptors of the day. Christie's sold a marble of Lord Chesterfield by Louis François Roubiliac in 1985 for the record price of £480,000 ($880,000). On the other hand, by the late 18th and early 19th centuries, an extensive industry of

portrait sculpture was established by sculptors such as Nollekens, which cost a fraction of this.

The early part of the 19th century continued the Neo-classicism of the late 18th. The most prominent sculptor of the period was the Italian Antonio Canova, outstanding not only for his own technical excellence and pure compositions, but also for his widespread influence on the many gifted young sculptors from France, Scandinavia, Germany and England working in his studio. This style of sculpture was particularly popular in England, where it found generous patrons. John Gibson, for example, returned to England much influenced by Canova and treasured by the British; his 'Sleeping Boy' sold at Christie's in 1988 for £48,000 ($88,800) illustrates this phenomenon. Towards the end of the century, a small group of English sculptors broke away from this academic tradition and formed a freer style known as The New Sculpture. This is typified by the fluid and romantic work of Frederick Leighton, Alfred Gibson, Alfred Drury and Henry Onslow Ford.

☞ *left*

ANTOINE-LOUIS BARYE

AN INDIAN ELEPHANT

CRUSHING A TIGER

FRENCH Mid-19th c.
This bronze of an
elephant mounted by a
Mahout is cast from a
model by Barye, an
exponent of the French
Animalier school of
sculpture.

☞ *below*

LEOPOLDO ANSIGLIONI

GALATEA RIDING A

DOLPHIN

ITALIAN c.1880
The Industrial
Revolution introduced
sophisticated mechanical
techniques which allowed
sculptors like Ansiglioni
to produce pieces full of
movement.

On the continent, new trends such as the French 'Animalier' school developed slightly earlier. Sculptors such as Antoine Louis Barye and Pierre Jules Mêne enjoyed great popularity, both at home and abroad. Their charming bronzes of animals, which introduced a new naturalism to the subject, were produced in large quantities and varying quality, which is reflected in the diverse prices they now fetch. They remain, nevertheless, within reach of more modest collectors, the smaller versions costing between £1,000 ($1,850) and £5,000 ($9,250). Simultaneously, a romantic tradition imbued both private and public sculpture, firstly in France and then spreading to the whole of Europe. The range of subject matter and of sculptors was immense, and examples of these decorative bronze and marble works of allegorical, mythological, realistic and religious subjects can still be found at reasonable prices. The appearance of wealthy patrons, stimulated by the Industrial Revolution and the development of sophisticated and mechanical techniques, encouraged the production of these decorative sculptures. At the top end of the market, an Italian marble group of Galatea on a Dolphin by Ansiglioni was sold at Christie's in February 1991 for £80,000 ($148,000), and grandly illustrates the frivolous and charming aspect of much later 19th century sculpture.

There are, obviously, many areas of sculpture and works of art which merit more attention, and many specialist monographs have been published to help the discerning collector. Thanks to its diverse nature, sculpture is a subject which will never weary an enthusiast.

DECORATIVE ARTS MOVEMENTS

☞ *above*

GILT BRONZE LAMP

FRENCH *Early 20th c.*
*This lamp was cast from a model by Raoul Larche, 'Scarf
Dance', inspired by the dancer Loie Fuller.*

THE ARTS AND CRAFTS MOVEMENT

LYDIA CRESSWELL-JONES

The Arts and Crafts movement originated in England as a reaction to the growing materialism and over-ornamented styles of the 1850s. Despite the effects of the Industrial Revolution, the improved methods of manufacture and the employment of new materials, stylistically pieces were still echoing the decorative themes of the past. As manufacturers adapted themselves to the new machinery, they began to lose sight of the aesthetic qualities of their products and furthermore became distanced from their consumers.

The need for a defined manifesto was recognized by a few enthusiastic pioneers, and William Morris (1834–96) was one of the main originators. Morris embodied the embryonic movement; a painter, poet, craftsman, lecturer and militant pamphleteer, he wanted to unify all the arts and crafts to bring about comprehensive reform, from architecture to the minutest aspects of interior design.

William Morris

MORRIS HAD studied at Oxford from 1853, and had developed an affection for the culture of the Middle Ages and what he saw as the honesty and simplicity of the Gothic. He had also become familiar with the works of John Ruskin (1819–1900), who believed that a respect for materials and all their qualities was paramount to the craftsman. Writing in *The Seven Lamps of Architecture* (1849), Ruskin stated: 'I believe the right question to ask, respecting all ornament, is simply this: was it done with enjoyment – was the carver happy while he was about it?'

Morris pursued a widely publicized philosophical argument, continuing Ruskin's and A. W. N. Pugin's (1812–52). All believed that the character of the living and working environment affects the character of the individual, and that the character of a nation is expressed by its architecture and ideas. Pugin believed that

 right centre

WILLIAM MORRIS AND DE MORGAN TILE PANEL

ENGLISH c.1876
One of six known identical tile panels by Morris and Co. commissioned by the architect George Devey for Membland Hall, Devon (demolished in 1928). This panel was sold for £42,000 ($77,700) in 1989.

☞ *left*

MORRIS THREE-FOLD SCREEN

ENGLISH 1889
This Morris & Co. screen was made for the drawing room of Bullerswood, a house in Kent designed for the Sanderson family by Ernest Newton.

☞ *top*

MORRIS HAND-KNOTTED CARPET

ENGLISH c.1900
A Morris & Co. 'Hammersmith' carpet, designed by Henry

Dearle. It was made for Robert and Joanna Barr-Smith, who were friends of May Morris. This carpet was sold for £200,000 ($370,000) in 1990.

Victorian buildings should adhere to the pure style of the Gothic and Middle Ages, reflecting an integrity and simplicity of function without fuss or unnecessary artifice.

At Oxford Morris worked for two years in the office of the architect George Edmund Street (1824–81), where he met Philip Webb (1831–1915) with whom he developed a lifelong friendship. In 1859 Webb designed the Red House at Bexley Heath in Kent for Morris and his bride, Jane Burden. The structure and furnishings of the house are as significant as the way in which it was built. Groups of workers were involved throughout the building process and it stood for everything that Morris and his artistic friends believed in. Simple lines and internal coherence were visible in the furnishings throughout the house. Together with Dante Gabriel Rossetti (1828–82) and Edward Burne-Jones (1833–98), Morris and Webb searched for truth, beauty, function and originality in what they made. Morris' artistic theories were shaped by, and helped shape the ideas and concepts of socialism. His principles of design for living were based upon the ideals of individuals working within a community to contribute to the richness and happiness of the group.

It was partly the Red House project, and the tangible evidence that the collaboration of artists worked, that inspired Morris to set up in business and move some way towards his goal to provide 'a manufactory of all things necessary for the design of a house'. The firm of Morris, Marshall, Faulkner & Co, Fine Art Workmen in Painting, Carving and Furniture and the Metals, was established in 1861 and was the first such collaborative venture in existence. The aim of the firm was to search for 'truth', without compromising themselves to commercialism or the machine age. They believed that the artist should be involved with the total environment and in the unity of the arts which had been latent in Pre-Raphaelite theory.

The firm first showed at the 1862 International Exhibition at South Kensington in two classes – decorated furniture, tapestries etc, and stained glass windows. They were awarded medals in both classes and, in fact, the stained glass was so good an imitation of medieval ware that some competitors in the trade believed that they had used original glass.

Morris' followers

As the followers of Morris urged for the practical and less ornamental, so more guilds based on Morris' cooperative

☞ *above*
MACKMURDO MAHOGANY CABINET
ENGLISH c.1886
One of William Morris' closest friends and followers, A. H. Mackmurdo, founded the Century Guild of Artists, for which he designed this mahogany cabinet. Made in Manchester, the painted panels may be by Selwyn Image.

☞ *right*
VOYSEY HIGH-BACKED CHAIRS
ENGLISH 1898
A pair of oak high-backed chairs designed by C. A. Voysey for Mr Ward Higgs' London home in Bayswater. Modified versions went into production and were exhibited at the Arts and Crafts exhibition of 1900.

began to be established. In 1882, Arthur Heygate Mackmurdo (1851–1942) founded the Century Guild of Artists. Mackmurdo's friendship with Morris had been established by 1877, with the formation of the Society for the Protection of Ancient Buildings. Mackmurdo also aimed to re-define the contemporary arts and their position within society. Through the Guild's magazine *The Hobby Horse* first published in April 1884, Mackmurdo questioned some of Morris' beliefs, but also acknowledged that 'as an artist and craftsman, he is our master'.

Although not officially a member of Mackmurdo's guild, Charles Annesley Voysey (1857–1941) worked with it, and applied many of the same principles to his furniture. Voysey had originally trained with the cabinet-maker, John Pollard Seddon, and the architect, Saxon Snell, but in 1881–82 he had decided to set up on his own as an architect. Voysey had travelled with Mackmurdo in Italy, and in 1883 started to collaborate with the guild on designs for wallpapers and textiles. He

End Road, where he attempted to train recruits, many of whom had no trade experience and were therefore ready to absorb the guild's ideals and standards. In practice this was a slow process and many of the early guild pieces have an amateurish quality.

When the lease on Essex House expired in 1902, Ashbee moved the guild in its entirety to Chipping Camden in Gloucestershire. By now it comprised 150 men, women and children, and the decision to re-locate was taken by a poll of the members. As the guildsmen worked to restore and convert the cottages in the village, Ashbee revived the educational aspects of his work, persuading his friends to visit and lecture. The guild

produced silver and jewellery with lightly hammered finishes and delicate enamels, leatherwork and woodwork. The work had a distinctive style in design and execution and the stylistic influences were varied, including simple forms reminiscent of medieval silverwork. Many included semi-precious stones, and almost all had a hammered surface, stressing the fact that the pieces were hand-made rather than manufactured by machine. The guild furniture, too, had a hand-crafted appearance. Made from large pieces of oak, rather than veneered, and often decorated with inlay with the joints evident, the means of their making were perfectly obvious.

By 1905 the guild was suffering

felt that there was nothing too small to deserve the attention of the architect, and his furniture designs with their plain surfaces, simple mouldings and decoration confined only to structural features, soon became recognized by both the public and critics for their artistic merits.

While training as an architect, Charles Robert Ashbee (1863–1942) had attended a meeting of the Hammersmith Branch of the Socialist League held in Morris' house, and he was struck by the ideas and beliefs of the assembled group. He was living at the time at Toynbee Hall, an educational charity in the East End of London, where he was the only architect in residence. He started a Ruskin reading class and, inspired by its success, began to teach drawing and decoration. It was this group that gave Ashbee the impetus to found the Guild of Handicraft in 1888, with three members and a working capital of £50. Its aims were to re-educate its members and train them for a specific industry. In the early years Ashbee and his guildsmen were all self-taught, since he believed that this was the way to master a craft, and that through trial and error skills could be acquired and an individualistic style develop. In 1890 Ashbee moved the Guild to Essex House, Mile

☞ *above*

VOYSEY MANTEL CLOCK

ENGLISH *c.1895*
The original design of this oak clock was for C. A. Voysey's own house, The Orchard, at Chorleywood. The design was later manufactured in aluminium by W. H. Tingey.

☞ *right*

ASHBEE CABINET

ENGLISH *c.1906*
A Guild of Handicraft Ltd cabinet designed by C. R. Ashbee.

financially. The constraints in terms of time due to the amount of manual work resulted in pieces priced considerably higher than those of other local workers who were embracing the new machinery. Ashbee's trial and error methods, athough noble, were expensive, and as the strain began to show, so more of the guildsmen began to look for work elsewhere. Eventually the guild was forced into liquidation in 1907.

In 1890, Ernest Gimson (1864–1919), W. R. Lethaby (1857–1931), Ernest and Sidney Barnsley, Mervyn MacCartney and Reginald Blomfield founded the firm of Kenton & Company. Named after a street near their workshop in Bloomsbury, and allegedly inspired by Morris' shop window, the group purposefully avoided an idealistic 'guild' title. Each member of the group contributed £100 towards the cost of setting up and turned their attentions towards experimenting with daring technical innovations and making one-off pieces of furniture rather than following a manifesto in the way that Ashbee had. However, the firm was to be short-lived, disbanding after two years due to lack of capital. Nevertheless, at their first exhibition at Barnards Inn, Holborn in December 1891 and at the Arts and Crafts Exhibition Society show of 1890, they received much critical acclaim, and Lethaby's walnut cabinet with its

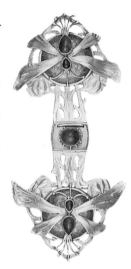

☞ *above*
ASHBEE CLASP
ENGLISH *c.1902*
A buckle or cloak clasp designed by C. R. Ashbee for the Guild of Handi-craft Ltd in silver, enamel and amethyst.

☞ *bottom*
WILLIAM DE MORGAN LUSTRE DISHES
ENGLISH *Late 1880s–1900*
Three lustre dishes designed by William de Morgan and painted by Charles Passenger.

severely rectilinear lines was praised as 'an exemplar of modern design'.

It was not as a designer or craftsmen that Lethaby is most relevant in the Arts and Crafts movement but as a teacher and theorist. At the Central School of Arts and Crafts which he founded with George Frampton in 1896, he excelled in spotting talent in others and hired Edward Johnston, the silversmith Henry Wilson and the enameller Alexander Fisher as teachers. The Central School was consequently the most advanced and dynamic art school in Europe until the foundation of the Bauhaus.

After the demise of Kenton and Company, Gimson and the Barnsley brothers moved to Golden Valley, near Cirencester in Gloucestershire, and in 1902 problems with their landlord forced another move to Sapperton. Gimson and Ernest Barnsley briefly operated in partnership here, producing simple, strong pieces of furniture and metalwork, enriched with smoothly sculptural details, a style developed by the Dutch cabinetmaker Peter Waals, who collaborated with Gimson. The visitors to their workshops were many and the difficulty was only to complete the orders that they received. Without the enforced vision of Ashbee, Gimson's workshop and community based on rural craftsmanship long outlived the Guild of Handicraft.

☞ *above*
INLAID MAHOGANY TABLE
ENGLISH *1890–91*
Designed by W. R. Lethaby for the hall of Lord Manners' house, Avon Tyrrell in Hampshire, this table was probably made in the Kenton & Co. workshops.

The philosophy spreads

PUBLIC AWARENESS of the Arts and Crafts movement was developed through exhibitions and competitions held under the auspices of various design reform movements. At the same time rivalry amongst the participants raised the standard of entries. Lectures on art and craft were given by Ashbee, Dr Christopher Dresser (1834–1904) and Walter Crane (1845–1915) and mail order companies and speciality shops were established.

The Arts and Crafts Exhibition society, founded in 1888 with Walter Crane as president, was set up in revolt against the exclusive view of art encouraged by the paintings-biased Royal Academy exhibitions. The work it showed was sound in quality and individuality, including furniture by Edward Barnsley, Lethaby, Voysey and Walter Cave, silver and jewellery by Ashbee, Henry Wilson and Nelson Dawson, and glass by James Powell. The Society also held lectures and demonstrations as part of an attempt to publicize the aims of the movement, as also typified in the writings of such periodicals as *The Studio*.

If England led the way in Arts and Crafts and the inspired style of working

that it encouraged, then the rest of Europe and America was not far behind. As similar problems of industrialization were recognized abroad, the theories of Ruskin and Morris began to reach a wider audience. In Vienna, Josef Hoffman and Kolomon Moser established the Wiener Werkstätte in 1903, said to be based on Ashbee's Guild of Handicraft. In Germany, too, similar workshops were growing in the 1880s and 1890s. Whilst in America, a number of craftsmen began to adapt to the English craft ethic as dictated by Morris and his followers.

The lack of direction for design in America had been highlighted by an exhibition – the 1876 Centennial exhibition in Philadelphia – where rather than celebrating a century of independence, the style of the exhibits underlined the dependence of American taste on elaborate and flashy decoration.

One of the main exponents of Arts and Crafts ideals in America was Gustav Stickley (1857–1942). He had trained as a stonemason and applied many of the qualities involved in stonemasonry to his monumental furniture. Stickley was deeply influenced by Ruskin and in 1898 travelled to England where he met Voysey and Lethaby, among other designers. On his return to America he began to produce his 'Mission' furniture, huge yet simple oak pieces. His company

was called 'The United Crafts' and the workshop was organized along the lines of the guilds in England.

In Chicago and the Mid-West the work of Frank Lloyd Wright (1869–1959) culminated in a movement now known as the Prairie school of architecture. The founder of the school, Louis H. Sullivan (1856–1924), was a revolutionary architect and pioneer of skyscrapers. As chief draughtsman from 1888 to 1893 Wright absorbed many of his theories, notably that 'ornament is mentally a luxury, not a necessary' and that 'it would be greatly for our aesthetic good if we should refrain from the use of ornament for a period of years'.

Wright's early designs in furniture showed him more as a sculptor, confronting pieces in terms of mass and form, and avoiding all ornamental embellishment. The stark exteriors of his buildings contrasted well with the uncluttered interiors, reflecting what became a life-long admiration of Japanese architecture.

As the Arts and Crafts movement developed into the 20th century it became apparent that a total rejection of the machine age did not spell long-term success. Despite the disparagement of the mass-produced furniture of Richard Riemerschmid in Germany, it appeared to be the way forward. Although the guilds and workshops provided the impetus for many other more forward-seeking enterprises such as the Design and Industries Association and the Council of Industrial Design, their ideals were generally too insular and idealistic. Their search for a standard of goodness, their opposition and suspicion to anything new, and preference for the supremacy of man as the creator rather than for profit did not represent a sound business ethic. The new society that Morris and his followers envisaged bore little resemblance to the contemporary reality of the Victorian industrial economy, and Morris' belief that he could 'never be contented with getting anything short of the best' often meant that it was only the wealthy who could afford to become his clients.

ART DECO

OLIVIER BROMMET

Born of a period of great change in society as well as in interior decoration, fashion, music and architecture, the Art Deco style draws its name from the Exposition des Art Décoratifs et Industrielles, held in Paris in 1925.

The 1925 exhibition is often cited as the high point of Art Deco. Originally planned for 1915, it was to be a forward-looking event, presenting the latest in decorative arts. Instead, however, because of postponements resulting from the war and its aftermath, it became very much a retro-spective look at the developments over the previous 20 years.

The exhibition included contributions from most industrialized countries, although Germany was excluded and the USA, the land of Art Deco skyscrapers, declined the invitation to attend saying it had no decorative arts worthy of repre-senting it. Despite the many different styles on show, it was quite apparent that there was one prevalent style, that of the French exhibitors. The French were, in-deed, the most important exponents of the style, so much of the best of Art Deco is French in origin.

☞ *left*

ART DECO POSTER

FRENCH 1935

Art Deco was particularly suited to the clean uncluttered lines combined with luxury that typified transatlantic travel.

☞ *top right*

SILVER-LEAFED WOOD COMMODE

FRENCH 1923

Manufactured by Atelier Martine, the gently serpentine form of this extraordinary commode in silver-leafed wood and onyx is offset by an outlandish design by Leo Fontan depicting women in a garden with a motor car approaching.

☞ *opposite page, bottom*

ROSEWOOD AND IVORY DESK

FRENCH 1927

A kidney-form desk with ivory knobs and the top inset with an ivory starburst pattern, which was made at the firm of Jacques-Emile Ruhlmann, whom many regard as the heir to the great 18th century French tradition of cabinetmaking.

Furniture

Art deco really goes back to when the fashion designer Paul Poiret (1879–1944) released women from the confinement of the corset, and shortened skirts, allowing women to show their ankles in public. In the same year Sergei Diaghilev and his Ballets Russes came to Paris for the first time. His bold and colourful ballets, with costume designs by Leon Bakst, inspired Poiret to design brightly coloured panta-loons with exotic fashion accessories, and the rest of the fashion world responded enthusiastically.

The following year the Salon d'Automne produced a similar turning-point in French furniture design. The German stand at this Salon shook the French artists and designers, leaving them with little faith in their own received ideas about decorative arts. While the French were still very much involved with the sensuous whiplash motifs of Art Nouveau, the Germans showed refreshingly pro-gressive modern styles, based largely on re-interpretations of Neo-Classicism. This encouraged the French to look back at the 18th and early 19th centuries with re-newed interest and, more specifically, with an abstract eye. Furniture design became more geometric and decoration was reduced to abstract motifs intended to break the symmetry.

Once again fashion designers were at the forefront of this change. Paul Poiret visited Vienna and Brussels in 1911, and met Josef Hoffmann and Koloman Moser, the founders of the Wiener Werkstätte. Impressed by their geometric designs Poiret created l'Atelier Martine, named after one of his daughters, upon his return to Paris. This was a school and workshop combined, where young girls were given a free hand to design textiles, rugs, wallpapers and furniture, mainly with bright floral patterns. L'Atelier Martine was a decided success, and later artists such as Raoul Dufy became associated with it.

Without doubt the most important *ébeniste* (a French term for which there is no exact English translation, but which implies somebody who combines all the skills of a master designer and cabinetmaker) of the period was Jacques-Emile Ruhlmann. He established his own firm, Ruhlmann et Laurent, shortly after the war, following considerable successes at the various salons where he exhibited. It was to become the most prestigious decorating firm in France. His simple but elegant designs, mostly inspired by Neoclassicism, were all executed in exotic woods and rare veneers, the natural pattern in the wood often being the only decoration on the piece. He also used very fine ivory inlays.

By using expensive woods and hiring the best craftsmen to execute his designs Ruhlmann effectively put his furniture out of reach of all but the rich, but the middle classes also wanted modern furniture, so the big department stores set out to satisfy their needs. These stores provided modern furniture, and a whole range of accessories in a unified style, designed and manufactured in their own workshops. The first store to open such a workshop, based on Poiret's Atelier Martine, was Le Magazin du Printemps, under the name Atelier Primavera. Galleries Lafayette followed three years later, entrusting the supervision of their Atelier La Maîtrise to Maurice Dufrene, a designer who had made his name in the Art Nouveau period but who was equally successful in the Art Deco style. Bon Marché created Atelier Pomone, headed by Paul Follot, another famous designer from an earlier period who was responsible for

☞ *top*
PAINTED WOODEN TABLE
FRENCH 1925
This table has a square bevelled mirror top supported by two moulded square sides. Attributed to Primavera, it was used to display jewellery at the 1925 Exposition International des Arts Decoratifs Modernes in Paris.

☞ *above*
AFRICAN-STYLE STOOL
FRENCH Early 20th c.
This lacquered stool designed by Pierre Legrain is inspired by African art forms.

some of the best designs of the twenties. Finally, the shop Le Louvre set up its Atelier Stadium in 1923.

The best Art Deco furniture is very expensive to buy nowadays. The work of Ruhlmann, Dufrene, Süe et Mare and Pierre Legrain is very much sought after by collectors. It is, however, still possible to pick up attractive pieces of quality furniture if one is prepared to go for lesser names.

Glass

FRANCE HAD a long and distinguished history of glassmaking, which peaked during the Art Nouveau period. Artists like Emile Gallé and Antonin Daum, both from Nancy, revived many old techniques and, more importantly, invented some of their own. Both men's factories participated at the 1925 exhibition, but as with furniture, the floral motifs that had been so much in demand at the turn of the century had fallen out of fashion and were replaced by more geometric and abstract designs. Daum had responded well to this new demand for abstraction and presented heavy glass vessels with deep, acid-etched geometric motifs.

These vessels were influenced by Maurice Marinot (1882–1962), one of the two leading glassmakers of the period. Originally trained as a painter who then worked in the Fauve style, Marinot became attracted to glass in 1911. He started working in the medium with decorative enamels executed after his designs at the glassworks of some friends, the Viard brothers. But he slowly lost interest in enamelling processes as his knowledge and understanding of glass working grew. Instead, he started to create heavy glass vases and bottles, sometimes internally decorated with coloured powders, sometimes with airbubbles carefully controlled to create motifs. He is best known, however, for his use of hydrofluoric acid to cut deep geometric motifs in glass. Marinot's examples were followed by many of the other top glassmakers of the period: Marcel Goupy and Auguste Heiligenstein were enamellers working in a similar vein, while André Thuret, Henri Navarre and Jean Luce were all influenced by his later work. Marinot's work is widely represented in museums but appears only rarely on the market.

In contrast, the work of René Lalique (1860–1945), one of the most important artists of the period between 1890 and 1945, is more widely available and therefore more collectable. Lalique was first a highly influential jeweller. His women

DECO GLASS VASES
FRENCH Early 20th c.
[Left] An internally decorated green bottle vase by Maurice Marinot. [Right] An internally decorated vase by André Thuret.

with flowing hair or life-like insects, in gold and with precious stones often set with *pliqué-à-jour* enamel, brought him worldwide acclaim. He then became interested in glass and started experimenting in 1902, creating glass jewellery. The possibilities of this new medium fascinated him and he started to create vases and figures in the lost-wax technique, hitherto only used for bronze. His first commission came in 1906 when he was asked to design scent bottles for the firm of Coty. At the end of the war he purchased a large glassworks and started producing vases, figures and other glass objects in large quantities. In contrast to Marinot he did not concentrate on creating unique pieces, but used the latest technology for high-quality mass-production, and by using a stamping press to press glass in a mould, he produced large editions of the same design.

Lalique's commissions included fountains for the city of Paris, fountains and other glass decorations for ocean liners, panels for the Pullman rail coaches, and in 1932 he decorated the interior of St Matthew's church in Jersey. Although his work was widely copied by firms such as Sabino, Verlys and Etling in France, Red-Ashay and Jobling in the United Kingdom and Val Saint-Lambert in Belgium, none of them ever achieved the same degree of detailed decoration or brilliance of colour.

Another glass technique that became popular in postwar years was *pâte-de-verre*.

In this process, crushed and powdered glass is mixed with a binding agent and metal oxides as colouring agents to create a paste, which then lines a mould. The mould is placed in a kiln at a temperature high enough to vitrify the paste.

The most important and popular artists to work in this medium were François Décorchemont, Almaric Walter and Gabriel Argy-Rousseau. Although all three worked in the same technique, their styles were very different. Often using lost-wax technique, Décorchement produced heavy-bodied vases cast with natural or geometric motifs. Almaric

PATE-DE-VERRE VASE
FRENCH Early 20th c.
This vase by Gabriel
Argy-Rousseau, moulded
with a central decorative
band and four cartouches,
set the record for the
artist's work, and indeed
any pâte-de-verre item,
when it was sold for
£107,755 ($211,200) at
auction in 1990.

☞ *below*
LALIQUE GLASS
FRENCH Early 20th c.
A group of opalescent
glass pieces by René
Lalique. They were sold
in 1989 for prices ranging
from £1,400 ($2,500)
and £3,800 ($7,000).

Walter, who started working in pâte-de-verre at Daum but set up his own workshop in 1919, is best known for heavy, opaque objects, including *vide-poches,* paperweights, small sculptures and vases. All are in controlled colours and more in the spirit of Art Nouveau. Gabriel Argy-Rousseau produced a semi-opaque substance, richly coloured, but unlike Décorchement's and Walter's, surprisingly lightweight. His work consisted of bowls, panels, vases, lamps and sculptures. His early work was decorated with classical motifs, but he changed his style in the 1920s, and animals, mythological creatures and geometric patterns appeared on his work. This later work is very much in demand by collectors today.

Ceramics

WHILST THE ceramics of the Art Nouveau period show the clear influence of Japanese Art, Art Deco ceramics reflect the interest there was at the time in Chinese and Islamic art as well as in Greek mythology. The two most important artists in the twenties were Emile Decoeur and Emile Lenoble. Decoeur worked in stoneware and porcelain, putting emphasis on form rather than decoration. Around 1925 he created vessels covered in magnificent plain coloured glazes, rendering any decoration obsolete. Emile Lenoble on the other hand, put the emphasis on decoration, using coloured glazes or engraving to adorn his creations.

André Metthey was working at the same time as Decoeur and Lenoble. He gave up stoneware as early as 1906 and worked in earthenware, which he had decorated by painters such as Odilon Redon, Matisse, Derain and Vlaminck. Other important artists are Jean Mayodon and René Buthaud, both originally trained as painters, who used Greek mythology as a source of inspiration. Mayodon became artistic director of the Manufacture de Sèvres. Buthaud was technical and artistic director of the ceramics department of Primavera (the artistic studio within the

Printemps department store) before taking up a senior teaching post at the Bordeaux Ecole des Beaux Arts.

The two largest factories, Havilland in Limoges and the Manufacture de Sèvres, benefited from the experiments of these individual artists. Sèvres set up a *faience* department under the leadership of Chevallier-Chevignard in order to prepare themselves for the 1925 Exhibition by asking artists and decorators like Lalique, Ruhlmann, Dupas and many others to design for the factory. Theodore Havilland called on Suzanne Lalique (René's daughter) and Jean Dufy.

England produced some very good work in ceramic in this period. Royal Doulton ceramic sculptures designed by Richard Garbe as well as their 'Sung' and 'Chang' wares are widely collected today, but probably the most sought-after English 'Deco' potter today is Clarice Cliff. Her brightly coloured 'Bizarre' wares, introduced in 1928, are widely available from antique fairs, auctions and dealers from a mere £50 ($90) to thousands. Much rarer than her 'Bizarre' pottery are her creations decorated after designs by well known artists including Duncan Grant, Laura Knight, Ben Nicholson and Frank Brangwyn.

Susie Cooper painted strong cubist and abstract patterns in bright colours although often her colour schemes were not as bold as those of Clarice Cliff. She eventually became a leading designer for Wedgwood. Wedgwood vases designed by Keith Murray have seen a steady rise in prices over the past few years. These elegant objects are usually decorated with parallel grooves finished in soft matt colours.

As with everything else in Art Deco it is still possible to buy quality ceramics at reasonable prices if one looks for the lesser known names. The French factory of Robj produced a range of novelty bottles in the shape of figures dressed in bright costumes. These are amusing and attractive and sell for around £100 ($180). In the same price bracket one can also find very attractive objects by Shelley potteries of Staffordshire.

Metalwork and lacquer

~

THE INTERWAR years saw a great demand for decorative metalwork. The strict geometry of contemporary architecture invited the use of metal and new technology made the manufacturing of metal easier; new alloys and patinas were also discovered at this time.

Edgar Brandt was without doubt the most successful of the metalworkers. He was responsible for the Porte d'Honneur at the 1925 exhibition, and also for a room in the Pavilion d'une Ambassade Française. Many public commissions came his way, including the tomb of the unknown soldier and its eternal flame under the Arc de Triomphe in Paris. He also created a variety of light fixtures, fire-screens and radiator grills, the light fittings often in conjunction with glass shades by Daum. Other successful metalworkers were Gilbert Poillerat, Paul Kiss, Jules and Michel Nics and Richard Desvallières, who executed designs for Süe et Mare.

Jean Dunand (1877–1942) used metal in a totally different way. After having trained and worked as a sculptor, he concentrated on *dinanderie*. In this process a single sheet of copper is hammered into a shape, and then decorated by means of patination, chasing, embossing or the inlay of other metals. Jean Serrier and Claude Linossier, a pupil of Dunand, produced work along similar lines.

Dunand is, however, more famous for his lacquer work. Influenced by oriental lacquerwork, he started applying lacquer on to metal vases: they were either monochrome or decorated with abstract geometric motifs. He soon moved on to large objects such as screens, panels and even furniture, which he decorated by using various colour pigments in the lacquer, by incising motifs, by inlaying mother of pearl or crushed eggshell, or by a combination of all these techniques. He also lacquered furniture created by other designers such as Eugene Printz, Jacques-Emile Ruhlmann and Pierre Legrain. The only other two Art Deco artists who worked successfully in lacquer were Eileen Gray and Leon Jallot.

☞ *left*
WROUGHT-IRON MIRROR
FRENCH Early 20th c. Titled 'Les Jets d'Eau', this mirror from the firm of Edgar Brandt is octagonal, mounted by a stylized fountain.

☞ *below*
LACQUER PANEL
FRENCH c.1928 A lacquer and coquille d'oeuf wooden panel by Jean Dunand, after a design by Francois-Louis Schmied showing strong Oriental influence.

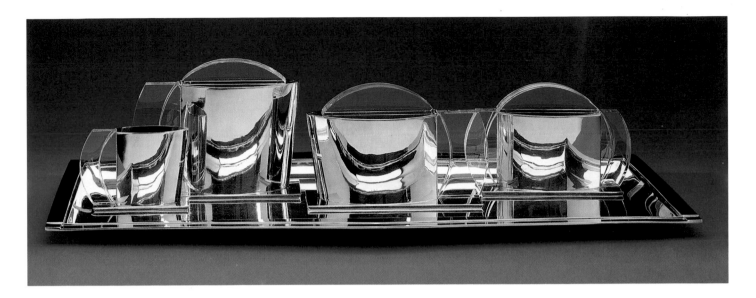

Silver and jewellery

THAT GEOMETRIC motifs and clean lines of Art Deco appeared early on in silver-work is largely due to the metalwork company Christofle, which responded to new demands by commissioning artists such as Paul Follot and Gio Ponti to design for it. It was also responsible for most of the tableware on the prestigious ocean liner, *Le Normandie*. This tableware was electroplated, a process Christofle had introduced in the mid-19th century and made its speciality.

The leading silversmith of this time was Jean Puiforcat (1897–1945). Trained by his father, he came from a family of silver-smiths, and first exhibited his own work in 1921. Puiforcat designed objects of geometric design with plain surfaces, doing away with the decoration and hammered patterns that had been popular for so long. He combined silver with hardstones such as lapis lazuli, rock-crystal and jade, and with rare woods like ebony.

One of the major exceptions to French domination of Art Deco was Georg Jensen (1866–1935). Born in Denmark, he came to silver via sculpture. His designs are simultaneously classical and modern, providing an alternative to the modernist designs of Puiforcat and his like. His designs were so popular that he opened retail outlets in Berlin, Paris, London, New York and Stockholm between 1908

and 1930. Jensen's stylish but cheap silver jewellery has remained so successful that most of his designs are still in production today.

The changes in fashion also had an effect on jewellery. Women cut their hair short so there was no longer any need for combs or tiaras. Large hats were replaced by small *cloche* hats, making hatpins obsolete. Instead short hair encouraged a fashion for long ear pendants. Dresses with deep necklines, open backs and short sleeves were ideal for showing off long necklaces, set with diamonds, multi-coloured stones, pearls, onyx, enamel, carved jade or coral, or a combination of these. Long gloves that had been in fashion

☞ *above*

SILVER AND GLASS TEA AND COFFEE SERVICE
FRENCH 1925
Designed by Jean Puiforcat in 1925, this four-piece set comprises a coffeepot, teapot, covered sugar bowl, cream jug and six-sided tray.

☞ *below*

'MAGNOLIA' TEA AND COFFEE SET
DANISH Early 20th c.
Designed by Georg Jensen, this five-piece set is typical of the 'Jensen style' which has been much copied.

up to now disappeared and were replaced
by bracelets and bangles, or wristwatches.
Cigarette cases and powder compacts
became exquisite works of art, often influenced by oriental motifs, and decorated
with finely carved plaques of jade, coral
or rock-crystal set in gold boxes and
highlighted with enamel, mother of pearl
inlay and coloured stones.

The most important jewellery firms
making these were Cartier, van Cleef and
Arpels, Janesich, Lacloche Frères, Boucheron and Chaumet, a number of whom
remain the finest jewellers of today. Apart
from these large firms a few individuals
managed to make their mark, particularly
Jean Fouquet, Raymond Templier,
Gerard Sandoz and Paul Brandt. Their
work could be seen as sculpture rather
than jewellery, with strictly geometric
designs often using contrasting matt and
polished metals in combination with
lacquer work, rock-crystal or coloured
gemstones.

Introduced by Coco Chanel, costume
jewellery became very popular during this
period. Chanel's plastic and paste creations
were widely accepted as fashionable and
fashion houses such as Schiaparelli started
producing them too. Art Deco costume
jewels are now widely collected and sold
through auction houses and galleries.

Modernism

MODERNISM ran parallel with Art Deco.
The creed of this style was that form
should follow function, and the modern-
ists thought that objects and interiors

should be devoid of any unnecessary decorative clutter. Unlike Ruhlmann, they
wanted to make modern design accessible
to everybody, making maximum use of
possibilities offered by machines. Tubular
steel combined with glass and wood was
therefore widely used for furniture, as it
was cheap and more durable than wood
on its own. Some classics of design still in
production today continue to have a
modern feel though designed in the 1920s,
for instance Marcel Breuer's tubular steel
cantilevered chair designed at the Bauhaus
in 1924, and Le Corbusier's reclining chair
designed in 1928. In France a modernist
group of artists formed an organization
called L'Union des artistes modernes.
René Herbst, Francis Jourdain, Helène
Henri, Robert Mallet-Stevens and Raymond Templier were its founders, soon to
be joined by other major artists of the
time, including Jean Puiforcat, Eileen
Gray and Pierre Charreau. They were
responsible for some of the best modernist designs.

☞ *right*
LIMOGES PORCELAIN
DINNER SERVICE
FRENCH 1925
Titled 'Les Pivoines',
this 121-piece service was
designed by Jean Dufy
and manufactured by
Theodore Haviland for
the 1925 Paris exhibition.

☞ *left*
CARD TABLE
FRENCH c.1920
Height: 62 cm (24 in)
A rosewood and
mahogany card table
designed by Pierre
Chareau.

☞ *below left*
MARCEL BREUER
'WASSILY CHAIR'
GERMAN c.1920
The design of this
chromed steel chair was
influenced by the
handlebars of a bicycle.
It was named after
Kandinsky.

☞ *below*
SEVRES PORCELAIN VASE
FRENCH 1946
A large vase designed by
Emile Decoeur and
decorated by P. Gaucher
with a narrative frieze of
mermaids, nereids and sea
creatures.

ART NOUVEAU

···

JANE HAY

Art Nouveau is above all a 'look', a visual style so distinctive as to be instantly recognizable, easier to describe than to define. Spanning the period from 1880 to the outbreak of the First World War, it was part of the great reaction to industrial machine age ethics which took place in the West at the end of the 19th century. Although its roots are to be found in Britain where it evolved out of the Arts and Crafts movement led by William Morris, in its heyday it swept across Europe as the fashion style *par excellence* of the era.

Celts, Japanese and maidens
～

IN BRITAIN during the 19th century the Pre-Raphaelite movement with its brotherhood of painters was one of the precursors of Art Nouveau. Two members of this group, Edward Burne-Jones and Dante Gabriel Rossetti, made lavish use of the image of the maiden to convey purity and innocence: this image was also to be particularly attractive to exponents of Art Nouveau because it confronted the facelessness of industry with the language of love and poetry. A bi-product of Pre-Raphaelite medievalism was the introduction of Celtic *entrelac* motifs, intertwining linear cartouches of serpents or foliage, for example, which were also to become leitmotifs of the new style.

In 1859 Japan opened its doors to the West for the first time in over 100 years, and at the 1862 London International Exhibition a stand was mounted displaying new wares from the East. The company of Farmers and Rogers had a trade licence with the Japanese government and, at the close of the exhibition, one of its employees, George Lazenby Liberty, purchased the remaining stock and opened a shop in Regent Street, London.

There was also a shop in Paris selling similar products: blue and white porcelain, textiles, bamboo work and prints. The well-known American painter James McNeill Whistler was seduced by these new aesthetics and promptly set about introducing them into his work, while the architect E. W. Godwin decorated his home in the Japanese style in 1862. As we can see, *japonaiserie* was introduced to the public by a combination of retailers, artists and designers.

One cannot overemphasize the impact of Japanese design and aesthetics on the West. In general terms it introduced new spatial concepts and new attitudes to light, rhythm and harmony, whose perfect expression was to be found in the natural works. For Art Nouveau this meant pale colour schemes; flowing, rhythmic and organic patterns derived from Japanese textile designs; the use of vertical lettering; and a certain delicacy of execution. A marriage of Japanese sinuous linear patterns and Celtic entrelac motifs

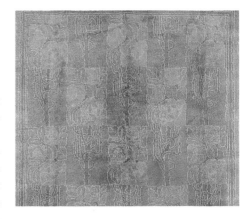

☞ *above*
ART NOUVEAU CARPET
ENGLISH 1890s
The Liberty company through its central London store was at the forefront in promoting the Art Nouveau style, known in Italy in fact as 'style Liberty'.

☞ *below*
TEMPLETON'S CARPET
ENGLISH 1930
A late example of Art Nouveau style, this carpet was designed by Frank Brangwyn for the Glasgow firm Templeton's and featured in a special exhibition of Brangwyn's work.

combined to produce what is now commonly known as the whiplash motif, another hallmark of the new style. Finally, the Western Symbolist movement in painting easily reinforced Oriental attitudes to organic design, with the result that foliate patterns were to become not just decorative but also meaningful: the organic was seen as a powerful emotional antidote to mechanization. Three Art Nouveau motifs, the maiden, the whiplash and organic design, can therefore be traced back to these influences.

British Art Nouveau

It is important to remember that there was a considerable amount of crossover between Art Nouveau and Arts and

Crafts, especially in Britain, where one evolved from the other. Both movements were reacting to the same conditions, namely the depersonalization of both workman and product, and at the same time they were inspired by the same sources. Where the Art Nouveau response was primarily on an emotional level Arts and Crafts sought political solutions in such concepts as 'fitness for purpose' and 'honest workmanship', resurrecting the old craft guild as the means by which these ideals could be expressed. In a sense Art Nouveau was concerned with the visual expression of a piece, while Arts and Crafts placed emphasis on production itself. For Morris and his followers this was not just a style but also a way of life, and therefore they rejected Art Nouveau as merely decorative. Nonetheless, they were not afraid to adopt its motifs in their work, which means that when one considers British Art Nouveau one must include the work of many who were actually wedded to the Arts and Crafts ideal.

While the maiden, whiplash and rhythmic foliate patterns were three essential components of Art Nouveau, they were only one aspect of it. At the other end of the spectrum was a rectilinear and geometric formal style introduced by the Scottish architect Charles Rennie Mackintosh. Arts and Crafts had wrestled with the vexed question of form and function in design but it was the Glasgow School, under the aegis of Mackintosh, which offered a solution in the geometry of forms, especially the cube. In many ways this represented a radical departure from what had gone before, and consequently opinion differs as to whether it properly falls within the scope of Art Nouveau. However, because the Glasgow School had such a great impact on European developments, and because they and their adherents incorporated so many Art Nouveau motifs into their work, it would be difficult to separate them entirely.

The movement was disseminated and made popular through three major retail outlets: Liberty in London, Tiffany in

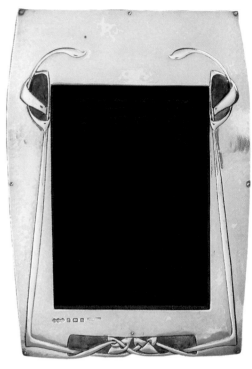

New York which opened in 1878 and, from 1895 Siegfried (commonly known as Samuel) Bing's Maison de l'Art Nouveau in Paris. It was Bing's establishment that gave the movement its name. *The Studio*, a British arts magazine first issued in 1893, was also to play a vital role in educating public taste and providing a platform for the cross-fertilization of ideas. This debt to Britain was acknowledged abroad in such names as 'Style Anglais' or 'Style Liberty'; in every country where it took root architects, designers and artists worked together in the new style, developing and ultimately transforming it from those British beginnings.

☞ *left*
ART NOUVEAU JEWELLERY
ENGLISH *Early 20th c.*
The brooch was designed by C. R. Ashbee. Though a member of the Arts and Crafts movement, his designs are allied to Art Nouveau.

☞ *above*
LIBERTY PICTURE FRAME
ENGLISH *Late 19th c.*
A Liberty 'Cymric' silver and enamel picture frame designed by Archibald Knox and incorporating Celtic entrelac motifs.

A seminal influence in England was the designer Arthur Heygate Mackmurdo (1851–1942). He was co-founder of the Century Guild in 1882 which introduced sinuous foliate tendrils into furniture and textiles, and through his magazine *Hobby Horse* (first issued in 1884), and its reproduction of William Blake's poems, he provided a showcase for graphic arts. Aubrey Beardsley (1872–98) is also considered an important innovator: in a brief and brilliant career he worked on book designs and illustrations for the mediaeval epic *Morte d'Arthur,* Oscar Wilde's *Salomé,* and the first issue of *The Studio*. Another influential figure was the illustrator Walter Crane (1845–1915). He introduced the new style into ceramics at Pilkington's, with larger factories such as Doulton with its Art Pottery studio and Minton with its 'Secessionist' range designed by Leon Solon following suit.

The architect M. H. Baillie Scott (1865–1945) designed furniture which, though still rectilinear in form, was profusely decorated with foliage in bright colours. Moving to the Isle of Man, he worked briefly with Archibald Knox (1864–1933), before being commissioned in 1897 to decorate the palace of the Grand Duke of Hesse in Darmstadt, Germany. In his capacity as designer for Liberty's ranges of metalware marketed under the names 'Cymric' for silver and 'Tudric' for pewter, Knox did much to popularize Art Nouveau and in particular the entrelac motif. The store had a stable of mostly anonymous designers and churned out relatively inexpensive items for the consumption of the middle classes, as well as being the main outlet for Silver Studio textiles.

Soon the new style became established in every field of decorative art, especially

☞ *left*
AUBREY BEARDSLEY
SALOME
ENGLISH *1894*
One of Aubrey Beardsley's celebrated, and at the time notorious, illustrations for Oscar Wilde's Salome.

jewellery, as seen in work of such diverse nature as Oliver Baker, Charles Ashbee and his Guild of Handicrafts, Kate Harris, Alexander Fisher, Henry Wilson, the Murrle Bennett company, and Charles Horner.

French organic motifs

IN BELGIUM groups and magazines promoting the new decorative arts had been proliferating since 1881, culminating in the formation of the 'Libre Esthétique' in 1894. Initially the Belgian scene had been greatly influenced by its contemporaries in Britain, many of whom had regularly exhibited there, but under the influence of Victor Horta (1861–1947), Henry van de Velde (1863–1957) and Gustave Serrurier-Bovy it was to move towards a much more refined curvilinear and abstract style. This is especially notable in the architecture and metalwork of Horta, while the furniture designed by Serrurier-Bovy and Van de Velde was sophisticated and elegant, divested of floral motifs and much more concerned with curvilinear forms. It is in many respects the bridge between the rectilinear British style and the great explosion of organic design in France.

It was in France that Art Nouveau undoubtedly found its spiritual home, where a heritage of rococco design combined in perfect synthesis with the new aesthetic ideals. Bing's Maison de l'Art Nouveau became the focus for the decorative and applied arts, with objects and interior designs contributed by, among others, Georges de Feure, Eugène Gaillard and Hector Guimard, the latter famed for his Paris Metro buildings. By now any residual angular simplicity left over from Arts and Crafts had completely disappeared, to be replaced by elegant and sophisticated curves and the total integration of flora and fauna into form and decoration. Famous women of the day became icons for their times, for example the commercial artist Alphonse Mucha (a Czech by birth) was inspired by the

actress Sarah Bernhardt, and the sculptor Raoul Larche by the American dancer Loïe Fuller.

In the provinces the creative hub was to be found at Nancy, where Emile Gallé (1846–1904), the Daum Brothers and Louis Majorelle all had their factories. Gallé specialized in acid-etched and carved cameo glass decorated with land-scapes, flowers and insects depicted with botanical accuracy, which are generally regarded as the most accomplished work in glass of this period. His great rivals Daum emulated their naturalistic style and produced some very fine work of their own. Gallé also designed furniture decorated with marquetry panels, but it is the decoration rather than the structure of these pieces which is their main appeal. The best École Nancy furniture came from Louis Majorelle (1859–1926) who managed completely to subordinate func-tion to form and decoration: his designs in furniture and metalwork have an un-rivalled plasticity which confound the restrictions normally considered inherent in wood and metalwork.

☞ *opposite, left*
ALPHONSE MUCHA
LA PEINTURE
FRENCH Early 20th c.
Although a Czech by
birth, it is with France
that Mucha is most
associated. His graphic
work, such as this
watercolour, epitomizes
Art Nouveau in the
popular mind.

☞ *opposite*
DAUM TABLE LAMP
FRENCH Early 20th c.
A Louis Majorelle design
for the French
glassmakers, Daum,
who were closely
associated with the Art
Nouveau movement.

☞ *right*
SUITE OF FURNITURE
FRENCH Early 20th c.
This extraordinary suite
of silvered metal furniture
in archetypically organic
Art Nouveau style
features a single chair; a
single chair with arms; a
double chair with arms; a
table, and a free-standing
coat-hanger.

Some decorative arts literally became organic, most notably Lalique's jewellery. René Lalique (1860–1945), the most famous jeweller of his day, combined precious metals and stones with glass and natural materials such as horn to produce the most fantastic and sumptuous pieces. All of this, however, was decorative arts for the exclusive and moneyed classes and this excellence in design did not often survive translation into mass-production.

Formalism and Geometricism
~

IN SCOTLAND the architect Charles Rennie Mackintosh (1868–1928) was to design his most famous commissions between 1896 and 1906, namely the Glasgow School of Art and the Cranston Tea Rooms. Mackintosh worked in close collaboration with his wife Margaret, her sister Frances and brother-in-law Herbert McNair: this was the nucleus of the

'Glasgow School' which included George Logan, E. A. Taylor, George Walton and Jessie M. King. Furniture designs by Walton, Logan and Taylor were executed by Wylie and Lockhead; of austere rectilinear design they were usually in plain oak set with stained glass panels of curvilinear motifs, often including a rose, while Mackintosh favoured white painted wood and maidens. Margaret and her sister worked in metal, stained glass,

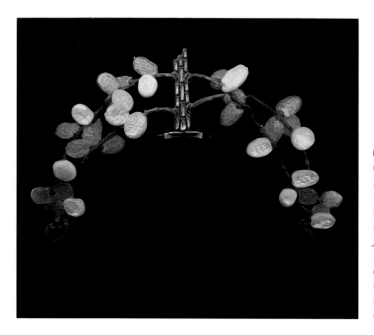

☞ *left*

LALIQUE DIADEM
FRENCH Early 20th c.
René Lalique worked in
many media, but he is best
known for his organic
jewellery designs, often
incorporating several
disparate materials, as in
this gold, horn, enamel,
rock crystal and mother-
of-pearl diadem.

iate move towards linear abstraction. Germany was fortunate to have a wealthy enthusiast in the form of the Grand Duke of Hesse who funded a school of art and design at Darmstadt, inviting both Behrens and Joseph Maria Olbrich to take part in the venture. Geometric design, via Austria, added counterweight to van de Velde's linear abstraction and typical Darmstadt design combines flowing lines with geometric decoration.

Art Nouveau spreads into mass-production

WHEN ONE considers the manufacturing side of decorative arts in Germany and Austria certain names immediately spring to mind as being common today, which is a good indication of their contemporary popularity. In glass the firm of Loetz specialized in curvilinear forms in iridescent glass much influenced by the American Louis Comfort Tiffany, although it also produced many pieces by Werkstätte designers. Similarly the great porcelain factories of Dresden and Meissen would take on the work of new designers to add to in-house designs. Iridescent decoration was also produced by the ceramic factory Zsolnay Pecs in what is now Hungary. Zsolnay produced many classic pieces of naturalistic design with floriform vases, whiplash motifs and romantic scenes. Other factories such as Royal Dux and Amphora mass-produced centrepieces decked with Art Nouveau maidens in flowing robes and surrounded by curvilinear foliage: this may have been working to a more restricted formula but was no less popular. In metal work the firm Würrtembergerische Metal Fabrik (W.M.F.) followed their example by mass-producing inexpensive pewter items decked with romantic maidens, of which candlesticks, letter trays, wall plaques and centrepieces are the best known examples. This contrasts with the more restrained output of their rivals Kayserzinn and Huecke, which preferred the abstract curvilinear design of Behrens and

textiles, jewellery and graphics, especially favouring the image of the ghostly ethereal maiden. The artist and illustrator Jessie King (1875–1949) specialized in delicate but detailed line drawings inspired by fairy stories and medieval epics, but she also designed jewellery for Liberty.

The geometric formalism combined with heavy symbolist overtones of Mackintosh's circle was not well received in England and one must look to Austria to see its true impact. Finally, it is worth mentioning the carpet factory Templeton, which executed many Art Nouveau designs for English artists, notably Frank Brangwyn.

In Vienna in 1898 the painter Gustave Klimt led a group of artists, designers and architects to form a group which could show its work independently, outside the established arts scene, with their own magazine *Ver Sacrum* to promote their work. Notable among the 'Wiener Sezession' (from which Austrian Art Nouveau derives its name) were Otto Wagner (1841–1918) and his pupils Joseph Hoffman (1870–1956), Koloman Moser (1868–1918) and Joseph Maria Olbrich (1867–1908).

Olbrich was a master of the restrained curvilinear style and was ultimately to move to Germany where he proved a

decisive influence, but Hoffmann and Moser were inspired by the Glasgow School which was invited to take a stand at their third exhibition in 1900. They went on to form the Wiener Werkstätte (Vienna Workshop) in 1903, taking a leaf from Ashbee's Guild of Handicraft. The Wiener Werkstätte developed an uncompromising geometric style popularly known as 'chessboard' which eliminated virtually all surface decoration not integral to an object, in all designs ranging from metalwork and jewellery to textiles and glass; it also executed architectural commissions and designed modestly priced mass-produced bentwood furniture to be manufactured by Thonet Brothers. Included in this group were Dagobert Peche, Michael Powolny and Otto Prutscher, and it is interesting to note that their trademark was a stylized rose within a square, obviously inspired by Mackintosh.

In Germany Jugendstil (youth style) began with organic and symbolist motifs and quickly progressed to the geometric after the Glasgow School had shown its hand at the 1900 Vienna exhibition. Early figures include Hermann Obrist, an artist turned embroiderer, architect-designer Richard Riemerschmid and Peter Behrens. Henry van de Velde, both designer and theorist, moved to Berlin in 1899, and one can see an almost immed-

Olbrich, while the jewellery company Theodor Fahrner produced pieces at both ends of the stylistic spectrum.

Tiffany

LAST OF all we must consider the work of Louis Comfort Tiffany (1848–1933) who in many respects stands apart from the rest in America, where Arts and Crafts dominated. He was much influenced by changes in Europe, exploring the style with great creativity. Today he is chiefly remembered for his leaded glass windows and light fittings depicting flowers, insects and birds, and his 'Favrile' range of hand-blown iridescent glass vases. These were often floriform in shape, such as the famous 'Jack in the Pulpit' vase, and were the main influence on the German manufacturers Loetz and Pallme-König and Habel.

The eclipse of the style

IN THIS survey it is not possible to enumerate all the different forms of Art Nouveau, nor to examine its impact on every region. The principal themes and areas have been explored but they should not be considered exhaustive; some of the most interesting architecture, for example, is to be found in Spain in the work of Antonio Gaudì, whose fluid structures of poured concrete are still considered revolutionary today.

In many ways Art Nouveau was an anachronism, an attempt to reinvent romantic images of women and organic design in an era when the telephone, motor car and electricity were part of a snowballing technological culture. It is ironic that the forces which generated it, mass-production and mechanization, were also the ones which ultimately led to its eclipse: the work of Art Nouveau designers was nearly always exclusive and expensive, and in the main failed to cater for mass consumption. On another level, because it did not have the intellectual

☞ *above*
THE 'SITZMACHINE'
AUSTRIAN Early 20th c. This restrained yet complex chair designed by Joseph Hoffman is typical of the Wiener Werkstätte 'chessboard' style.

foundation of Arts and Crafts, and once all the stylistic possibilities had been explored and exhausted, it came to a natural conclusion without leaving any obvious imprint on the next generation. Perhaps this is why it first fell into disregard and later into obscurity until it was rediscovered in the late 1960s. Nonetheless, it left behind many works of great beauty and in the process helped to sweep away the excesses of 19th century Rococo. In retrospect one can trace Art Deco and Bauhaus back to these early attempts to create a new grammar of ornament, and in particular to the work of Mackintosh and the Wiener Werkstätte. These may have been radical outposts of the movement but they contain the seeds of Modernism, and for all these reasons Art Nouveau is an important staging post in the history of decorative arts.

NORTH AMERICAN ART AND ARTEFACTS

☞ *above*

AMMI PHILLIPS
PORTRAIT OF TWO BROTHERS
AMERICAN c.1850
76 × 96cm (28¾ × 39¼in)
Phillips is one of a handful of folk artists whose work has
been positively identified. This portrait by Phillips is
thought to be of Edward and Henry Bronson of Winchester,
Connecticut.

NATIVE AMERICAN ARTEFACTS
JOE RIVERA

Early in the 20th century American Indian arts were considered the exclusive province of anthropology and natural history museums. However, during the last 25 years there has been a remarkable development of interest in Native American art. In the early 1970s, two of the greatest contributions to the popularity of Native American art among collectors were Sotheby's two sales of the Green Collection, and the Norman Feder exhibition at the Whitney Museum, New York. Among collectors, this art has become internationally recognized as an excellent investment because of the power of its aesthetic beauty, its historic significance, its inherent spiritual nature, and its rarity. Even so, it is still considered to be one of the best kept investment secrets in the fine art field.

The tremendous increase in the collection of Native American art by private collectors and museums has resulted in a rapidly increasing rise in prices. We have also seen the birth of a successful American magazine devoted exclusively to Native American art which has been a great tool

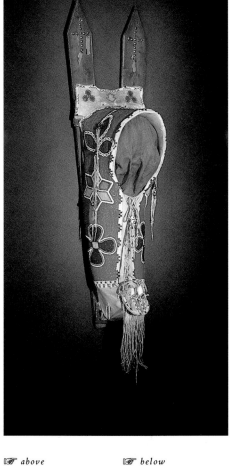

☞ *above*

KIOWA CRADLE

NATIVE AMERICAN c.1890
A baby carrier with a fully beaded cover decorated with abstract floral designs on fruitwood boards, which protected the baby's head. This example was sold in 1991 for $65,000.

☞ *below*

ACOMA STORAGE JAR

NATIVE AMERICAN c.1885
A polychrome storage jar coil-built with clay from local pueblo sources, pit fired and hand painted with natural pigments. Historic pueblo pottery is among the finest aboriginal American arts.

 ☞ *above centre*

TSIMSHIAN PUPPET

NATIVE AMERICAN c.1850–70
A marionette from the Northwest Coast, with a carved and painted face, movable legs and arms and accented with human hair.

☞ *right*

CROW WAR SHIRT

NATIVE AMERICAN c.1850
Made of native tanned deer hide, self-fringed at edges and cuffs, the shirt is decorated with quill-wrapped horsehair. This masterpiece of Crow craftsmanship sold for $250,000 in 1989.

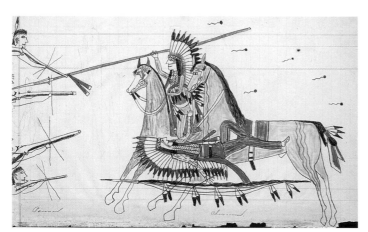

☞ *left*

KIOWA LEDGER DRAWING

*NATIVE AMERICAN c.1885
One of the drawings done
by adult males which
illustrated the
pictographic chronicles of
the Plains Warrior
Societies.*

in educating the general public in an appreciation of the Native American heritage.

Native American art, which ranges from the Pacific Northwest to the Eastern Woodlands, can be enjoyed both for its visual merit and for the meaning it holds. The artwork was created by employing such skills as weaving, basketry, pottery-making, embroidery, and the applied arts of bead, quill and featherwork. The decoration not only made the piece more beautiful but also gave an object its significance.

Much of the art was made to emphasize the importance and rank of the individual who owned and used it. Also many objects were made as gifts given at the coming of age of a young male or female, a marriage and the birth of a child. Others were made for religious purposes, and often decorated with representations of the spirits whose help was sought and realized through visions.

The coming of the white man brought not only new materials but also styles and objects that were incorporated into the clothing and artifacts of the Native American people. Venetian glass beads, brightly coloured silks, brass tacks, mirrors and commercial blankets are only a few of these new materials. Vests, shoulder bags, epaulettes and gauntlets were all incorporated into Indian costume. Also, the American Flag became a very popular subject and was used quite extensively in bead work. A group has evolved who specifically collect works containing the American Flag, and in 1975 there was an exhibition and accompanying catalogue published on this material entitled 'The American Indian/The American Flag'.

Wherever designs were taken from and whatever materials were used, the artifacts have always indicated the Indian belief in the unity between art and life. Every creation expressed features of style that clearly identified and separated it from the art of any other part of the world.

Collecting Native American art

~

THE PRICE of an American Indian artifact is determined by the age, condition, authenticity and rarity of the object and has increased significantly in price over the last ten years. For example, a war shirt which sold for $1,200 in 1981 was offered for sale in 1991 at a well-known gallery for $18,000. Current prices range from $675 for a pair of child's moccasins, to $250,000 for a wonderful war shirt.

Antique Native American art can be purchased from reputable galleries such as Morning Star Gallery, Zaplin and Lampert and Fenn Gallery, all located in Sante Fe, New Mexico, which is the centre for authentic American Indian art. It can also be purchased from well known auction houses like Sothebys, Butterfields and Skinners, during their Tribal Art Sales.

☞ *above*

**NAVAJO WEARING
BLANKET**

*NATIVE AMERICAN c.1880
Finely woven of
commercially spun
Germantown and
homespun yarns, this type
of classic Navajo Moki
blanket was traded
extensively, especially to
the buffalo-hunting
tribesmen of the Plains.*

☞ *below*

**WESTERN APACHE
STORAGE BASKET**

*NATIVE AMERICAN
c.1890–1915
This storage 'ollas' and
platter tray are of coil-
built technique. Western
Apaches made little
pottery and needed baskets
for transporting
everything from grain to
firewood.*

AMERICAN FOLK ART

DAVID SCHORSCH

The term 'Folk Art' as applied in America has been described as the art and artifacts of the common man, made by and for those individuals who first settled and nurtured what was to become the United States. And just as the United States has been termed 'a melting pot of society', the traits and differences which combine in creating the unique community which is America are exemplified in the best of American folk art.

Contrary to popular belief, folk art was not restricted to rural communities, nor cut off by economic bounds. As a general category, American folk art reflects and expresses the development and growth of the American middle class. Folk artists prospered throughout the country, from Maine to New York, to the Southern States and to the Midwest. American folk art in countless variations was made by individuals who had a great gift and capability, who had an intuitive and an instinctive feeling for art, but not necessarily formal training. The exclusion of a formal guild system in the United

States, combined with the climate of an open society, gave artists and craftsmen the independence and freedom to express themselves in ways that were unattainable to the academically trained or schooled artists. This peculiar environment enabled a number of folk artists to develop styles

David C. Knowles. Aged 31 Years Septr 12 1836.   Mary Knowles. Aged 31 Years Novr 5th 1836.

shoes. Sailors on board whaling ships would engrave whales' teeth and fashion canes and other utilitarian and decorative forms from whalebone and wood, as well as mending nets and performing other mundane functions. Ladies and young girls, who were trained in the 'feminine arts' at home and in academies, produced delicately painted watercolours, stitched intricate samplers and embroideries, and made strikingly beautiful quilts, coverlets, hooked rugs and table covers as well as

of artistic expression that often anticipated elements of abstraction encountered hundreds of years later by Modernist and other artistic movements in Europe and America.

As was typical of many professionals during the 18th and 19th centuries, the folk artists and crafts people were often required to wear many expert hats. For example, Edward Hicks painted coaches and signs as well as his well-known paintings. In addition to being a working physician, Rufus Hathaway is acknowledged as a talented and prolific 18th century portrait painter. Skilled carvers produced sculptural pieces such as carousel animals, ship figureheads, or architectural ornaments, and metal smiths fashioned elaborate and sophisticated weather vanes, whirligigs, lighting devices or horse

☞ *bottom left*
JOHN BREWSTER, JR.
PORTRAIT OF COMFORT
STAR MYGATT AND LUCY
MYGATT
AMERICAN c.1850
137 × 99.5cm (54 × 39¼in)
Brewster was a talented deaf-mute working in a three-state area between New York, Connecticut and Massachusetts.

☞ *above*
JOSEPH H. DAVIS
PORTRAIT OF DAVID C. AND
MARY KNOWLES
AMERICAN 1836
25.4 × 39cm (10 × 15½in)
Joseph Davis specialized in watercolour portraits depicting the rural citizens of Maine and New Hampshire.

☞ *left*
WILLIAM W. KENNEDY
PORTRAIT OF A LITTLE
GIRL
AMERICAN c.1840
73.5 × 61cm (29 × 24in)
This oil painting of a
little girl in a pink dress is
typical of the Prior-
Hamblen School's 'flat'
style of facial features.

graphy in the 1850s, the pictorial record of most of the American people was largely recorded by folk artists. Although a small number of these artists have been identified and their work researched, the majority of the painters responsible for the customary folk paintings remain anonymous. Among the most famous folk painters of the 18th and early part of the 19th century is Winthrop Chandler (1747–1790), who worked in Connecticut during the 1770s, painting portraits and over mantles. Significant works by Chandler have sold for over $250,000 at auction and in private sales. Two folk portrait painters whose works can encompass a very broad price range are John Brewster, Jr. (1766–1854) and Ammi Phillips (1788–1865). An unimportant work by either painter may fetch $7500, while a major example can sell in excess of one million dollars. Brewster was a

mending clothing and doing other routine domestic chores. And then there were the often anonymous professional crafts people who plied their trades by specializing in the production of any manner of utilitarian objects, such as hardware, signboards, trade figures, painted and punched tinware, pottery, toys, fire buckets, ornamental painting, decoys, and weavings.

All of these objects share a boldness of form, a brilliance of colour, a delight in skilful and pleasing use of pattern, an overriding sense of imagination and sure design ability which made the lack of technical proficiency almost irrelevant. As the famous Boston collector and noted connoisseur Maxim Karolik said, 'While the folk artist might lack the ability to describe, he did not lack the ability to express.' We are speaking of poetry rather than prose.

Folk paintings
—

PERHAPS THE most prolific and popular forms of American folk art are portraits, weather vanes and textiles. Before the widespread popularity of photo-

☞ *above*
EDWARD HICKS
THE PEACEABLE KINGDOM
AMERICAN c.1838
44.5 × 59.5cm
(17½ × 23½in)
A charming oil painting
typical of the work of this

Quaker preacher and sign
painter from Newtown,
Pennsylvania.

remarkably talented deaf-mute artist who worked in Connecticut in the 1790s, and in Maine in the 1820s. Phillips was one of the most prolific and celebrated of folk painters. He worked in a three-state area between New York, Connecticut and Massachusetts, between 1811 and 1862.

During the first quarter of the 19th century a large group of folk portrait painters was active, including Joseph H. Davis, who specialized in watercolour profile portraits depicting the rural citizens of Maine and New Hampshire during the 1830s. Works by Davis have ranged in price from about $3500 to over $50,000. Jacob Maentel was another watercolourist who worked in Pennsylvania and Indiana between the 1820s and 1840s. Maentel executed profile as well as frontal portraits, and his portraits have ranged from about $4500 to over $100,000.

Probably the most prolific and recognizable folk portrait painter in the 19th century was William Matthew Prior (1803–1873), and members of the so-called 'Prior-Hamblen School'. These painters worked in the New England states during the 1840s and 1850s. Prior-Hamblen portraits can be recognized for their 'flat' style of facial rendering. Prior and his counterparts were also capable of a more sophisticated and academic method of facial rendering which was available for a higher cost to the patron.

The most sought-after and popular of all folk paintings are the charming works of Edward Hicks (1780–1847). Hicks was a Quaker preacher and sign painter from Newtown, Pennsylvania, who worked between 1825 and 1845. He has taken his place as one of the most important and desirable of American artists of the 19th century for his delightful renditions of 'The Peaceable Kingdom' and 'Penn's Treaty with the Indians', both of which were taken from print sources. Important works by Hicks often sell in the low seven figures.

Weathervanes

~

ALTHOUGH THERE existed a small number of weathervanes in 17th and 18th century America, the majority of the hollow bodied copper and cast iron weathervanes were produced by small factories located in New England and New York during the second half of the 19th century. These makers included the

☞ *above*

REARING HORSE WEATHER VANE
AMERICAN c.1860
122 × 91.5cm (48 × 36in)
A moulded copper and cast zinc weather vane made by J. Howard and Company of West Bridgewater, Massachusetts.

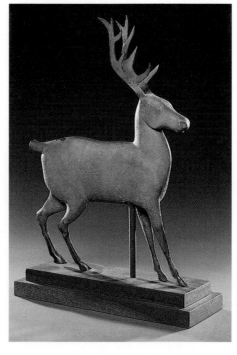

☞ *left*

MINIATURE DEER WEATHER VANE
AMERICAN c.1860
30.5 × 23cm (12 × 9in)
A moulded copper and cast zinc miniature weather vane, painted yellow, and made by J. Howard and Company, West Bridgewater, Massachusetts.

☞ *left*
ROOSTER WEATHER VANE
AMERICAN c.1840
48 × 67cm (19 × 26½in)
The maker of this weather vane has not been identified, but it probably comes from New England or New York State. It is made of pine with the original painted decoration.

firms of H. L. Washburn, J. L. Mott, Rochester Ironworks, J. W. Fiske, A. L. Jewell, and L. W. Cushing and Sons. One of the earliest and most acclaimed makers of factory-produced weather vanes was J. Howard and Co. of West Bridgewater, Massachusetts. The weather vanes produced by the Howard firm are highly distinctive, made with cast zinc front parts, with the balance of moulded hollow copper. The unidentified artist responsible for the designs of the Howard weather vanes gave his creations a unique classical elegance, with highly stylized forms that may have been inspired by antiquities.

Copper weather vanes of rare and desirable forms which retain their original gold leafing or green verdigris patination are highly prized. Many charming and desirable weather vanes were 'home-made', created in rural communities utilizing materials at hand. An excellent example of this type of one-of-a-kind weather vane is the silhouetted wooden rooster, with original painted decoration and leather cockscomb. Weather vanes which have been resurfaced, repaired, or refinished greatly diminish in value. Nineteenth century weather vanes have sold at auction from about $2,500 to $770,000.

Bed 'ruggs' and quilts

THE EARLIEST form of bed covering made in the United States consists of the 'bed rugg', which is a form of heavy woollen bedspread. Most bed ruggs were

☞ *below*
BED RUGG
AMERICAN 1806
244 × 228.5cm (96 × 90in)
Attributed to a member of the Packard family of Jericho, Vermont, this wool bed rugg sewn with a running stitch is initialed 'BNP' and dated.

produced during the 18th century in New England, one of the earliest being dated 1724. Fewer than fifty bed ruggs survive today; the majority reside in museum collections. Bed ruggs have sold at auction for as much as $55,000.

Pieced and appliquéd quilts have been produced in America since the mid-to-late 18th century. The majority of quilts date from the 19th and 20th centuries. Quilt-making reached its zenith during the mid-19th century in Baltimore, Maryland. One of the most splendid and best preserved examples of a 'Baltimore Album Quilt' is the example attributed to Mary Evans made for Mary and Sarah Pool, circa 1846. The superb quality of the appliquéd and stuffed elements combined with the density of the composition make this one of the supreme achievements of American textile folk art. Depending on quality and condition, Baltimore Album Quilts have sold at auction from about

numerous stylized pictorial elements in silk threads on a linen ground, and is inscribed 'Susan Rabsom Her Work 1789'. Eighteenth century American samplers have sold at auction from about $3,000 to $198,000.

Collecting American folk art

INTEREST IN collecting and studying American folk art dates to the last decade of the 19th century. Among the earliest collectors and scholars in this newly emerging field was Edwin Atlee Barber, whose speciality was Pennsylvania German folk art. The recognition of folk art as a category of 'American art' began in 1924 with an exhibition organized by Juliana Force at The Whitney Studio Club, in New York City. Throughout the 1930s Holger Cahill assembled exhibitions at the Newark Museum, in New Jersey, and at the Museum of Modern Art in New York City, with folk art borrowed from the collections of contemporary artists of the day, including Charles Sheeler, Charles Demuth, Elie Nadelman, and Robert Laurent. These artists saw in this 'primitive' work an anticipation of the kind of abstract art that they were creating.

Cahill's exhibitions brought folk art to the attention of such early collectors as Abby Aldrich Rockefeller, whose collection now comprises The Abby Aldrich Rockefeller Folk Art Center at Colonial Williamsburg, Virginia. Electra Havemeyer Webb's collection now forms the Shelburne Museum, in Vermont. Henry Ford also collected and his collection has become the Henry Ford Museum in Dearborn, Michigan; finally Henry Francis du Pont's collection now forms the Winterthur Museum in Delaware. These private collections, which in turn became the nucleus for the public institutions which bear their names, did much to legitimize and popularize a wonderful vernacular art form, and to bring this material to the attention of the public and scholar alike. The process of defining,

$10,000 to as much as $176,000, and in private transactions they have exceeded $250,000. More modest examples can be found but prices are still around $1,000–$5,000.

Samplers and needlework pictures

ONE OF the most popular areas of collecting are samplers and needlework pictures. A sampler differs from a needlework picture by including the alphabet. The advanced scholarship in this area has made it possible to identify distinctive samplers and needlework pictures specific to schools, towns and regions, and samplers are often rich in potential biographical information about their makers. A particularly fine example is the Susan Rabsom sampler from Philadelphia, Pennsylvania. It incorporates

☞ *above*
ALBUM QUILT
AMERICAN c.1850
269 × 273cm
(106 × 107½in)
Attributed to Mary Evans of Baltimore, Maryland, this beautiful cotton quilt was made for the Sarah and Mary J. Pool family.

legitimizing, and building public awareness of American folk art has been
influenced by museum exhibitions,
scholarly publications, and the marketplace. Through the advanced scholarship
generated by this new awareness, an
entire generation of dealers, collectors and
museum professionals has seen the market
for the finest American folk art literally
expand by leaps and bounds. This period
is highlighted by the establishment of The
Museum of American Folk Art in New
York City in 1960.

The development of the market

BETWEEN 1930 and 1960, when popular
interest and awareness of American folk
art was beginning to emerge, there were
only a handful of dealer-specialists. The
most dramatic expansion of the folk art
market occurred in the mid-1970s and
coincided with a landmark exhibition at
the Whitney Museum of American Art,
in New York City, 'The Flowering of
American Folk Art'. At the same time the
first of a series of seven auctions at
Sotheby Parke Bernet in New York
offered a superb group of folk watercolours from the renowned Garbisch
collection. These folk art auctions
attracted worldwide attention because of

the rarity, quality and diversity of the pieces, and the fact that the audience for folk art had grown in both number and sophistication. In the forty-odd-years since the Garbisches had begun to collect, the world of folk art collecting had made a quantum leap from simply being considered 'quaint decorations' to serious works of early American art.

The landmark auction sale of the Stewart E. Gregory folk art collection in 1979, at Sotheby Parke Bernet in New

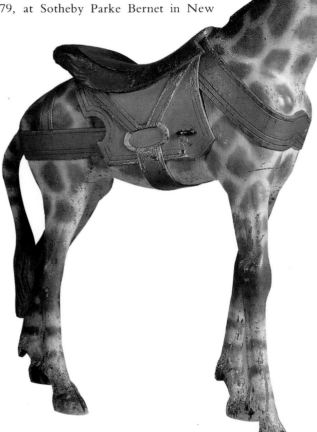

☞ *opposite page, top*

TRADE SIGN

AMERICAN *c.1820*

54.5 × 132cm (21½ × 52in)
An oil painted pine trade sign for Edward Hall, Hatter and Furrier of Randolph, Vermont, by an unknown artist.

☞ *opposite page, bottom*

EMBROIDERY SAMPLER

AMERICAN *1789*

45.5 × 33.5cm (18 × 13¼in)
A sampler of silk threads on linen embroidered by Susan Rabsom of Philadelphia.

☞ *left*

CAROUSEL GIRAFFE

AMERICAN *c.1900*

Height: 188cm (74in)
A Carousel animal made by the Gustav A. Denstzel Carousel Company of Philadelphia and carved by Daniel Muller.

York, marked an escalation of prices for the best folk art that has yet to pause. Many auction records were set at this sale, and the $1.3 million total was a record for a single owner auction of American folk art. It was a breakthrough as a major event in the art world, creating an international awareness and monetary appreciation for American folk art. Numerous record prices were established at the Gregory sale. A moulded copper weather vane in the form of an Indian, estimated at $8000–$10,000, sold for $27,500. A portrait of a child painted by

John Brewster, Jr., estimated at $25,000–35,000, sold for $74,000. A painted box in the form of a lectern that was expected to sell for $4000–6000 brought $18,700. A pair of portraits painted by Ammi Phillips that was estimated to bring $20,000–30,000, sold for $68,000.

Throughout the 1980s outstanding items entered the marketplace through the disposal of folk art from a number of distinguished collections. Another record price seemed to be achieved at each of these auctions. At the four sales of the Barbara Johnson Whaling Collection

there were numerous records set for scrimshaw. The Pottery Collection of William E. Wiltshire III established many record prices, including a record for redware when a John Bell lion sold for $18,000. At the sale of the Theodore H. Kapnek Collection of American Samplers a record was set when a Matilda Filbert sampler sold for $41,800. At the Howard and Jean Lipman sale a record was set for painted furniture when a Pennsylvania decorated blanket chest brought $41,000. At the Thomas G. Rizzo Sale a record was set when a weather vane in the form of the Statue of Liberty brought $82,500. At the Fred Wichmann Sale a fraktur of a man feeding a bear an ear of corn brought $24,000, and at the M. Austin Fine Sale, a Baltimore Album Quilt sold for $176,000.

The unprecedented quantity of high calibre offerings combined with the rapidly expanding interest in the field, caused the majority of the records that were established during the 1980s to be rapidly eclipsed. The record for a weather vane now stands at $770,000, paid for a horse and rider vane made by J. Howard and Company, W. Bridgewater, Massachusetts, circa 1865. The record for a sampler is now $198,000, paid for an 18th century Marblehead needlework picture inscribed Ruthy Rogers. A portrait painted by John Brewster, Jr., depicting a father and daughter, sold for $852,500. A portrait of a little girl wearing a red dress painted by Ammi Phillips sold for $682,000. A rendition of Penn's 'Treaty with the Indians' painted by Edward Hicks now holds the auction record for a folk painting at $990,000. An 18th century Pennsylvania fraktur drawing depicting Lady Washington on horseback sold for $110,000. A watercolour on silk depicting Aurora riding through the clouds probably painted by a Rhode Island schoolgirl sold for $374,000. A carved and painted Connecticut wall box ornamented by an eagle and floral devices sold for $187,000. A Virginia painted tall clock decorated by Johannes Spitler sold for $203,500.

THE ARTS OF
THE EAST

☞ *above*

POTTERY HORSE

CHINESE *Tang Dynasty (618–906) 50.5cm (20in) high*
Many of the figures of animals produced in the Tang
dynasty were funerary ware. This small pottery horse was
sold for £11,000 ($20,350).

CHINESE WORKS OF ART

RODDY ROPNER AND PETER TUNSTALL-BEHRENS

Chinese Jade

JADE IS a generic term covering nephrite, a silicate of calcium and magnesium, and jadeite, a silicate of sodium and aluminium. Both are extremely hard stones, ranking 6.5 and 6.75 on the Moh's scale, where talc is 1 and diamond 10. In its purest form, jade is white and translucent, but often at least partially coloured by inclusions of mineral impurities including browns and greens in nephrite, and brilliant greens and lavenders in jadeite. It is the sensitivity with which the lapidarist incorporates any of these natural flaws in his carving which is critical to its success.

Unavailable in China proper, nephrite was originally found in pebbles and boulders from two rivers in Khotan in the Taklamakan Desert until supplies were exhausted in the 18th century, when it was mined in larger quantities near Yarkand, 200 miles further northwest. Jadeite, imported from Upper Burma, has only been carved since the 18th century. For the Chinese, jade carries reverential auspicious symbolism; as a metaphor it stands as a supreme commendation, and it represented heaven, purity, loyalty and intelligence for Confucius.

In the Neolithic and early Historical period, jade was carved for practical purposes such as blades and belt hooks and ritual burial ornaments in the form of pierced discs (*bi*), squared cylindrical objects (*cong*) and numerous plaque pendants (*huang*) often decorated with the geometric and zoomorphic patterns found on contemporary bronze objects. From the Han to Ming period, these shapes continue as archaisms alongside the development of small, independent, mythical and naturalistic animal and figural sculptures and vessels.

The mining of nephrite and accompanying technical developments resulted in larger and more virtuosic pieces. Loose copies of archaic bronze vessels, vases and censers as well as smaller animal and figural groups were produced in large numbers during the great period of jade carving under the Emperor Qianlong (1736–95). The 19th century witnessed a gradual decline in quality although highly intricate if somewhat sterile carvings in both nephrite and jadeite are still produced.

Chinese bronzes

THE ARCHAIC bronzes of China are the most dramatic testimony to the sophistication of early Chinese Society. The Bronze Age of China (*c*. 2000BC–500BC) saw the introduction and development of bronze tools, weapons and ritual vessels. Tin and lead were added to copper to reduce the latter's melting point (1083°C) and increase its hardness. Early bronzes were cast by pouring the molten metal into a gap between a central core and an outer casing of section moulds; the interior of these moulds could be incised with designs in negative image.

Rituals during the Shang dynasty (*c*. 16th–11th century BC) demanded sacrifices to ancestors, and bronze vessels were cast

for these ceremonies. They included wine and food vessels. Initially performed as state rituals, these sacrifices were later enacted by aristocratic families. Technically the vessels developed from the earliest thin bodied *jue,* a tripod wine vessel, with a narrow band of decoration, to storage vessels with ornate and dramatic decoration. The most popular motif was the *taotie,* a form of hybrid bird and beast probably used to ward off evil spirits.

Initially the Zhou dynasty (*c*. 11th century BC–221BC) continued the rituals and bronze techniques of the Shang. There was, however, less emphasis on wine vessels, as alcohol had been associated with the demise of the Shang. Inscriptions, which during the Shang were limited to two or three characters, were now extended to lengthy passages explaining the circumstances in which the bronze was commissioned and extolling the virtues of the owners' ancestors. After a period of decline, new techniques were introduced and during the Spring and

☞ *above*
CELADON AND RUSSET JADE BOULDER
CHINESE 18th c.
19cm (7½in) long
For the Chinese, jade has always carried special significance, being associated with
intelligence, heaven and purity. This piece was sold by Christie's for £3,850 ($7,120).

☞ *top*
BRONZE WINE VESSEL AND COVER
CHINESE 11th–9th c. BC
33cm (13in) high
Bronze was commonly used during the first half of the Zhou dynasty (which ran from c.1207
BC to 221 BC), *but wine vessels are relatively rare, and this fetched £28,600 ($53,000) in 1990.*

Autumn period (770–476BC) we find copper, turquoise, silver and gold inlays.

The lost wax method of casting developed during the Warring States period (475–221BC). The significance of ritual vessels declined and a greater range of utilitarian wares appeared, including chariot fittings and mirrors which were made in large quantities from the 4th century BC until the Tang dynasty. These were usually circular discs cast with one smooth surface and the reverse with detailed ornament, some with geometric patterns such as the so-called TLV mirrors. The decoration of mirrors became more naturalistic during the Tang with motifs like the 'lion and grape'.

The Song dynasty saw a period of archaism, where the shapes of the Shang and Zhou were reverentially imitated. The Ming and Qing continued this practice and these later wares are largely decorative.

☞ *right*
FAMILLE ROSE ARMORIAL SAUCER DISHES
CHINESE mid-18th c.
31.5cm (12½in) diameter
This pair of saucer-dishes, which sold for £2,860 ($5,290) at Christie's, date from early in the reign of Qianlong.

☞ *above*
SILVER-BRONZE CIRCULAR MIRROR
CHINESE Tang dynasty (618–906)
24cm (9½in) diameter
Decoration of mirrors became more naturalistic during the Tang dynasty. This example was sold by Christie's for £9,500 ($17,575) in 1990.

☞ *bottom right*
'QUAIL' BOWL
CHINESE late 18th c.
38.5cm (15¼in) diameter
Polychrome wares like this 'famille rose' piece, were widely produced during the reign of the emperor Qianlong (1736–95). This sold for £2,530 ($4,680) at auction.

Lacquer

LACQUER IS produced from the sap of the lac tree. It can be coloured with dyes and hardens when kept in a warm damp atmosphere. Layers of lacquer are usually applied to a wooden or cloth core to give the object a light but sturdy foundation.

Lacquer began to flourish during the Warring States with the development of numerous shapes including carved cups, bowls and boxes. These were painted with geometric designs or figures such as musicians. Production of lacquer increased dramatically during the Han dynasty. Lacquer inlaid with mother-of-pearl dates back to the Tang dynasty but it is not until the Song dynasty that lacquerware is again found in large quantities. Monochrome bowls and dishes were especially popular. The simplicity of forms was closely linked to other decorative arts such as ceramics. The technique of carving through alternately coloured layers with the design of cloud scrolls, to produce what is known as *guri* lacquer, was started during the Song and was widely practised during the Yuan.

Under the Ming and Qing there was a profusion of techniques including carved and inlaid lacquers in both monochrome and polychrome. Flowers, dragons, phoenixes and figures amidst pavilions and terraces were especially popular.

Chinese Export art

THE CHINESE began to export art to the West on a regular basis after the colonization of Macau by the Portuguese in 1517. The mainstay of the China Trade comprised tea and silk, but the thin white body of porcelain found a ready market in the West and the fashion for Orientalism eagerly absorbed other Chinese products. The Portuguese dominated activities for a century and early pieces of porcelain which survive are Chinese or Middle-Eastern forms decorated in blue and white with the coats of arms of individual seamen squeezed in amid Ming decorative motifs. Trade began in earnest during the 17th century under the Dutch East India Company. Quite roughly potted pieces including dishes, bottles, mustard pots and brandy bowls decorated in blue and white with floral-filled panel designs were very popular in the West. These date from the mid-century and are known as 'Kraak porselein'. Cargoes of finer quality pieces

☞ *left*
'KRAAK PORSELEIN' DISH
CHINESE late 16th or early 17th c.
47.5cm (18¾in) diameter
Late Ming potters made this form of porcelain for Dutch traders. This example from Wanli fetched £3,850 ($7,120) at auction in 1990.

☞ *below*
BLACK LACQUER HARDWOOD SCREEN
CHINESE 19th c.
40.5 × 182.5cm (16 × 71½in) each
Screens were widely exported from China in the 19th century. This example was sold at auction in 1990 for £4,950 ($9,100).

slackened, although it continued with America and Europe throughout the 19th century. Other examples of Export art include screens, sewing boxes and games boxes decorated in lacquer, wall-paper, silver, fans and furniture. In addition, a large number of paintings depicting views of the Treaty ports through which the trade was directed, and watercolours accurately illustrating Oriental species or the manufacture of Oriental porcelain were sent back to the families of the Traders and to museums and schools for educational purposes.

Chinese ceramics

THE HISTORY of Chinese ceramics charts the progression from earthenware, pottery fired up to 1100°C, to stoneware, fired between 1200°C–1300°C to produce a vitrified body, and culminates with porcelain which in the West is considered to be a ceramic body achieved by combining kaolin or China clay with petuntse or China stone fired between 1280°C–1450°C to achieve a fine white-bodied vitrified ware. Chinese ceramics are discussed in detail on page 25.

Amongst the most refined of all Chinese ceramics are the stone wares and porcelains of the Song Dynasty. Long prized for their emphasis on understated elegance, their beauty is largely derived from simple forms and monochrome glazes. Many wares are associated with individual kilns from which they derive their names but are known to have been produced at a number of sites. These wares of Northern China include the ivory-white Ding, the green-glazed, grey-bodied Yaozhou, the distinctive Jun with its turquoise glaze often splashed with purple and the simple grey-green Ru; at their finest all were produced for Imperial use. Contrasting with these were the boldly carved, incised and painted Cizhou pieces which formed the largest body of popular wares.

The flight of the Imperial Court south to Hangzhou in 1127 encouraged the

dating from *c.*1650 and 1750, including the famous Nanking Cargo, have been recovered from sunken ships. These comprise both Western and Chinese forms, still decorated in blue and white, and include purely utilitarian objects such as teapots, teabowls and saucers and decorative garnitures of beaker vases and jars.

The 18th century witnessed the introduction of the English to the trade and the use of polychrome decorations labelled *famille rose, famille verte* and *famille noir.* These were used to decorate human and animal models and specially-commissioned dinner services enamelled with family and Masonic arms and historical and mythological 'European subject' designs. As factories in Europe began to manufacture porcelain offering a cheaper and not inferior alternative, the China Trade

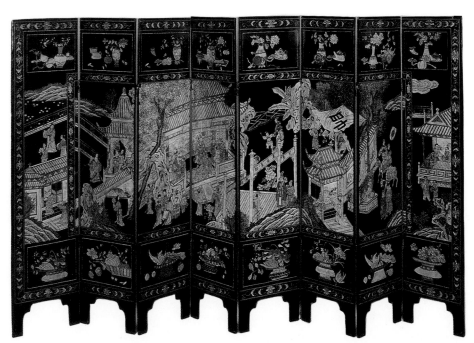

growth of the southern kilns. The crackled wares of Guan and Ge have enjoyed a special position because of their Imperial associations. The most prolific wares of this period are the so-called celadons of Longquan which are typified by an opaque green glaze on a grey stoneware body which fires red where exposed in the firing. Also popular were the pale blue *qingbai* 'bluish white' porcelain produced at the Jingdezhen kiln complex, which was to become the most important centre of ceramic production throughout the Yuan, Ming and Qing dynasties.

The date of the earliest blue and white decorated porcelain is still debated; however, sophisticated blue and white porcelains were being produced at Jingdezhen by the mid-14th century. The colour blue is produced from cobalt oxide, one of the few oxides that remain stable at the temperatures used to fire porcelain. The oxide is painted onto the body which is then glazed and fired.

Initially produced in response to a demand created by Middle Eastern traders in China during the Yuan dynasty (1279–1368), blue and white came to be appreciated by the Chinese and reached its apogee in the 15th century under the emperors Yongli (1403–1424), Xuande (1426–1435) – who was the first to have his reign mark painted on Imperial blue and white wares – and Chenghua (1465–1487). During the late Ming period, with China under threat of invasion from the North, Imperial patronage of Jingdezhen declined. During the late 16th and 17th centuries the potters sought new markets (see above). The mid-17th century, referred to as the 'Transitional' period sees a profusion of new shapes and subjects, many of the latter derived from romantic novels.

The Ming dynasty was overthrown by the Manchu Qing (1644–1912) dynasty and the emperor Kangxi (1662–1722) reasserted control over the Imperial kilns at Jingdezhen. They were responsible for producing perhaps the most technically perfect porcelain of either the Ming or Qing dynasties during the reigns of

☞ *below*

JAR

CHINESE Yuan dynasty (1276–1368)

46.5cm (18¼in) high

Blue and white porcelain was first produced during the Yuan dynasty, but output did not peak until 100 years later. This jar is hence rare, and was auctioned for £110,000 ($205,350).

☞ *above*

BLUE AND WHITE DISH

CHINESE 1403–24

40.5cm (16in)

A fine piece from the reign of the Ming emperor Yongle, this was sold at auction for £132,000 ($244,200) in 1990.

Kangxi, Yongzheng (1723–1735) and Qianlong. More recently, however, collectors have begun to appreciate the wares of subsequent dynasties.

While blue and white porcelain forms the largest section of wares from China's last two dynasties, other decoration was widely employed. These include monochromes such as the Imperial yellow glazed wares, and also polychrome wares including *doucai* and *wucai* enamelled pieces. *Famille verte* and *famille rose* were also produced, but only during the Qing dynasty.

Buying Chinese works of art

As with other antiques, there are two main methods for buying Chinese works of art, through the auction houses or through dealers. The main auction houses hold regular sales often devoted to either Chinese taste or export market works of art. The lots are normally on view for several days prior to the auction and provide the potential buyer with an excellent opportunity to study the pieces at leisure with the aid of a detailed catalogue description and estimate for guidance. Departmental staff are happy to provide further information and condition reports if requested. While dealers carry stock around the year, many hold specialized exhibitions and can offer an excellent individual service. Many dealers also exhibit at annual fairs held in major cities.

Chinese works of art vary in price considerably within any given category. The discrepancy in prices is largely dictated by two main factors: quality and condition. The quality can only be assessed by studying as large a range of examples as possible. The finer quality pieces will inevitably cost more but are more likely to hold their value. Condition is an equally important consideration. Chips, cracks and repairs can greatly reduce the value of most pieces, particularly ceramics, where a premium is currently paid for items in perfect condition.

ISLAMIC WORKS OF ART

JOHN CARSWELL

What is Islamic art? The term is so all-embracing that it is as well to define some of its parameters. Chronologically, it covers the 1,400 years since Muhammad revealed a new religion, Islam, in the 7th century, to the present day. Geographically, Islam spread from Arabia throughout the Middle East and North Africa to Spain and the Atlantic, and eastwards to India, south-east Asia and China. Culturally, Islam is even more complex, for over the centuries the ancient, indigenous civilizations and dynasties of Central Asia and the Near and Far East were absorbed by conversion, but never entirely lost their own identity. One has only to think of the Umayyads and Abbasids, the Seljuks and the Timurids, the Persian, Ottoman and Mughal empires, and the present-day nation-states, all linked by the common thread of a single faith, but all so different in their aesthetic expression.

Can one identify anything specifically 'Islamic' in the art of these different peoples and times? Not in the religious sense, for although there is obviously an art and architecture directly concerned with the practice of Islam – the mosque, minaret, shrines and holy places, and the Holy Qur'an itself – there is a whole secular world which is also an integral part of Islamic culture. However, various common elements can be perceived. First is the artistic inheritance and incorporation of pre-Islamic cultures, such as that of the Graeco-Roman world, and Sassanian Persia. There is a tendency to expression through the use of geometric forms and patterning, to such a degree of complexity that they become a metaphor for the infinite. But there is also a love of the natural world, with floral and faunal motifs tailored into lively arabesques. The old dogma that Islam prohibits the representation of the human form is simply not true; but figural representation belongs to the secular world, of manuscript painting and the minor arts, and certainly not the mosque. The one single most striking aspect of Islamic art is calligraphy – the calligraphy primarily of the Qur'an, but also the Arabic and Persian inscriptions found on monuments, in manuscripts and throughout all the minor decorative arts.

Carpets and textiles

~

WHAT KIND of Islamic art is one likely to encounter today in the West? Perhaps the most obvious form, and not immediately perceived as Islamic, is the carpet. With a long tradition stretching back at least as far as the ancient Near East, most carpets combine the two predominant Islamic themes – geometric forms and the arabesque – with infinite degrees of invention. This also applies to the rarer Islamic textiles – Persian silks and Turkish velvets spring to mind. For the collector the choice is vast, in size, style and range. Quite recently, a Persian carpet (once in the collection of the British Rail Pension Fund) sold for an all-time record of £236,500 ($437,525). But a pretty Susani hanging could cost less than £2,000 ($3,700), and a nice rug or Turkish textile half that. Carpet scholarship, if not exactly in its infancy, is still marked by imprecision; for the buyer, the surest ally is a reputable dealer, and a careful perusal of specialist literature on carpets and textiles, of which the highly attractive and well-designed journal *Hali* is way ahead of its competitors.

Ceramics

~

AFTER CARPETS, Islamic ceramics constitute a rich field for appreciation. Islamic pottery has been one of the predominant crafts since the 7th century, and in the early days of Islam represented a local

☞ *left*

SHRUB AND ARABESQUE CARPET

PERSIAN Late 16th – early 17th c.

Carpets are amongst the most widely encountered Islamic works of art. This Persian example was sold on behalf of the British Rail Pension Fund for £236,000 ($437,525) in 1990, a world record.

response to the wonders of imported Tang dynasty Chinese porcelain. But the Moslem potters were no mere imitators, and added a number of technical and stylistic innovations of their own to the history of world ceramics. In the early centuries they were renowned for the production of beautifully toned golden lustre-ware, again combining both figurative and naturalistic motifs. Originally found in Mesopotamia in the Abbasid period, the technique then appears in Fatimid Egypt, and later still in 12th century Iran, at Kashan and other centres, where it was used not only for the decoration of vessels but also for star-shaped and moulded tiles. There was even a revival of the technique in Persia in the Safavid period, in the 17th century. In 9th century Persia a unique form of earthenware was produced, with a cream-coloured slip decorated with symmetrically designed calligraphic inscriptions. This elegant, aristocratic ware was associated with the Samanids, and many examples were excavated by the Metropolitan Museum, New York, at Nishapur in North East Persia.

From the 14th century onwards, Chinese blue-and-white porcelain made its impact on the Middle East, and potters in Persia, Syria, Egypt and Turkey all came up with their own solutions to produce a blue-decorated ware in the Chinese style. Again, these imitations were distinctly Islamic, and the looser asymmetrical Chinese forms were standardized and used within more strictly geometric de-

☞ *right*

POTTERY DISH

TURKISH c.1580
This dish from the Iznik pottery, which was sold for £55,000 ($101,750) in 1990, bears the characteristic cintimani lattice pattern.

☞ *bottom left*

IZNIK TILE

TURKISH Early 16th c. Iznik was one of the most dominant Turkish potteries. Its early geometric tiles were tightly drawn. This was sold by Sotheby's for £12,000 ($22,385) in 1989.

signs. Particularly fine examples of hexagonal tiles in this style can be seen in the Murad II mosque at Edirne, the Ottoman Turkish capital on the European mainland in the 15th century, before the capture of Constantinople in 1453. In Turkey in the 16th century the famous potteries at Iznik initially produced tightly drawn designs for tiles and vessels in cobalt blue and turquoise; this monochromatic phase then evolved into a highly sophisticated combination of subtle colours and swirling, arabesque designs, and by the 1560s reached its peak with the introduction of a brilliant tomato red in relief under a flawless transparent glaze.

Court art in 16th century Turkey was epitomized by its consistency of style, whether the objects were of pottery, wood, metal, leather or any other medium. This was because many of the patterns were produced by the *nakkashane*, or court designers, to be executed by individual craftsmen. One of the most characteristic motifs were *cintimani*, combinations of three crescents and pairs of tiger-stripes. Probably of Central Asian origin, these unmistakably Turkish designs can be found on ceramics, textiles and woodwork. Depictions of the guild crafts-

☞ *above*

MAMLUK QUR'AN

EGYPTIAN 1488 A Qur'an, of which the frontispiece is shown, dedicated to Sultan Qa'it Bey and dated 894 AH. It fetched £88,000 ($162,000) at auction in 1982.

men in the Ottoman processions also show them at work on their floats – the glass-blowers with their furnaces, the potters with their wares for sale.

Woodwork and metalwork

WOODCARVING in the Islamic world in the early period survives in a series of panels with deeply cut arabesques. Fine examples can be found in Egypt, where the dry climate has helped preserve the organic material, and others come from Samarra, the Abbasid capital on the Euphrates north of Baghdad. In the Mamluk period, particularly in the 14th century in Syria and Egypt, the arts again have the sort of homogeneity found in Ottoman Turkey and Safavid Persia. Mamluk manuscripts have an unmatched refinement of style, in calligraphy and decoration, the latter frequently based on elaborate extensions of complex geometric forms. Exactly the same idiom can be found on Mamluk woodwork, on the carving of mosque furniture and fittings, such as doors; on Mamluk stonework, such as the decorative domes of tombs and shrines in Cairo and Jerusalem; and

even on leather, on the endcovers of Mamluk Qur'ans tooled with identical patterns. The Qur'an, indeed, may have been one of the major transmitters of style. Every year there was a great fair at Mecca at the time of the pilgrimage, and it is not difficult to imagine Qur'ans changing hands on that occasion, to be dispersed throughout the Islamic world.

Mamluk metalwork – brass basins, platters, stands, lamps and other forms – was inlaid with silver and gold, not only with abstract geometric patterns but also floral motifs often derived from Chinese sources such as the lotus, and – most

☞ *top*

CANDLESTICK

SYRIAN 13th or 14th c. Syrian enamelwork was every bit as splendid as Mamluk metalwork, as evidenced by this enamelled and gilt glass candlestick.

☞ *left*

AYYUBID EWER

EGYPTIAN Early 13th c. A brass, silver inlaid ewer, sold at auction in 1989 for £20,900 ($38,650). The best of Mamluk metalwork is without parallel.

interesting of all – figural medallions depicting rulers and courtiers, and even more curiously, scenes from Christian iconography. The eclectic splendour of Mamluk metalwork is unequalled. Parallel with it is the production of enamelled glass, beakers and hanging lamps, probably from Syria. A unique object, now in the Corning Museum of Glass, is an enamelled lamp, following a metal prototype in form. The enamelled patterns can be compared with those on a famous Mamluk glass beaker, the 'Luck of Edenhall', once in a private family collection in England and now in the Victoria and Albert Museum in London.

Western influences

INFLUENCES on Islamic art came not only from the East and Central Asia, but also from the West from the 16th century onwards. European goods filtered into the Islamic world, through Turkey, Syria and Persia, and had all the attraction of novelty. An English organ-builder, Thomas Dallam, took an example of his work, a mechanical organ, to Istanbul as a present from Elizabeth I to the Sultan. Gentile Bellini visited Istanbul and worked for several months for the Sultan Mehmet II in the late 15th century. French jewellers and European craftsmen are known to have been employed at the court of Shah Abbas I in Persia in the 17th century. In the 18th century and later, the emergence of an affluent middle class in the Islamic Near East meant that there was a new market for European textiles, and other goods.

In the 19th century western influences became even stronger with the advent of mass tourism. For instance, there were numerous photographers practising in Istanbul, Beirut, Jerusalem and Cairo in the second half of the century. In architecture, a style evolved in Ottoman Turkey which combined local necessity with European forms, and 'Ottoman Baroque' was born. The same style can be seen in Turkish silver.

JAPANESE WORKS OF ART
WILLIAM TILLEY

With Japanese art, we incline to think first of Commodore Perry, the bluff American naval officer who in 1853 started the process which ended for ever the two and a half centuries of peaceful seclusion which had kept Japan hidden from the world. In fact, the West had begun to take note of Japan and its art much earlier, and Japan's art had already long exercised its sway over the West.

Leaving aside Marco Polo, contact began with the missionary efforts of the Portuguese. They arrived in Japan in 1543 and were soon under the leadership of the Basque Jesuit Saint Francis Xavier. They were followed by the trading ventures of the Dutch through their East India Company, the famous VOC, or Vereenigde Oostindische Compagnie. This continued to function even after Japan closed its doors to foreigners and the company's members were confined to tiny Dejima island in the bay of Nagasaki. The second half of the 16th century and the first part of the 17th thus formed a great trading period between Japan and Portugal and Holland.

Portuguese (and to some extent Spanish and Italian) influence was largely responsible for the Momoyama style of decoration of this time. It mostly comprised

animals and birds among flowering trees and shrubs, executed in gilt painted lacquer and shell inlay. These features are found on religious objects such as shrines, missal-stands, and host-boxes made for the missionaries and their followers, and on coffers and chests-on-stands, many of which may still be found in western palaces, castles and country houses. To the Dutch the West also owes the vast importation of porcelain, made in the Arita area of Kyushu island and exported via the small port of Imari to the larger one of Nagasaki, and thence by Dutch ships to Holland.

As well as ordinary porcelain known as Imari, a particularly fine quality was pro-

duced, called Kakiemon after its originator, and this too was much favoured by western royalty and aristocracy. Attempts to copy it led to the creation of the European porcelain industry. These two art forms were largely intended for the export market and cannot therefore be called typically Japanese, although they would have been the earliest Japanese objects encountered by many westerners before the 20th century. Today, many of us have become familiar with such things as excavated Jomon pottery, bronze mirrors copied from the Chinese, bronze bells called Dotaku, Haniwa figures in terracotta, cypress-wood sculptures and other objects from Japan's early artistic history, but to our recent forbears Japanese art would have been mainly confined to the Edo period (sometimes called the Tokugawa period, from 1603 until 1868). The art of this period included painted screens and scrolls, woodcut colour prints, books, calligraphy, sculpture, ceramics, lacquer, costumes, armour, weapons and other metalwork.

The export market since the Edo Restoration

ALTHOUGH lacking the grand sculptural tradition of Heian and Kamakura, and the golden splendour of Momoyama, the Edo period was especially rich in the diversity and ingenuity of its art. The minor, or perhaps one should say miniature, arts flourished, such as, for example, the small sectional lacquer boxes known as *inro* or seal containers, and *tonkotsu* or tobacco containers; both of these were carried on the person, suspended from the *obi* or sash by means of a small carved toggle known as a *netsuke*. Small works of art such as these appealed greatly to the collecting instinct which prevailed in Europe during the prosperous years of the late 19th century, and quite fortuitously it was at this time that the Japanese decided to discard such objects.

Commodore Perry's arrival served as a trigger in releasing pent-up opposition to

☞ *left*
MOMOYAMA PERIOD CHRISTIAN PORTABLE SHRINE
JAPANESE c.1590
45.5 × 32 × 4.5cm
(18 × 12½ × 1¾in)
This Namban lacquer rectangular box is one of the few relics of Christianity's brief flowering in 16th century Japan. The Virgin and Child oil painting is Flemish.

☞ *opposite page*

IMARI TUREEN AND COVER

JAPANESE c.1700
29.5cm (11½in) diameter
This large tureen is decorated in iron red enamel and gilt on a blue underglaze. The decorative flowers include chrysanthemums, peonies and cherry blossom.

☞ *right*

GOD OF LONGEVITY NETSUKE

JAPANESE 18th c.
8.5cm (3¼in) high
This dancing figure of Fukurokuju, the God of Longevity, is from the Kuyoto school.

the Shogunate which had for years ruled Japan in a reactionary and tyrannical manner. The defeat in 1868 of the Shogunate and the restoration of real rather than symbolic power to the emperor in the person of the youthful Emperor Meiji began a fresh period marked by the new government's decision to embark on the complete westernization of the country. In the Meiji period, 1868–1912, vast quantities of objects which reminded the Japanese of their feudal past were labelled 'curios' and exported to the west. There they formed the bases of many collections of Japanese art.

Besides the *inro* and *netsuke* already mentioned, these exports included woodcut colour prints, looked on as a rather plebeian art by the Japanese, and swords and sword-fittings – not regarded as plebeian, but after the prohibition of sword-wearing sold in increasing numbers by the often impoverished *samurai* class. Collec-

tions were soon being formed of *tsuba*, or sword-guards, which, with *netsuke*, became extremely popular; they vary between the simple iron types with Zen-inspired designs favoured by the *samurai*, and the elaborately decorated soft-metal ones, often produced for the rich Edo merchant class.

Some other very collectable sword-fittings were the *kozuka*, or handle, of a small knife, the *kogatana*, carried in the scabbards of some swords; the *fuchi-kashira*, or paired fittings from each end of a sword's hilt, and the *menuki* – small metal fittings placed on each side of the hilt, usually under the hilt-binding which revealed them and the white sharkskin beneath them in regular diamond-shaped openings.

Even pottery tea-bowls and other items from the tea-ceremony joined the flood of objects shipped to the West. Since the Japanese were at heart a nation of potters

☞ *bottom*

INRO PIECES

JAPANESE 19th c.
A four-case dark brown ground inro decorated with gold inlay; a two-case 'roironuri' inro inlaid with gold; and a three-case Kinji inro inlaid with mother-of-pearl and showing Chinese figures.

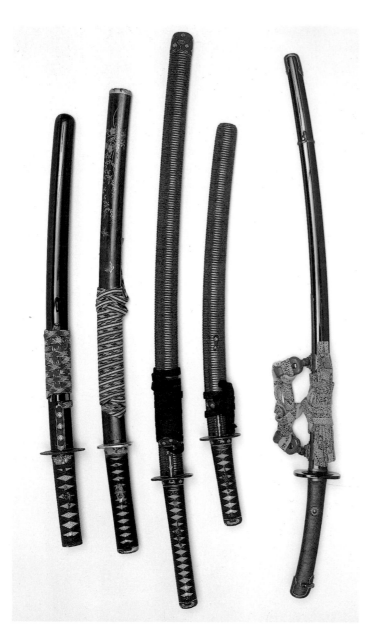

plates, elaborately detailed ivory carvings and richly decorated bronze vases and similar objects decorated in high relief with birds, flowers, insects and the like, all done with the greatest realism.

The makers of this 'Meiji Art', as we call it today, were often the sword-fittings craftsmen and other artists who had lost their former employment and now turned to new enterprises, sometimes organized by their old patrons, the better-educated *samurai*. There are, of course, some items of this type which predate 1868, often made for International Exhibitions, but it was in Meiji (1868–1912) and Taisho (1912–1926) that the trickle became a flood.

☞ above

SUZURIBAKO

JAPANESE 17th c.
A richly decorated writing box in gold, bronze and pewter showing bamboo, paulownia and hibiscus.

Key terms

RESTRAINT WAS hardly ever a feature of this new export art, and much of it can be described by the Japanese word *hade*, meaning flowery or florid, the converse being *shibui*, meaning astringent or restrained. Some knowledge of these terms may be helpful to the student of Japanese art. Another which he will encounter is *yugen*, literally meaning profound or mysterious, but difficult to define precisely since it is applied to something that really lies beyond art and can only be sensed intuitively. Sometimes translated as 'occult', it is evoked by simple forms which have in them 'the lines of eternity'.

Another word is *aware*, originally an expression of delight but later meaning gentle pleasure tinged with melancholy, a sadness that comes from the knowledge that beauty soon passes away. The terms

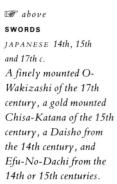

☞ above

SWORDS

JAPANESE 14th, 15th and 17th c.
A finely mounted O-Wakizashi of the 17th century, a gold mounted Chisa-Katana of the 15th century, a Daisho from the 14th century, and Efu-No-Dachi from the 14th or 15th centuries.

rather than decorators of porcelain, these were available in great quantity, and with them came beautifully decorated lacquer boxes, for example tiny ones to hold incense (*kogo*), larger incense boxes (*kobako*), writing boxes (*suzuribako*), document boxes (*bunko*, often made to match the *suzuribako*), and many others.

But the import of these Japanese art objects is only a part of the story of this 'age of enlightenment', for, as if its antique arts were not enough, Japan now turned to the wholesale manufacture of art for the western world. To this period belong ubiquitous Kaga and Satsuma wares, vividly coloured cloisonné enamel

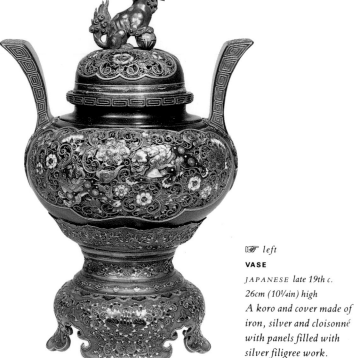

☞ *left*

VASE

JAPANESE late 19th c.
26cm (10¼in) high
A koro and cover made of
iron, silver and cloisonné
with panels filled with
silver filigree work.

☞ *above*

SATSUMA WARE

JAPANESE late 19th c.
48cm (19in) high
This large oviform vase is
decorated in various
coloured enamels and gilt.
The flowers in the basket
include peonies, wisteria,
and plum blossom.

☞ *right*

ANDO CLOISSONNÉ VASE

JAPANESE Meiji period
(1868–1912)
32cm (12½in) high
This ovoid vase is
decorated in various
coloured enamels on grey-
green ground, and shows
persimmons growing from
a branch.

wabi and *sabi* are better known and seem
to be passing into the western artistic
vocabulary, the first meaning rustic simplicity and unpretentiousness, while the
second is applied to things that are old or
imperfect, worn, tarnished or patinated.

To the collector, Japanese art brings the
special pleasure that comes from learning
something of the history and culture associated with an object, while it is always
pleasant to know, purely coincidentally,
that virtually all Japanese art collections
formed in living memory have shown a
steady increase in monetary value.

Many Japanese artists sign their work,
often adding a date and other information,
so that another pleasure lies in developing
the ability to read these inscriptions. It is
not difficult, and calls only for perse-
verance.

Finally, there is the subject-matter of
Japanese art, where the beginner/collector
enters a world rich in myth and legend, a
world of heroes, demons and monsters,
and strange creatures with supernatural
powers, yet always a world where the
Japanese artist shows his love of nature,
his curiosity and his acute observation of
the things around him. It would be difficult to find a form of art more satisfying
to collect.

ARMS AND ARMOUR

FRED WILKINSON

☞ *above*

DUELLING PISTOLS

ENGLISH *Late 18th c.*
*Duelling pistols were normally supplied in pairs with all
the necessary accessories. This pair was made by H. W.
Mortimer, one of the finest gunmakers of his time.*

Collecting arms and armour was a minority taste until after the end of World War II. It was probably the influx of American forces, many of whom were keen gun collectors, during the war which stimulated an interest among British collectors. Since then it has been a field that has constantly expanded with an increasing number of specialist dealers and books covering the many aspects of a fascinating and absorbing hobby.

Rising demand and value

As with any market the rising demand over the years has inevitably led to rising prices. This trend has slowed somewhat over the past year or so but in certain areas such as armour the upward rise continues. Good quality armour has more than retained its value even allowing for the rate of inflation and there is still a strong demand for good pieces. Next in popularity come antique firearms, followed by edged weapons and then, with a slightly smaller following, come sundry military objects lumped under the title of militaria.

No matter what is collected, knowledge is power and for those wishing to concentrate on arms and armour there are many good, reliable books to help the amateur. Similarly, there are a number of specialist auction houses and dealers who can be most useful to both the beginner and the expert.

In practical terms it is only possible to collect arms and armour dating from the 16th century onwards, although a few items of an earlier date may occasionally appear on the market. Most armour available to the collector is of the late 16th and 17th centuries. Swords from the Middle Ages and earlier periods do become available but the majority of edged weapons seen will be no earlier than the 16th century. Firearms have only been in general use from the 15th century.

☞ *above left*

HEAVY CLOSE HELMET

GERMAN c.1560
Probably made in Augsburg, this helmet was intended for battle, yet it is still well decorated with bands of etching and gilding.

☞ *above centre*

MEDIEVAL SWORDS

ITALIAN 1360–1400
Comparatively few swords from the Middle Ages survive. The rare Italian example on the right dates from about 1400, while the tapered blade sword on the left is earlier, dating from about 1360.

☞ *right*

THREE-QUARTER ARMOUR

EUROPEAN c.1650
Three-quarter armour was worn by some heavy cavalry units, the cuirassiers.

The development of armour

THE STORY of arms and armour is generally the story of an age-old competition between the weapon-maker and the armourer. Each sought to defeat the other and each advance in one field was usually matched by the other. Armourers were faced with a difficult task for they had to offer protection which would not hamper the wearer. Thus the old story of armoured knights falling and being unable to rise is nonsense. A trained knight could carry out any normal movements although he might well be hot and uncomfortable. The plates of the armour had to allow him to move with minimum restriction. The surface of the armour needed to be smooth so that there were no projections to catch an enemy's blade.

One of the earliest forms of armour was mail which was made up of small metal rings cleverly intertwined to allow ease of movement whilst protecting against a cut or thrust. Mail was limited in the amount of protection that it could offer for it was very vulnerable to the point of a weapon which could pierce the gaps or even the rings themselves. The armourer countered this by fixing plates to the mail, and as the process continued the body was more and more covered by plates until by the 15th century the warrior was protected from head to foot by a complete outer skin of plate armour.

The head was protected by a helmet which could be of many forms. The earliest which are available to collectors are mostly of the late 16th century such as the close helmet which completely enclosed the head. The lighter, less enclosing types were the morion and the cabasset which left the face unprotected. The most common 17th century forms were the burgonet and the pikeman's pot. The harquebusier or light cavalry man wore a helmet with a neckguard, two cheek pieces and a simple face guard. This might be a single bar which could be adjusted or a three bar guard fitted to a pivoted peak. The pikeman's pot was usually plain with a broad rather drooping brim. Nearly all these 17th century helmets are made of two sections whilst earlier examples have the skull cover fashioned from a single piece.

The body was protected by the cuirass, made up of a breast and back plate. Their styles changed over the centuries, ranging from the fluted Maximilian style to the late 16th century peascod shape and on to those worn by the heavy cavalry of the Napoleonic armies. Many breastplates will be found with a bullet mark on them but sadly the romantic idea of a soldier saved in battle is unlikely to be the case for these are almost certainly 'proof' marks. To demonstrate the quality of the plates they were tested by firing a musket at them and if the bullet failed to penetrate the subsequent dent demonstrated its strength.

By the 18th century most troops had abandoned armour. Although some cavalry retained a helmet and a cuirass, the arm defences and leg defences were no longer considered necessary. But armour was never completely discarded and a number of patented types were used during the American Civil War (1861–1865) and its use is continued today with soldiers and police wearing body armour. Some armour was also retained for bodyguards and ceremonial units, and examples of all such items do appear on the market.

Helmets, cuirasses and gauntlets which protected the hand are the most popular items sought after by collectors. They are more accessible and easier to handle and display than larger items of personal armour. Trench warfare in World War I led to the introduction of metal helmets for the troops and these can form an interesting and fairly cheap field of collecting.

Armour outside Europe

WHILST EUROPE used less and less armour from the 17th century onwards it was still worn by many Oriental warriors. In India, Persia, Turkey and parts of Africa the armour was often a mixture of plate and mail. The helmets usually had only an adjustable bar to guard the face but the neck and sides of the head were protected by a curtain of mail hanging from the rim of the helmet. In addition to the armour many of the troops carried a circular shield sometimes fashioned from elephant, hippopotamus or buffalo hide but also frequently of metal.

In Japan the armour was very different in construction and much of it was composed of small lacquered plates laced together into larger defences. The helmets, commonly surmounted by crests of many forms, usually have a metal skull and a neck defence of lacquered plates.

☞ *left*
SWORD
GERMAN *c.1570*
A superb sword from the armouries of the Elector of Saxony in Dresden. It has the long blade and blued hilt typical of these swords.

Swords and spears

AGAINST THE armoured soldier was ranged a formidable armoury of weapons intended to pierce his defensive shell. Some, like the spear and pike, were long and designed to make him keep his distance. Others, like the halberd, were a combination of axe and spear intended to chop and pierce. These were popular with ceremonial guards and many were richly decorated. Since they were fairly common they often appear at sales but their size makes them difficult to display.

The sword changed greatly over the centuries, developing from a weapon intended mainly to cut to one that was intended to thrust at undefended parts of the body or, in the hands of the cavalry, to slash at foot soldiers from above.

Swords came in all sizes up to the large two-handed swords nearly six feet in length. These were intended as a slashing weapon swept around in circles above the head and they proved formidable in the hands of the German and Swiss mercenaries of the 16th century. Some two-handed swords were never intended as weapons but were carried in procession as a status symbol.

In the 16th and 17th centuries there was a marked change in use and the rapier with its long, thin, stiff blade was developed as a thrusting weapon. The sword-hand was protected by a metal bowl – the cup-hilted rapier – or a pattern of metal bars – the swept hilt rapier.

The rapier encouraged the development of swordplay, and fencing schools were common during the 17th and 18th centuries. One style of fencing especially popular in Spain and lands around the Mediterranean featured the use of a sword and dagger. The rapier was wielded in the right hand whilst the left hand held a short dagger which was used to parry an opponent's blade. The left-hand dagger or *main gauche* was often decorated *en suite* with the rapier. Those from Spain usually have a wide, curved, triangular guard pierced with intricate patterns.

The need for a sword declined from the late 17th century. The rapier was reduced in size and became more decorative – less a weapon and more a costume accessory. These swords were known as small-swords and were often made with hilts of silver, brass or chiselled steel. They were worn by men of fashion until around the 1770s.

The military sword

THE SERIOUS weapon carried by soldiers was far less decorative and much more functional. The British infantry relinquished their short swords or 'hangers' around the mid-18th century but officers continued to carry theirs. From the end of the 18th century the design of the military sword was regulated by the government. This development took place throughout most of Europe and these 'official pattern' weapons form an interesting group on their own and are generally not too expensive. The details of the various patterns are fairly well documented and most are easy to identify. The type of sword differed for infantry and cavalry, and specialist units, like the pioneers, artillery and transport, had their own patterns.

There were many arguments over which type of sword was the best for the military. Some argued for a long, narrow-bladed thrusting weapon but others claimed that a broad-bladed sword designed to slash and cut would be much better. Many swords were designed to serve both purposes but nearly all these failed to serve well in either capacity. Much of the discussion was pointless anyway, since by the 19th century new technology meant that in Europe the sword could hardly be considered a serious military weapon.

In the East, however, the sword continued to play an important role. In India the range of shapes and types was considerable. The tulwar was probably the most common. It usually had a slightly curved single edged blade and a simple hilt with a disc pommel and a short cross-guard. The bladesmiths of Asia also produced a wide range of daggers, some of which, like their swords, were beautifully decorated.

The finest swords in the world were produced by the Japanese, and their simple lines and superb quality have attracted a keen following of collectors. The warrior class of Japan regarded their swords as an object of veneration and worthy of respect. However, by the 19th century they too were forced to realise that the day of the sword was over and the firearm was taking over.

☞ *left*

CEREMONIAL HALBERDS

*GERMAN Early 17th c.
Early halberds were
intended solely as
weapons, but as tactics
changed they became more
ceremonial.*

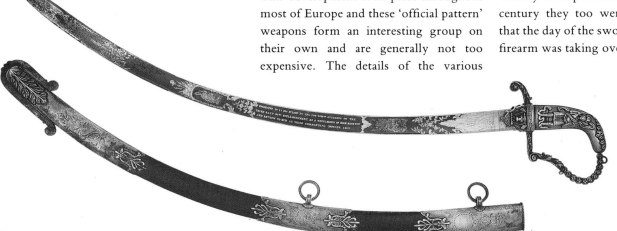

Early firearms

GUNPOWDER, a mixture of sulphur, charcoal and saltpetre, was first discovered in China, probably in the 11th century. The secret of its manufacture and use travelled slowly across the world and reached Europe probably in the 13th century. The first positive proof of guns is to be found early in the 14th century but from then on development was brisk. By the end of the 15th century many infantry were armed with muskets and armour was proving no longer to be an effective defence.

Muskets were loaded by pouring powder down the barrel and pushing the bullet down to sit on top of the powder. A small hole, the touch hole, was bored in the side of the near end of the barrel – the breech – and a small amount of powder was placed in a small pan adjacent to the touch-hole. This powder, known as the priming, was fired by pressing the glowing end of a piece of smouldering cord (the match) into it. The match was held in the jaws of a pivotted arm which was pushed down into the pan by pressure on the trigger. The flame from the priming passed through the touch hole and set the main charge alight which then exploded

and the expanding gases drove the bullet along the barrel. The 'matchlock' musket was simple and cheap but was at the mercy of wind and weather and the match had to be kept constantly glowing whenever action was likely.

In the 16th century a new system of generating fire to ignite the priming was developed. Sparks were produced by the friction between a piece of mineral, pyrites, and the roughened edge of a steel wheel. The great advantage of this mechanism, the wheel-lock, was that it could be loaded and the mechanism set so that the weapons could be made ready to fire in an instant. The system had some drawbacks as the mechanism was rather intricate and liable to malfunction.

Gunmakers continued to search for simpler methods and eventually perfected the flintlock. This system generated sparks by striking a piece of flint down the face of a steel plate. The sparks fell into the priming and so fired the weapon. The flintlock was efficient and was to continue in service for some two and a half centuries until it was displaced by an even simpler method.

Development

A SCOTTISH CLERGYMAN, Alexander Forsyth, devised a system of using certain chemicals known as fulminates to generate a flash to ignite the priming. These

fulminates detonated when they were struck a hard blow, and if a small quantity was placed over the touch hole and struck by a small swinging arm known as the hammer, it detonated, produced a flash and so ignited the powder.

There were difficulties in depositing a small amount in the right place but eventually in the 1820s a simple copper cap containing some fulminate, the percussion cap, was designed. This made a push-fit onto a small pillar known as the nipple which was connected by a small tube to the powder in the breech.

The mechanism was fairly robust and was soon being used in a whole range of weapons, including revolvers. The idea of the revolver had been around for many years but it was very difficult to produce an efficient flintlock revolver. The percussion cap changed this and soon American makers such as Colt, Smith and Wesson, and Remington were producing serviceable percussion revolvers. In Britain the leading manufacturers were Adams, Tranter, and Webley and by the middle of the century there were many types to choose from.

The percussion system was to last from about 1810 until 1865. This was when the new metal cartridge loaded directly in the breech was developed in America and England. The modern firearm had arrived. In general terms modern firearms are outside the ordinary collectors' scope since there are so many legal restrictions surrounding their possession.

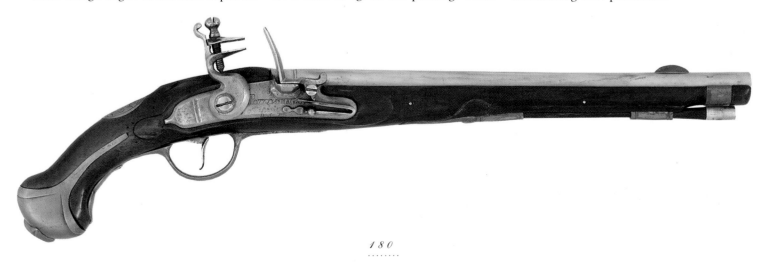

☞ *left*
**BREECH-LOADING
WHEEL-LOCK PISTOL**
GERMAN *c.1560*
*An extremely rare pistol
made in Augsburg, and
decorated overall with
inlay of horn plaques
engraved with hunting
topics. It was sold in 1983
for £50,000 ($92,500).*

Some people query the propriety of
collecting weapons with their connection
with violence but most collectors see
them as objects of craftsmanship. Many
are decorative works of art in their own
right and much armour has a grace and
beauty of form.

Militaria

MILITARIA RELIES less on its beauty and
more upon its intrinsic interest. Medals
obviously recall battles and bravery
whilst the uniforms and headdress sym-
bolize the glamour and colour of the past.
One great attraction of militaria must be
the range of material; books, medals,
buttons, uniforms, maps, postcards,
badges and equipment which can be collected at a cost well within the price range
of most collectors.

☞ *opposite page, bottom*
**PRUSSIAN FLINTLOCK
PISTOL**
GERMAN 1787
*A sturdy military pistol
from the Potsdam
Arsenal, it is dated 1787
although the pattern was
first introduced to the
cavalry in 1742.*

☞ *below*
PERCUSSION REVOLVER
ENGLISH *c.1865*
*A fine cased percussion
revolver made by one of
the best British
gunmakers William
Tranter. The revolver
has a double trigger which
allowed the weapon to be
fired quickly and
accurately.*

☞ *right*
FLINTLOCK BLUNDERBUSS
ENGLISH *Late 18th c.*
*The blunderbuss with its
wide muzzle was popular
as a defence weapon and
was carried by mail coach
guards. This example is
unusual in being decorated
with silver wire inlay.*

COINS,
MEDALS AND
STAMPS

☞ *above*

24c INVERTED JENNY

AMERICAN 1918

*Stamp errors are of particularly high value to collectors. In
1989, a collector bid $1 million for the unique 1918 24 cent
Inverted Jenny plate block.*

COINS AND MEDALS

RICHARD BISHOP

Coins have been collected for their own sake for many centuries. There are references to Greek coins among collections of precious vases and gems in Roman literature, and the cabinets of Renaissance princes were crowded with ancient coins and medallions. A find of English silver pennies of the 12th century recently caused experts to wonder if a 'coin collector' had buried his collection to protect it from the bands of mercenaries devastating the country during the early years of the reign of Henry II. Coins are depicted with loving attention to detail in the decorated margins of medieval manuscripts and printed books on coins date from the earliest years of printing.

In England the hobby has traditionally been the preserve of the parson, the academic and the country gentleman. Recently the appearance of investors and speculators, eager to spend large sums of money but not at all keen to devote time to serious study, has caused a few ripples on what is otherwise a tranquil scene. True coin collectors care less about commercial value than intrinsic historical interest but are prepared to pay for the rarest pieces.

The appeal of coins

To ANYONE unfamiliar with numismatics all coins look much the same, and the assumption is that if it is old, it must be valuable. Apart from that, coins are something of a mystery. Not many could be said to be beautiful, while some are quite crudely made and unappealing. Most are covered with illegible legends and indecipherable symbols, and have portraits which are of necessity simple and two-dimensional. They are not easy to display and usually end up in a small box in the bank. They do not inspire lively after dinner conversation except among like-minded enthusiasts, and then the conversation can become heated and obscure, so the question is a fair one – what makes numismatics such a fascinating subject, and coin collecting such an absorbing hobby?

The emphasis will vary from one collector to another but all will agree on one

basic principle. The numismatist must be a student of history. The very word, from the Greek *nomisma,* has its roots in ancient civilization and literally meant anything that was used as currency, not just the piece of metal we know today as a coin. *Nomisien* means 'to have in current use' and embraces all forms of wealth which were used in trade and for barter. The citizens of Sparta were not encouraged to accumulate wealth, and so they used heavy metal bars instead of coins. The early Romans used a bronze 'coinage' which frequently took the form of large blocks of bronze, cast in oblongs and simply decorated. They were exchanged by weight and quickly fell into disuse with the introduction of silver and gold. Numismatics includes such primitive forms of currency as wampum, shell or bead money used in North America, tea-

brick money used in China, the many forms of shell and feather money used in the Pacific islands, and even the massive and still mysterious great stone money of the island of Yap. The list is very long indeed, and each form of currency is an open door to a different culture, or an ancient civilization.

The root word *Nomisien* also gives a strong indication as to what numismatics is *not* about. It is not about modern proof commemorative sets of so-called coins, produced only for collectors and never intended to be used as currency. Such modern products usually have an intrinsic value far above their face value, and are sold with special packaging and numbered certificates. If they lose their carefully prepared proof surfaces, and become separated from their elaborate packaging, the majority of these coins are reduced to the level of bullion. They have almost no historical interest, and the collector who buys such a set must understand that he has strayed beyond the boundaries of numismatics and has entered the realms of the speculator.

The introduction of coinage

RECOGNIZABLE coins made their first appearance in the Eastern Mediterranean in about 600BC. There is no exact time or place, though the kingdom of Lydia under the immensely powerful and wealthy king Croesus (560–546BC) has long been regarded as the birth place of regular coinage. The speed with which precious metal coins ousted all other media of exchange was remarkable, and this has been the case whenever coinage has been introduced. Some regard the

☞ *left*
BRONZE COIN
ROMAN 37–41AD
A bronze coin struck under the Emperor Caligula, showing the head of Germanicus, the adopted son of the Emperor Tiberius.

☞ *centre, top*
DOUBLE DUCAT
DUTCH 1800
The ducat was used throughout Europe from the 12th century.

more primitive forms of money as the most interesting, revealing more about early civilizations than the more centralized and later mechanized products of a mint. For most, however, the story begins with the arrival of the true coin.

☞ *right*
BRONZE MEDAL
ITALIAN c.1655
A bronze medal in honour of Pope Alexander VII (1655–1667), commissioned by Domenico Jacobacci and engraved by Gioacchino Travani, after a design by Bernini, and valued in 1991 at £1000–1,200 ($1,850– 2,220).

Early collectors

THE EARLIEST coin collections were almost exclusively ancient Greek and Roman coins. The demand for good quality Roman bronze coins was so great in Italy in the late 14th century that elaborate copies, or even fantasies, were made by professional medal engravers. Petrarch was one of the earliest of these Italian collectors, while at the same time that great patron and collector, Jean, Duc de Berry,

☞ *above*
GOLD PRESENTATION MEDAL
GERMAN Late 17th c.
A very rare gold medal struck for presentation purposes by Johan Hugo von Orsbeck, Archbishop of Trier (1676–1711). Medals were universally popular from the 17th to 18th centuries, and huge quantities were privately commissioned. One like this was valued at £10,000–15,000 ($18,500–27,750) in 1991.

was including coins and medals among his many purchases. During the 17th and 18th centuries medals became as popular, if not more so, than coins. As a means of communicating political or religious ideas, the medal was ideal, being durable, portable and relatively inexpensive to produce. The coin and medal cabinet became a natural part of the educated man's library.

Alongside the interest in history, which at times was no more than superficial, there developed an appreciation of the artistic qualities of the best coins produced by the ancients and their Renaissance imitators. When an English collector placed an Anglo-Saxon penny, bold but crudely engraved, alongside a finely engraved ancient coin, the gulf separating the two was apparent. The demand for a more artistic coinage was frequently made then in Western Europe and North American from the 18th century, and is still to be heard today.

Collecting modern currency

IN THE United States the criticism of 19th century coinage grew to such a pitch that by the turn of the century it had become a matter of some urgency to find an acceptable series of designs for a planned

☞ *below*
'HIGH-RELIEF' 20-DOLLARS
AMERICAN 1907
Designed by the sculptor Saint-Gaudens, this is considered by many to be America's most beautiful coin. Its value to collectors was assessed in 1991 at about £8,000–12,000 ($14,800–22,200).

☞ *left*
MEDAL CABINET
FRENCH Mid 19th c.
25.4 × 20.3 × 22.8cm (10 × 8 × 9in)
A leather-covered mahogany medal cabinet, with 12 trays pierced to hold 127 medals of the Napoleonic era. Small cabinets were very popular among the wealthy middle classes in Europe. Complete with medals this cabinet is valued at £4,000–5,000 ($7,400–9,250).

new coinage. The sculptor Augustus Saint-Gaudens was commissioned to design the gold 10-dollar and 20-dollar pieces, and his 'Indian Princess' and 'Standing Liberty' designs won universal approval. The 20-dollar was struck in high relief, and at some considerable expense, in 1907. It was considered a coin which could rival those of the ancients in excellence of design and quality of workmanship. Unfortunately the experiment was too costly, and a much flattened version of the high relief coin eventually made its way into circulation. The modern coin however had taken its place among the best products of the ancients and the collecting of modern coins as a serious hobby was now accepted.

Collecting in Britain and Europe

IN ENGLAND there was less emphasis on artistic merit and more attention paid to historical context. Collectors were intrigued by the numerous issues of silver pennies put out by the Anglo-Saxon kings, their archbishops, and the Viking invaders who settled in the north of England and issued their own coinage in imitation of their southern neighbours. There was more interest in mint names, and the possible relationships between different coin types. When the Gothic Revival in England finally made an appearance on the coins of Victoria there was an outcry, not against the heavily crowded Gothic design of the

coins, but because the letters D.G. for Deo Gratia had been omitted from the 1849 florin. This so-called 'Godless' florin was quickly redesigned and the missing letters restored. The conservatively-minded English coin collector was very much a product of Victorian society.

All over Europe coin collectors concentrated on the coins of their own countries. Coins reflect both a country's history and its aspirations and it was natural that collections based on place of origin should develop. Today the coin markets in the industrialized West are for the most part distinct, with domestic coins dominating, sometimes to the point of totally excluding all others. It is not uncommon for a large coin auction to be held in Germany or the United States in which every one of the thousands of coins on offer are exclusively of German or American origin.

Coin grading

OVER THE YEARS various systems of grading coins have developed. In America a numerical system based on a scale of 1 to 70 has been introduced, in which 1 is the lowest grade possible – the coin would be flat and with a hole in it to warrant this grade – and 70 is flawless, and so probably unobtainable. The European grades, verbal descriptions, correspond roughly to every ten of the American grades. Thus good = 20, fine = 30, very fine = 40, extremely fine = 50 and mint state = 60. Numerical grading has until recently been applied only to American coins, but the intention is that eventually these numbers will be used for all types of coins from all periods. Whether this will ever come about is not certain, but it is certainly true that to date there is no agreement among American numismatics about the detailed working of this numbered system. The collector who wishes to specialize in American silver dollars must worry about the application of these numbers, but for the majority of coin collectors adjectival descriptions are sufficient.

☞ *above*

ANGLO-SAXON SILVER PENNY

ENGLISH *Early 9th c.*
This silver penny in the name of Wulfred, Archbishop of Canterbury (805–832), is an extremely fine example of the vigorous, simple portraiture on Anglo-Saxon coinage. It was valued at £4,000–6000 ($7,400–11,100) in 1991.

☞ *above*

GEORGE III HALF-GUINEA PROOF STRIKING

ENGLISH *1787*
The portrait is clearly inspired by the busts of Roman coinage while the whole design has been reduced to the bare essentials. It was valued at £600–800 ($1,110–1,480) in 1991.

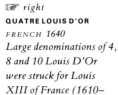

☞ *right*

QUATRE LOUIS D'OR

FRENCH *1640*
Large denominations of 4, 8 and 10 Louis D'Or were struck for Louis XIII of France (1610–1643), apparently for use at the king's gaming table. Louis D'Or are valued at £50,000–60,000 ($92,500–111,000).

Acquiring coins

☞ *above*

GOLD 20-YEN

JAPANESE 1880
*A gold 20-yen coin of the
Emperor Mutsuhito
(1867–1912), dated
Meiji 13 (1880), a rare
early example of the
largest of Japan's machine
made gold coins. It was
valued in 1991 at
£80,000–100,000
($148,000–185,000).*

☞ *left*

**QUEEN MARY 30 GOLD
SOVEREIGN**

ENGLISH 1553–1554
*A 'fine' gold sovereign of
30 shillings from the short
reign of Mary Tudor. It is
a good example of the
crowded Gothic style
which was evident in
English coinage until the
mid-17th century. This
one was valued at
£3,000–4000 ($5,550–
7,400) in 1991.*

☞ *above*

CHARLES I GOLD UNIT

SCOTTISH c.1625
*This Scottish gold unit of
Charles I was engraved
by Nicholas Briot. Briot
was so proud of his skill
that he frequently signed
his work. In this example
his tiny 'B' can be seen
above the king's head.
The coin's value is about
£1,800–2,200 ($3,330–
4,000).*

THE COIN MARKET has grown rapidly since the 1970s. There have been several 'boom' periods, but also some corresponding slumps. Most experienced coin collectors are not seriously affected by these movements in the market. Nowadays, specialist markets and dealers provide an almost overwhelming choice, with every type of coin now available, and even the most obscure collecting interests catered for. The popularity of some types of coin is universal – ancient Greek and Roman are the most popular, while others are hardly in demand at all. This is the result of the recent growth in the economies, and therefore the increase in the numbers of collectors, of some countries. For example, Japanese coin prices have soared in response to a huge increase in demand.

The novice collector however need not be daunted by the wide range, both historical and geographical, available today through public auctions and dealers' lists. For most the question of what to collect is answered automatically by a natural inclination to a certain type of coin, the gold sovereign, the silver coin or the copper token. Alternatively it may be an attraction to a certain period, such as the age of the 'Twelve Caesars' (the 1st century AD), or the Tudor and Stuart monarchs (the 16th and 17th centuries).

For many the choice is also determined by how much the collector is prepared to spend on any particular coin. Roman gold coins are on the whole expensive, but Roman silver coins can be collected for as little as £20–£50 ($37–$90) each, while small Roman bronze coins can cost even less than this. Age is in fact not relevant when pricing a coin. What matters is how desirable is the coin, not necessarily how rare, and how many collectors actually want it.

☞ *left*

THE MILLION POUND NOTE

ENGLISH
*Perhaps the most famous
of banknotes, this
example was allowed to
be kept by a high-ranking
Treasury official only
after it had been officially
cancelled. Collecting
banknotes is a small but
important part of
numismatics and this one
was valued in 1991 at
£20,000–25,000
($37,000–46,250).*

The importance of condition

WHETHER HE specializes, or remains a general collector, the novice quickly comes to appreciate the importance of condition. The value of a coin can vary greatly according to its quality, and indeed some coins which are common in very worn condition are practically unobtainable in mint state. This is particularly true of base-metal coins, which were not precious enough to be carefully looked after at the time they were in circulation, and is less true of gold coins which tended to be handled with care from the moment they were produced. A collector who decides to concentrate only on the highest quality of anything other than modern issues must be prepared to spend a very long time building up his collection.

The best compromise between rapidly buying whatever is available and never acquiring a coin because the finest quality cannot be found, is to buy as good as you possibly can and be ready to up-grade whenever possible. All sale catalogues and dealers' lists offer coins that are graded, enabling the collector to buy with confidence. If the grade stated is wrong or misleading and the dealer is reputable, then the coins can always be returned.

There has been some concern among collectors recently about the increase in the number of coin hoards being discovered. The sophistication of metal detectors makes hunting for 'buried treasure' a far simpler and more lucrative task than it was 20 years ago. Hoards of ancient and medieval coins are discovered in Britain and mainland Europe every week of the year, many of them containing hundreds, some even thousands, of coins. There is always the danger that what is rare and valuable today will be plentiful and inexpensive tomorrow. Underwater exploration has been developed to a point where wrecks can be located and examined, and even the contents salvaged, by remote control. Hundreds of wrecks around the world are currently being examined in this way.

None of this need worry the coin collector unduly if he has collected for pleasure, not for profit. The pleasure to be derived from finding and acquiring interesting and beautiful coins cannot be dulled by the activities of speculators or treasure hunters, and can only increase as the collection grows. The coins illustrated on these pages are all in extremely fine condition and in many cases are very

expensive. It must be remembered that these are examples of exceptional quality. An excellent coin collection can be made for a fraction of this cost and the modest collector can find good examples of medieval or modern coins for under £50 ($95). Coins can be collected at every level, and the history, religion, portraiture, heraldry, mythology and artistry of 2,500 years of civilization can be enjoyed by all.

☞ *left*

THE PONTEFRACT UNITE
ENGLISH *1648–49*
The unique gold Pontefract Unite, part of the emergency coinage struck during the siege of Pontefract in the name of Charles I. Siege pieces were often struck from silver plate using locally prepared dies. Gold examples are very rare and could be worth £25,000–30,000 ($46,250–55,500).

☞ *left*

BADGE OF THE GARTER
ENGLISH *Early 17th c.*
An extremely fine sash badge of the Garter, possibly a gift from Charles II to the 1st Duke of Beaufort. Orders of Knighthood and other decorations come under the heading of numismatics though they bear little resemblance to coins. A badge of quality would be worth £50,000–70,000 ($92,500–129,500).

STAMPS

TIMOTHY HIRSCH

The first adhesive postage stamp was brought into official use on 6 May 1840 and even at the time attracted considerable interest. One of the earliest chronicled stamp collectors in London was a solicitor, Robert Cole, working during the 1830s in Throgmorton Street and, from 1840, in Lothbury.

Robert Cole's collection, housed in a scrap book, comprised in part a number of first day cover cancellations including those for 5 December 1839 – the first day of the penny postage for the London District. More importantly, it contained a fine '1d black' used on a wrapper dated 6 May 1840 from Robert's daughter Augusta to her father, bearing his endorsement 'the first day of the use of postage stamps'. The collection was sold in a

series of 29 lots at auction by Christie's in September 1986 and the 6th May cover realized £8800 ($16,250), from a total of over £20,000 ($37,000) for the whole collection.

In many respects, Robert Cole was a collector of the future and was ahead of his time with his specialization and his emphasis upon postal history – the changing postal rates and postal markings. This aspect of collecting really developed as a separate discipline during the 1930s and only in more recent years has its full potential been realized.

For many Victorians, postage stamp collecting was generally unsophisticated and the aspirations of most were limited to gathering a collection of as many different stamps as possible from as wide

a range of countries around the world. There was little degree of specialization and concepts of completion were of lesser importance. The primary concern lay with the design image and questions of paper type, perforation, watermark or shade were unnecessary complications.

Valuing stamps

MANY FAMILIES have a collection of stamps which has been passed down, and frequently they hope that within such old accumulations there may be items of value and importance. However, the two key factors which must be carefully assessed are rarity and condition. Unlike most works of art which are unique or produced in very small or limited editions, stamps, in most cases, are prepared in essentially limitless quantities. For example, over 60 million 1d blacks were produced for use, so what gives a Penny Black value is more its condition or aspects of its usage rather than the fact that the stamp is a Penny Black. A space-filler example, suitable for inclusion in a young person's collection, might be obtainable for a few pounds or dollars whilst a very fine used example for a specialized collector might achieve an auction realization over £100 ($185). A fine unused example with the original cement or gum on the reverse would bring over £1,000 ($1,850); a premium

☞ *left*
PENNY BLACK
BRITISH 1840
A 1d black first day cover – 6 May 1840 – the very first adhesive postage stamp. This was sold in 1986 for £8,800 ($16,280).

☞ *opposite page, top*
CHRISTMAS ISSUE PROOFS AND ARTWORK
CANADIAN 1898
The proofs and artwork for this 1890s Christmas

stamp issue from the Canadian Bank Note Archives were sold in New York in 1990 for $60,500.

☞ *opposite page, bottom*
LARGE DRAGON COVER
CHINESE 1885
A Chinese large dragon cover sent to Copenhagen, and sold in Zurich in 1990 for Swf. 32,625 (about £10,000/ $18,500).

would be paid for pairs, blocks or multiples of larger size. A similar emphasis upon condition also applies to the renowned triangular stamps of the Cape of Good Hope and the classic stamps of most other countries from around the world.

In other instances, rarity is the crucial factor in determining the value of a stamp. Rarity is a difficult concept to define as different collectors may look at it from a range of standpoints. What is rare to a young collector may simply be unobtainable with the limited means at his disposal whilst an experienced collector may consider a rarity to be a stamp which is unique or virtually so. Rarity must also reflect demand or popularity. A unique stamp from a country which has little following at a given moment in time may achieve a much lower price than a numerically more plentiful stamp from a country actively sought after by a number of monied collectors from around the world. Stamps are not unique in being subject to the prevailing forces of supply and demand.

For example, for the 1d red stamps of Great Britain issued between 1858 and 1879, most are of minimal value but examples from plate 77 are worth around £50,000 ($92,500)! There are nine recorded examples (one of which was unfortunately lost in the San Francisco earthquake) from this plate which was rejected at the time of printing because of the irregular spacing of the stamp subjects.

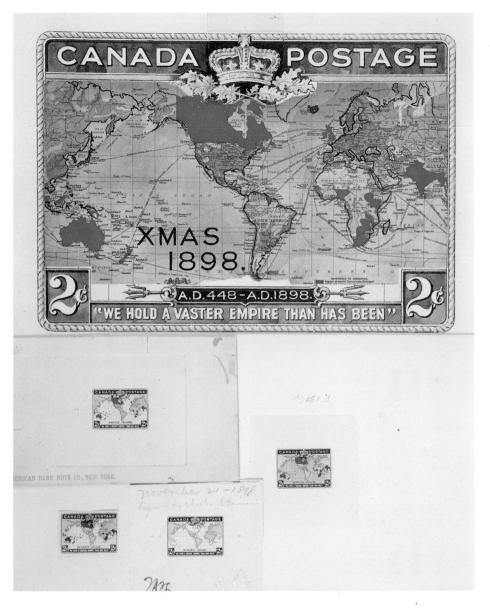

Specialized collecting

THE LAST 150 years of collecting have resulted in a market of increased specialization, with most collectors today concentrating on the stamps of one country or a group of countries. There is a greater emphasis on collecting proofs and essay material relating to the production of stamp issues, featuring items from the archives of the various security printers such as De La Rue, Bradbury Wilkinson or the American Bank Note Company.

During the late 1980s and early 1990s the market in the stamps and postal history of the Far East has expanded considerably, with strong interest not only from Europe and the United States but more importantly from the Far East itself. This rising interest has been broadly based embracing the market for early issues of China, Japan and Thailand.

Probably the most well known stamp of China – the Small Dollar provisional of 1897 – ranks amongst the world's rarest and most valuable stamps. There are 32 recorded examples and in November 1989 an example brought SwFr 315,000 ($270,000) at auction in Zurich.

Generally the issued stamps which are

the most valuable are the classic stamps of countries from the 19th century, although almost without exception the condition of such stamps must be very high to attract the greatest interest. The early issues from many European countries are popular, including the various German and Italian states as well as the first issues of Switzerland.

☞ *left*
INVERTED FRAME 1s
JAMAICAN 1920
A 1/– variety stamp with inverted frame which sold in 1990 for £13,200 ($24,400), showing the value to collectors of unusual errors.

Errors and varieties

WITHIN TRADITIONAL philately, errors and varieties have always been popular and have achieved high prices at auction. Such errors may be variations of printing or perforating, or may arise at other stages in the production of the stamps themselves. Whilst there may have been many hundreds of thousands, or in more recent times, many millions of a particular stamp printed, only a few examples might exist showing some error of printing or production.

An outstanding illustration of the remarkable prices achieved for major errors at auction is also the highest price ever paid for a US stamp. In October 1989, at a Christie's auction for the sale of the Weill brothers' stock, a collector bid $1 million for the unique 1918 24 cent Inverted Jenny plate block. A single sheet of 100 24¢ airmail stamps was purchased for $24 by a William T. Robey on May 14, 1918, at the New York Avenue Post Office in Washington, D.C. The sheet was shortly afterwards sold for $15,000 and was subsequently broken up for sale.

☞ *left*
A SELECTION OF COLLECTOR'S ITEMS
BRITISH 1840–7
An 1840 1d black plate 2 marginal block, sold in 1990 for £6,600 ($12,200). An 1840 1d black plate 7 block of four on experimental thin paper, sold for £5,720

($10,500). An 1840 2d blue marginal block of six, sold for £14,300 ($26,400). An 1847 10d mint corner block of four, sold in 1990 for £9,900 ($18,300).

With stamps printed in more than one stage, errors are more likely to occur in printing. The US Inverted Jenny may be a spectacular example but other such inverts are known. These may not have achieved the same level of value at auction but have nevertheless still excited the interest of specialized collectors.

The 1920 one shilling stamp from Jamaica comprises two parts to the design printed in similar colours – orange-yellow and red-orange. In March 1922 about ten examples were found with the frame inverted, these being the remains of a half sheet of 30 stamps sent to Manchioneal Post Office. It is believed that the other half sheet was sent to Kingston G.P.O. Only about 20 examples in total are known. In May 1990 a mint example brought £13,200 ($24,000) at auction in London.

Other mistakes may occur in the printing of multicoloured stamps. In 1964 a set of four stamps was issued by the Falkland Islands to commemorate the 50th Anniversary of the Battle of the Falklands. A single sheet of the 6d value was printed in error with the centre design showing HMS Glasgow instead of HMS Kent. The error was not noticed when the sheet was broken up for distribution by a new issue dealer in the United States at the time of issue and was only recognized later. A maximum of sixty examples exist and as yet the vast majority still remain to be identified. Examples of this error achieve between £7,000 and £12,000 ($13,000–22,000) at auction, depending upon condition.

Examples of other printing errors include the 1879 Western Australia 2d stamp printed in lilac (the colour of the 6d) instead of yellow. A very few examples of the 3d Baden Powell stamp from the Siege of Mafeking during the Anglo-Boer war are known to exist with the design printed in reverse – with the portrait looking to the left instead of to the right and with the lettering backwards. It is thought that only a single sheet of twelve of this variety was produced. Both this and the Western Australia error of colour would fetch several thousand pounds when offered at auction.

Another notable error occurred in 1953 when the definitive stamps of Malta were re-issued overprinted 'SELF GOVERNMENT' and the 1½d denomination was issued in a revised colour – green. The stamp was never officially issued without the overprint although about five used examples are recorded. In March 1990 an example realized £8,800 ($16,200) at auction in London whilst a further example, although slightly less fine, was sold for £5,500 ($10,000) in November of the same year. The normal stamp would be worth no more than 5 pence (10 cents).

Postal history

THE CONCEPT of postal history and the illustration of the history of the postal service and the conveyance of mail has developed as an area of collection during the last twenty years. During this time, there has also been an increased emphasis upon specialization and popular themes include airmail postal history or military mail. This might include covers from members of the British Armed Forces serving overseas, from the Zulu Wars in southern Africa or from the many conflicts in the Middle or Far East.

As an illustration, early pioneer flights have always captured the imagination of stamp collectors and the early attempts to fly the Atlantic are no exception. In 1919 Captain F. P. Raynham and his navigator Major Charles Morgan first attempted the crossing on 19 April. A second attempt was made on 19 July but in both cases Raynham and Morgan only managed to fly a few hundred yards. On 21 July Captain Raynham set sail for England on the S.S. Grampian taking with him the bag of mail salvaged from the Raymoor. This contained some sixty envelopes. It was not until January 1920 that the bag of mail was delivered to the postal authorities in London, when the contents were postmarked '7 January 1920' and delivered the following day. Of the 60 envelopes about 30 were franked with a special manuscript overprint by W. C. Campbell, the Secretary to the postal department. An example, addressed to the Rt. Hon. Albert H. Illingworth, Postmaster General of Great Britain 1919–21, recently brought £18,700 ($34,000) at auction.

The appeal of stamps

THE ALLURE of stamp collecting lies in the broad appeal of the hobby, the freedom which it gives to the collector to pursue his own line of acquisition, tailored to his own financial resources. In the long term, stamps have increased in value, reflecting not only inflationary pressures but also the vagaries of fashion and popularity. Some stamps today are cheaper than ten, 20 or even 50 years ago whilst others are worth infinitely more. The financial rewards from collecting stamps generally accrue to those who have formed a specialized collection over a reasonable period of time. Such a collection would include the major rarities and would have an even balance between stamps, production proofs and essays as well as the postal history of a particular country or subject. Those who have attempted to speculate in a narrow portfolio of generally unrelated items greatly increase the risk of incurring a loss associated with their investment and are most subject to changing fashion and market levels. As with most investments, stamps can move up or down in value.

During the late 1970s there was a rapid but unsustained increase in stamp values underpinned by investment speculation. In 1980 the market reversed and, even after ten years, many prices did not recover to the levels of 1978–1979.

For many people, a collection of stamps from countries overseas may have been their first introduction to the history and geography of those territories. For most, the sense of collecting was far removed from the investment potential of their collection and ideally that is the basis upon which most people should pursue a collection of stamps.

☞ *below*
MANUSCRIPT
MARTYNSIDE
PROVISIONAL
CANADIAN 1919

A Newfoundland provisional on airpost cover, which was sold for £18,500 ($34,500).

CLOCKS, WATCHES AND SCIENTIFIC INSTRUMENTS

☞ *above*

AUGSBURG MASTERPIECE

TABERNACLE CLOCK

GERMAN c.1600

This Augsburg 'Meisterstuck' gilt-metal tabernacle clock
has 18th century enamelled dials.

CLOCKS AND WATCHES

RICHARD GARNIER

The first mechanical clocks were made sometime in the late 13th century for monasteries to call the monks to prayer, but by the mid-14th century most European cities had at least one public clock. These early clocks were sited near ground level and did not strike the hours. It was not until the mid-16th century that public clocks were first placed in towers, so that the sound of their bells could be heard over the city.

Meanwhile the earliest domestic clocks had been developed in Northern Italy, Switzerland, Germany and France. Made to be hung on walls, these chamber clocks were, of course, smaller than public clocks, but were still quite bulky. Of open-frame construction, they were decorated with Gothic pinnacles and crockets and surmounted by a bell housed within a spire.

Tower and chamber clocks were driven by weights. However, it was not until the late 15th century that the mainspring (a coiled driving spring) was made, thereby making portable clocks possible. The earliest surviving examples date from the early 16th century and they are relatively common from about 1550 onwards.

The first watches were really just small portable clocks that could be slung on a cord round the neck. They originated in Nuremberg in the early 16th century, but the art of making them soon spread round the courts of Europe. These early clocks and watches had drum-shaped cases made of engraved gilt-brass. By the end of the 16th century watches were often oval in shape, and after 1600 they could also be octagonal or modelled after naturally occurring objects and animals, such as flowers and skulls. These are known as form watches. The cases are constructed of gilt-brass, silver or gold, often set with rock crystal or gem stones, or are enamelled.

Early decoration

~

Until the early 17th century enamelling was either in the Limoges tradition of painted enamel or of colours separated by dividing strips of raised metal. However, around 1630 the goldsmith Jean Toutin of Blois developed the art of painting in coloured enamels on an opaque white ground. This technique required successive firings of the enamel but produced exquisite miniatures of flowers, religious subjects or, sometimes, portraits. The Blois enamellers did not sign their work.

☞ *left*
HUAUD WATCH
SWISS c.1680
This watch is typical of the work of the Huaud family of Geneva in its bright colours.

☞ *above*
BLOIS FLORAL WATCH
FRENCH c.1650
Blois enamellers produced exquisite renditions of flowers on very small surfaces, as on this gold floral watch.

The leading enamellists in the last quarter of the 17th century were the Huaud family of Geneva. Their subjects were not original, being generally copied from early 17th century paintings, but they achieved unsurpassed richness of colour in their garnet red, bright blue and yellowy-orange watch-cases, which were signed on the band.

In reaction to the profuse decoration of much early 17th century casework, some English makers produced a completely undecorated type of oval watch with bowed covers, known as a Puritan watch. At the same time, while weight-driven chamber clocks were declining in popularity elsewhere, the English developed a local form, known as the lantern clock. These are of posted-frame construction (like the frame of a four-posted bed) but with turned columns rather than Gothic pillars. Pierced frets fill the space between the top of the frame and the bell above. The style was established in London by 1620, and they continued to be made there until about 1700, whereas in country towns their production continued up to the end of the 18th century.

17th century German clocks

WEIGHT-DRIVEN clocks were more suited to the skills of the English makers who had less of a tradition of clockmaking behind them. In Germany, on the other hand, most clocks made in the 17th century were spring-driven. By 1580 most canister-cased clocks were square and in the 17th century many were hexagonal, both types with the dial on the horizontal upper surface. The bases, which contained the bells, were hinged and stood on feet. These feet were at first cast in the form of animals or fruit but by 1620 were mainly of turned shapes. Another type of German table clock of the same time was the tabernacle clock. It was made in the form of a miniature tower, with the dials on the vertical sides, and

with subsidiary dials that had complex calendar indications. The most complicated of these are known as masterpieces as they could serve as qualification pieces for an apprentice to become a master clockmaker under guild regulations. Tabernacle clocks continued to be made until the end of the 17th century and hexagonal table clocks until well into the 18th century.

German fantasy clocks of the 17th century are the counterpart to form watches of the same date. They exhibit an extraordinary variation in design, many being in the form of animals, urns or monstrances, while others depict a Calvary with the crucified Christ flanked by two saints. Some of these clocks have an automaton action working in time to the strike of the hours.

English bracket and longcase clocks

UNTIL THE invention of the pendulum, none of these clocks was more accurate than a quarter of an hour fast or slow in a day. Galileo first realized the likely effect of a pendulum, but it was the Dutchman Christian Huygens who, in 1656, first

successfully applied one to a clock. He then put Salomon Coster of the Hague to making pendulum clocks under his patent. The Fromanteel family in London heard of the new invention and sent a younger son, Johannes, over to Coster in 1657 to learn the art. On his return in 1658 the Fromanteels were able to advertise clocks that 'go exact and keep equaller time than any now made without this Regulater'.

The pendulum rendered clocks accurate to within three minutes a week and resulted in two new types of clock in England: bracket and longcase clocks. The first are spring-driven and intended to stand on pieces of furniture, but occasionally were provided with the wall brackets that have given them their name. Longcase clocks are floor standing weight clocks. What immediately marks both out from their predecessors is that the cases are made of wood, in contrast to the metal cases of most clocks previously. These cases had classical columns at the angles supporting a full entablature of frieze and cornice, topped by a pediment, and as a result the years 1660 to 1675 are known as the architectural period in English clockmaking.

By 1675 bracket clock cases had become a rectangular box with a base moulding reflecting the cornice and topped by a cushion-shaped moulding. Longcase clocks retained an architectural vestige in angle columns (now either straight or spiral) and a frieze and cornice. But their tops were no longer pedimented, being left flat or having a cushion-moulded caddy as with bracket clocks. A gradual progression occurred in the size of longcase dials in the late 17th century, from 8 inches square in 1660 to 12 inches square after 1700. Then from about 1720 the basic square shape was augmented by an arched extension at the top, and this arched shape was repeated in the long door to the trunk about ten years later. Meanwhile, also in about 1720, the throat moulding between the hood and the trunk of the case was reversed from convex to concave. Bracket clock dials were initially

☞ *left*

TABLE CLOCK

GERMAN c.1630
German 17th century clocks were usually spring-driven, enabling them to be made to table size.

☞ *left*
ARCHITECTURAL
LONGCASE CLOCK
ENGLISH *c.1675*
This Charles II ebony
architectural longcase
clock has an 8 inch dial
made by Joseph Knibb.

☞ *centre*
BRACKET CLOCKS
ENGLISH *1690–1790*
Bracket clocks are spring-
driven and hence can
stand on pieces of
furniture. However, they
were often fixed to the
wall with brackets, hence
the name. They remained
very popular throughout
the 18th century.

☞ *far right*
LONGCASE CLOCK
ENGLISH *c.1740*
Japanning replaced
marquetry on English
longcase clocks in the
early 18th century.

7 or 8 inches square, but by 1670 had shrunk to 5 or 6 inches square, although they too became arched from the early 1720s. In about 1710 the tops of bracket clocks started to develop an ogee outline of two opposing curves known as an inverted bell top. These curves were reversed by 1760 into the shape known as the bell top.

The earliest of these longcase and bracket clock cases were of ebony or ebonized pearwood veneered on an oak carcass. Such black finishes soon fell out of favour for longcase clocks, but for bracket clocks remained just as fashionable as showier woods up to the end of the century. By 1670 burr walnut was starting to be used, initially with parquetry inlay of geometric stars or ovals on longcase trunk doors. Floral marquetry, at first (1673–8) with pieces of green-stained bone for the leaves in the design, followed parquetry. Initially in oval or shaped panels on the case plinth and trunk door, this floral marquetry by 1685 has coalesced into one composition on the plinth

and trunk door. Then seaweed marquetry (sinuous foliage patterns) came into vogue, and by 1710 had spread over the whole front surface of the case. It must, of course, be remembered that there were more plain burr walnut than marquetry cases made, although some have been 'improved' with new marquetry in the late 19th century in order to increase their value. By now these altered cases can be difficult to detect from completely 'period' examples.

From 1700 marquetry decoration fell out of favour in relation to japanned (imitation oriental lacquer) decoration. The most popular (and therefore expensive) japanning today are the bright colour examples in yellow, scarlet, blue and green. However, the most frequently found lacquer cases are of a comparatively dark colour. Over all the ground colours there is normally a raised gilt decoration of chinoiserie landscape scenes with figures. About 1750 walnut, which had for 30 years been used in straight grained veneer, was superseded by mahogany,

after a similar changeover in furniture. By the end of the 18th century some cases were veneered with satinwood, and in the Regency and Victorian periods rosewood was frequently used. From the 1760s longcase clocks made in country districts had much fussier cases than London ones, often with clustered columns at the angles and with pointed Gothic doors.

Longcases had ceased being made in London by 1820, and died out in the provinces a few years later. Bracket clocks were made until around 1830, when they became smaller (and often with a flat top) and are known as mantel clocks.

All through the 18th century English clocks and watches were considered superior to any others. In England the clockmakers dictated the form of their cases, whereas in France it was the *ébenistes* (cabinetmakers) who controlled the piece. French clocks therefore follow closely the decorative fashions prevalent in furniture, metalwork and porcelain, without the time lag there is in England.

composition. A common type of clock has the movement and dial supported on the back of an animal (an elephant, bull, rhinoceros or horse, generally). Others have cast ormolu or porcelain figures on rock bases surrounded by a bower of flowers in porcelain. In the second half of Louis XVI's reign with the rise of Neo-classicism, a more sober style prevails, characterized by rectilinear forms and a return to architectural decoration. The 19th century saw an abundance of ormolu and porcelain-mounted mantel clocks fashioned in a series of revivals of previous Gothic, Renaissance, Baroque, Régence and Rococo styles, often in an eclectic mix.

Watches

THE INTRODUCTION of the balance-spring to watches had as revolutionary an effect on timekeeping as the pendulum had had on clocks.

Watches were invariably circular through the 17th and 18th centuries. French examples of 1680–1720 are known as *oignons* because of the onion-like shaped single cases, whereas in England slightly flatter watches were developed

with a pair of cases. These pair-cased watches were the envy of all Europe and copied widely, especially in Holland where Swiss movements were assembled with local dials and cases (often bearing spurious hallmarks), and are known as 'Dutch forgeries'. These carry invented names such as 'Tarts, London'.

Watch dials of the earlier 17th century had been composed of a narrow chapter ring for the hour superimposed on a profusely engraved plate, but from about 1675 these were superseded by a *champlevé* single sheet dial of gold, silver or gilt-metal. These had sunken matted areas between the hour and minute chapters which were left raised and polished. From 1700 enamel dials began to be used in

French clocks

THE FIRST French clocks were based on the Hague clocks developed by Huygens and Coster in Holland. These had rectangular cases with lunette crestings and velvet covered dials. In France this boxy shape soon developed into more flowing forms, so that by 1735 the typical bracket clock has a waisted form. By mid-century the ormolu mounts no longer fit closely to the outline of the case, being composed of openwork foliage at the hips, shoulders and on the cresting.

As with French furniture, much use is made of boulle (brass or pewter inlay in a tortoiseshell ground) in the Louis XIV, Régence and Louis XV periods. Louis XV's reign also saw other decorative finishes such as green-stained horn or *vernis martin* (a gilt imitation lacquer decorated with sprays of flowers).

French mantel clocks were made in a profusion of fantastical designs in Louis XV's reign. Dials were commonly circular, whether central or incidental to the

☞ *left*
SELECTION OF FRENCH WATCHES
FRENCH Early 17th c.
An early verge watch, a rock crystal stackfreed watch, an octagonal silver and giltmetal verge watch, and a silver paircased verge watch in a pique case.

☞ *top left*
BRACKET CLOCK
FRENCH Mid-18th c.
French bracket clocks became curvaceous in the early 1700s, eventually taking on a waisted form. This one is finished in the gilt imitation lacquer known as vernis martin.

☞ *top right*
ELEPHANT MANTEL CLOCK
FRENCH Mid-18th c.

France, but they did not become current in England until the mid-1730s, from when many of the earlier watches with champlevé metal dials were newly fitted with replacement ones in enamel.

Oignon cases could be either engraved or left plain. Pair-cased watches, on the other hand, commonly had a plain inner case and any decoration was applied to the outer case. This could be engraving or a veneer of leather or tortoiseshell, often with a pattern of gold or silver studpins (*piqué* work). Enamel decoration was quite popular in 18th century France, but was not much used in England, particularly before 1760, the English favouring *repoussé* decoration (embossed by hammering the inner surface) instead. Many of these repoussé cases have by now been worn down or even pierced through on their highlights, unless fitted with a protective third case. Such protecting cases became more common once enamelling was popular in England.

Genevan watch enamellers
~

EIGHTEENTH century enamelling does not have the same charm as the work of the Huauds at the end of the previous century, and subject painting was generally reduced to an oval on the back of the case, often framed by bands of translucent and opaque enamel. From the 1760s increasing use was made of translucent enamel over an engine-turned ground, known as *guilloché* enamel. This frequently covered the whole back panel, which was then framed by a band of real or white enamel pearls. By the end of the 18th century the Genevan enameller's work surpassed French and English work and during the Empire period and shortly afterwards (to about 1835) they specialized in exquisitely enamelled gold and pearl-set musical watches and automata. The early 19th century also saw the revival of form watches modelled after flowers or musical instruments. Otherwise many cheaper watches in England were veneered with horn painted on the underside with

☞ *above*

FORM WATCHES
Early 19th c.
Seventeenth-century-style form watches came back into fashion in the early 19th century, often, as here, with guilloche enamel cases.

Arcadian, urban or shipping subjects.

Whilst the Genevan enamellers in the 19th century produced cases decorated with landscapes, portraits, bouquets of flowers or scrolling foliage in abundance, but varying in quality, it must be remembered that the majority of watches were cased in plain silver or gold. Watches had first been made thinner in fashion-conscious France from the 1780s, and in the 19th century were universally of flatter, thinner form. Until the mid-century dials were either of enamel or engine-turned gold, silver or giltmetal,

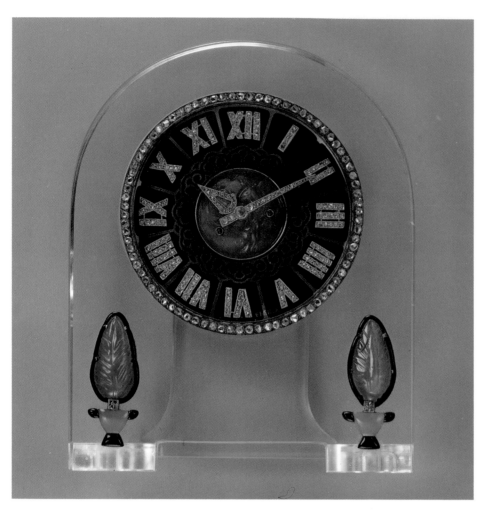

Watchmakers in America seized on this idea of standardized parts, which they produced by machines from the mid-century, resulting in a cheap, reliable, mass-produced watch that was exported worldwide. As standards of mechanization improved, the Americans, with all manufacturing processes of making a watch concentrated in single companies, lost their lead to the Swiss, where skilled specialized outworkers were the norm. In this way the Swiss also captured the quality market from the English in the early 20th century.

In France the principle of standardization of parts had been applied to travelling clocks, known as carriage clocks, from around 1840. Over the next ten years their manufacture became very organized, the movements and cases being made to set sizes and in varying grades of quality and decoration, which could then be assembled in various combinations. The simplest do not strike but merely tell the time, while the most complicated strike the hours and quarter hours at each quarter and have calendar indications.

The organization of the carriage clock industry was such that they were often dispatched around the world already bearing the retailers' names, but the First World War disrupted this trade and the industry did not recover. Something of a revival, however, was seen in France in the 1920s and 1930s when fine quality enamelled bedside or travelling clocks and watches were made in the Art Deco style. These were to be amongst the last collectable timepieces of quality.

but from then on increasingly of plain white enamel.

The spread of mechanization
~

THE SWISS and French introduced keyless winding via the crown button from about 1860, but this was resisted by the English for 20 years. The commonest form of English watch in the second half of the 19th century was the hunter, in which a glazed dial is protected from damage by a hinged cover. In a half hunter this cover is pierced in the centre in order to read the time without opening the watch. The majority of Continental watches at this date were open-faced.

The late 18th-century had seen the beginning of part making by home-based outworkers in Switzerland, while the watch was assembled at the watchmaker's.

☞ *bottom left*
CARRIAGE CLOCK
SWISS AND FRENCH 19th c.
Carriage clocks were often exported around the world, appropriately so as they were made for travellers. The lacquered brass example is of a type known as 'grande sonnerie' from its ability to strike hours and quarters.

☞ *top left*
ART DECO CLOCK
FRENCH 1920s or 1930s
Art Deco rock crystal desk clock made by Cartier.

SCIENTIFIC INSTRUMENTS

JEREMY COLLINS

Interest in the art of science and the production of scientific instruments can be traced back to the late 15th and early 16th centuries, when the makers of instruments and experimental apparatus were among the more important artisans in cities such as Florence, Augsburg, Nuremberg and Louvaine. No king, prince, bishop, or successful merchant at that time would have been without his cabinet of fine instruments, which would have demonstrated not just his wealth but his scholarly understanding of astronomy, mathematics, surveying and the physical sciences. Makers such as Schissler, Habermel, Bürgi, Coignet and others were in great demand, and the output of superlative, and in some cases extremely complex, instruments was prodigious.

During the late 18th century enthusiasm for scientific instruments and apparatus began to wane, possibly with the exception of microscopy, and 100 years later many fine instruments would have appeared in collections which were held in little regard by their owners. The lack of understanding and appreciation of the craftsmen of the Renaissance and later, who produced the most wonderful instruments now to be seen in museums around the world, is quite astonishing.

To the tutored modern eye these beautiful creations should be seen and considered against their historical background. The energy and skill of those that made them are gradually, once again, being appreciated. Over the last two decades there has been a considerable increase in interest in antique scientific instruments. Within the last decade prices have more than trebled for many items, and in some cases values have gone up by more than fivefold.

The tragedy has been that because of the low value and low regard to which many instruments have hitherto been subjected, many of the finest 19th century items have, for decorative purposes, been buffed up and polished to take their place on boardroom tables or as sideboard decorations in the home.

All this is now changing and the major auction houses in London, Paris and New York have, between them, with the understanding of the trade, begun to repair the damage by producing a marketplace in which the very best can once again be purchased. Prices, in some cases, have risen dramatically. For example, in 1977, a 2 inch pocket globe by a maker such as Price would have commanded a figure of approximately £350 to £400 ($650–740). In 1989, only 12 years later, a fine example of such a globe could command, on a good day, somewhat in excess of £5,000 ($9,250).

Microscopes have always been of interest, particularly as they are of use in discovering the unknown, but have a certain decorative value. Nevertheless, they remain cheap by today's standards, with even the best 19th century instruments costing under £3,000 ($5,500), most hovering around the £200 to £800 bracket ($375–1500). Interest in microscopy was

☞ *above*

ASTROLABE

FLEMISH 1559
A gilt brass planispheric astrolabe made by Walter Arsenius, one of the leading makers of astronomical instruments in the 16th century.

☞ *top centre*

PLANETARIUM

ENGLISH 18th c.
22cm (8¾in) diameter
A lacquered and silvered brass planetarium, with sun ball, two planets with moons and a face plate engraved with zodiac and calendar scales.

☞ *left*

POCKET ASTRONOMICAL COMPENDIUM

ENGLISH 1579
Case 5.5cm (2¼in) diameter
This rare pocket compendium comprises of a perpetual calendar and table of saints' days, magnetic compass, equinoctial sundial, table of latitudes, nocturnal, shadow square and unequal hour diagram.

☞ *left*

'NEW UNIVERSAL'
MICROSCOPE

ENGLISH mid-18th c.
The London instrument
maker, George Adams,
invented the object glass
changer, or rotating
nosepiece, for his 'New
Universal' microscope.
This rare example is
valued at around £20,000
($37,000).

menon has passed, then prices tend to fall, showing that interest can be paper thin.

Fluctuating prices

THERE IS and always has been a great interest in scales, weights and measures. However, since the establishment of a Standard measure in Britain, the variety of objects within this category has become legion. Many are marked with Borough coats of arms and maker's name, and these, if in their original condition, being both signed and dated, are eagerly sought after by collectors.

Prices over the last decade have risen dramatically and then almost done a 'U' turn and fallen equally quickly, which only goes to prove that like many other works of art one does not 'invest' in instruments, but buys them because one likes them and because of the craftsmen and their craftsmenship.

The more exotic instruments such as astrolabes, astrolabe-quadrants, quadrants and dials of various varieties can sell for huge sums in the London, European and American salerooms. However, if taken into the context of their value when new, prices are still remarkably low, and we are perhaps living in a period where scientific instruments represent one of the finest long term bargains to be had anywhere within the world of Fine Art.

If one considers the low survival rate of such objects and the lack of space which

☞ *above*

BINOCULAR TELESCOPE

FRENCH c.1900
128cm (50½in) high in
lowered position
The binocular eyepieces
allowed two people to
look through the telescope
simultaneously. The
triple ocular revolver
gives magnification of
×33, ×53 and ×73.

at its zenith in the late 19th century, when many wonderful instruments and a great variety of slides were made for study in the home.

Surveying instruments, that is to say the level and theodolite, have always appeared in great variety, constructed by many makers, some good, some bad. Collecting surveying instruments today gives the would-be enthusiast an enormous range of exciting, delightful and eccentric instruments from which to choose. Prices range from a lofty £30,000–£40,000 ($55,000–75,000) for the very best examples of the 17th century to under £100 ($185) for superbly made 20th century instruments but with little decorative appeal.

Astronomy has always fascinated the professional and amateur alike, and since the days of Galileo there have been many keen collectors of telescopes and other astronomical instruments. It is of interest to note that as and when a particular astronomical event hits the headlines, such as the recent sighting of Halley's Comet, prices tend to rise sharply and almost anything in the line of astronomy sells to an eager public. Once the pheno-

they take up in the modern home, delicate, small and unobtrusive instruments of the 16th and 18th centuries can be collected, even today, with relative ease by the enthusiast with even a very modest pocket.

To encourage collectors world-wide, the Scientific Instrument Society was formed in the early 1980s and now caters for hundreds of enthusiasts. It holds up to six international meetings a year, and has held meetings with visits to great collections in the USA, Spain, France, Italy, Germany, Austria and Czechoslovakia. Among many of its members there are museum curators, academics, members of the trade and collectors.

Of considerable interest, and some concern, to the Society is the growing number of forgeries that are beginning to appear on the market, principally as the result of the successful sale of similar but original objects at auction. The amateur collector should be wary of such objects, purely by making note of originals that appear in public and private collections and the sudden mysterious arrival of similar pieces on market stalls and in antique shops.

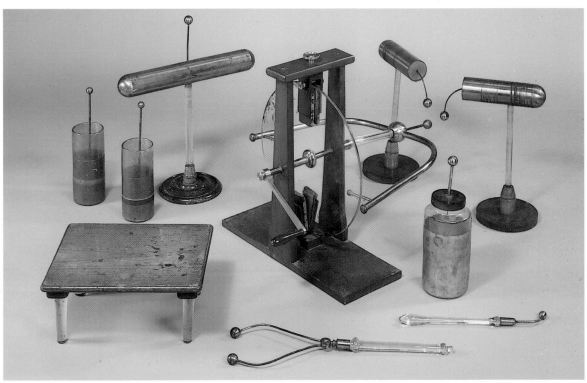

☞ *top left*

SELECTION OF SCIENTIFIC INSTRUMENTS

GERMAN 18th c.
Instruments assembled by Josef Pieter Zallinger (1730–1805). Most of them were commissioned from the Augsburg maker Georg Friedrich Brander.

☞ *left*

SELECTION OF SCIENTIFIC INSTRUMENTS

ENGLISH 19th c.
Apparatus assembled by Charles Wheatstone (1802–1875), a professor of Experimental Philosophy at King's College, London. A prolific inventor himself, especially of electrical instruments, Wheastone worked with the great Victorian scientist James Maxwell.

BOOKS AND MANUSCRIPTS

SARAH SOAMES

☞ *above*

ABRAHAM ORTELIUS

THEATRUM ORBIS TERRARUM

FLEMISH 1573

*Ortelius' epoch-making work was the world's first regularly
produced atlas. Although it ran to 42 printings, complete
sets are rare today and this one sold for £15,000 ($27,750)
in 1990.*

Before Johann Guttenberg discovered the art of printing from movable type over 500 years ago, books were written by hand, mostly in Latin. These medieval manuscripts, the result of immense labour, generally produced in monasteries and for wealthy patrons, would sometimes take their scribes and illuminators years to complete. Generally speaking, only ephemeral texts were written in the vernacular and are of great rarity. Such is our appreciation today of the work of these masters that many of these early manuscripts have been cut up and the individual miniatures and leaves of calligraphy sold separately. A single initial 'P' cut from a large illuminated manuscript on vellum with a charming scene of the Nativity, produced around 1490, alone fetched £36,000 ($66,600) at a recent Christie's auction.

Guttenberg's first book, his Bible of 1455, of which only 45 copies are known to exist, is understandably the most valuable printed book in the world today. Since then the Bible, in an astonishing range of languages, has been printed more often than any other book. By 1500 the Latin Vulgate had already been reprinted 94 times. However, it is true to say that the great majority of printed Bibles, in particular the vast quantities which appeared in the 19th century, are in little demand.

Books from the press of England's first printer, William Caxton, are naturally some of our greatest treasures. A single leaf from Caxton's first edition of Geoffrey Chaucer's *Canterbury Tales,* 1477, will command a price in excess of £1,000 ($1,850). The whole book contains 374 leaves.

The spread of printing

I N T H E second half of the 15th century, following Guttenberg's invention, printing presses sprang up with surprising speed all over Europe. The books they printed are termed 'incunabula' from the Greek word meaning cradle. In effect they are the crade of printing and as such have ever since been collectors' items. The goal of some past collectors was to obtain an example from each press established before 1500, but this would be almost impossible to achieve today.

The invention of printing transformed the world. Books were produced in large quantities, to the great benefit of schools; public libraries became larger and more numerous, and the standard of literacy rose dramatically as a whole range of ancient thought became available to the curious. However, much of what was printed in the following centuries was to be of little lasting interest. The main philosophers, scientists and historians of the Middle Ages had been printed, so too had the writings of antiquity – in large quantities, mainly in Latin. Today, in spite of their age, much of this material of the 16th and 17th centuries is in little demand. The exception of course, is the work of the new authors and thinkers of the Renaissance. The scarcity and importance of a first edition of Sir Thomas More's *Utopia,* 1516, is reflected in the price of £100,000 ($185,000) or so that it commands today.

William Shakespeare's *First Folio,* the first collected edition of his *Comedies, Histories and Tragedies,* published in 1623 by his friends and admirers after his death, is as near as we can get to a Shakespeare 'first', nearly all the original copies of many of the individual plays having been lost or worn out by the original

☞ *top left*
**INITIAL P FROM
ILLUMINATED
MANUSCRIPT**
ITALIAN *c.1490*
*This large historiated
initial was cut from an
illustrated manuscript
created by the
Lombardian artist Da
Crema.*

☞ *below*
**HARTMANN SCHEDEL
LIBER CHRONICARUM**
GERMAN *1493*
*This woodcut map is from
the Nuremberg Chronicle
by Hartmann Schedel, a
fine example, sold
by Christie's in 1990 for
£44,000 ($81,400). It is
hand-coloured.*

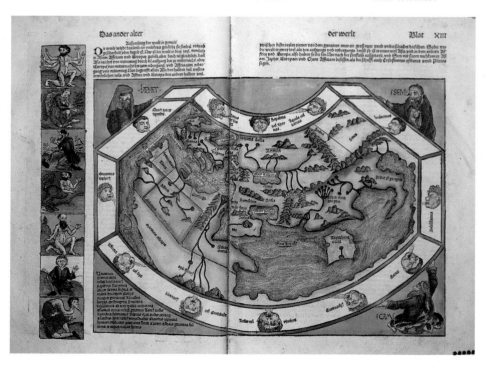

actors. However, a *First Folio* is beyond the reach of most of us. The most important book ever printed in English, it contains 20 plays that had never been printed before. But, with this exception, the general guideline for collectors of English literature is to go for the first editions of the classic authors, the household names – Alexander Pope, Jonathan Swift, Jane Austen, Charles Dickens, Charlotte Brontë, and so on. The 'Collected Works' of most authors, although essential on library shelves for readers, are not what are sought by the bibliophile.

Illustrated books
—

THE OBVIOUS appeal and delight of illustrated books of all periods ensures them a permanent place on collectors' shelves. From block-books and the earliest medicinal herbals, psalters, histories, technological books, etc. with their charming woodcut illustrations, right through to children's books of recent times, Edmund Dulac, Arthur Rackham, Beatrix Potter and the like, there are enthusiasts for all

categories. French illustrated books of the 18th century deserve a special mention with their exquisite engravings after the greatest artists of the day: Boucher, Fragonard, Watteau, Oudrey, and others. They attained a peak of excellence recognized by all, and many were also bound in the highest quality gilt-tooled bindings of the period. Those bound in red morocco, with the sides decorated with the gilt armorials of the original owner or library, are the most highly prized.

In the early 19th century came the great period of the English book with coloured plates. Watercolour painting, one of England's major contributions to the visual arts, reached its height at the time when the technique of aquatint engraving was perfected. The Napoleonic wars provided exciting scenes of battle, picturesque uniforms and never-ending inspiration for caricature. Artists' watercolours were reproduced by means of hand-coloured aquatint in an enormous range of publications: landscape gardening, costume, travel, guide books and, above all, remarkable topographical productions. Outstanding was the publisher Rudolph Ackermann, famous for his sporting books and prints, whose massive output

☞ *above*
RUDOLPH ACKERMANN
VIEW OF THE HIGH STREET,
OXFORD
ENGLISH 1814
The publisher Ackermann's hand-coloured aquatint is from his book, History of the University of Oxford.

☞ *left*
BEATRIX POTTER
FROM THE TALE OF
PIGLING BLAND
ENGLISH Early 20th c.
20 × 16.5cm (8 × 6½in)
The early 20th century is often seen as the Golden Age of illustrated children's books. This original drawing was sold for £5,000 (£9,250) at auction in 1988.

botanical books in London in the mid-1980s, no less than ten individual books were sold for over £100,000 ($185,000) each, including two by Redouté and two English books of the same period, Robert John Thornton's *Temple of Flora* with its massive coloured plates, and John Sibthorp's *Flora Graeca* in ten volumes with almost 1,000 coloured plates of the flora of Greece. These are some of the great books, but even little-known, privately printed, books by amateur Victorian lady botanists are avidly collected today.

The same is true of bird books. John James Audubon's famous four elephant folio volumes of *The Birds of America*, published in 1827–38, are already legendary, and so is the price – millions in any currency. Britain's Audubon is Prideaux John Selby, one of Audubon's own pupils. He, too, produced fine folios of life-sized ornithology, worth £30,000 ($55,000) or so today. Perhaps Britain's most loved and most prolific ornithological artist was John Gould. His output includes, amongst others, monographs of the *Birds of Great Britain, Europe, Asia, New Guinea, The Humming Birds,* and eight folio volumes on *The Birds of Australia,* a complete set of which today is worth upwards of £150,000 ($275,000).

Gould's coloured plates were reproduced by means of lithography, a method of engraving on stone which was used with great success during most of the 19th

included three fine works on Regency England, the *Microcosm of London,* histories of the universities of Oxford and Cambridge, and a history of the Public Schools. All have numerous aquatint illustrations after various artists including Pugin, Westall and Nash. A large set of the three works was recently sold at Christie's for £28,000 ($51,800).

This was also the heyday of natural history, in particular botany and ornithology. Pierre Joseph Redouté's mastery of flower painting has seldom been equalled, nor the sheer quantity of superb books he illustrated, especially his masterpieces on the rose and lily families. In an auction of

☞ *above*

ROBERT JOHN THORNTON PLATE FROM THE TEMPLE OF FLORA

ENGLISH 1800

The Temple of Flora *is one of England's finest botanical publications, and was the first to have life-sized flower prints with landscape backgrounds.*

☞ *right*

PRIDEAUX JOHN SELBY ILLUSTRATIONS OF BRITISH ORNITHOLOGY

ENGLISH 1833–4

century. David Roberts' *The Holy Land, Syria, Idumea, Arabia, Egypt and Nubia* in six volumes was another *magnum opus* to employ this method. It has been described as 'one of the most important and elaborate ventures of nineteenth-century publishing, and the apotheosis of the tinted lithograph'. The technique ideally suited Roberts' romantic landscapes of the Middle East. A coloured copy of the whole set has fetched as much as £95,000 ($175,750) at auction.

Architecture is a very important, and extensive, branch of the illustrated book and has recently become an increasingly popular one. From early editions of Palla-

☞ *above*

JOHN GOULD

PLATE FROM THE BIRDS OF AUSTRALIA

ENGLISH *1840–69*
Gould's extraordinary work on Australian ornithology contained 681 hand-coloured lithographs across its eight large folio volumes.

dio to architects of this century such as Frank Lloyd Wright, all are enthusiastically collected. This applies also to voyages and travel books. Accounts of Christopher Columbus' discovery of America and subsequent early voyages to the continent are amongst the gems, as are first accounts of Australian discoveries. The price of a set of Captain James Cook's three famous voyages (1773–84), illustrated with fine engraved charts and plates, has increased rapidly over the years and now can be as high as £10,000 ($18,500).

A mention too must be made of atlases. The Dutch were the pre-eminent cartographers of early years, and the 16th and 17th century engraving of maps and charts of the old and new world, often artistically embellished and coloured by hand, then bound, often in vellum, into splendid folio atlases, assured that no literate person was without a knowledge of geography. The fact that every home today has an atlas of some sort is probably due to their industry. The *Theatrum Orbis Terrarum* of Abraham Ortelius, published in Antwerp in 1570, was the world's first regularly produced atlas. Such was its popularity that no less than 42 folio editions, in seven different languages, were printed between 1570 and 1612. In spite of this, today they are rare, so many having been broken up and the maps framed and sold individually.

Amongst the many other areas of antiquarian books, perhaps the first printed accounts of all man's greatest intellectual achievements, whether in science, mathematics, economics, politics, philosophy, art, history, poetry, or fiction, are of especial importance and value to the bibliophile. So too are many dictionaries, encyclopedias and reference books of all kinds, not forgetting bibliographies.

Modern first editions and fine bindings

MODERN FIRST editions are nearer the financial reach of most of us than many of the books mentioned above. Here again, it is important to concentrate on authors of high standing and the condition and rarity, as with all books, are also paramount. To take Ian Fleming's James Bond novels as an example, it is the first, *Casino Royale,* published in a far smaller quantity than the later ones, which, complete with dust-jacket, can fetch £1,000 ($1,850) today, the others nearer £100.

To be a fine and desirable copy, a book of any period must be complete. Once it is defective, lacking any part of the text or illustrations, down to a word or even a letter, the value is immediately impaired. Any indication of an interesting provenance, on the other hand, can greatly enhance the value, whether it be an ownership or other inscription, bookplate or binding.

Book bindings present another whole field of interest. Leather bindings have been created for books since long before the invention of printing and these can be some of the greatest treasures to be found, sometimes regardless of the book they encase.

☞ *top left*
LUIGI ROSSINI
RACCOLTA DI
PROSPETTIVE DELLE PIÙ
BELLE FABRICHE DI ROMA
ITALIAN 1822
Architecture has been an important category of illustrated books from Palladio onwards. An edition of Rossini's 50 views of Rome was sold at auction in 1990 for £23,000 ($42,000).

☞ *bottom left*
DAVID ROBERTS
PLATE FROM THE HOLY
LAND, SYRIA, IDUMEA,
ARABIA, EGYPT AND NUBIA
ENGLISH 1842–9
The technique of hand-colouring engravings possibly reached its peak with the 241 plates of Roberts' magnificent though romanticized work.

DOLLS AND TOYS

☞ *above*

ARMY SUPPLY COLUMN

GERMAN c.1920

*Every aspect of both army and civilian life was reproduced
in exact detail in this Heyde supply column. The products
of this company were exported to many countries, and they
would make up sets to order.*

DOLLS AND DOLLS HOUSES

OLIVIA BRISTOL

The collecting of dolls is not a recent phenomenon. Collectors such as Alice K. Early were forming important collections in the 1930s and 1940s. Christie's have been holding specialist sales since March 1969, although they did sell the original Golliwog and Dutch dolls used for the illustrations to Florence K. Upton's books, in 1917.

Although dolls have been known since ancient times, most that appear on the market date from the 18th century or later. It must be said that some ancient dolls, such as the beautifully carved Egyptian doll in the Scottish National Museum, may have been adapted from religious figures and given joints when their usage changed, although the 1st century roman doll in the Museo Capitolini with her gold jewellery appears to have been made originally as a doll, and survived because it was buried with its young owner.

These two dolls also show another point to the survival of their species. Although most small children who had any time in which to play, may well have had some sort of companion, these do not generally survive, but an expensive professionally made doll was a household article of value, and was more likely to be passed on to future generations. Indeed, the condition of some dolls still surviving in near original condition from the 17th, 18th and 19th centuries, point to their being a status symbol that children were made to treasure most carefully.

Surviving dolls

WOOD WAS the most common material used in the 17th and 18th centuries. Although finer examples do exist, most English dolls of this period had the head and torso turned on a lathe, the back sliced off, nose and ears carved and

☞ *top*
TURNED AND CARVED WOODEN DOLL
ENGLISH 1760
A severe looking turned, carved and painted wooden doll in excellent condition.

☞ *above*
GESSO COVERED WOODEN DOLLS
ENGLISH *Early 19th c.*
Two typical turned and carved, gesso covered and painted dolls, both in contemporary clothes.

enamel eyes inserted before being covered with gesso and brightly painted. They had simply jointed legs, roughly painted, white, stick-like arms with crudely carved fingers and hoof-like feet. They seem to have been dressed before sale, judging by the professionalism and fit of many of the surviving clothes. By the beginning of the 19th century this type of rather heavy doll appears to have declined in popularity. Cheap peg wooden dolls with carved heads, some with yellow painted combs were now being imported from the Grodner Tal. In sizes from half an inch, to three feet, some were very fine indeed with chiselled hair effects and red, green or blue painted slippers.

Wax and papier maché dolls

THERE WERE also English wax dollmakers at this time. Beautiful poured bees wax heads were produced, the first real 'baby' dolls, with high waisted robes, cloth bodies and even sleeping eyes, worked by a wire through the body. A cheaper form of English doll, made from the late 18th century to the 1860s, was a crude, very lightweight papier maché shoulder head, brightly painted and then dipped in a thin layer of wax to give a more subtle flesh-like effect. Occasionally the address of the shop may be written or stamped on the cloth body. The arms are generally of coloured kid or of the same construction as the heads, and the wigs were of mohair, sometimes inserted in a slit from forehead to nape.

The papier maché dolls coming from Germany on the other hand, were highly sophisticated ladies, with elaborate moulded hairstyles, painted eyes and slim kid bodies with wooden arms and legs. Usually the attachment to the body was concealed by a coloured paper band. Sometimes these survive in their original sewn-on clothes; others have home-made clothes, as the contemporary toy catalogues show that they were usually sold undressed. Many importers and retailers, especially in France, probably ordered them in bulk and had them dressed for sale in the clothes most likely to appeal to their customers.

By the middle of the century porcelain heads from Germany and bisque heads from France were in production. The German heads from the 1840s were often of exceptional quality, with well modelled coiffures, sometimes with flowers and later with hair ornaments, bands, necklaces, earrings and even bodices. The early French bisque heads have a marvellous translucent quality; those made for Mesdames Rohmer and Huret often have plump cheeks and an almost child-like appearance, although dressed in rich fashionable clothes.

French luxury dolls

IT WAS FROM the middle of the century that French dolls began to surpass their German rivals in quality and invention. While the Germans had always had and continued to have the mass market, the French produced superb dolls for the luxury trade. There were fashionably dressed dolls, modelled as women, with a variety of ingenious body designs, and they also introduced *bébé* dolls. Jules Nicholas Steiner was the most inventive of the Paris makers. Dolls that walked,

cried, moved their arms, kicked their legs and closed their eyes, were all patented by him. The *bébé* first appeared in the 1870s, and epitomized the current ideal of an exceptionally pretty child. The main makers were Leon Casimir Bru, Jules Nicholas Steiner and Emile Jumeau. Most collectors would like to own a French *bébé* of this period. The quality of the bisque is usually very fine, with lustrous glass eyes, closed mouths, pierced ears, mohair wigs, jointed wood and composition bodies and expensive fashionable clothes.

Each firm had its own distinctive facial type. Bru's was typified by his unusual small pouting mouths, sometimes with the suspicion of a tongue showing, and his kid bodies with bisque-plated shoulders and forearms. Steiner had several facial types in two lettered groupings, some letters having open and closed mouth versions, the open mouth dolls usually having a speaking mechanism. Jumeau dolls are remarkable for their large and jewel-like eyes, heavy brows, and on the early models for their shaded eyelids. During the 1890s the Germans were also producing bisque-headed dolls, usually with sweet dolly faces, sleeping brown or blue eyes, open mouths, blonde or brown mohair wigs and jointed wood and composition bodies. They were often sold in chemise, shoes and socks, ready to be dressed by a loving mother or aunt. Many survive in their contemporary home-made clothes. The most prolific

☞ *left*
GOOGLI-EYED DOLLS
GERMAN
Two googli-eyed dolls, both by J. D. Kestner. The larger has a mould number 221, the smaller, all-bisque mould is number 179.

☞ *far left*
SCHMITT *BÉBÉ* DOLL
FRENCH
A fine example by Schmitt of Paris, a maker whose work does not often appear on the market.

☞ *top centre*
JUMEAU *BÉBÉ*
FRENCH
A Jumeau bébé showing the stunningly effective original clothes. Although the construction is quite cheap, the overall effect is one of luxury.

firms were Armand Marseille, J. D. Kestner, Gebruder Heubach and Simon and Halbig, although by the 1920s there were hundreds of others making bisque-headed dolls of all qualities and sizes.

The early 20th century

IN 1909 there seems to have been an explosion in the doll world. It was not only the birth of the so-called character doll, that is a doll modelled as a real child, but Kathe Kruse and the stuffed toy firm of Steiff also produced marvellous ranges of cloth child dolls, and Marion Kaulitz made the Munich Art dolls in composition with painted soulful faces.

These dolls are very sought after by collectors. Prices depend on the rarity of the mould, its quality and size. The originality and type of body are also impor-

tant, as are the clothes. It is possible to have every expression from tears, rage, yells and naughtiness to sulks, pensive looks and joy. Bisque character children are also made as figures for use as ornaments or as tiny solid standing dolls with only the arms jointed at the shoulder.

In recent years not only Steiff and Lenci cloth dolls have become popular but also English firms, such as Dean's Rag Book Co., Chad Valley, Farnell's, Merrythought and Norah Wellings. The prices of these cloth dolls depend primarily on their condition and the survival of their original clothes. Chad Valley made two versions of Her Majesty the Queen when Princess Elizabeth, and also Princess Margaret Rose and Prince Edward, later Duke of Kent. They also made a set of Snow White and the Seven Dwarfs. Dean's dolls were at first simply printed on cotton and stitched round the sides. Later felt and cotton was used with only the faces printed on a moulded mask. In the late 1930s rubber heads were made. Chad Valley inserted glass eyes on their Bambina range.

Collecting dolls

WHEN COLLECTING old dolls it is better to go for a doll in mint condition from a cheaper category than to spend a lot on a poor-quality specimen from a rarer form, such as a French bisque *bébé*, badly repainted, re-wigged with new clothes and an over-painted or replaced body.

A good way of acquiring knowledge both of different types of doll and their market value is to attend specialist sales where dolls can be examined freely and prices reached can be marked in the catalogue for future reference. Celluloid, tiny dolls of the 1920s and '30s can still be bought for a few pounds or pence and come in a huge variety of mouldings, often of popular children's characters of the period and with brightly painted clothes. A bit more expensive are the North American composition and mama dolls from the 1920s to the end of the

Second World War when hard plastic began to take over.

Dolls' houses

THE COLLECTING, or perhaps the furnishing of dolls' houses, has been a compulsive hobby since the 16th century, the most fabulous being the Dutch cabinet houses of the 17th and 18th centuries.

Houses that appear on the market now date mainly from the 19th and 20th centuries. They normally fall into three main types, the first being early large strongly made baby houses of the late 18th and early 19th centuries. These usually have good lines and architectural details, such as painted stonework, quoining, pillasters, pediments, glazed windows and chimney stacks. Each is unique, and it is probable that they were made by estate carpenters, their weight and size pointing to their having been made for a well-to-do local child or children.

The second type are the toy-man houses dating from the last quarter of the 19th century, that is those made by small craftsmen for sale through toy shops. These are generally rather crude in construction, the emphasis being on low price rather than quality. Because of the general simplicity of design, home-made houses may be in this group as well, although some made after elaborate pattern book designs can be very fine.

The third type, and one that is now highly sought after, are the smaller manufactured houses, many from firms such as Christian Hacker, Moher of Bavaria, Muller, Gottschalk, Lines Bros., Bliss, Amersham, Tri-ang, Silber and Fleming and Swan. Here prices depend on architectural detail, much of it supplied, particularly on the German and American houses, by colour lithography.

Furnishing, once one has acquired a house, is a long term project, particularly if one is determined to have items of the correct scale and period for the house. It is the lucky collector who finds one already furnished, and prices will reflect this.

ANTIQUE TOYS

JAMES OPIE

It could be said that many of the toys keenly collected today are not old enough to qualify as antiques. This results from the strong nostalgic tug exerted by the memories of childhood playthings, an attraction that seems to be strongest at the age of about 35 onwards. As each generation of children grows up, the enthusiasm for the toys they played with causes a boom in new collecting subjects; for instance, in the 1980s, the most popular collectable by far was the die-cast model, reflecting the most popular toy of the 1950s.

Collecting more recent toys is made easier by the much wider availability, and therefore lesser expense. Earlier toys are much more directly related to the normal criteria by which antiques are judged, their decorative attraction and intellectual interest. It is unlikely that an antique toy would be bought for practical use by a modern child in the same way as antique furniture.

The history of toymaking

THE HISTORY of toymaking closely parallels that of industrial development, since toys are an item for which there was a huge demand once they were able to be manufactured cheaply enough. In the 18th century, toymaking was a cottage industry turning out wooden trinkets for pedlars and fairs, or at its most developed, a sideline for jewellers, clockmakers and metalworkers. In a practical age where craftsmen lived close to many basic skills, turning out a toy would utilize the handmade dexterity available, and occasionally someone would become sufficiently well-known at making a particular type of toy that he could earn a large part of his living at it.

The urge to make toys was certainly just as well developed then as now, it was just that the means were not to hand. The instinct to create working model objects, tableaux and wondrous curiosities was often manifested in centrepieces at the feasts of the rich or royal, powered by water, weights or clockwork. Part of the attraction was in the ostentation. The first model of the State Coach of England was that made for George III to see if he liked

☞ *left*

GROUP OF COLLECTABLE TOYS

EUROPEAN AND AMERICAN 19th and 20th c. A typical spread of collectable toys, representative of items on offer through leading toy auctioneers. Toy soldiers, die-cast cars and aircraft, toy trains, tin toys, teddy bears and dolls are all well represented, the current auction value of the items in this picture amounting to over £40,000 ($74,000).

☞ *opposite*

TINPLATE TOYS

EUROPEAN AND AMERICAN 20th c. Medley of tinplate toys, some appealing by their novelty action, others by their realism.

☞ *left*

DINKY TOYS

ENGLISH 1930–55

A range of Dinky Toys, including some of the earliest models of 1932– 40 in the front row and mint boxed 1950s production models further back. Toys in this condition are worth 20 times those which are scratched.

☞ *below*

EARLY ROYAL HORSE ARTILLERY SET

GERMAN 19th c.

A fascinating early Royal Artillery set made by Sonnenberg in Germany. The figures are unusual for their large size, excellent standard of paintwork, and the springs on which they are mounted to simulate a galloping motion.

the concept. It was not until 150 years later that mass production of models of the same coach began, as souvenirs of the Coronation of 1937.

The main categories of toys are as follows: automata, board games, cast iron toys, character toys, construction toys, die-cast toys, dolls, doll houses and furniture, jig-saws, lead figures, mechanical toys, money banks, optical toys, paper toys, penny toys, plastic toys, robots and space toys, teddy bears, tin toys, toy guns and soldiers, toy theatres, and train sets.

Toys can date from the Renaissance (automata) to the present day (robots) and prices range from a few pounds to thousands. Broadly speaking, toys can be divided into categories by purpose, i.e. baby play objects such as rattles, companions such as dolls or teddy bears,

models of the real world and its activities, entertainments by way of games, sports or spectacles, puzzles providing various challenges of intellectual or physical prowess, or constructive activities where something is built. Many toys cover more than one category, and the specializations within sub-divisions are equally diverse, including a choice of manufacturer, manufacturing process or subject matter.

Character toys, for instance, include the popular choice of toys showing characters from Disney cartoons, sometimes known as Disneyana. Of course, merchandize other than toys has been sold in association with Disney characters, and toys possessing the added attraction of fitting into other collections can fetch prices out of all proportion to similar non-character items. These toys, dating from the beginning of this century, can be bought for as little as £5 ($9) but varieties have reached five figures.

Many toys, however old, are so damaged, home-made, or plainly unattractive that they are worth very little. The British International Toy and Hobby Fair 1991

Product Locator Service lists 286 categories of toys, old examples of some of which, for instance Noah's Arks, may be worth up to £5,000 ($9,250), while building bricks from the same period of about 1890, even by the premier firm of Richter, are worth at best only a few pounds. There is no hard and fast rule, but the more intricate and attractive the toy, the more expensive it is likely to be.

☞ *above*

WOODEN NOAH'S ARK

GERMAN 19th c.
A traditional wooden Noah's Ark. The religious significance of this toy made it a favourite for families to buy for Sunday use.

☞ *below*

TIN PLATE LINER

GERMAN c.1920
Made by Bing, this is an example of the aristocrat among tinplate toys. This example was sold for £3,200 ($5,920) in the late 1980s – even though it had some parts missing.

same way for well over a century. Early hand-made marbles can be spectacularly interesting compared to most modern machine moulded specimens, but there is not sufficient depth of literature, sequence of development, history of manufacture, story of commercial endeavour and competition simply in glass marbles as there is in the types of toy previously listed, each of which is the subject of many books and the objective of thousands of specialist collectors. Indeed, judging by the number of toy collector's fairs held each weekend, it is possible to estimate that there are some hundreds of thousands of people collecting toys in Britain alone.

As the industrial age gathered momentum, so did the toymakers become major companies and thrive as businesses. Often it is by manufacturer that toys are collected. For instance, among the best-known for tin toys are Arnold Gunthermann and Lehmann of Germany, Bandai in Japan, Bergmann in America, Mettoy in Britain and Jep in France. Hornby is of course the best-known manufacturer of toy trains, but Bassett-Lowke (another British company) predates them and both Bing of Germany and Ives of America made trains, as did Rossignol of France. Specialist books give details of the enormous range.

High quality toys

COSTLY TOYS have always been fashion objects of great prestige both for their owners and their parents, and such toys are very often still the most desirable today. Certainly there is no more beautiful an artifact than a well-crafted toy, and individual toys can be as decorative in the right setting as any painting, furniture or ornament. It is in this context, where toy collecting meets the art world, that the highest prices are to be found, for instance in the cunning mechanisms of the automata, where prices are always in the thousands, the breathtaking realism of the master models, the sheer elaboration of a frigate made in bone by a Napoleonic prisoner-of-war, or the lithographic fantasies of the tinplate circus performers.

Consider how much art there is to be found in the humble glass marble, a toy sold in millions every day, yet with an almost infinite variety of shape and swirl held within the rattling spheres. They are much collected by children, who know their play value, but not much by adults, since they have been made in much the

☞ *above*

TINPLATE CAR

GERMAN Early 20th c. The hand painted tinplate car is from Carette of Germany. Good quality tin toys are highly valued: this one could sell for £10,000 ($18,500).

☞ *below*

TOY TRAINS

BRITISH, FRENCH AND GERMAN 20th c. The two rear engines were originally made for the British market, front left for France and front right for Germany.

MUSICAL
INSTRUMENTS

☞ *above*

LYRAFLUGEL

GERMAN c.1820–30

*A lyraflugel by J. G. Schleip of Berlin. This is typical of
the curiosities made by early 19th century instrument-
makers.*

COLLECTING INSTRUMENTS

FREDERICK W. OSTER AND SARAH McQUAID

The history of musical instruments is bound together with the social and technical history of music. As new contexts for music-making arose and as new forms of musical language came into being, musical instruments evolved in response to these developments. Some instruments were rendered obsolete, and others changed in size and appearance; new instruments are being invented even today.

Throughout recorded time, musical instruments have served many social purposes. They have been used to entertain small and large groups, to frighten enemies, to inspire religious devotion, to facilitate dancing, to rally troops. Often, new social situations necessitate changes in musical instruments. During the American Civil War, for example, it was common for a band to march in front of the troops. This created a need for the 'over-the-shoulder' horn, the bell of which pointed back toward those marching behind.

The effect of technical developments

~

INNOVATIONS have also been dictated by the technical aspects of music. By the beginning of the 19th century, for instance, the violin had acquired a longer neck and fingerboard, a larger bass bar, a thicker soundpost, and a more highly pitched neck angle. While these changes occurred in part in order to produce the more powerful sound needed for the new

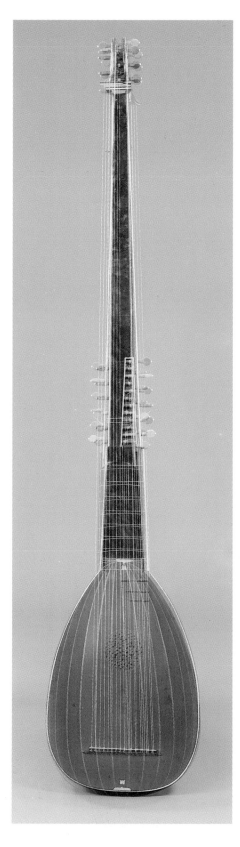

☞ *right*

TECCHLER CHITARRONE

GERMAN 1725
Length: 179.7cm (70¾in)
A fine chitarrone by David Tecchler, the neck veneered front and back with tortoiseshell.

concert halls, they were also directly related to developments in the music of the time. Composers were increasingly writing pieces that required musicians to use the 7th and higher fingering positions; in addition, a higher concert pitch necessitated instruments that could bear greater tension.

Developments in technology have had a significant effect on musical instruments. Before the late 18th century, nearly all instruments were hand-made in small workshops, and were available in relatively limited numbers. Most were made for the use of peasants or townspeople; only a few makers catered to the nobility. With the evolution of mass-production, a new and more significant distinction arose: that between hand-made and commercially produced instruments. Joseph Guarneri del Gesù, for instance, was in his day thought to be a maker of 'rough' instruments; today, his instruments command prices in some cases equal to those of Antonio Stradivari, whose refined productions were made for the aristocracy.

The 19th century was a turning point for musical instruments. New manufacturing methods made instruments available and affordable to the public at large, and it became fashionable to take up music as a hobby. By the 1840s brass bands had become a fad in America: within 30 years, every town, social organization, and military unit, as well as some businesses, had a band. By the 1880s, nearly every household had a piano. Minstrel bands popularized the five-string banjo in both England and America, creating a vogue for banjo orchestras. The musical fervor of the 19th century generated a profusion of musicians, music instructors, instrument-makers, and music publishers. Makers continued to produce hand-crafted instruments, but their creations were outnumbered by millions of commercially manufactured instruments.

Many of the commercially made instruments were altered to make them appear older, and it was common

to insert into factory-made violins of this period facsimile labels of such famous makers as Stradivari, Guarneri, Guadagnini, Amati, Maggini, and Stainer. These instruments were seldom produced as intentional forgeries; rather, the label indicated that the violin was inspired by or styled after one of these makers. They were commonly sold through music shops and catalogues and today constitute the bulk of available old violins. Deliberate forgeries do however exist. Leopoldo Franciolini (1844–1920), perhaps the most infamous instrument forger, produced a great many fake early stringed instruments and altered others to make them appear older or more ornate.

Factors that Determine Price

In general, the highest prices for musical instruments are commanded by violins, followed by historical keyboards and early stringed and wind instruments. The current record auction price for a musical instrument was set in November 1990, with the sale at Christie's of the Mendelssohn Stradivari violin of 1720 for £902,000 (about $1.76 million). A number of criteria work together to determine the value of a musical instrument. These include the maker, model, provenance, date, condition and availability.

The most important of these factors is the maker. Violins by Antonio Stradivari (1644–1737) and Joseph Guarneri del Gesù (1686–1744) have been the choice of great virtuosi, as have bows by Francois Tourte of Paris (1747–1835). Consequently, they are universally acknowledged to represent the apex of violin and bow making, and will always occupy the top tier of the market. Below that level, it is largely a question of trends; makers may come in and out of favour as musical styles change. Outside the violin family, there are no makers that have achieved a status equivalent to that of Stradivari, Guarneri del Gesu and Tourte; however, instruments by great innovators within an instrument classification are highly sought

☞ *left*
MAGGINI VIOLA
ITALIAN c.1600
Length of back: 42.9cm
(16⅞in)
A viola made by Giovanni Paolo Maggini. Maggini is almost as important today as Antonio Stradivari.

(active 1829–55), inventor of the piston valve, and by Johann Moritz (1777–1840), inventor of the tuba and the 'Berliner' valve.

The model of an instrument is in some cases of even greater importance than the maker. As the needs of musicians change with prevailing musical forms, certain physical characteristics become more or less desirable. In violins, for example, a preference has arisen for instruments with a flatter arch to the back and table, especially those based on the designs of Stradivari and Guarneri del Gesù. Such instruments are more likely to produce the louder and more powerful sound currently in favour among orchestra players.

☞ *above*

KIRKMAN HARPSICHORD

ENGLISH 1761
A very fine double manual harpsichord by Jacob Kirkman.

after. These include pianos by Bartolomeo Cristofori (1655–1731), who is credited with the earliest pianos, and more refined fortepianos by Johann Andreas Stein (1728–92). Other revolutionary instruments that fetch high prices include: harps by Sebastian Erard (1752–1831), inventor of the modern double-action pedal harp; flutes by Theobald Boehm (1794–1881), creator of the modern key system for the flute; early flutes and woodwinds by Johann Christoph Denner (1655–1707) and by members of the Hotteterre family (late 17th to early 18th century); bassoons by Johann Heckel (1812–77); saxophones and brasswinds by Adolphe Sax (1814–94); and brasswinds by Francois Perinet

☞ *right*

THE COLOSSUS VIOLIN

ITALIAN 1716
Length of back: 35.8cm (14⅛in)
Another important violin by Stradivari, sold in 1987 for £440,000 ($814,000).

☞ *right*

IMPORTANT

DEVELOPMENTAL

INSTRUMENTS

FRENCH, ENGLISH AND
AMERICAN 19th c.
Left to right: a serpent-
Foreveille, by Foreveille,
Paris, c.1830; an English
keyed bugle, c.1830; a
mid-19th century side-
drum; a clarinet in
boxwood with six keys,
by Asa Hopkins of
Litchfield, Conn.,
c.1825; a flute in
boxwood with four keys
by Firth, Pond & Co.,
New York, mid-19th
century; a stained maple
bassoon with 13 keys,
American c.1820; and an
early American bass viol
or 'Church Bass' by
William Green of
Medway, Mass., 1806.

Highly arched violins such as those of the Florentine and Roman makers are still popular, however, with chamber musicians. Similar examples can be drawn for other stringed instruments: flat-backed mandolins after the designs of Orville Gibson replaced Neapolitan-style round-backed mandolins; larger 'dreadnought' model guitars like those developed by the C.F. Martin Company in Pennsylvania have replaced the smaller parlour guitars popular before the 1930s.

The provenance of a musical instrument – its history – is also a significant consideration in determining market value. An instrument that has been used by a famous musician is often worth a great deal more than one with a less distinguished history. In 1986, for example, Christie's New York auctioned a platinum flute made in 1939 by Verne Q. Powell of Boston. The market price for this instrument might normally have been about $25,000 (£13,500). This flute, however, had belonged to William Kincaid, a member of the Philadelphia Orchestra

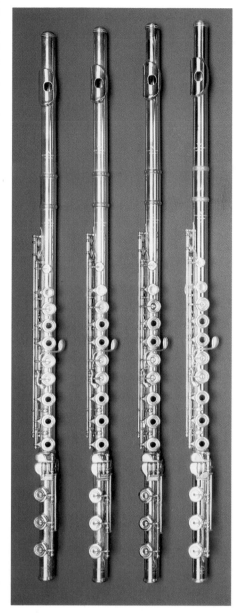

☞ *right*

POWELL FLUTES

AMERICAN 19th c.

Four flutes by Verne Q. Powell of Boston, made from precious metals – two silver, one gold and one platinum, previously the property of William Kinkaid.

☞ *left*

ALTO RECORDER

GERMAN Mid-16th c.

A rare columnar alto recorder by Hans Rauch von Schratt. This sold in 1988 for £44,000 ($81,000).

who was widely considered to be the greatest flautist and most influential teacher in the United States. A collector bought the flute for $187,000 (£101,000) – five times the previous world record for a wind instrument. More recent examples come from the pop music world: in April of 1990, a white Fender Stratocaster electric guitar made in 1968 which had been played by Jimi Hendrix at the Woodstock festival sold at auction for £198,000 ($366,300); a similar guitar might normally have been worth about £650 ($1,200). Buddy Holly's *c.* 1945 Gibson J-45 guitar – a model also commonly valued at about $1,200 – sold in June of 1990 at

auction in New York for $242,000 (£130,800).

The value of some instruments may be affected by their date and 'period of making'. The two are closely related, although a period of making is often associated with a region rather than a number of years. Giovanni Battista Guadagnini, for example, worked in five different cities, each inspiring a different style; violins from his Turin period are worth more than his earlier work. Violins by Antonio Stradivari made before the year 1700 are far less valuable than his later instruments.

The condition of an instrument is also an important criterion. This is especially true for violins. While no one expects a 250-year-old violin to look exactly the way it did the day it was made, it must meet certain basic standards. Investment-grade instruments should be free of 'post cracks' to the back (a post crack being any crack that appears in the region of the soundpost), be free of poorly executed or unsightly repairs, retain a large amount of original varnish, and be original in all their essential parts (back, table, ribs, and scroll). For other instruments, condition is not quite as crucial, although an instrument in an overall original state is far more desirable. If an instrument is playable, its value is often greatly increased.

The final factor that determines the value of a particular musical instrument is availability. Some instruments, such as those of the Renaissance, are valuable simply because so few have survived. In March of 1988, a rare mid-16th century columnar alto recorder by Hans Rauch von Schratt sold at auction at Christie's for £44,000 ($81,840), a record price for an early wind instrument (only four columnar instruments by the maker are known to exist). In a few cases, however, lack of availability can lead to a lower value. This applies to makers whose output was so small that they never achieved wide renown, or to those lesser-known workers whose productions were destined to bear the label or brand of a more significant maker, or the master maker of a workshop.

THE VIOLIN FAMILY

FRANCES GILLHAM

The most popular type of antique musical instrument is the violin family – violins, violas, violoncelli and bows. This is the field that commands the highest prices and captures the imagination of the world at large. There is something undeniably romantic and perhaps mystifying about the idea of 250-year-old violins selling for around a million pounds and appearing subsequently in concert halls across the globe.

This brings us to the central point that must never be forgotten in consideration of the field. Unlike other antiques, the violin family should not be viewed primarily as works of art. Essentially they are tools and this is their *raison d'être*. The violin was conceived and produced to function – the majority of purchasers will earn their living by using them. Those attending auctions of musical instruments will invariably be a wide cross-section: professional players (both soloists and orchestral), teachers and students, dealers, makers, restorers, and amateur musicians.

The violin market has developed substantially in the last ten years, and this applies equally to other members of the violin family. Sales have expanded, prices moved upwards and new shops and restorers have sprung up all over the world. One of the main reasons for this growth has been the entry into the field of the Japanese, and more recently, the Koreans and the Chinese. Western classical music has gained enormous appreciation in the Far East during the last few decades and performance standards attained there are now of top international quality. Naturally these exponents require instruments – similarly so do Suzuki-school students, many of whom start playing at the age of three. Demand as a result spans the whole range of instruments, from Stradivaris to childrens' violins.

The most sought-after instruments are Italian, then French, with English and

German makers in general less popular. During the 16th century, the design of the violin as we know it now had more or less taken shape. Musically, instruments of the viol family were still in the ascendant and little was written for the violin at this time. During the 17th century, however, the violin increased in popularity as its design permitted more fluid and gymnastic display than the viols. Louis XIV had a court orchestra of violins, an idea copied by Charles II in England. The musical forms of the sonata and concerto, ideal vehicles for the violin, were being actively developed and expanded. By the early 18th century, composers such as Bach, Handel and Vivaldi were all writing prolifically for violin. The concept of the violin virtuoso was already in its early stages and violins were required and being made in many parts of Europe.

Stradivari and the Cremona workshops

THE MOST famous Italian violin-making centre was Cremona, and it was here that Antonio Stradivari was apprenticed to Nicolo Amati before setting up his own workshop. Amati had inherited a substantial business from his father and uncle and Cremona was already considered to be at the forefront of this craft. Violins are generally made of maple, with pine fronts facilitating resonance. These raw materials grew in abundance along the Po River valley. Since the end of the 18th century Stradivari has been considered to be at the zenith of violin-making, and his instruments have never been surpassed either tonally or visually.

Other celebrated names are also attached to Cremona: the Guarneri family, Carlo Bergonzi, Francesco Rugeri and Lorenzo Storioni. However, there were other thriving centres as well. Venice attracted names such as Domenico Montagnana, Carlo Tononi, Matteo Goffriller and Pietro Guarneri. Naples could boast several generations of the Gagliano family, and Giovanni Battista Guadagnini worked in

☞ *opposite*
BERGONZI VIOLIN
ITALIAN 1739
*Front and back views of
the Carlo Bergonzi violin
which was sold in 1984 in
New York for $132,000.*

☞ *above*
CAPPA VIOLONCELLO
ITALIAN 1697
*Views of the front, back
and scroll of a cello by
Gioffredo Cappa, made
in Mandovi.*

several towns: Cremona, Piacenza, Parma and Turin. During the 19th century, Cremona lost its position as the top violin-making town and the Turin makers of that period are considered worthy successors. Instruments by Giovanni Francesco Pressenda and Joseph Rocca have become particularly desirable in recent years, combining as they do high standards of craftsmanship with a powerful tone well-suited to the demands of the modern concert hall. All these makers also made violas and violoncelli of comparable quality.

Assessing the quality

WHAT DO people seek in a violin? Condition and tonal qualities are the most important as well as proportion and appearance. Tone is without doubt a personal and subjective matter. Even in the rarified world of Stradivaris, one soloist may be enraptured, another disappointed and a third may find a specific example difficult to play. Much can be done to alter the way a violin responds. Sometimes it may be a very minor consideration, such as simply experimenting with different strings. In other cases an instrument may need structural work, such as changing the angle of the neck. Old internal repairs might need to be redone and some instruments have been fitted inside with so-called tonal improvement patches which could have the opposite effect. Restoration of instruments is highly skilled work which should only be carried out by well-respected repairers.

Assessing string instruments

ASSESSING VIOLINS remains the preserve of the dedicated specialist. It is virtually impossible to explain to the layman how to recognize an instrument of quality. Throughout the history of violin-making there have been copies, fakes and mis-labelling, not always with the intention of deception. It is very simple to place a label inside any violin in order to improve its saleability. Generations of makers have copied and followed the models of earlier great makers without dishonest intent. Others, however, have attempted to recreate not only the pattern, but the signs of ageing and wear in order to pass the instrument off as the work of a more substantial master. In Germany and France during the last century huge numbers of violins were produced. Made for students and amateurs, many carried a copy of the maker's label on whose model these commercial instruments were based. Hundreds of thousands of violins bearing reproduction Stradivari labels have survived. Other labels were also popular, ranging from Amati and Guarneri to the English maker Richard Duke. These instruments cost about 25 shillings in 1900, complete with case, strings and bow and were not meant as fakes. However, with a further 90 years of ageing and the dream of substantial sums of money, these instruments are constantly retrieved from attics, sheds and even skips by hopeful, but ultimately disappointed, owners from all over the world. Their value is rarely more than a few hundred pounds.

WINE

....

DUNCAN McEUAN

☞ *above*

VINTAGE COGNAC

*Cognac needs time to achieve quality, and good vintages are
sold regularly at auction together with fine unfortified wine.*

It is a common complaint that there is never enough time to spend on the serious laying down of a cellar. The fact that the space in which to lay it down does not exist is neither here nor there. Time is the critical factor; the availability of a fairly modest amount of money, and the interest in collecting, are the corner stones on which to build.

Why wine?

COLLECTING AND laying down wine can be a rewarding and fascinating pastime, as well as an efficient investment. Income from the investment should be seen as the money saved by buying early and consuming later, when the price of the wine will have risen, due to scarcity, and strong demand in the market for a ready-to-drink product. Capital appreciation has been self-evident over the past 20 years, although performances like that of Château Latour 1961 – opening offer in 1962 around £25 ($45) per case, recent price at auction £5,000 ($9,000) per case – are going to be hard to match, medium term. However, as long as patience is exercised and the rules followed, profits can be made and perhaps used to purchase new vintages and help contribute towards free drinking.

Why buy at auction?

BUYING AT AUCTION is the simplest method because of the vast range offered and encapsulated in one well laid out catalogue. For instance, Christie's Wine Sales take place twice a month, one sale devoted entirely to Bordeaux wines – classed growth reds and sauternes, vintages 1955 to 1986; the second sale to smaller lots of more mature wines, across the board from rare old Bordeaux, through fine red and white burgundy, German wines and champagne to vintage port and cognac.

Catalogues can be obtained from the auctioneers by subscription and the wines, which lie in various locations, can be delivered for a charge, depending on distance. Considerable care is taken to check on condition and provenance before cataloguing takes place and whenever possible wines and cellars are inspected. Many of the wines offered at auction lie in bonded warehouses where ideal conditions prevail and often private collectors who have had their stocks stored in wine merchants' cellars, decide to sell and are steered by their merchant to an auctioneer. These stocks of impeccable provenance have the advantage of being offered generally in small quantities and are of undoubted quality.

The catalogue arrives well in advance of

☞ *right*
SELECTION OF VINTAGE BORDEAUX AND BURGUNDY
FRENCH Mid-20th c.
Château Mouton Rothschild, 1959, Romanée Conti, 1926, Château d'Yquem, 1921, Montrachet, 1965, and Château Lafite Rothschild, 1953.

the sale date and so gives ample time for the contents to be studied and decisions made. With advance notice, advice can be sought from the auctioneer, and here the advantage of time at the buyer's disposal can be best used to make unhurried choices and a study of prevailing market conditions.

What to buy

THE CRITICAL factor is what to buy. At a time of recession, an undoubted buyer's market prevails. Prices, which for several years have moved upwards, have now settled. Enormous pressure was placed on a hitherto willing market by the opening prices demanded by the producers for each new vintage. This resulted in strong price resistance, and while considerable stocks were taken up, even more remained in growers' and *negociants'* cellars in France. The wine market is international, and when the dollar is weak,

demand from the United States is muted. As this is such an important market the result is that good recent vintages can be bought elsewhere cheaply, providing there is a good quantity. In 1990 some of the abundant vintages of the 1980s could be bought for less, in real terms, than was being asked when they were first available, providing that you weren't buying in dollars.

In the space available it is only possible to give broad outlines of what should be purchased. Red Bordeaux and vintage port are the safest bets. Red Bordeaux is produced in a ratio to vintage port of 90:10. Modern methods of production, coupled with some pretty hot summers, have ensured a plethora of good vintages in the last decade. The best Bordeaux vintages to go for with a view to medium term investment, say five to ten years until the wines are ready to drink and therefore running short in supply, and so increasing in value are: 1982, 1983, 1985 and 1986. You can buy these for as little as

£60 ($110) a case. For vintage port 1977, 1983 and 1985 are the years to look for, at upwards of £96 ($180) a case.

There is no doubt that as with pictures, silver or furniture, buying the best produces the best results. Avoid dubious vintages such as 1984 and 1987. These will provide attractive drinking wines, but definitely not good investments. Which châteaux to buy? Safe bets are first growths, such as Lafite, Mouton-Rothschild and Latour, or 'super-seconds', such as Palmer, Pichon-Lalande, Ducru-Beaucaillou, Canon, Lynch-Bages or Léoville-Las-Cases. However, these are expensive – anywhere between £150 ($275) and £800 ($1,500) per case for one of the good vintages. For reasonable prices, good drinking and a perfectly safe investment, châteaux such as Beychevelle, Gruaud-Larose, Gloria, Grand-Puy-Lacoste, Giscours, Cissac, d'Angludet and Chasse-Spleen, to name but a few, fit the bill. For vintage port, the choice is much easier. The top shippers, in commercial terms, are Taylor, Graham and Fonseca, closely followed by Cockburn, Dow, Warre, Croft and Sandeman.

Burgundy has become very expensive in recent years, and even new vintages fetch high prices. With a smaller output than Bordeaux, many of Burgundy's better labels fetch as much as first growth clarets, and there is little of quality at the cheaper end of the range. In contrast, many good Californian wines are as highly valued as high-quality French ones. Labels to look for include Robert Mondavi, Diamond Creek and Joseph Phelps, and the best of recent years (for reds) are 1976, 1984 and 1985.

Storage

ONCE YOU HAVE bought your wine, how you store it is important. A cellar or basement is preferable. If one is not available, then use a cool cupboard, on a north-facing wall in a bedroom or under the stairs, even a secure garage. A steady temperature, ideally 13–16°C (55–60°F), darkness and stillness are advisable. If it is any warmer, the wine matures a trifle faster, perhaps no bad thing! Storage in a public warehouse is easily available, providing ideal conditions and at a fairly reasonable cost.

Finally, the above information provides a mere skeleton of a complex and fascinating subject. With time at your disposal and with plenty of wine books and specialist magazines bursting with knowledgeable articles, further study will open up a whole new vista of vinous enjoyment: a modicum of knowledge is strongly recommended. If a problem does arise a corkscrew pleasurably disposes of it.

☞ *below*

VINTAGE PORT AND MADEIRA

PORTUGUESE AND SPANISH

Like fine French red wine, good port improves with age and can be a profitable investment. Madeira does not enjoy the high prestige it had a hundred years ago, and so is cheaper than port but a less reliable buy.

COLLECTOR'S
SECTION

☞ *above*

**A SELECTION OF LADIES'
SHOES**
EUROPEAN 17th–19th c.

Buying and Selling

⌒

ANYONE ENTERING the field of antiques as a potential purchaser has essentially three options to choose from: they can attempt to 'go-it-alone', building a collection by themselves on the basis of trial and error, word-of-mouth, and information derived from magazine articles and books such as this; they can purchase primarily at auction, taking their chances and competing with experts and professionals, but at least being assured that the auction house is, to a degree, acting in their interest as well as that of the seller: or they can form a relationship with a dealer in their chosen category, who can become, if the dealer is a good one, not only a supplier, but also a guide and mentor.

Of the three, the first can be the most fun, and in some categories – say collecting comic books or cigarette cards, where individual purchases are at a price which is seldom likely to be financially threatening – it is a route to be highly recommended. There is nothing more exciting to the collector-acquirer (as opposed to the collector-investor, who is an entirely different animal) than browsing and rummaging at street-markets, trade fairs, second-hand shops or front-yard sales in order to find that vital finishing piece for their collection, or that mythical item (there is one in every collectible category) such as a missing Shakespeare manuscript, a lost van Gogh, or a Ming vase that someone has been using as a door-stop for the last twenty years, which will launch them to collecting fame and fortune (recently in England an Italian Renaissance bronze discovered at the back of a garden shed fetched over £650,000 at auction – so such things do happen).

However, buying without expert guidance, especially where significant sums of money are involved, can be hazardous and fraught with dangers: purchasing on a regular basis by trial and error is obviously out of the question for the vast majority of us as soon as the price of any individual item in the category we choose climbs over the £30–$50 mark, and that is when professional advice becomes essential. A book such as this is able to furnish the background information and factual data that any collector will want to refer to regularly, but when it comes to making important, high-value decisions on the spot, a definitive and confident assessment is necessary which can best be made by someone whose professional life has been devoted to discussing, handling, and, most importantly, buying and selling items in very specific disciplines. Remember, even some of the experts who have contributed to this volume, some of whom have been in the antiques business for upwards of forty years, will have made mistakes themselves while they were learning their trade: it is these hard knocks, and the sometimes costly lessons they teach, that fashion authority and expertise. There is no need for the average collector to 'learn by experience' (i.e. by expensive, or at least frustrating, errors) when such professional help is at hand, and need not cost a penny.

By buying at a reputable auction house, or by buying through a trustworthy dealer, the collector can be assured of certain things: firstly, the item for sale will have been thoroughly appraised by someone who knows what they are doing; secondly, that it will be accurately described; and thirdly, that the auctioneer or dealer will be considering their own reputation (worth considerably more to them than the commission on any individual piece, whatever its price) as well as the possibility of making a profit. After that, it is a question of 'Caveat Emptor' (Buyer Beware): after all, the buying and selling of antiques these days is big business, and people are in it to make money, as well as for reasons of aestheticism and enthusiasm. The majority of traders in antiques maintain high professional standards and deal with honour, but that does not stop them from driving a very hard bargain, and from quite rightly attempting to make the profits that their training, initiative, knowledge and energy deserve. Indeed, that is one of the most exciting aspects of antique collecting: once the ground has been laid for a fair contest, there are few things so exhilarating as the cut and thrust of making the deal. The best traders, and the best collectors, are those who never lose their appetite for excitement, and who never let excitement affect their judgement.

The Advantages of Buying at Auction

• The leading auction houses are household names – often businesses that have been trading for several centuries. They would not have done so – and would not continue to do – unless they maintained the highest standards of integrity, and that serves as a guarantee to the buyer as well as to the seller, of fair play within reasonable commercial parameters. That having been said, it is also fair to point out that the *first* duty of the auctioneer is to the client – to sell the piece, and to get as much as possible for it. An auctioneer's catalogue, like any sales brochure, is not going to dwell on the bad points of the product it is advertising, so although what *is* mentioned in the description will be scrupulously accurate, the buyer has to retain a normal and sensible level of cynicism. Items purchased at auction are bought 'as seen' – there is no going back later to point out a blemish, as the responsibility ultimately devolves onto the buyer to ensure prior to purchase that the piece is in the anticipated condition.

• For many potential sellers – and often quite remarkable objects are in the hands of ordinary folk who have inherited family treasures and so on – the major auction houses are the obvious first point of contact when for any reason they decide to, or need to, consider parting with their heirloom. The best houses offer free appraisal services without commitment, allowing the sellers to discover the value of their objects, and then the time to decide, on the basis of the valuation, whether they wish to put them up for auction or not. The benefit to the auctioneers of offering this service is obvious, in that it provides them with a regular, varied, and often fascinating source of items to handle. The benefit to the buyer is the potential these sources offer for bargains, and also the regular influx they provide of fresh material into the market place.

• Auction houses always provide the opportunity for the items at any forth-coming sale to be viewed several days in advance. At these viewings the sale pieces are on display, usually with experts on hand. Under supervision, virtually all the objects can be examined in detail and handled. This opportunity is absolutely invaluable for the collector: while learning, there is no substitute for close examination and touching (obviously where allowed and appropriate), and any-one seriously interested in developing an expertise for themselves should attend as many viewings as possible. It goes without saying that, unless you know a piece and its current condition already, it is highly

inadvisable to bid at auction on an item without having viewed it thoroughly.

• Auction houses are fine 'documenters' for the antiques business. For their own purposes, and as a service to their clients, they keep thorough and accurate records of items and transactions, thus building up excellent libraries and databases. Their photographic libraries are particularly good, as can be seen from the illustrations in this volume, most of which were provided by the individual experts with the support and professional assistance of the photographic department of the auction houses involved. The particular benefit this sound practice of recording affords the buyer is in the provision of exceptionally well-produced sale catalogues, which are circulated some way ahead of the main auctions. It is very easy to get on the mailing lists for these catalogues, though, depending on the auction house, and sometimes on the particular sale, there may be a charge. The catalogues are use-

ful to the serious collector for two reasons: principally to let them know what will be available for sale on a specific date (they are, after all, essentially promotional literature); but also, as they tend to be lavishly illustrated, to contain detailed descriptions, and to specify upper and lower likely sale prices as guidance, they form an excellent record of activity and current pricepoints in particular categories. A library of these catalogues can quickly build into an invaluable professional reference source.

• Perhaps the most important advantage to most buyers is that, given that most auction houses take a commission of around 10–12.5%, and that a private dealer could be attempting to mark up an item by anything from 50% to 200% or more, it can obviously be very much cheaper to buy at auction. Naturally this depends on how hot the competition for a piece is on a certain day: who is at the auction, whether the item has generated professional interest, and even whether it is raining outside!

☞ *opposite*

PIPE BAG

NATIVE AMERICAN c.1880
An early and excellent example of a Blackfoot pipe bag. Very few were made in this style, with its triangular beaded drop.

☞ *left*

JAPANNED BRACKET CLOCK

ENGLISH c.1760
The highly reliable English bracket clocks were much in demand overseas; this scarlet one was made for export to Turkey.

The Advantages of Buying from Dealers

• The main advantage of buying from a dealer is without doubt the benefit of personal contact. This benefit is substantially diluted if items are purchased piecemeal from a variety of sources, and for this reason most collectors who favour this route will prefer to work closely with a small circle of dealers. However much you like and trust a particular trader, it is still a good idea to build a relationship with more than one, and to make sure that each of the dealers you work with knows about the others: that will keep them on their toes and keep prices competitive. Good dealers will take the time and trouble to get to know their clients, even if no immediate purchases arise, both because they have a personal love of their subject, and wish to share their interest with others, and for the very sound commercial reason that, in the long term, if their advice, service, and contacts are good, business will be done.

One of the main advantages good dealers offer is, ironically, that they will often actually *prevent* their clients from purchasing. All collectors make mistakes early in their careers: they over-buy through enthusiasm (both in quantity and price); or they are tempted to diversify too soon into new areas, acquiring pieces which are not central to their true interest, which later become at best superfluous or peripheral, and, at worst, an embarrassment. Commonly the sympathetic dealer, with greater experience than the client, may have a better idea of the shape that the overall collection is taking, and can nurture and focus attention in the right direction.

The best dealers offer a much broader service than merely having their goods on display and 'selling from stock'. Once they know the needs of a particular collector they can actively seek specific items to fill gaps in the collection. Because it is their business, to which they devote themselves full-time, they will inevitably have a much wider network than any non-professional collector can ever develop. As a matter of course they can enquire about the availability of pieces from dealers in other cities and, most vitally in some categories, from overseas. In addition they will be routinely circulated with news of all auctions and important private sales, and should be well-enough connected to get wind, occasionally, of items which are not yet quite on sale but might be available for a certain price. In turn, they can circulate their own contacts with 'want-lists' of desired items or subjects, radically multiplying their client-collectors' chances of expanding their collections.

Purchases from dealers, depending on individual arrangements, can be less risky than those from auctions. The 'as seen' element need not apply, as most reputable dealers are happy to issue receipts and guarantees that a piece is in a certain condition, backed up by a full professional description. Once a relationship has been formed, many dealers are even prepared to offer a piece on a trial basis – allowing the client to keep it for a while to see how it sits with the rest of the collection, and to see how they feel about it before a final decision is made and money changes hands (or the piece is returned). Purchases from dealers are very often made on the understanding that if ever the client changes their mind the piece will be repurchased by the dealer at the original price paid – though this should be clarified at the time that the deal is made. It is not in the long-term interest of the dealer to force goods on their clients, or to persuade them to take items which are not suitable – though there are, of course, many less scrupulous traders around who do not view business in quite these terms.

Restoration, Care and Display

THE BEST advice commonly given about repairing and restoring antiques is: don't. If you are weighing up this option, then your piece is already imperfect, and the damage is done. In virtually every antique category there is very little or no difference in price between a damaged item and a repaired or restored item, so there is

unlikely to be any financial benefit. Prevention is better than cure: think very hard before you purchase a piece knowing that it is imperfect; and transport, store and display your antiques in the most careful manner possible – however much it adds to your expenditure of time and money the care taken is always worth it.

If you have some personal or aesthetic reason for wishing to restore or repair a piece, do not attempt to carry out the work yourself. There are highly talented professionals who specialize in all categories – from pictures to dolls to watches – who have spent their lives perfecting their skills and who will be able to carry out the work much more quickly and attractively than you, however lovingly you proceed. Their involvement will at least ensure that the damage will not be made worse. If repair work is to be carried out, then invest carefully in having it done properly and sympathetically. It is satisfying to use techniques and materials current at the time the piece was originally made, and, if possible and necessary, to incorporate replacement parts from similar contemporary objects. Specialist craftspeople may have access to such material from items they have 'cannibalized' in the past.

Cleaning antiques is a highly controversial subject, and advice will vary from category to category and from expert to expert. As usual, the best practical guidance is that if you have any doubts, leave it alone. Certainly never ever attempt to touch any antique with any form of proprietary cleaner, especially anything abrasive or corrosive. Even if you are a reasonably old hand and confident in the advice you have been given, cleaning is still a task best left to a paid professional. Even the final decision about whether an item needs cleaning or not is a decision to be taken by an expert. What might look, to the untrained eye, like a blemish, ugly stain, or layer of dirt may well be the essential mark or authentic patina which makes a piece of particular interest when viewed by an experienced dealer.

Caring for and maintaining your antiques is something quite different, and a topic to which any serious collector will give a lot of emphasis. There is little point in investing a large amount of money in a piece if its quality and condition are then allowed rapidly to deteriorate. It is difficult to cover the subject of care and maintenance in a comprehensive volume such as this, as each category of antique has its own rules and guidelines: the right condi-

tions for storing wine, for example, are obviously totally unsuitable for a quilt or etching. Many specialist articles and books have been published on the care of items within the individual antique disciplines, and anyone collecting in a specific category must thoroughly familiarize himself with this information. Particular attention should be paid to the three essential variables of temperature, humidity and light, all of which can be great allies or very dangerous foes.

If you have purchased an item from a dealer he will almost certainly give you detailed instructions on how to care for it – whether you want them or not! Listen carefully and you will not regret it. If you are buying for the love of a piece, then you will want to keep it in the best possible condition: and if you are buying with an eye to financial gain, then, if anything, care is even more vital to safeguard your investment.

Displaying antiques is one of the most enjoyable aspects of collecting: there is no point, after all, in investing a large amount of time, money and effort in assembling a fine group of items if you do not then take an enormous amount of pride in displaying it to the best effect. Nothing is sadder than to hear of fine pieces locked away, stored in bankers' vaults, or hidden in basements because of lack of display space (some of our greatest museums and galleries are, of course, guilty of this crime against collecting, though this is not always a situation of their own choosing). Regrettably there can often be a tension here between the best conditions for storing and caring for a piece, and the best conditions for displaying it. For example, sometimes the best light for viewing can be the worst possible light for conservation, and where this is the case it is unfortunately necessary to veer heavily towards the line of caution.

Once you are certain that your planned display system will not contribute to the deterioration of your collection, then great fun can be had in creating storage systems, display cases, and lighting effects. Some collectors prefer to stick to traditional methods – the plan chests, multi-drawered cabinets and glass-fronted cupboards, for example, so beloved of the Edwardian archaists – while others commission simple modern shelving systems and invest more heavily in various forms of indirect or spot-lighting. The main thing is to choose a style that you feel comfortable with and that attractively complements the nature and feel of the antiques you are collecting. On a grander scale a whole house interior or room can be designed around the theme of your collection: one collector of musical instruments and ephemera, for example, has created a complete period music room in which his collection is naturally and perfectly arrayed.

Good display adds an extra intangible dimension to a collection. In addition, if you have any intention of dealing in antiques, even at the most basic level, and you are ever likely to invite a fellow collector to view an item and make an offer on it, it is undoubtedly the case that good display can add value to the piece on offer. One constantly hears the complaint from buyers that the piece that looked so charming, striking, dignified, or colourful in the shop, and for which they therefore paid such an exorbitant sum of

money, became miraculously charmless, inconsequential, vulgar, or subdued as soon as they got it home. This is because the clever merchant, after years of experience, has thought carefully about the character of the item and designed a setting in his shop to accentuate its finest virtues; whereas the buyer has hurried home to put it on the mantelshelf, resting it at an angle in a shadow against the orange wallpaper next to his unpaid bills.

Care and display are fundamental elements of the collector's art, but are too often neglected, one reason being that they are, unavoidably, relatively expensive. A rough estimate might be that 10% of the value of a collection should be set aside for its care and display, especially when the cost of insurance is taken into consideration. Items such as sophisticated temperature and light controls, and burglar alarms or other security measures are costly, but worth every penny, if for no other reason than to give the collector peace of mind. It is good advice to budget for these 'hidden' costs of collecting when planning purchases. If all of your financial allocation goes on the pieces themselves, you might very well quickly assemble ten fine items, but be forced to jumble them ad hoc around the house, or even to keep

them at your bank for fear of robbery. How much better to have nine pieces arranged as an attractive centrepiece to your home, set on complementary shelving, with subtle lighting, protected by the security of a burglar alarm, and kept in top condition by the most up-to-date humidity modifier. By disciplining yourself to spend, in round numbers, only $90 or £45 of every £100 or £50 of your collecting budget on actual antiques, and allocating the residual 10% to these peripheral elements, you will obtain much greater pleasure, satisfaction, and, in the long term, value from your collection.

Recording and Cataloguing
—

METICULOUS RECORDS should be kept from the first day a collection is started. Most collectors enjoy this aspect, as the urge to collect normally reflects a well-organized and retentive personality, but

☞ *below*
SELECTION OF TOYS
VARIOUS COUNTRIES
20th c.
The archetypal boys' toys are soldiers and trains, as the archetypal girls toys

are dolls. In spite of the huge variety of other toys, these three subjects remain the most widely respected individual specialities.

even for those who find this an unexciting prospect, it is nevertheless vital that scrupulous documentation should be maintained, for the following reasons:

- In order to develop as a collector, it is important to be able to look back at previous buying and selling activity in the light of experience. At minimum, notes on the date of purchase, the piece, the seller's address, and the price are obviously crucial, and you can very usefully add personal details covering your reasons for buying that particular antique, how you located it, the way the negotiation or bidding was handled, your view of the person who sold the item to you, and your feelings once the deal was done. This will force you to ask questions of yourself and to analyze your collecting practices. It is only by constantly reviewing your motivation, successes and mistakes that you will improve as a collector, and that improvement will be quickly reflected in higher quality pieces at lower prices, and a generally more satisfying collection.

- As well as your personal records, you will need to keep the basic details of any transaction, including a sales receipt and any other documentation provided, for both tax and insurance purposes. These should be kept together in a safe place, probably outside your home. Get in the habit of administering this element in an organized way – it may be a chore, but nowhere near as bad as desperately trying to recreate several years of your collecting history from torn scraps of paper and crumpled receipts to satisfy a suspicious tax collector or to make an insurance claim in the aftermath of a robbery or fire.

- Recording prices and keeping documentation is also essential in order to allow a piece to be sold. Whether you set off to be a trader or not, as a collector you will inevitably end up by being, at least in part, a dealer. Unless you are lucky enough to have unlimited resources you cannot continue to acquire endlessly: a stage will be reached when you will need to sell some pieces in order to buy others. In addition, you may have made mistakes early in your career – pieces which are not up to standard, or which are no longer central to your interests – which you will want to shed. Just as the tendency is to upgrade the type of house we live in or the car we drive as tastes and resources change, so a collection will go through several distinct phases, dependent on variables such as the collector's disposable income, personal style and experience. Items which seemed strange and exciting early in a collector's development may turn out to be commonplace, and these pieces will be traded in for finer or more expensive antiques. Obviously when an item has to be sold, the new buyer will want some details as to its provenance, and at the very least some proof that you own what you are selling: this will be provided by the original receipt you have kept. And just as importantly, you will want an accurate reference as to how much you paid for the piece, and how long ago. In order to get the maximum benefit to reinvest in your collection, and the additional resources to improve it, you need to be sure that you are selling these items for more than you paid for them – allowing for inflation – and this, again, is where good record-keeping is absolutely vital.

Starting a Collection

THERE ARE two basic elements which link all collector-acquirers, whatever their speciality: these are a love of their subject, and, principally, a love of collecting. As

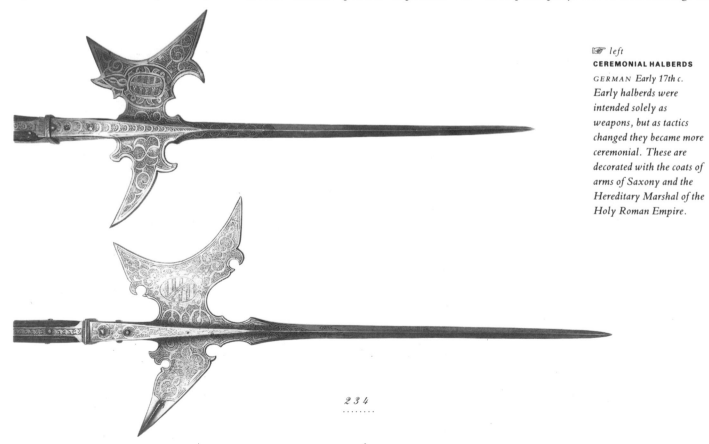

☞ *left*
CEREMONIAL HALBERDS
GERMAN *Early 17th c. Early halberds were intended solely as weapons, but as tactics changed they became more ceremonial. These are decorated with the coats of arms of Saxony and the Hereditary Marshal of the Holy Roman Empire.*

the urge to collect generally precedes the selection of the item to be acquired, it is worth examining a few basic rules to be followed when planning a collection and choosing a subject:

● Although collectors are probably born, rather than made, it is still the case that most collections are started by accident rather than deliberately. Perhaps the latent collector inherits one or two items and decides to build on this nucleus; or, at a very young age, the person takes on an enthusiasm, perhaps influenced by friends or a current craze at school, which lives on in them after the initial impetus is long forgotten. This latter motivation is particularly common in the fields of coin, stamp, model soldier, comic book, cigarette card, doll, and train collecting, while the former is more closely associated with items that are often passed down in families, such as watches and clocks, china and glass, and furniture. In both these sets of circumstances, the collection exists almost before the collector knows or acknowledges it, and all that is needed to transform it into a collection proper is a slightly more serious and formulated approach to things like cataloguing, display, the seeking of expert information and advice, research, and a programme of budgetting and acquisition. It may well be, having experimented with a juvenile collection in one specialization, or having been given one or two objects in a category, that those pieces cease to be of interest, but the collecting bug remains, in which case a new field will need to be researched.

● Whether you have previously experimented with a collection of one sort, or are starting completely from nothing, the most important thing is to combine your urge to collect with your personal taste and other interests – to be involved with a category that you are comfortable with, find aesthetically pleasing, and personally satisfying. One well-known collector started with a practical interest in needleworking, and acquired all sorts of accessories to use and experiment with

before specializing in thimbles and eventually forming one of the best collections in the world: it is this combination of collecting enthusiasm and personal passion that is likely to shape the most successful collections.

● If you are genuinely unsure about a category to collect, then visit some general antique fairs, markets, and viewings to look at a wide range of objects. Only by looking at items close up and handling them will you know if you have an empathy with the subject. Talk to as many people as you can and read about the history of the categories you are considering: the stories, both of the pieces themselves and of the people who made, purchased and collected them, can be fascinating, and may inspire you in a particular direction.

● Think hard about the practical aspects before committing yourself to a subject. If you live in a small flat or apartment, there is little point, even if you are wealthy enough, in setting out to build a collection of large-scale stone sculpture or Tudor oak furniture, as you won't have the space to display it. Similarly if you have a limited amount of time to allocate to your collection, the main sales and dealers you need to attend and see regularly should be situated locally: if the principal auctions in your chosen specialization are held only on weekdays, and 300 miles away, then your collecting hobby will come into tension with your work or other aspects of your life, and both will suffer.

● Principally, think about the amount of money you have to spend in relation to the prices you will have to pay. If you are starting from nothing you will want very quickly to form a nucleus of four or five items which can legitimately be described as 'a collection'. After that you will want to add to it regularly, and just how regularly will depend on how much the pieces cost in proportion to your resources. You will probably become very frustrated if

☞ *above*

NICHOLAS HILLIARD
A GENTLEMAN
ENGLISH Late 16th c.
Height: 5.5cm (2⅛in)
This portrait is thought to be of George Clifford, 3rd Earl of Cumberland.

you cannot splash out on a new piece at least once every six months, and if that is the case, then the calculations and decisions become straightforward. If the items in your chosen subject category cost, in round figures, about £50/$100, then you will need an initial input of around £250/$500 (plus a little extra for display, insurance and so on), and a minimum of £100/$200 per year to keep the collection growing and developing at anywhere near a satisfying rate.

Think hard about the budget and your own collecting urges and style: too often what should be a great pleasure is spoiled either because collectors get themselves into financial difficulties to support their hobby, or because the collector has chosen to operate in an area which is too expensive to allow purchasing at exciting and satisfying intervals. The advice most commonly given is to buy less frequently in order to devote your budget to purchasing the best quality you can: if you have the patience to adopt this tactic you will never be disappointed. If this simply does not suit your personality, then try to choose a category in which the best items are inexpensive enough to allow you to buy relatively frequently within your resources.

INTERNATIONAL DIRECTORY
···
MUSEUMS, AUCTIONEERS AND
SPECIALIST DEALERS

AUSTRALIA

ASA STAMPS CO PTY
138–140 Rundle Mall, Adelaide, SA 5001
Tel: 223 2951
auctioneer
~

ASSOCIATED AUCTIONEERS PTY
800–810 Parramatta Rd, Lewisham, NSW 2049
Tel: 560 5899
auctioneer
~

BRIGHT SLATER PTY
Brisbane Club Building, Isles Lane, Brisbane,
Queensland 4000 Tel: 312415
auctioneer
~

CHRISTIE, MANSON & WOODS
298 New South Head Road, Double Bay, Sydney,
NSW 2028 Tel: 326 1422
auctioneer
~

JOHNSON BROTHERS
328 Main Road, Glenorchy, Tasmania 7011
auctioneer
~

SOTHEBY PARKE BERNET
115 Collins Street, Melbourne, Victoria 3000
Tel: 633 900
auctioneer
~

H E WELLS & SONS
326 Rokeby Road, Subiaco, WA Tel: 381 9040
auctioneer
~

AUSTRIA

CHRISTIE'S
A-1030 Wien, Ziehrerplatz 4–22 Tel: Vienna 732644
auctioneer
~

KUNSTHISTORISCHES MUSEUM
Vienna
museum: general collection
~

BELGIUM

CHRISTIE, MANSON & WOODS
33 Boulevard de Waterloo, Bruxelles B-1000
Tel: Brussels 512 8830
auctioneer
~

MUSÉE HORTA
Brussels
museum
~

SOTHEBY PARKE BERNET
32 Rue de l'Abbaye, Bruxelles 1050
Tel: Brussels 343 5007

CANADA

CHRISTIE'S INTERNATIONAL
1055 West Georgia Street, Vancouver, BC V6E 3P3
Tel: 685 2126
auctioneer
~

MUSEUM OF FINE ARTS
1379 Sherbrooke Street, Montreal, Quebec
Tel: 514 285 1600
museum: general collection, Native art
~

ROYAL ONTARIO MUSEUM
100 Queen's Park, Toronto, Ontario
Tel: 416 586 5736
museum: general collection, arts of the East
~

SOTHEBY PARKE BERNET
156 Front Street, Toronto, Ontario M5J 2L6
Tel: 416 596 0300
auctioneer
~

WINNIPEG ART GALLERY
300 Memorial Boulevard, Winnipeg, Manitoba
Tel: 204 786 6641
gallery: general collection, Native and Canadian folk art
~

FRANCE

DE CAGNY
4 rue Drouot, Paris 75009 Tel: 246 0007
auctioneer
~

CHRISTIE'S
17 rue de Lille, Paris 75007 Tel: 261 1247
auctioneer
~

MUSÉE DE LOUVRE
Paris
museum: general collection
~

SOTHEBY'S
3 rue de Miromesnil, Paris 75008 Tel: 266 4060
auctioneer
~

GERMANY

ANTIQUITAETEN LOTHAR HEUBEL
371 Odenthaler Strasse, Koln 1 Tel: Cologne 601825
auctioneer
~

AUKTIONSHAUS TIEJEN
30 Spitaler Strasse, D-2000 Hamburg 1 Tel: 330368
auctioneer
~

BAYERISCHES NATIONALMUSEUM
Munich
museum: general collection
~

AUGUST BODIGER
4 Oxfordstrasse, Bonn Tel: 636940
auctioneer
~

CHRISTIE'S
Maximilianstrasse 20, D-8000 Munich 22
Tel: 229539
auctioneer
~

GERMANISCHES NATIONALMUSEUM
Berlin
museum: general collection
~

GERMANISCHES NATIONALMUSEUM
Nuremberg
museum: general collection
~

GERNET DORAU
2 Johann-Georg Strasse, D-1000 Berlin 31
Tel: 892 6198
auctioneer
~

HISTORICHES MUSEUM
Dresen
museum: general collection
~

SOTHEBY PARKE BERNET
Odeonsplatz 16, D-8000 Munich 22 Tel: 222376
auctioneer
~

HOLLAND

CENTRAAL MUSEUM
Utrecht
museum: general collection
~

CHRISTIE, MANSON & WOODS
Rokin 91, Amsterdam 1012 KL Tel: 231505
auctioneer
~

RIJKSMUSEUM
Amsterdam
museum: general collection
~

SOTHEBY
Rokin 102, Amsterdam 1012 KZ Tel: 246215
auctioneer
~

HONG KONG

SOTHEBY PARKE BERNET
64 Queen's Road Central, Hong Kong
Tel: Hong Kong 225454
auctioneer
~

ITALY

CHRISTIE'S
114 Piazza Navona, Roma 00186 Tel: Rome 6541217
auctioneer
~

FINARTE
Piazzetta Bossi 4, Milano 20121 Tel: Milan 877041
auctioneer
~

GALLERIA DEGLI UFFIZI
Florence
gallery/museum: mainly paintings

~

SOTHBY PARKE BERNET
Via Gino Capponi 26, Firenze 50121
Tel: Florence 571410
auctioneer

~

VATICAN MUSEUM
Rome
museum: general collection

~

NEW ZEALAND

ALEX HARRIS LTD
377 Princess Street, Dunedin Tel: 740703
auctioneer

~

DUNBAR SLOANE LTD
32 Waring Taylor Street, Wellington Tel: 721 367
auctioneer

~

THORNTON AUCTIONS
89 Albert Street, Auckland 1 Tel: 30888
auctioneer

~

D J VISSER
90 Worcester Street, Christchurch Tel: 67297
auctioneer

~

SOUTH AFRICA

SOTHEBY PARKE BERNET
Total House, Rissik Street, Braamfontein 2017
Tel: 393726
auctioneer

~

SPAIN

CHRISTIE'S
5 Casado del Alisal, Madrid Tel: 228 9300
auctioneer

~

UNITED KINGDOM

ADAM & SONS
26 St Stephen's Green, Dublin Tel: Dublin 760261
auctioneer

~

ALDRIDGES
130 Walcot Street, Bath, Avon Tel: 0225 62830
auctioneer

~

ALFIES ANTIQUE MARKET
13–25 Church Street, London NW8
Tel: 071 723 6066
market; over 350 stands including; desks & bureaux;
clocks & watches; paperweights; samplers; sporting items
and ephemera; ceramics; silver; jewellery; marine items;
lighting; radios; Art Deco furniture and artefacts;
bohemian glass; fireplaces; French mirrors; Art Deco
ceramics; scientific instruments; postcards; handbags;
paintings of all types; rare books; mechanical items;
Victoriana; carpets and textiles; corkscrews; etc

THE AMERICAN MUSEUM IN BATH
Claverton Manor, Claverton, Bath, Avon
Tel: 0225 463538
Americana and American folk and decorative arts

~

AMERSHAM AUCTION ROOMS
125 Station Road, Amersham, Bucks
Tel: 0494 729292
auctioneer

~

ART DECO CERAMICS
The Ocsbury, 10 Mill Street, Warwick CV34 4HB
Tel: 0926 498068
dealer; specializes in Art Deco ceramics

~

THE ASHMOLEAN MUSEUM
Beaumont Street, Oxford Tel: 0865 278000
museum; fine and decorative arts

~

AVON ANTIQUES
25–27 Market Street, Bradford-on-Avon, Wilts
Tel: 02216 2052
dealer, eight showrooms; specializes in 17th, 18th and
early 19th century furniture, also clocks and barometers,
etc

~

GILBERT BAITSON
The Edwardian Auction Galleries, 194 Anlaby
Road, Hull Tel: 0482 865831
auctioneer

~

BATE COLLECTION OF HISTORICAL
INSTRUMENTS
Faculty of Music, Oxford University, St Aldate's,
Oxford Tel: 0865 276139
museum; musical instruments

~

BAYLES
Childs Farm, Cottered Buntingford, Herts
Tel: 076381 256
auctioneer

~

BETHNAL GREEN MUSEUM OF CHILDHOOD
Cambridge Heath Road, London E2
Tel: 081 980 3204
museum: dolls, dolls houses, toys, costume, ephemera,
juvenilia

~

BIGWOOD AUCTIONEERS
The Old School, Tiddington, Stratford-on-Avon,
Warwicks. Tel: 0789 69415
auctioneer

~

BIRMINGHAM MUSEUM AND ART GALLERY
Chamberlain Sq., Birmingham B3
Tel: 021 235 2834
museum; comprehensive general collection

~

BONHAMS
Montpelier Street, Knightsbridge, London SW7
Tel: 071 584 9161
auctioneer

~

BONHAMS (WEST COUNTRY)
Devon Fine Art Auction House, Dowell Street,
Honiton Tel: 0404 41872
auctioneer

~

BRIGHTON MUSEUM AND ART GALLERY
Church Street, Brighton, East Sussex
Tel: 0273 603005
museum; decorative arts, decorative arts movements,
general collection

~

BRITISH ANTIQUE DEALERS'
ASSOCIATION
20 Rutland Gate, London SW7 1BD
Tel: 071 589 4128
trade association; will provide lists of accredited members,
lists of antiques fairs, and various other consumer services
to collectors on request

~

BRISTOL MUSEUM AND ART GALLERY
Queen's Road, Bristol BS8 1RL, Avon
Tel: 0272 251470
general collection

~

BRITISH MUSEUM
Great Russell Street, London WC1
Tel: 071 636 1555
museum; general collection, antiquities

~

WILLIAM BROWN
11–14 East Hill, Colchester, Essex Tel: 0206 868070
auctioneer

~

BRUTON, KNOWLES & CO
111 Eastgate Street, Gloucester, Glos Tel: 0452 21267
auctioneer

~

BURRELL COLLECTION
Pollok Country Park, Glasgow Tel: 041 649 7151
museum; general collection, silver, applied arts, decorative
arts, fine arts

~

CARLESS & CO
58 Lowesmoor, Worcester, Worcs. Tel: 0905 612449
auctioneer

~

CHANCELLORS
32 High Street, Ascot, Berks
Tel: 0990 872588
auctioneer

~

CHEFFINS, GRAIN & COMINS
2 Clifton Road, Cambridge, Cambs.
Tel: 0223 358721
auctioneer

~

CHELTENHAM ART GALLERY AND
MUSEUM
Clarence Street, Cheltenham, Glos.
Tel: 0242 237431
museum; Eastern ceramics, textiles, arts and crafts
movement, general collection

CHRISTIE'S
8 King Street, St. James's, London SW1
Tel: 071 839 9060
auctioneer

~

CHRISTIE'S SOUTH KENSINGTON
85 Old Brompton Road, London SW7
Tel: 071 581 7611
auctioneer

~

CHURCHGATE AUCTIONS
66 Churchgate, Leicester, Leics. Tel: 0533 621416
auctioneer

~

CLARE'S AUCTION ROOMS
70 Park Street, Birmingham Tel: 021 643 0226
auctioneer

~

CLEVELAND CRAFTS CENTRE
57 Gilkes Street, Middlesborough, TS1 5EL,
Cleveland Tel: 0642 226351
permanent display of ceramics and jewellery

~

COOPER HIRST
Granary Saleroom, Victoria Road, Chelmsford,
Essex Tel: 0245 25814
auctioneer

~

THOS COULBORN & SONS
Vesey Manor, Sutton Coldfield, West Midlands
B72 1QP Tel: 021 354 3974
*dealer; general antiques, fine arts, clocks, silver and works
of art*

~

COURTAULD INSTITUTE GALLERY
Somerset House, Strand, London WC2
Tel: 071 873 2526
gallery; the art collection of the University of London

~

THE CUMBERLAND TOY AND MODEL MUSEUM
Bank's Court, Market Place, Cockermouth,
Cumbria Tel: 0900 827606
20th century British toys

~

DARLINGTON RAILWAY CENTRE AND MUSEUM
North Road Station, Darlington, Co. Durham
Tel: 0325 460532
museum; railway equipment and ephemera

~

DERBY MUSEUM AND ART GALLERY
The Strand, Derby, Derbys. Tel: 0332 293111
museum/gallery; general collections

~

ENTWISTLE GREEN
The Galleries, Kingsway, Lytham St. Annes, Lancs.
Tel: 0253 735442
auctioneer

~

GH EVANS
The Market Place, Kilgetty, Dyfed Tel: 0834 811151
auctioneer

~

FAIRFAX HOUSE
Castlegate, York YO1, N. Yorks. Tel: 0904 655543
*private collection open to the public; general collection,
furniture, clocks*

~

THE FAN MUSEUM
10 Crooms Hill, London SE10 8ER
Tel: 081 858 7879
museum; fans

~

FITZWILLIAM MUSEUM
Trumpington Street, Cambridge, Cambs.
*museum; antiquities, coins, tribal art, books and
manuscripts, etc*

~

FRASERS
28 Church Street, Inverness Tel: 0463 232395
auctioneer

~

GALLERY OF ENGLISH COSTUME
Platt Hall, Platt Fields, Rusholme, Manchester
Tel: 061 224 5217
exceptional collection of costume and textiles

~

GA AUCTION GALLERIES
40 Station Road West, Canterbury, Kent
Tel: 0227 763337
auctioneer

~

GA FINE ART
Royal Auction Rooms, Queen Street, Scarborough,
Yorks Tel: 0723 353581
auctioneer

~

GEFFRYE MUSEUM
Kingsland Road, London E2 Tel: 081 739 8363
*museum; antiquities, period decor, decorative arts, books
and manuscripts, furniture, Art Deco*

~

STANLEY GIBBONS AUCTIONS
399 Strand, London WC2 Tel: 071 836 8444
auctioneers; stamps; coins

~

THE GINNEL ANTIQUE CENTRE, HARROGATE
Corn Exchange Building, Parliament Street,
Harrogate, Yorks HG1 2RB
*40 shops, including jewellery, linen & lace, longcase
clocks, prints, arms & armour, porcelain and glassware*

~

GLASGOW ART GALLERY AND MUSEUM
Kelvingrove, Glasgow Tel: 041 357 3929
*gallery/museum; fine and decorative arts, arts and crafts
movements*

~

GLOUCESTER CITY MUSEUM AND ART GALLERY
Brunswick Road, Gloucester, Glos. Tel: 0452 24131
museum; general collection

~

GRAYS ANTIQUE MARKET
58 Davies Street, London W1 Tel: 071 629 7034
*nearly 80 stalls, including the following specialities: lace
(Diana Harby, 629 5130); glass and drink-associated*

antiques (Ronald Falloon, 499 0158; and Vintage, 483
9457); cameras, lighters, and watches (Cozy World, 409
0269); netsuke and oriental objects (David Bowden, 495
1773); antique weapons, arms and armour (Armada
Antiques, 499 1087; and Armoury Antiques, 408 0176);
jewellery (JM Davies, 493 0624; Abacus, 629 9681;
Renate, 408 1059; R&R Jewellery, 629 6467;
Westminster Group, 493 8672; Trianon, 491 2764;
Ventura-Pauly, 408 1057; Sandra Ventura, 495 6147;
RBR Group, 629 4769; and A&G Antiques, 493
7497); tools and instruments (David Hogg, 493 0208);
smoking antiques (Kunio Kikuchi, 629 6808); quilts and
textiles (Sue Maddon, 493 1307); thimbles (The
Thimble Society, 493 0560); scientific instruments
(Steven O'Donnell, 491 8852); and toys (Pierre Patau,
499 0539)

~

GRAYS MEWS
1–7 Davies Mews, London W1 Tel: 629 7034
*c. 80 stalls, including golf collectibles; oriental objects;
silver; boxes; jewellery; toys; mechanical toys;
needlework; Art Deco; watches; Victoriana; dolls; arms
and armour; pictures and paintings; bronzes; tribal
antiquities; fine books; Art Nouveau glass; Islamic
objects; netsuke; chinese textiles; and chess books and
ephemera*

~

GREENSLADE
13 Hamet Street, Taunton, Somerset
Tel: 0823 277121
auctioneer

~

HALL AND LLOYD
South Street Auction Rooms, Stafford, Staffs
Tel: 0785 58176
auctioneer

~

HALL, WATERBRIDGE AND OWEN
Welsh Bridge Saleroom, Shrewsbury
Tel: 0743 60212
auctioneer

~

HAMPSHIRE AND BERKSHIRE AUCTIONS
82 Sarum Hill, Basingstoke, Hants.
Tel: 0256 840707
auctioneer

~

HAMPTONS
71 Church Street, Malvern, Worcs. Tel: 0684 892314
auctioneer

~

HEATHCOTE, BALL & CO
Albion Auction Rooms, Commercial Street,
Northampton Tel: 0604 22735
auctioneer

~

CECIL HIGGINS ART GALLERY AND MUSEUM
Castle Close, Bedford, Tel: 0234 211222
museum; general collection, decorative arts, lace

~

HOBBS AND CHAMBERS
15 Royal Crescent, Cheltenham, Glos.
Tel: 0242 513722
auctioneer

~

HORNIMAN MUSEUM
100 London Road, London SE23 Tel: 081 699 2339
museum; tribal art, musical instruments, crafts,
design

~

ILFRACOMBE MUSEUM
Wilder Road, Ilfracombe, Devon
museum; general collection

~

IMPERIAL WAR MUSEUM
Lambeth Road, London SE1
Tel: 071 735 8922
museum; arms and armour, militaria, uniform

~

RAYMOND INMAN AUCTION GALLERIES
35 Temple Street, Brighton, Sussex
Tel: 0273 774777
auctioneer

~

JOHN JEFFREY & SON
The Livestock Market, Christ's Lane, Shaftesbury,
Dorset Tel: 0747 52720
auctioneer

~

A JOHNSON & SONS
Nottingham Auction Rooms, Meadow Lane,
Nottingham Tel: 0602 869128
auctioneer

~

LACY SCOTT
10 Risbygate Street, Bury St Edmunds, Suffolk
Tel: 0284 763531
auctioneer

~

THE LEICESTERSHIRE
MUSEUM AND ART GALLERY
New Walk, Leicester Tel: 0533 554100
museum

~

LEIGHTON HOUSE
ART GALLERY AND MUSEUM
12 Holland Park Road, London W14
Tel: 071 602 3316
museum/gallery; decorative arts, arts and crafts
movements

~

LEWES AUCTION ROOMS
56 High Street, Lewes, Sussex Tel: 0273 478221
auctioneer

~

LITHGOW SONS & PARTNERS
The Auction House, Station Road, Stokesley,
Middlesborough Tel: 0642 710158
auctioneer

~

LIVERPOOL MUSEUM
William Brown Street, Liverpool, L3
museum; general collection

~

LUTON MUSEUM AND ART GALLERY
Wardown Park, Luton LU2 7HA, Beds.
Tel: 0582 36941
museum; general collection

~

MAGGS BROS
50 Berkeley Sq., London W1 Tel: 071 493 7160
dealer; rare and antiquarian books

~

MAIDSTONE MUSEUM AND ART GALLERY
St Faith's Street, Maidstone, Kent Tel: 0622 54497
museum

~

MANCHESTER CITY ART GALLERY
Moseley Street (061 236 5244) and Princess Street
(061 236 9422) Manchester
galleries; one of the best collections in the UK

~

MILLER
Lemon Quay Auction Rooms, Truro, Cornwall
Tel: 0872 74211
auctioneer

~

THOMAS MILLER
18 Gallowgate, Newcastle, Tyne & Wear
Tel: 091 232 5617
auctioneer

~

J MILNE
9 North Silver Street, Aberdeen Tel: 0224 639336
auctioneer

~

PAUL MITCHELL
99 New Bond Street, London W1Y 9LF
Tel: 071 493 8732
dealer; picture frames

~

MORGANS AUCTIONS
Dunroe Crescent, Dunroe Road, Belfast
Tel: 0232 771552
auctioneer

~

WILLIAM MORRIS GALLERY
Water House, Lloyd Park, Forest Road,
Walthamstow, London E17 Tel: 081 527 3782
museum; based at Morris' childhood home, arts and crafts
movement

~

MUSEUM OF CHILDHOOD
38 High Street, Edinburgh Tel: 031 225 2424
museum; costume, toys, ephemera, dolls

~

MUSEUM OF COSTUME
Assembly Rooms, Bennett Street, Bath, Avon
Tel: 0225 461111
Costume from the 1500s to the present day

~

MUSEUM OF COSTUME AND TEXTILES
51 Castlegate, Nottingham Tel: 0602 483504
museum; lace, textiles, costume

~

MUSICAL MUSEUM
368 High Street, Brenford, Middx. Tel: 081 560 8108
museum; musical instruments of all periods

~

NATIONAL ARMY MUSEUM
Royal Hospital Road, London SW3
Tel: 730 0717
museum; uniform, militaria, weaponry

~

NATIONAL GALLERY
Trafalgar Square, London WC2 Tel: 071 839 3321
gallery

~

NATIONAL GALLERY OF SCOTLAND
The Mound, Edinburgh
gallery

~

NATIONAL MOTOR MUSEUM
Beaulieu, Hants.
Tel: 0590 612345
museum; over 250 motor cars and vehicles

~

NATIONAL MUSEUM OF IRELAND
Kildare Street and Merrion Street, Dublin
Tel: 0001 618811
museum; fine and decorative arts

~

NATIONAL MUSEUM OF WALES
Main Building, Cathays Park, Cardiff
Tel: 0222 397951
museum; general collection, paintings

~

NATIONAL POSTAL MUSEUM
King Edward Street, London EC1 Tel: 071 432 3851
museum; stamps and associated items

~

JAMES' NORWICH AUCTIONS
33 Timberhill, Norwich, Norfolk Tel: 0603 624817
auctioneer

~

OUTHWAITE & LITHERLAND
Kingsway Galleries, Fontenoy Street, Liverpool
Tel: 051 236 6563
auctioneer

~

PA OXLEY
The Old Rectory, Cherhill, Nr. Calne, Wilts.
Tel: 0249 816227
dealer; clocks and barometers

~

PEACOCK
26 Newnham Street, Bedford, Beds.
Tel: 0234 66366
auctioneer

~

PERCIVAL DAVID FOUNDATION
OF CHINESE ART
53 Gordon Square, London WC1 Tel: 071 387 3909
private collection open to the public; arts of the East

~

PHILLIPS
17 East Parade, Leeds, Yorks Tel: 0532 448011
auctioneer

~

PHILLIPS
101 New Bond Street, London W1
Tel: 071 629 6602
auctioneer

~

PHILLIPS
Armada Street, North Hill, Plymouth, Devon
Tel: 0752 673504
auctioneer

~

PHILLIPS, BROOKS
39 Park End Street, Oxford, Oxon Tel: 0865 723524.
auctioneer

~

PHILLIPS IN CHESTER
150 Christleton Road, Chester, Cheshire
Tel: 0244 313936
auctioneer

~

PHILLIPS FINE ART
56 Machen Place, Cardiff Tel: 0222 374320
auctioneer

~

PHILLIPS FINE ART
Baffins Hall, Baffins Lane, Chichester, Sussex
Tel: 0243 787548
auctioneer

~

PHILLIPS FINE ART
71 Oakfield Road, Clifton, Bristol Tel: 0272 734052
auctioneer

~

PHILLIPS FINE ART
Millmead, Guildford, Surrey Tel: 0483 504030
auctioneer

~

PHILLIPS FINE ART
114 Northenden Road, Sale, Manchester
Tel: 061 962 9237
auctioneer

~

PHILLIPS FINE ART
Cinque Ports Street, Rye, Sussex Tel: 0797 222124
auctioneer

~

PHILLIPS FINE ART
49 London Road, Sevenoaks, Kent
Tel: 0732 740310
auctioneer

~

PHILLIPS FINE ART
The Red House, Hyde Street, Winchester, Hants
Tel: 0962 62515
auctioneer

~

PHILLIPS IN SCOTLAND
65 George Street, Edinburgh Tel: 031 225 2266
auctioneer

~

PHILLIPS IN SCOTLAND
207 Bath Street, Glasgow Tel: 041 221 8377
auctioneer

~

PITT RIVERS MUSEUM
South Parks Road, Oxford Tel: 0865 270927
museum: tribal art, antiquities

~

PLYMOUTH CITY MUSEUM AND ART GALLERY
Drake Circus, Plymouth, Devon Tel: 0752 264878
museum; general

~

POOLEY & ROGERS
9 Alverton Street, Penzance, Cornwall
Tel: 0736 63816
auctioneer

~

JAMES REEVE
9 Church Street, Warwick Tel: 0926 498113
*dealer; specializes in 17th, 18th and early 19th century
English furniture*

~

RIDDETTS
26 Richmond Hill, Bournemouth, Dorset
Tel: 0202 25686
auctioneer

~

RIPLEY ANTIQUES
67 High Street, Ripley, Surrey Tel: 0483 224981
dealer; specializes in 18th and 19th century furniture

~

ROYAL COLLEGE OF MUSIC
Prince Consort Road, London SW7
Tel: 071 589 3643
*museum; over 450 musical instruments of all types and
periods*

~

ROYAL MUSEUM OF SCOTLAND
Chambers Street, Edinburgh Tel: 031 225 7534
*museum; general collection, scientific instruments,
decorative arts*

~

THE ROYAL PAVILION
Brighton, East Sussex Tel: 0273 603005
*historic pleasure pavilion; regency furniture and decor,
chinoiserie*

~

**RUSSELL-COATES ART GALLERY
AND MUSEUM**
East Cliff, Bournemouth, Dorset
museum; general collection

~

THE SCIENCE MUSEUM
Exhibition Road, London SW7 Tel: 071 589 3456
*museum; scientific and medical instruments from all
periods, motor cars, aircraft*

~

ALLAN SMITH CLOCKS
162 Beechcroft Road, Upper Statton, Swindon,
Wilts. Tel: 0793 822977
*dealer in and restorer of clocks, some furniture. Call for
appointment.*

~

SNEDDON'S SUNDERLAND AUCTION ROOMS
30 Villiers Street, Sunderland, Tyne & Wear
Tel: 091 514 5931
auctioneer

~

SOTHEBY'S
28 Watergate Street, Chester, Cheshire
Tel: 0244 315531
auctioneer

~

SOTHEBY'S
34–35 New Bond Street, London W1
Tel: 071 493 8080
auctioneer

~

SOTHEBY'S SUSSEX
Summers Place, Billingshurst, Sussex
Tel: 0403 783933
auctioneer

~

HENRY SOTHERAN
2–5 Sackville St, London W1 Tel: 071 734 1150
dealer; rare and antiquarian books, maps and prints

~

HENRY SPENCER & SONS
1 St James Road, Sheffield, Yorks. Tel: 0742 728728
auctioneer

~

STEPHENSON & SON
Livestock Centre, Murtom, York, Yorks.
Tel: 0904 489731
auctioneer

~

SWORDERS
Northgate End Salerooms, Bishop Stortford, Herts.
Tel: 0279 651388
auctioneer

~

TATE GALLERY
Millbank, London SW1 Tel: 071 821 1313
gallery

~

TATE GALLERY LIVERPOOL
Albert Docks, Liverpool L3 Tel: 051 709 3223
*gallery; houses overflow and special exhibitions from Tate
in London*

~

TENNANTS AUCTIONEERS
27 Market Place, Leyburn, N. Yorks Tel: 0969 23780
auctioneer

~

THEATRE MUSEUM
Russell Street, London WC2 Tel: 071 831 1227
museum; costume, masks, manuscripts, ephemera

~

TIFFIN KING & NICHOLSON
12 Lowther Street, Carlisle, Cumbria
Tel: 0228 25259
auctioneer

~

TOWER OF LONDON
Tower Hill, London EC3 Tel: 071 709 0765
*one of the finest collections of arms, armour, and
weaponry; also costume, textiles, furniture, jewellery,
and decorative arts*

~

UNIVERSITY OF HULL ART COLLECTION
The Middleton Hall, Cottingham Road, Hull
Tel: 0482 465192
gallery

~

VICTORIA AND ALBERT MUSEUM
Cromwell Road, London SW7 Tel: 071 589 6371
*museum; decorative arts from all parts of the world, lace,
textiles, costume, furniture, decorative arts movements*

~

THE WALLACE COLLECTION
Hertford House, Manchester Square, London W1
Tel: 071 935 0687
*private collection open to the public; paintings, decorative
arts*

~

JOHN WALTER
1 Mint Lane, Lincoln, Lincs. Tel: 0552 525454
auctioneer

~

WARRINGTON MUSEUM AND ART GALLERY
Bold Street, Warrington WA1 1JG, Cheshire
Tel: 0925 444400
museum; general collection

~

WEDGWOOD MUSEUM
Josiah Wedgwood and Sons, Barlaston, Staffs
ST12 9ES Tel: 0782 204218
*museum of Wedgwood pieces and manufacturing
equipment*

~

WHEATCROFT & SON
39 Dale Road, Matlock, Derbys. Tel: 0629 584591
auctioneer

~

WHIPPLE MUSEUM OF THE HISTORY
OF SCIENCE
Free School Lane, Cambridge, Cambs.
Tel: 0223 334540
museum; scientific instruments 1500s–1800s

~

WHITTON AND LAING
32 Okehampton Street, Exeter, Devon
Tel: 0392 52621
auctioneer

~

WHITWORTH ART GALLERY
Oxford Road, Manchester Tel: 061 273 4865
gallery

~

ARNOLD WIGGINS & SONS
4 Bury Street, London SW1   Tel: 071 925 0195
dealer; picture frames

~

WOOLEY & WALLIS
Castle Street, Salisbury, Wilts. Tel: 0722 411422
auctioneer

~

UNITED STATES OF AMERICA

ABERDEEN ORDNANCE MUSEUM
Aberdeen, MA
museum specializing in firearms and weapons of the world

~

ALABAMA AUCTION ROOM
2112 5th Ave Nth, Birmingham, AL 35203
Tel: 205 252 4073
auctioneer

~

ALLEN ART MUSEUM
Oberlin College, Oberlin, OH
museum: general, glass

~

AMERICAN CARNIVAL GLASS ASSOCIATION
PO Box 273, Gnadenhutten, OH 46629
information service

~

THE AMERICAN CLOCK AND WATCH MUSEUM
Bristol, MA
museum: clocks and timepieces

~

W GRAHAM ARADER III
1000 Boxwood Court, King of Prussia, PA
auctioneer

~

ART DECO SOCIETIES OF AMERICA
3447 Sheridan Ave., Miami Beach, FL
Tel: 305 538 8352
information service

~

ART INSTITUTE OF CHICAGO
Michigan Ave at Adams, Chicago, IL
Tel: 312 4453 3500
gallery/museum: primarily paintings and decorative arts

~

BARRIDOFF GALLERIES
242 Middle Street, Portland, ME 04101
Tel: 207 772 5011
gallery: auctioneer

~

BALTIMORE MUSEUM OF ART
Charles between 31st and 32nd Streets, Baltimore,
MD Tel: 301 396 7100/7101
museum: painting, sculpture, general

~

JN BARTFIELD GALLERIES
30 W 57th Street, New York, NY 10019
dealer specializing in art of the American West

~

BEINECKE RARE BOOK AND MANUSCRIPT
LIBRARY
121 Wall Street, New Haven, CT Tel: 203 432 2977
at Yale University; books and manuscripts

~

BENNINGTON MUSEUM
West Main Street, Bennington, VT
Tel: 802 447 1571
museum; Americana, folk art

~

BERGSTROM ART CENTER AND MUSEUM
Neenah, WI 54956
museum; specializes in glass and paperweights

~

BOSTON MUSEUM OF FINE ARTS
465 Hungtingdon Ave., Boston, MS
Tel: 617 267 9300
museum; Americana, arts of East, impressionists, general

~

RW BRONSTEIN
3666 Main Street, Buffalo, NY 14226
Tel: 716 835 7666
auctioneer

~

BROOKLYN MUSEUM
200 Eastern Parkway at Washington Ave.,
Brooklyn, NY Tel: 718 638 5000
museum; general and Americana

~

BUCKINGHAM GALLERIES
4350 Dawson Street, San Diego, CA 92115
Tel: 714 283 7286
gallery; auctioneer

~

BUSHELL'S AUCTION
2006 2nd Ave., Seattle, WA 98121
auctioneer

~

BUTTERFIELD & BUTTERFIELD
1244 Sutter Street, San Francisco, CA 94109
auctioneer

~

CARNEGIE INSTITUTE: MUSEUM OF ART
4400 Forbes Ave., Oakland, Pittsburgh, PA
Tel: 412 622 3131
museum; general collection of international renown

~

CHAPEL HILL RARE BOOKS
143 W Franklin Street, Chapel Hill, NC 27514
Tel: 919 929 8351
dealer; books

~

CB CHARLES GALLERY
825 Woodward Ave., Pontiac, MI 48053
Tel: 313 338 9023
gallery; auctioneer

~

CHRISTIE'S EAST
219 East 67th Street, New York, NY 10021
Tel: 212 570 4141
auctioneer

~

CINCINNATI ART MUSEUM
Eden Park Drive, Cincinnati, OH Tel: 513 721 5204
museum; general collection, Islamic, musical instruments

~

MARVIN COHEN AUCTIONS
Box 425, Route 20 & 22, New Lebanon, NY 12125
auctioneer

~

COLONIAL WILLIAMSBURG
Williamsburg, VA
*authentically recreated and preserved historical site,
featuring Americana, decorative arts, costume, and early
American furniture*

~

COOPER-HEWITT MUSEUM
2 East 91st Street, New York, NY Tel: 212 860 6894
museum; arts, crafts, design

~

CORNING MUSEUM OF GLASS
1 Museum Way, Corning, NY Tel: 607 937 5371

DEGENHART PAPERWEIGHT AND GLASS MUSEUM
Cambridge, OH 43725
museum

~

DENVER ART MUSEUM
100 W 14th Ave., Denver, CO Tel: 303 575 2793
museum; fine collection of Native American artefacts

~

DETROIT INSTITUTE OF ART
5200 Woodward Ave., Detroit, MI Tel: 313 833 7900
museum; general collection

~

DUMOCHELLE ART GALLERIES
409 East Jefferson, Detroit, MI 48226
Tel: 313 963 6255
gallery; auctioneer

~

THE FINE ARTS COMPANY
2317 Chestnut Street, Philadelphia, PA 19103
Tel: 215 564 3644
auctioneer

~

HENRY FORD/GREENFIELD VILLAGE MUSEUMS
Interstate-94, Dearborn, MI Tel: 313 271 1620
12 acre site, mainly featuring Americana, American folk art, and American decorative arts, American ephemera, scientific instruments, machinery, motor cars, aircraft, carriages, etc.

~

FORDEM GALLERIES
3829 Lorain Ave., Cleveland, OH 44113
Tel: 216 281 3563
gallery; auctioneer

~

JACK FRANCIS AUCTIONS
200 Market Street, Lowell, MA 01852
Tel: 508 441 9708
auctioneer

~

THE FRICK COLLECTION
1 East 70th Street, New York, NY Tel: 212 288 0700
private collection open to public; mainly paintings; some sculpture and furniture

~

GARTH'S AUCTIONS
2690 Stratford Road, Delaware, OH 43015
Tel: 614 362 4771
auctioneer

~

MM GOLDBERG
215 Nth Rampart Street, New Orleans, LA 70112
Tel: 504 522 8364
auctioneer

~

GRAMERCY AUCTION GALLERIES
52 East 13th Street, New York, NY 10003
Tel: 212 477 5656
gallery; auctioneer

~

GREENFIELD VILLAGE MUSEUM
(see Henry Ford)

~

CHARLTON HALL GALLERY
930 Gervais Street, Columbia, SC 29201
Tel: 803 252 7927
gallery; auctioneer

~

HANZEL
1120 South Michigan Ave., Chicago, IL 60605
Tel: 312 922 6234
auctioneer

~

HARRIS AUCTION GALLERY
873 Nth Howard Street, Baltimore, MD 21201
Tel: 301 728 7040
gallery; auctioneer

~

HART
2311 Westheimer, Houston, TX 77098
Tel: 713 524 2979
auctioneer

~

GR HAWKINS
7224 Melrose Ave., Los Angeles, CA 90046
Tel: 213 550 1504
auctioneer

~

THE HEARD MUSEUM
22 E Monte Vista, Phoenix, Arizona
Tel: 602 252 8848
museum; Native American arts and crafts, general

~

HIGH MUSEUM OF ART
1280 Peachtree Street, Atlanta, GA Tel: 404 892 4444
museum

~

WILLIAM HILL AUCTIONS
Route 16, East Hardwick, VT 05834
Tel: 802 472 6308
auctioneer

~

HOUSTON MUSEUM OF FINE ARTS
1001 Bissonet, Houston, TX
Tel: 713 526 1361/713 639 7300
museum; general collection

~

FB HUBLEY
364 Broadway, Cambridge, MA 02100
Tel: 617 876 2030
auctioneer

~

HERBERT JOHNSON MUSEUM OF ART
University Ave at Central Ithaca, NY
Tel: Ithaca 255 6464
museum; Islamic, painting, general

~

KENNEDY ANTIQUE AUCTION GALLERIES
1088 Huff Road, Atlanta, GA 30318
Tel: 404 351 4464
auctioneer

~

KENNEDY GALLERIES INC
40 W 57th Street, New York, NY 10019
dealer; art of the American West

~

LIBRARY OF CONGRESS
Independence and 1st Street, Washington, DC
Tel: 202 707 5000
books and manuscripts

~

LIPTON
1108 Fort Street, Honolulu, HI 96813
Tel: 808 533 4329
auctioneer

~

LOS ANGELES COUNTY MUSEUM OF ART
5905 Wilshire Boulevard, Los Angeles, CA
Tel: 213 857 6000/6111
museum; arts of the East, painting, largest general collection in any individual museum in North America

~

MAIN AUCTION GALLERY
137 W 4th Street, Cincinatti, OH 45202
Tel: 513 621 1280
gallery; auctioneer

~

METROPOLITAN MUSEUM OF ART
5th Ave at 82nd Street, New York, NY
Tel: 212 879 5500
museum; general collection

~

MILWAUKEE ART MUSEUM
750 N Lincoln Memorial Drive, Milwaukee, WI
Tel: 414 271 9508
museum

~

MILWAUKEE AUCTION GALLERIES
4747 West Bradley Road, Milwaukee, WI 53223
Tel: 414 355 5054
gallery: auctioneer

~

MONGERSON-WUNDERLICH
704 North Wells, Chicago, IL 60610
dealer; art of the American West

~

MUSEUM OF THE AMERICAN INDIAN
Broadway at 155th Street, New York, NY
Tel: 212 283 2420
specialist collection; Native American art

~

NATIONAL ASSOCIATION OF DEALERS IN ANTIQUES
PO Box 421, Barrington, IL 60011 Tel: 312 381 7096
professional trade association; its listings and code of behaviour are available on written request

~

NATIONAL ASSOCIATION OF WATCH AND CLOCK COLLECTORS
Columbia, PA
information service and collector's club

~

NEDRA MATTEUCCI'S FENN GALLERY
1075 Paseo de Peralta, Sante Fe, NM 87501
dealer; art of the American West

~

NELSON-ATKINS GALLERY OF ART
45th Terrace at Rockhill, Kansas City, MO
Tel: 816 751 1278/816 561 4000
gallery/museum; arts of the East, general collection
~

NEW BEDFORD GLASS MUSEUM
New Bedford, MA 12742
museum; glass
~

NEW ENGLAND RARE COIN AUCTIONS
89 Devonshire Street, Boston, MA 02109
Tel: 617 227 8800
auctioneer; coins
~

NORTHGATE GALLERY
5520 Highway 153, Chattanooga, TN37443
Tel: 615 842 4177
auctioneer
~

NORTON SIMON
(see Simon)
~

O'GALLERIE
537 SE Ash Street, Portland, OR 97214
Tel: 503 238 0202
gallery; auctioneer
~

PEABODY MUSEUM OF ARCHAEOLOGY
11 Divinity Street, Cambridge, MS
Tel: Cambridge 495 1310
at Harvard University; early Native American art
~

GERALD PETERS GALLERY
439 Camino del Monte Sol, PO Box 908, Sante Fe,
NM 87504
dealer; art of the American West
~

PHILADELPHIA MUSEUM OF ART
Fairmount Park, Philadelphia, PA Tel: 215 763 8100
*museum; comprehensive and highly-regarded general
collection*
~

PHILLIPS
525 E 72nd Street, New York, NY 10021
Tel: 212 570 4852
auctioneer
~

PHOENIX ART MUSEUM
1625 N Central, Phoenix, AZ Tel: 602 257 1222
museum; general collection
~

POLLACK
2780 NE 183rd Street, Miami, FL 33160
Tel: 305 931 4476
auctioneer
~

PORTLAND MUSEUM OF ART
7 Congress at Free Street, Portland, ME
Tel: 207 775 6148
museum; mainly painting
~

LLOYD RALSTON TOYS
447 Stratfield Road, Fairfield, CT 06432
auctioneer; specializing in toys
~

RHODE ISLAND SCHOOL OF DESIGN
MUSEUM OF ART
224 Benefit Street, Providence, RI Tel: 403 331 3511
museum; arts of East, painting, general
~

ROSVALL AUCTION CO
1238 South Broadway, Denver, CO 80210
Tel: 303 777 2032
auctioneer
~

ST LOUIS ART MUSEUM
Forest Park, St Louis, MO Tel: 314 721 0067
museum; general collection
~

SEATTLE ART MUSEUM
14th Street E and Prospect, Volunteer Park, Seattle,
WA Tel: 206 625 8900/1
museum; general collection, arts of the East
~

BJ SELKIRK & SONS
4166 Olive Street, St Louis, MO 63108
Tel: 314 533 1700
auctioneer
~

NORTON SIMON MUSEUM OF ART
North Orange Blvd at Colorado, Pasadena, CA
Tel: 818 681 2484/818 449 3730
museum; mainly paintings and sculpture
~

ROBERT W SKINNER
585 Boylston Street, Boston, MA 02116
Tel: 617 236 1700
auctioneer
~

SMITHSONIAN INSTITUTION
The Mall, near the Capitol, Washington, DC
Tel: 202 357 2700 for general information
*a group of 14 museums and galleries, including American
history; African art; natural history; national gallery of
art; national portrait gallery; air and space museum; arts
and industries building (a recreation of the World's Fair of
1876), and the Freer gallery (arts of the East)*
~

SOTHEBY PARKE BERNET
980 Madison Ave., New York, NY 10021
Tel: 212 472 3400
auctioneer
~

JB SPEED ART MUSEUM
2035 3rd Street, Louisville, KY Tel: 502 636 2893
museum
~

SPRINGFIELD ARMORY MUSEUM
Springfield, MA
*museum; very comprehensive coverage of American small
arms and other firearms*
~

THE TIME MUSEUM
Rockford, IL
museum; clocks and timepieces
~

TUSCON MUSEUM OF ART
140 N Main, Tuscon, AZ Tel: 602 624 2333
*museum; general collection, excellent pre-Columbian art
and artefacts*
~

VIRGINIA MUSEUM OF FINE ARTS
Grove and N Boulevard, Richmond, VA
Tel: 804 367 0844
*museum; general collection, jewellery, Art Nouveau,
decorative arts*
~

WADSWORTH ATHENEUM
600 Main Street, Hartford, CT Tel: 203 247 9111
museum; fine painting collection
~

WALTERS ART GALLERY
Charles at Center Street, Baltimore, MD
Tel: 301 547 9000
gallery/museum; general, arms and armour
~

WHITE PLAINS AUCTION ROOMS
572 North Broadway, White Plains, NY 10603
Tel: 914 428 2255
auctioneer
~

THE WILLARD CLOCK MUSEUM
Grafton, MA
museum; clocks and timepieces
~

THE WILSON GALLERY
PO Box 102, Fort Defiance, VA 24437
Tel: 703 885 4292
gallery; auctioneer
~

WINTERTHUR MUSEUM
Winterthur, Route 52, Nr Wilmington, DE
Tel: 302 888 4600
museum; American decorative arts and general
~

JOHN WOODMAN HIGGINS ARMORY
Worcester, MA
*European and Far Eastern arms and weaponry from the
middle ages*
~

YALE UNIVERSITY ART GALLERY
1111 Chapel Street, New Haven, CT
Tel: 203 432 0600
gallery
~

GLOSSARY

AIRTWIST STEMS stems of drinking glasses containing hollow spirals created out of bubbles in the glass

ANNEALING process by which a metal or glass is repeatedly heated and cooled to prevent its becoming brittle

AQUATINT method of engraving, or print made by this method, that enables the engraver to produce tonal as well as linear variety

ARMOIRE a cupboard, usually grand in appearance with architectural details on the front

ASTROLABE disc-shaped instrument made for ascertaining the altitudes of stars and planets

BALUSTER a short pillar with a curving outline and a round section: commonly part of banisters, but also a furniture leg or glass stem of this shape

BISQUE unglazed white fired clay, especially of dolls

BRACKET CLOCK a sprung-driven clock, small enough to sit on a piece of furniture or to be hung from the wall

BRISÉ FAN a fan that has no leaf but consists of sticks pivoting at the base and then held together by ribbons

CABOCHON a smooth, uncut, oval gemstone

CABRIOLE LEG a furniture leg that curves outwards at the middle and then tapers inwards, finishing in a decorated foot

CHAMPLEVÉ (1) referring to a process in enamelling where grooves are cut into the object to be decorated, the enamel is poured in, and then rubbed down to the same level as the metal; (2) the technique of removing areas of coloured slip from ceramics to make a pattern through exposing the colour of the clay

CHASING process in metalworking whereby the metal is worked with a hammer to remove blemishes or to create raised patterns

CHINOISERIE style of decoration intended to imitate motifs and forms found in Chinese art

CLOISONNÉ referring to a process of enamelling whereby the surface is separated by metal bands and the coloured enamels poured into them. The bands make clear boundaries between the colours

CHEVRON a v-shaped pattern

CLARET any red wine from Bordeaux

CRISTALLO the name given by 15th century Venetian glass makers to soda glass, the earliest known form of glass, which uses sodium carbonate as a flux

CROSSHATCHING method of depicting shade and depth by intercrossing lines

DIPTYCH a painting consisting of two equal-sized panels which are joined – usually with hinges – to each other

ENTRELAC two ribbons of stone or other material carved into strips so as to appear interwoven

FAÇON DE VENISE type of glass-making practised by the Venetians in the 16th and 17th centuries using soda glass. It was very light and brittle

FAMILLE VERTE a form of Chinese porcelain in which the decoration is dominated by a bright green enamel

FAVRILE GLASS iridescent glassware made by the American Art Nouveau designer Louis Comfort Tiffany

FORM WATCH a watch made in the shape of an animal, plant or other feature from the natural world

GADROONS a continuous pattern of short repetitive reeding set vertically, diagonally or twisted

GUARDSTICKS the outer sticks of a fan

GUILLOCHE a continuous pattern of overlying strips in a plait

GUILLOCHÉ formed into a guilloche

GUM ARABIC a fine gum taken from the acacia tree, used to bind together pigments for watercolour paints

INCUNABLE (plural incunabula) a printed book from the early years after the invention of printing

JACQUARD LOOM loom invented in the early 19th century by Joseph-Marie Jacquard, needing only one person to work it but capable of producing elaborate designs

JAPANNING imitation Oriental lacquer, most commonly applied to wood, though sometimes also to metal objects

KNOP a component, usually spherical or oblate, of the stem of a drinking glass: it can be made in many styles, hollow or solid

LEAD CRYSTAL colourless clear glass made by mixing a silica with an alkali and lead

LIMNER a painter: in medieval times a manuscript illuminator, then in the Elizabethan and Jacobean periods a painter of miniatures

LONGCASE CLOCK pendulum-driven clock with weights that stands on the floor

LOST-WAX TECHNIQUE method of casting in which a model is made of wax and set in clay which is then baked: the wax is then run off and the clay forms a mould for the material of which the object is to be made

LUSTRE (1) a shiny decoration used on ceramics that is derived from metals; (2) a chandelier; (3) a Victorian vase with cut-glass drops hanging from the rim

MAINSPRING the coiled driving spring of a clock or watch

MAIOLICA tin-glazed earthenware, especially from Italy

MAMLUK from the period of the Mamluk rule in Egypt – 1250–1517

MARQUETRY a veneer applied to wooden furniture consisting of small pieces of wood assembled into a design

MENUISIER French furniture maker who would construct the frame of a piece: the menuisier's role was limited by the guild system to that of a joiner, also making small plain objects, while an ébéniste was a cabinet-maker, dealing with veneered furniture

MILLEFLEUR TAPESTRIES tapestries in which finely dressed figures appear against backgrounds of large numbers of brilliant flowers, small animals and birds

MOUNT material a picture is fixed on before framing: it is often deliberately exposed in framing to provide a border to the picture

ORMOLU decorative cast bronze, chased and fire-gilt

PARURE a set of jewels designed to be worn together

PEARLWARE a form of creamware but with a less creamy hue, developed by Josiah Wedgwood

POUNCING the application of a decorative surface by hammering, giving rise to a powdered appearance

PRUNT a decorative, shaped blob made of molten glass, on a glass object

PRUNTED bearing a prunt or prunts

RÉGENCE the style dominant in France during the early part of the reign of Louis XV, about 1710–30. It is a somewhat formal and extravagant form of Rococo.

REPOUSSÉ referring to metal embossed from within or underneath, by hammering the inner surface

SAMPLER a piece of embroidery in which the embroidress uses several stitches in order to manifest her skill: samplers were generally executed by children and often incorporate biblical quotations or religious exhortations

SLIP a mixture of clay and water applied to ceramic objects: it was originally used to make porous surfaces less porous, but then came to serve as a form of decoration, especially when coloured

SFUMATO technique in painting of merging colours so finely that there is no clear division between them: the word means 'smoked', in reference to the delicate blending

STRETCHER the wooden frame on which a canvas is stretched and then fixed prior to painting

SWAG material suspended from each end and falling into a loop, or wood carved to resemble this shape

TABLE of a violin, the flat front of the body over which the strings are suspended

TEMPERA technqiue of making artists' colours in which the pigment is mixed with egg – sometimes just the egg-white

TIN-GLAZING a glazing technique in which fired pottery is dipped in a mixture of tin and lead to give it a white surface

TOPOGRAPHIC PAINTING paintings intending to give an accurate record of a place

TRIFID divided into three lobes, as sometimes with furniture feet

TROMP L'OEIL the depiction of scenes or objects in a highly realistic way, designed to trick the observer into thinking that they are real

UNDERGLAZE COLOURS colours that are applied to ceramic objects before they are fired: not all colours are made from materials that can withstand the temperatures used in firing ceramics, so the development of a range of underglaze colours has involved a long history of discovery

VEDUTISTI painters of vedute, highly realistic depictions of urban scenes or landscapes

VELLUM a material for writing or drawing on, predating paper, and made from the skin of a calf

VERNIS MARTIN a gilt imitation lacquer decorated with sprays of flowers

WASH an area of single colour in watercolour painting

BIBLIOGRAPHY

··

Furniture

ENGLISH AND CONTINENTAL FURNITURE

HAYWARD, HELENA (ed.); World Furniture, Hamlyn, London. 1965.

KREISEL, HEINRICH; Die Kunste des Deutschen Mobels, Vols. 1, 2, 3, Munich 1968, 1970, 1973.

MACQUOID, PERCY AND EDWARDS, Ralph; The Dictionary of English Furniture, 2nd ed. 3 vols. London 1960.

PAYNE, CHRISTOPHER; 19th Century European Furniture, Woodford, 1981.

PRADORO, ALEXANDRO; French Furniture Makers of the Eighteenth Century, London, 1989.

AMERICAN CHIPPENDALE FURNITURE

BATES, ELIZABETH BIDWELL AND FAIRBANKS, JONATHAN L.; American Furniture – 1620 to the Present, Richard Marek, New York, 1981.

COOPER, WENDY A.; In Praise of America – American Decorative Arts, 1650–1830/Fifty Years of Discovery Since the 1929 Girl Scouts Loan Exhibition, Alfred A. Knopf, New York 1980.

HECKSCHER, MORRISON H.; American Furniture in The Metropolitan Museum of Art – Late Colonial Period: The Queen Anne and Chippendale Styles, The Metropolitan Museum of Art and Random House, New York, 1985.

KIRK, JOHN T.; American Chairs – Queen Anne and Chippendale, Alfred A. Knopf, New York, 1972.

SHAKER FURNITURE

ANDREWS, E. D. & F; Shaker Furniture, Dover, N.Y. and Constable, London. 1950.

China and Ceramics

CHARLESTON, R(ed.); World Ceramics, Paul Hamlyn.

CUSHION, J. P.; Handbook of Pottery and Porcelain Marks, Faber & Faber.

VALENSTEIN, SUZANNE G.; A Handbook of Chinese Ceramics, Metropolitan Museum of Art.

Glass

BATTIE, DAVID, AND COTTLE, SIMON (ed.); Sotheby's Concise Encyclopedia of Glass, Conran Octopus, London 1991.

KLEIN, DAN; Glass, A Contemporary Art, Collins, London, 1989.

KLEIN, DAN AND LLOYD, WARD (ed.); The History of Glass, Orbis London, 1989.

MARSHALL, JO; The Glass Source Book, Quarto London, 1990.

ROSSI, SARA; A Collector's Guide to Paperweights, Letts (London), 1990.

Silver

BLAIR, CLAUDE (ed.); The History of Silver, McDonald Orbis.

CLAYTON, MICHAEL; A Collector's Dictionary of Gold and Silver of the British Isles and North America, Antique Collectors Club.

TARDY (ed.); Les poincons de garantie internationaux pour l'argent, Tardy, 1985.

Jewellery and Fans

JEWELLERY

BURY, SHIRLEY; Jewellery, 1789–1910: The International Era, Vols I & II, Antique Collectors Club, 1991.

NERET, GILLES; Boucheron, Four generations of a world renowned jeweller, Rizzoli International Publications, 1988.

FANS

ALEXANDER, H; Fans, 1984.

ARMSTRONG, N; A Collector's History of Fans, 1974.

CUST, LIONEL; Catalogue of the Collection of Fans and Fanleaves presented to the Trustees of the British Museum by Lady Charlotte Schreiber 1893.

L'EVENTAIL; Miroir de la Belle Epoque, Exhibition, Palais Galliera Paris, 1985.

MAYOR, S; Letts Guide to Collecting Fans, 1991.

RHEAD, C. W.; Wolliscroft, The History of the Fan, 1910.

FANS FROM THE EAST, Victoria & Albert Museum, 1978.

VOLET, MARYSE; L'Imagination au service de l'Eventail, Vezenaz, Switzerland, 1986.

Textiles

BREDIF, JOSETTE; Toiles De Jouy, 1989.

COLBY, AVERIL; Patchwork, 1958.

JOHNSTONE, PAULINE; Three Hundred years of Embroidery, 1986.

KING, DONALD; Samplers, 1960.

KING, DONALD AND MONIQUE; European Textiles in the Kier Collection, 1990.

PARRY, LINDA; Textiles of the Arts and Crafts Movement, 1988.

ROTHSTEIN, NATALIE; Silk Designs of the 18th century, 1990.

SAFFORD, CARLETON L, AND BISHOP, ROBERT; America's Quilts and Coverlets, 1974.

SYNGE, LANTO; Antique Needlework, 1989.

THOMSON, W. G.; A History of Tapestry, 1930.

THORNTON, PETER; Baroque and Rococco Silks, 1965.

LACE

EARNSHAW, PAT; Identifying Lace, Shire Publications, 1980.

JOURDAIN, M; Old Lace, B. T. Batsford Ltd, London 1988, republished from original 1908 edition.

LAPRADE, MME LAUCRENCE DE; Le Poinct de France et les Centres Dentellieres au XVII et XVIII siecles, Paris 1908.

LEVEY, SANTINA M; Lace, A History, Victoria & Albert Museum, W S Maney & Son Ltd, 1983.

MRS. PALLISER; History of Lace, 1st Edition 1865, revised and enlarged by Margaret Jourdain and Alice Dryden (1902).

☞ *left*

ATTRIB. WINTHROP CHANDLER PORTRAIT OF MARY AND LUCY GAY

AMERICAN c.1776
69 × 112cm (27½ × 44in)
This portrait in oils is attributed to Winthrop Chandler, one of the most famous folk painters of late 18th century, who worked in Connecticut during the 1770s.

SHAWLS

AMES, FRANK; The Kashmire Shawl, Antique Collectors' Club.

IRWIN, J; The Kashmir Shawl, V&A Publications.

LEVY-STRAUSS, MONIQUE; The Cashmire Shawl, Dryden Press 1988.

COSTUME

MANSFIELD, A, & CUNNINGTON P; A Handbook of English Costume, 5 vols, Medieval, 16th, 17th, 18th, 19th and 20th century, Faber and Faber.

MCDOWELLS DICTIONARY OF 20TH CENTURY COSTUME – Muller.

Paintings

PAINTING:

E. H. GOMBRICH, The Story of Art, Phaidon, Oxford 1989.

KENNETH CLARK, Looking at Pictures, John Murray, London, 1960.

W. G. CONSTABLE, The Painter's Workshop, Dover Publications New York, 1979.

GETTENS STOUT, Painting Materials, Dover Publications, New York, 1966.

MICHAEL LEVEY, Giotto to Cezanne, Thames and Hudson, London 1989.

JOHN REWALD, A History of Impressionism, Weidenfeld & Nicholson, London 1973.

H. H. ARNASON, A History of Modern Art, Thames and Hudson, London 1989.

WATERCOLOURS:

MARTIN HARDIE, Watercolour Painting in Britain, 3 volumes, published B. T. Batsford, London, 1966;

IOLO WILLIAMS, Early English Water-Colours, published The Connoisseur, London 1952;

ANDREW WILTON, British Watercolours 1750 to 1850, published Phaidon, Oxford, and E. P. Dutton, New York, 1977;

HUON MALLALIEU, The Dictionary of British Watercolours up to 1920, published Antique Collectors Club, Woodbridge, 1976.

HUON MALLALIEU, Understanding Watercolours, Antique Collector's Club, Woodbridge 1985.

DRAWINGS:

JOSEPH MEDER, The Mastery of Drawing, translated by Winslow Ames, published Abaris Books, New York, 1978;

EDWARD J. OLSZEWSKI, The Draughtsman's Eye, published Cleveland Museum of Art, 1981;

REGINA SHOOLMAN AND CHARLES E. SLATKIN, Six Centuries of French Master Drawings in America, Oxford University Press, New York, 1950;

EGBERT HAVERKAMP–BEGEMANN AND CAROLYN LOGAN, Creative Copies, Interpretative Drawings from Michelangelo to Picasso, published Drawings Center, New York in association with Sotheby's, New York, 1988.

FRANCIS AMES-LEWIS, Drawing in the Italian Renaissance Workshop. Victoria & Albert Museum, London 1983.

FRITS LUGT, Les Marques de Collectione de dessins et l'estampes, Amsterdam, 1921.

U.S. IMPRESSIONISTS

BOYLE, RICHARD J; American Impressionism, Boston, New York Graphic Society Ltd. 1974.

GERDTS, WILLIAM H; American Impressionism, Seattle: The Henry Gallery Association, 1980.

GERDTS, WILLIAM H; American Impressionism, New York; Abbeville Press, 1984.

HOOPES, DONELSON F; The American Impressionists, New York, Watson-Guptill Publications, 1972.

PIERCE, PATRICIA JOBE; The Ten, Concord, Rumfold Press, 1976.

AMERICAN 19TH CENTURY LANDSCAPES

BAUR, JOHN I. H.; Trends in American Painting 1815–1865 in M. and M. Karolik Collection of American Paintings, 1815–1865, Harvard University Press, Cambridge, Mass., 1949.

CZESTOCHOWSKI, JOSEPH S; The American Landscape Tradition, E. P. Dutton Inc., New York, 1982.

HOWAT, JOHN K.; American Paradise; The World of the Hudson River School. The Metropolitan Museum of Art, Harry N. Abrams, Inc., New York, 1987.

NOVAK, BARBARA; Nature and Culture, Oxford University Press, New York, 1980.

WILMERDING, JOHN; American Light: The Luminist Movement 1850–1875. Harper & Row, National Gallery of Art, Washington, D.C., 1980.

ART OF THE AMERICAN WEST

AXELROD, ALAN; Art of the Golden West: Abbeville Press, New York, 1990.

BRODER, PATRICIA JANIS; The American West; the Modern Vision: Little, Brown & Co., Boston, 1984.

BRUCE, CHRIS. ET AL; Myth of the West, Rizzoli/The Henry Art Gallery/University of Washington, Seattle.

GOETZMANN, WILLIAM H. AND WILLIAM N.; The West of the Imagination: Norton & Company, N.Y., 1986.

HASSRICK, PETER H; Artists of the American Frontier, Promontory Press, New York, 1988.

ROSSI, PAUL A. AND DAVID C. HUNT; The Art of the Old West: Promontory Press, New York, 1981.

TYLER, RON; Visions of America; Pioneer Artists in a New Land: Thames & Hudson, New York, 1983.

TYLER, RON ET AL; American Frontier Life; Early Western Paintings and Prints: Abbeville Press, New York, 1987.

PORTRAIT MINIATURES

FOSKETT, DAPHNE, British Portrait Miniatures, 1963, London.

FOSKETT, DAPHNE, John Smart, the Man and his Miniatures, 1964, London.

FOSKETT, DAPHNE, Samuel Cooper, 1974, London.

FOSKETT, DAPHNE, Miniatures Dictionary and Guide, 1987, London.

FOSTER, J. J., British Miniature Painters and their Works, 1898, London.

FOSTER, J. J., Samuel Cooper and the English Miniature Painters of the XVIIth Century, 2 vols., 1914–16, London.

LEMBERGER, ERNST, Portrait Miniatures of Five Centuries, London, New York and Toronto.

LONG, BASIL S., British Miniaturists, 1929, London.

O'BRIEN, THE HON. D., Miniatures in the 18h and 19th Centuries, 1951, London.

REYNOLDS, GRAHAM, English Portrait Miniatures, 1988, Cambridge.

SCHIDLOF, LEO R., The Miniature in Europe, 4 vols., 1964, Austria.

STRONG, DR. ROY, Nicholas Hilliard, 1975, London.

STRONG, DR. ROY, The English Renaissance Miniature, 1983, London.

WALLACE COLLECTION, Miniatures and Illuminations Catalogue, W. P. Gibson, 1935, London.

WILLIAMSON, DR. GEORGE C., Richard Cosway, R.A., 1905, London.

WILLIAMSON, DR. GEORGE C., George Engleheart, 1902, privately printed.

WILLIAMSON, DR. GEORGE C., Andrew and Nathanial Plimer, 1903, London.

WILLIAMSON, DR. GEORGE C., The History of Portrait Miniatures, 2 vols., 1904, London.

WILLIAMSON, DR. GEORGE C., Catalogue of the Collection, the property of J. Pierpont Morgan, 4 vols., 1906–07, privately printed.

WILLIAMSON, DR. GEORGE C., Ozias Humphry, R.A. 1918, London and New York.

Sculpture
~

AVERY, CHARLES; Studies in European Sculpture, Vols I & II, Christies, London 1981 & 1988.

☞ *left*
DAUM TABLE LAMP
FRENCH Early 20th c.
A Louis Majorelle design for the French glassmakers, Daum, which was closely associated with the Art Nouveau movement.

BAXANDALL, MICHAEL; The Limewood Sculptors of South Germany, Yale University Press, New Haven and London, 1980.

KEUTNER, HERBERT; Sculpture: Renaissance to Rococo, Michael Joseph, London, 1969.

LICHT, FRED; Sculpture 19th and 20th Centuries, Michael Joseph, London, 1969.

RANDALL, RICHARD H, JR.; Masterpieces of Ivory from the Walters Art Gallery, Sotheby's Publications, London, 1985.

SALVINI, ROBERTO; Medieval Sculpture, Michael Joseph, London, 1969.

SOUCHAL, FRANCOIS, French Sculptors of the 17th & 18th Centuries, 3 Vols., London, 1977.

Decorative Arts Movements
~

THE ARTS AND CRAFTS MOVEMENT

KLEIN, DAN AND BISHOP, MARGARET; Decorative Art 1880–1980 Phaidon, Christies, 1986.

GARNER, PHILIPPE, Encyclopedia of Decorative Arts 1890–1940, Phaidon, Oxford 1978.

ART DECO

ARWAS, VICTOR; Art Deco, Academy Editions, London, 1980.

BRUNHAMMER, YVONNE; Le Style 1925, Paris.

DUNCAN, ALISTAIR; Art Deco Furniture, Thames and Hudson, London, 1984.

KLEIN, DAN, HASLAM, MALCOLM AND MCCLELLAND, NANCY; In the Deco Style, Thames & Hudson, 1989.

ART NOUVEAU

AMAYA, MARIO; Art Nouveau, London and New York, 1966.

BATTERSBY, MARTIN; The World of Art Nouveau, London, 1968.

BOUILLON, JEAN-PAUL; Art Nouveau, 1870–1914, Geneva, 1985.

BUFFET-CHALLIE, LAURENCE; The Art Nouveau Style, London 1982.

RHEIMS, M; The Age of Art Nouveau, London, 1966; L'Art 1900, Paris, 1965.

SCHMUTZLER, ROBERT; Art Nouveau, London, 1964.

TSCHUDI MADSEN, S; Art Nouveau, translated by R. I. Christopherson, London, 1970.

WARREN, G.; Art Nouveau, London, 1972.

WEISBERG, GABRIEL P; Art Nouveau Bing, Paris Style 1900, New York, 1986.

North American Art and Artefacts

BATKIN, JONATHAN; Pottery of the Pueblos of New Mexico, Colorado Springs Fine Arts Center, 1987.

CONN, RICHARD; Circles of the World, Denver Art Museum, 1982.

EWERS, JOHN; Plains Indian Sculpture, Smithsonian Institution Press, 1986.

FURST, PETER & JILL, North American Indian Arts, Rizzoli International Publications Inc., 1982.

HALL, BARBARA; Hau Kola, Haffenreffer Museum of Anthropology, 1980.

HARLOW, FRANCIS; Two Hundred Years of Historic Pueblo Pottery: The Gallegos Collection, Morning Star Gallery Publishers, 1990.

KENT, KATE; Navajo Weaving, School of American Research Press, 1985.

MCCOY, RONALD; Kiowa Memories, Morning Star Gallery 1987.

PETERSEN, KAREN; American Pictographic Images, Alexander Gallery and Morning Star Gallery, 1988.

WHITEFORD, ANDREW; Southwestern Indian Baskets, School of American Research Press, 1988.

The Arts of the East

CHINESE WORKS OF ART

DE BOULAY, A; Christie's Pictorial History of Chinese Ceramics, Phaidon Christie's, Oxford, 1984.

FONG, WEN (ed); The Great Bronze Age of China, The Metropolitan Museum of Art, New York, 1980.

HOWARD, D. AND AYERS, J.; China for the West, Sotheby Parke Bernet, London and New York, 1978.

MEDLEY, M., The Chinese Potter, Phaidon Oxford, 1976.

CHINESE JADE CARVING, CATALOGUE; Ip Yee, Hong Kong. 1983.

ISLAMIC WORKS OF ART

ALLAN JAMES; Islamic Metalwork; the Nuhad Es-Said Collection, London 1982.

ATIL, ESIN; The Age of Suleyman the Magnificent, Washington D.C. 1987.

CRESWELL, K. A. C.; A Bibliography of the Arts and Crafts of Islam, Vaduz, 1978 (with two later supplements).

ETTINGHAUSEN, RICHARD; Arab Painting, Skira/Rizzoli, 1977.

GRAY, BASIL; Persian Painting, Skira/Rizzoli, 1971.

HALI, London (leading journal for carpets and textiles)

LANE, ARTHUR; Early Islamic Pottery, Faber, London, 1947. Later Islamic Pottery, Faber, London, 2nd ed. 1971.

LENTZ, T AND LOWRY, G; Timur and the Princely Vision, Persian Art and Culture in the Fifteenth Century, Washington D.C. 1989.

ROBINSON, B. W. ET AL; Islamic Art In the Keir Collection, London 1988.

JAPANESE WORKS OF ART

BUSCH, NOEL F; A Concise History of Japan, Cassell, London.

COLLCUTT, JANSEN AND KUMAKURA; Cultural Atlas of Japan, Phaidon, Oxford.

EARLE, JOE (ed); Japanese Art and Design, Victoria & Albert Museum.

Arms and Armour

SWORDS

NORMAN, A. V; The Rapier and Small-Sword 1460–1820, Arms and Armour Press, London 1980.

RAWSON, P; The Indian Sword, Herbert Jenkins, London 1978.

ROBSON, B; Swords of the British Army, Arms and Armour Press, London 1971.

SOUTHWICK, L; The Price Guide to Antique Edged Weapons, The Antique Collectors' Club, Woodbridge 1982.

TARRASUK, L AND BLAIR, C; The Complete Encyclopaedia of Arms and Weapons, B T Batsford, London 1979.

SWORDS AND HILT WEAPONS, Weidenfeld & Nicholson, London 1989 (various authors).

WILKINSON, F; Edged Weapons, Guiness, London 1970.

MILITARIA

KIPLING, A AND KING, H; Head-Dress Badges of the British Army, Frederick Muller (2 vols) London 1972 and 1978.

ROSIGINOLI, G; The Illustrated Encyclopaedia of Military Insignia, Quarto, London 1987.

WILKINSON, F; Badges of the British Army, Arms and Armour Press, London 1987.

WILKINSON, F; Battle Dress, Guiness, London 1970.

WILKINSON, F: Collecting Military Antiques, Ward Lock, London 1978.

FIREARMS

BAILEY, D. W.; British Military Longarms 1715–1865, Arms and Armour Press, 1986.

BLACKMORE, H. L.; British Military Firearms, Herbert Jenkins, 1969.

FLAYDERMAN, N.; Flayderman's Guide to Antique American Firearms, Northfield, 1978.

WILKINSON, F; The World's Great Guns, Hamlyn, London 1972.

ARMOUR

BLAIR, C; European Armour, Batsford, London, 1972.

Coins, Medals and Stamps

COINS

GRIERSON; Coins and Medals: a select bibliography, Historical Association, London 1954.

CARSON, R. A. G.; Coins, Ancient, Medieval and Modern, London 1962.

CRIBB, J, COOK, J., AND CARRADICE, I; The Coin Atlas, London 1990.

HOBERMAN, G; The Art of Coins and their Photography, London 1981.

JONES, M; The Art of the Medal, London, 1979.

PORTEOUS, J; Coins in History, London 1969.

PRICE, M. J (gen. ed.); Coins, an Illustrated Survey, 650 BC to the Present Day, London 1980.

SUTHERLAND, C. H. V.; Art in Coinage, London, 1955.

STAMPS

STANLEY GIBBONS STAMP CATALOGUE PART 1 – British Commonwealth.

LOWE, ROBSON (ed); Encyclopaedia of British Empire Postage Stamps Vols 1–5, Christie's Robson Lowe.

MUIR, DOUGLAS; Postal Reform and the Penny Black, National Postal Museum.

WATSON, JAMES; Stanley Gibbons Book of Stamps and Stamp Collecting, revised by John Holman.

Clocks, Watches and Scientific Instruments

BRITTEN, F. J; Old Clocks and Watches and Their Makers, Antique Collectors' Club, Woodbridge, 6th edition, 1932, and then subsequent revised editions by Bailey, Clutton and Kent.

CAMERER CUSS, T. P.; Antique Watches, Antique Collectors Club, 1976.

CARDINAL, CATHERINE; The Watch, Wellfleet Press, Secaucus, N.J., U.S.A.

DAWSON, DROVER AND PARKES, Early English Clocks, Antique Collectors Club, Woodbridge, revised edition, 1985.

ROSE, R. E; English Dial Clocks, Antique Collectors Club, Woodbridge, 1988.

TARDY; French Clocks the World Over, Tardy, Paris, 1985.

WHITE, GEORGE; English Lantern Clocks, Antique Collectors Club, Woodbridge.

Dolls and Toys

DOLLS

KING, C. E.; The Price Guide to Dolls Antique and Modern, Antique Collectors Club, Woodbridge, updated 1982.

TOYS

ANTIQUE TOY WORLD MAGAZINE, P.O. Box 34509, Chicago, Illinois 60634, USA.

HILLIER, MARY; Automata and Mechanical Toys, Jupeter 1976.

FRASER, ANTONIA; A History of Toys, 1966.

LEVY, ALLEN; A Century of Model Trains, New Cavendish 1986.

O'BRIEN, RICHARD; The Story of American Toys, New Cavendish 1990.

OPIE, JAMES; Britain's Toy Soldiers 1893–1932, Gollancz 1985.

OPIE, JAMES (Ed.); Collector's Guide to 20th Century Toys, Letts 1991.

PRESSLAND, DAVID; The Art of the Tin Toy, New Cavendish 1976.

PRESSLAND, DAVID; The Book of Penny Toys, New Cavendish 1991.

RICHARDSON, MIKE AND SUE; Dinky Toys and Modelled Miniatures, New Cavendish 1989.

☞ *left*

GROUP OF CHARACTER DOLLS

GERMAN Late 19th and early 20th c.
A Lenci boy in typical knitted clothes and with side-glancing eyes; a 'dolly face' doll by Kestner in original red frock; a Kestner character baby with open and close mouth; and a Kammer and Reinhardt character child with glass eyes.

Musical Instruments

BAINES, ANTHONY; European and American Musical Instruments, New York, 1966.

HENLEY, WILLIAM; Universal Dictionary of Violin and Bow Makers, Brighton, 1973.

MARCUSE, SIBYL; Musical Instruments: A Comprehensive Dictionary, New York, 1964.

MONTAGU, JEREMY; The World of Medieval & Renaissance Musical Instruments, London, 1976.

MONTAGU; The World of Baroque and Classical Musical Instruments, London.

SACHS, CURT; The History of Musical Instruments, New York, 1940.

THE NEW GROVE DICTIONARY OF MUSICAL INSTRUMENTS, London, 1984.

THE NEW GROVE MUSICAL INSTRUMENT SERIES, London, 1989.

Wine

CHRISTIE'S WINE COMPANION, 4, Christie's Wine Publications in association with Webb & Bower.

BRADFORD, SARAH; The Story of Port, Christie's Wine Publications.

MICHAEL BROADBENT'S POCKET GUIDE TO WINE TASTING, Christie's Wine Publications in association with Mitchell Beazley.

JOHNSON, HUGH; The World Atlas of Wine, Mitchell Beazley, 1971 and reprints.

SPURRIER, STEPHEN AND MICHEL DUVAZ, Académie du Vin Wine Course, Christie's Wine Publications in association with Mitchell Beazley.

ABOUT THE CONTRIBUTORS
TO THIS VOLUME
···

These short biographies appear in the order of the contributions in the book:

~

DAVID BATTIE (Introduction) left Art School and became a Graphic Designer before starting a new career as a porter at Sotheby's in 1967. He worked in several departments including heading the Ceramics and Oriental Works of Art Department at Sotheby's Belgravia (now closed) since its inception in 1971. He became a Director in 1976.

He has written Price Guides to both *19th Century British Pottery* and *Porcelain,* is the Editor of *Sotheby's Encyclopedia of Porcelain,* and has contributed articles and chapters to various other publications.

He has appeared on the *Antiques Roadshow* since the first series in 1979 as well as making numerous other radio and television programmes. He lectures on a wide range of topics in this country and abroad to the National Association of the Decorative and Fine Arts Societies, other antiques societies, to business executives, and other groups.

~

JOHN TAYLOR (English Furniture; Continental Furniture) studied History of Art at Cambridge University, England, and worked in the Furniture Department at Sotheby's, London, for three years. He is now an independent consultant. He has contributed to *The Sotheby's Encyclopedia of Furniture* (Conran Octopus, UK; Harper Collins, USA, 1990), and to *The Antique Collector's Club Magazine.*

~

LEIGH R. KENO (American Chippendale Furniture), who holds a BA in the History of Art from Hamilton College (1979), has been active in the field of American antiques since childhood. In 1979 he became the Director of the American Furniture Department at the William Doyle Galleries in New York City, and between 1984 and 1986 he held the positions of Vice President of Appraisals and specialist in American Furniture at Christie's, New York. He left this position in 1986 to open his own gallery – Leigh Keno, 19 East 74th Street, New York 10021 (tel: 212 734 2381) – specializing in 18th and early 19th century American furniture and decorative arts. He lectures extensively throughout the United States and has written articles for *Art and Antiques Magazine* and *The Magazine Antiques.*

~

JOHN CUSHION (China and Ceramics) is a Fellow of the Royal Society of Arts. He has been a lecturer with the National Association of the Decorative and Fine Arts Societies since its founding over twenty years ago. He spent many years on the staff of the Victoria and Albert Museum, mostly in the Department of Ceramics, where he was the Senior Research Officer. From 1960–1980 he conducted courses in the History of Porcelain and Pottery for the University of London Extra-Mural Department. He has since lectured on behalf of the National Trust, Sotheby's and Christie's Art Courses, and the Society of Fine Art Auctioneers. He has lectured in many parts of the world, including the USA.

~

SIMON COTTLE (Glass) worked in Museums for ten years – at London, Newcastle and Glasgow – before joining Sotheby's, London in 1990 as a specialist in Glass and Ceramics. He has published several books and many articles on glass.

~

CHARLES TRUMAN (Silver) began his career at the Victoria and Albert Museum, London, where he spent nine years in the Department of Metalwork before becoming Assistant Keeper of the Department of Ceramics in 1980. Having been recruited to run the London silver department of Christie's in 1984, he was appointed a Director in the following year. In 1990 he left Christie's to set up his own business as an independent consultant. He has published extensively on the subjects of silver and gold boxes.

~

DAVID WARREN (Jewellery) is a Director of Christie's, London.

~

SUSAN MAYOR (Fans) is Head of the Textiles Department and a Director of Christie's South Kensington, London. She was educated at London's Lycée Français and joined Christie's in 1964. Since then she has made her Department an international venue for the sale of fans, textiles, lace, embroidery, and costume. She is married to the architectural historian Professor J. Mordaunt Crook, F.B.A.

~

DIANA FOWLE (Textiles) received a BA (Hons) in History from Oxford University, England. She has been with Christie's, South Kensington, London, for four years, where she is a Specialist in Textiles. She has contributed to *Samplers* (Studio Editions, 1990) and *The History of Textiles* (Studio Editions, 1991, Ed. Madeleine Ginsburg).

~

PATRICIA FROST (Lace, Shawls, and Costume) received a BA (Hons) in English at Cambridge University, England. She has been at Christie's, South Kensington, London, for four years, where she is Cataloguer of Costume, Lace, Shawls, and Islamic Textiles. She has contributed a section on Tapestry to *The History of Textiles* (Studio Editions, 1991, Ed. Madeleine Ginsburg).

~

JEREMY HOWARD (Oil Paintings; Drawings; and Watercolours) worked at the Clarendon Gallery for eight years before joining Colnaghi, the old master gallery of Bond Street, London, nearly four years ago. He has published numerous articles and contributed to many books on the subject of paintings.

~

LAUREN RABB (American Impressionists) graduated with honours from Rutgers University in 1981, and began working at the Princeton Gallery of Fine Art, Princeton, New Jersey, as a gallery assistant. She moved to Washington, D.C., in 1983, and after a brief stint at the National Gallery of Art was hired by Taggart & Jorgensen Gallery, of P Street, Washington, as the gallery manager, where she has remained since. She has written numerous essays on American art for the gallery, including catalogues for two major exhibitions: *In The Open Air,* a comparison of French and American Impressionism published in 1988, and *The Pennsylvania Impressionists, Painters of the New Hope School,* an exhibition which travelled to the James A. Michener Art Center in Pennsylvania in 1990.

~

HOWARD REHS (19th Century American Landscapes) is Managing Director of Schillay & Rehs Gallery in New York City. Mr Rehs is a recognized expert in the field of 19th century painting and has a personal love for the art and artists of the Hudson River School. Mr Rehs received a BA in art history from New York University and has been with Schillay & Rehs Gallery since 1981, first as a Director of European Operations, and then as Managing Director.

~

ROBYN G. PETERSON (Art of the American West) is Curator of Collections at The Rockwell Museum in Corning, New York. Raised in the American West, Ms. Peterson received a PH.D in art history and archaeology from the University of Wisconsin, Madison, in 1987, and has published articles on various cultural topics.

~

CLAUDIA HILL (English Portrait Miniatures) studied the History of Art at Reading University. Between 1984 and 1990 she was an expert in Portrait Miniatures at Christie's, London, and she is now an independent.

~

JAMES BRUCE GARDYNE (Picture Frames) is at Christie's, King Street, London, where he is a a Specialist in Old Master Paintings and Picture Frames.

~

IONA BONHAM-CARTER (European Sculpture) is an Associate Director of Christie's, London, where she runs the Sculpture Department.

~

LYDIA CRESSWELL-JONES (The Arts and Crafts Movement) is Cataloguer for the Applied Arts Department at Sotheby's, London.

~

OLIVIER BROMMET (Art Deco) is an Associate Director of the 20th Century Decorative Arts Department at Christie's. He is responsible for organizing the auctions in this field in the company's continental salesrooms, and has contributed to the *Ceramics and Glass International Auction Records.*

~

JANE HAY (Art Nouveau) graduated from Manchester University in 1982 with an honours degree in Modern History and Economics, going on to complete an MA at the School of Oriental and African Studies in London. She has worked for three years at Christie's, South Kensington, London, where she is a Specialist in the Decorative Arts Department.

~

JOE RIVERA (Native American Artefacts) was born, raised, and educated in New York City. He served as an ethnographer and Research Curator for the Museum of the American Indian, after which he moved to the Sioux Reservation at Rosebud, South Dakota, where he spent ten years engaged in fieldwork. He is currently the Director of the largest American Indian Artifact gallery in the United States – the Morning Star Gallery, 513 Canyon Road, Sante Fe, New Mexico (tel: 505 982 8187).

~

DAVID A. SCHORSCH (American Folk Art) was born in Philadelphia, and established himself at a remarkably early age (he started dealing aged fourteen) as one of the best-known antique dealers in America. In the field of folk art he is a market leader, having set numerous records at sales and auction in categories such as folk painting, folk sculpture, Shaker furniture, weather vanes, and needlework. He is frequently interviewed for both TV and magazines, including *The New York Times, Barrons, Antiques Monthly, Art and Auction Magazine, Americana Magazine,* and *The New Yorker.* He has published articles on American folk art and its associated categories in a wide variety of prestigious specialist magazines and journals, and he regularly organizes specialist exhibitions at his own gallery – David A. Schorsch, Inc, New York – which he catalogues himself.

~

RODDY ROPNER (co-author: Chinese Works of Art) is a Specialist in the Chinese Department at Christie's, King Street, London.

~

PETER TUNSTALL-BEHRENS (co-author: Chinese Works of Art) is a Specialist in the Chinese Department at Christie's, King Street, London.

PROF. JOHN CARSWELL (Islamic Works of Art) is a Director of Sotheby's, London, and Head of the Islamic Art, Rugs and Textiles Department.

~

WILLIAM TILLEY (Japanese Works of Art) studied at the Royal College of Art and at the Sorbonne and L'Ecole des Beaux Arts in Paris. He acquired his first Japanese sword in 1947, and began a lifelong commitment to the serious study of Japanese Art, developing an exceptionally fine personal collection. Since joining Christie's, London where he has worked for twenty-two years, he has supervised some of the largest sales of Japanese artifacts ever held, including the record-breaking sale of the Naga-sone Kotetsu blade and the Ichimonji Nobufusa blade at Christie's New York. More recently he has overseen the gift of 600 pieces from the Raymond and Frances Bushell Netsuke Collection to the Los Angeles County Museum, supervising the auctioning of a further 1080 lots from the collection in London, New York, and Los Angeles. He is currently the senior technical specialist in the Japanese Department of Christie's, London, of which he is a former Head. His published works include the editing of Sasano Masayuki's *Sukashi tsuba* – the standard reference work on this type of sword fitting.

~

FRED WILKINSON (Arms and Armour) is the President of the Arms and Armour Society, and a consultant to the Arms and Armour department at Sotheby's. He is also Vice-President of the Historical Breech Loading Small Arms Association, an Associate of the Royal Historical Society, a Fellow of the Royal Society of Arts, and the author of many well-known books.

~

RICHARD BISHOP (Coins and Medals) is an Associate Director of Christie's. He has been with the company for eleven years, four of which were spent in the New York branch. He is currently in charge of the Coins and Medals Department at Christie's, King Street, London.

~

TIMOTHY HIRSCH (Stamps) joined Stanley Gibbons Ltd in London in 1979 as a Junior Dealer, and was appointed Managing Director in 1986. In 1990 he joined Christie's in London as the Director responsible for Stamp auctions worldwide (London, New York, and Zurich).

~

RICHARD GARNIER (Clocks and Watches) has a BA in History. He is on the Livery of the Clockmaker's Company, and was the Director

of the Clocks and Watches Department at Christie's Auctioneers, London, between 1975–1990. He is currently Head of the Antique Clock Department at Garrads Crown Jewellers of Regent Street, London. He is a regular contributor to *Antique Collector's Club Magazine* and to *Country Life,* and a lecturer to Christie's Fine Arts Courses, to local branches of the Antiquarian Horological Society, and to the National Trust.

~

JEREMY COLLINS F.S.V.A. (Scientific Instruments) is a Director of Christie's, London, and heads the Scientific Instruments Department.

~

SARAH SOAMES (Books and Manuscripts) is an Associate Director of Christie's, London, and has been with the company for fifteen years.

~

OLIVIA BRISTOL contributed the section on Dolls and Dolls Houses.

~

JAMES OPIE (Antique Toys) is commonly recognized as one of the world's leading authorities on the subject of model soldiers and figures, and his expertise and experience also embrace the other types of toy discussed in his contribution. He has written a number of books about toys, including *British Toy Soldiers, 1893 to the Present* (Arms and Armour Press, 1985); *Britain's Toy Soldiers 1893–1932* (Gollancz, 1985); *Collecting Toy Soldiers* (Wm Collins, 1987), and, as Consultant Editor, *The Letts Guide To Collecting 20th Century Toys* (Charles Letts, 1991).

~

FREDERICK W. OSTER and SARAH MCQUAID (Collecting Musical Instruments): Mr Oster resides in Philadelphia, where he has been dealing in and appraising musical instruments for over twenty years. He has for ten years been Consultant to the Musical Instruments Department of Christie, Manson and Woods, and specializes in the violin family, early wind, and American fretted instruments. Sarah McQuaid works as Mr Oster's assistant.

~

FRANCES GILLHAM (The Violin Family) is the daughter of two professional musicians. She was educated at St Paul's Girl's school, going on to read music at St Catherine's College, Oxford. She joined Christie's in 1979, and was appointed a Director in 1990. She heads the Musical Instruments department of Christie's in London.

~

DUNCAN MCEUAN (Wine) is a Director of Christie's, London.

~

INDEX

ACKNOWLEDGEMENTS

THE PUBLISHERS and authors would like to thank the following for their kind permission to reproduce photographs in this book:

Agnew's, London: 96, 107 top. America Hurrah, NY: 154; 160 below, 161 (Joel and Kate Kopp collection). Asprey's London: 47, 49, 50, 52, 53 below right, 54, 56, 57, 58 top. Christie's: 63–95, 99 below, 101 below, 103 right, 104 top, 105, 112 below (Taggart & Jorgensen Gallery), 114 (Berry-Hill Galleries, NY), 119–122, 124–133, 140–142, 143 top, 147–153, 165–175, 182–189, 190 right (Major General Sir Leonard Atkinson Collection of Great Britain Stamps and Covers), 190 top left, 191–211, 216–27. Clandon Park (National Trust): 43 top. Colnaghi, London: 95 top, 97, 98, 100 below, 102, 103 left, 104 below, 106, 110 top. Richard Green, London: 99 top, 101 top. Leger Galleries, London: 109, 111. Leigh Keno: 17–21. Maas Gallery, London: 110 below. Morning Star Gallery, Santa Fe: 155, 156. Phillips Fine Art Auctioneers, London: 212–215. Private Collection: 40 below, 41 top, 107 below, 157 top. Rockwell Museum, Corning, NY: 117, 118. Schillay & Rehs, Inc., NY: 115 top. David Schorsch, Inc., NY: 22, 23; 157 below, 158, 159, 160 top, 162, 163 (G. William Samaha Collection). Sotheby's: 6–16, 21 top, 46, 48, 51, 53 left and top, 55, 58 below, 59–61, 134–139, 176–181, 123. Taggart & Jorgensen Gallery, Washington, D.C.: 112 top, 116. Victoria & Albert Museum: 24, 25, 27–32, 34 below, 35–39, 40 top, 41 below, 42–45. Richard York Gallery, NY: 115 below.

Claudia Hill writes: My obligations go to all the authors referred to in the bibliography of the miniature portrait section. I am however, particularly grateful to Mrs. Daphne Foskett, whose book *British Portrait Miniatures* supplied me with a general survey of the subject and descriptions of the various forms that it takes. The idiosyncracies of individual artists and the subject of collecting including the delicate matter of fakes is recorded in her scholarly book *Miniatures Dictionary and Guide*. This book is a valuable source of reference and any serious collector would be well advised to read it. I am also indebted to Graham Reynolds whose revised edition of *English Portrait Miniatures* has taken account of recent research.

The publishers particularly wish to thank Claudia Brigg, of the Christie's Colour Library, in London, for her expert advice and assistance.